Upper Cut

Upper Cut

Highlights of My Hollywood Life

Carrie White

ATRIA BOOKS

NEW YORK LONDON TORONTO SYDNEY NEW DELHI

ATRIA BOOKS

A Division of Simon & Schuster, Inc.
1230 Avenue of the Americas
New York, NY 10020

First Atria Books hardcover edition September 2011

ATRIA B O O K S and colophon are trademarks of Simon & Schuster, Inc.

This work is a memoir. It reflects the author's present recollections of experiences over a
period of years. Certain names and identifying characteristics have been changed. Dialogue
and events have been re-created from memory and, in some cases, have been compressed to
convey the substance of what was said or what occurred.

For information about special discounts for bulk purchases, please contact
Simon & Schuster Special Sales at 1-866-506-1949 or business@simonandschuster.com.

The Simon & Schuster Speakers Bureau can bring authors to your live event. For
more information or to book an event, contact the Simon & Schuster Speakers Bureau
at 1-866-248-3049 or visit our website at www.simonspeakers.com.

Designed by Kyoko Watanabe

Manufactured in the United States of America

10   9   8   7   6   5   4   3   2   1

Library of Congress Cataloging-in-Publication Data
White, Carrie.
   Upper cut : highlights of my Hollywood life / Carrie White.
      p. cm.
1. White, Carrie. 2. Beauty operators—California—Biography. 3. Substance abuse—
California—Biography. 4. Motion picture actors and actresses—California—Anecdotes.
I. Title.
   TT955.W54A3 2011
   646.7'24092—dc22
[B]   2010044571

ISBN 978-1-4391-9909-1
ISBN 978-1-4391-9911-4 (ebook)

For my children
Tyler, Adam, Daisy, Aloma, and Pitita

One day your life will flash before your eyes. Make sure it's worth watching.

—JOHN LENNON

My INNER contradictions interest only me, yet I cannot manage to get used to them. I am at once the most timid person on earth and the strongest, the gayest, and the saddest. Not that I am violent by nature, rather, these contrasts, these tremendous opposites RAGE within ME.

—GABRIELLE "COCO" CHANEL

It is not easy to cut through a human head with a hacksaw.

—MICHAEL CRICHTON

PART 1

Pacoima

1948–1958

First Drink

"Honey, could you make Mommy and Johnny a little drinkie-poo?"

I liked it when my mother included me. I picked up their glasses from that coffee table that never had coffee on it and walked to the bamboo bar. Mixing drinks was easy for me. I'd been doing it for my mother and her boyfriends for a while. Not much to figure out—there were only two bottles behind the bar. "Just a little ice, honey, and more bourbon than 7UP," my mother reminded me. I dropped one ice cube in the glass of bourbon and filled the rest with 7UP. If I filled the glass too full, I would sip from it to make it easier to carry.

I was six years old.

My mother was wearing a faded blue chenille robe; her red lipstick matched her Pall Mall cigarette package and two combs held up both sides of her fine golden brown hair. She was lying down on the couch with Johnny, listening to records in our living room. It was the same room where I saw my father beat my mother. Terrified, I'd hidden under the card table, viewing them through the wooden legs. It was the same room my father walked out of and never came back into. I'd felt sad watching him go, but I didn't want him to hurt my mother anymore. "Where are you going, Daddy?" I asked. He never answered me. I only remember his face from one photograph, slick black hair and bright white teeth. I would stare at this photo and wonder if he would ever return. It was the same room where I watched my mother sit alone crying. How could I console her? I knew that once she stopped crying, everything would get better for *both* of us. She never spoke one word about my father after he left. I thought, *Okay, that's how this is—I have my mother and we'll be fine.*

We were fine for a while, until the boyfriends started coming around, until *Johnny* was her only boyfriend. He was six-four and weighed 240 pounds. My mother talked about this fact like he was a famous building.

My mother inked and painted cartoons like *Tom and Jerry* and *Mr. Magoo*. One time she was away from her desk and I saw her coffee cup by her drawing board. Curious, I took a sip. It burned my throat, not because it was hot, but because it was laced with bourbon. I figured, *Oh . . . I get it . . . you put it in everything.* Sometimes I would mix a small drink for myself, which I kept tucked away behind that bamboo bar. It was warm and sweet. It felt good going down. It was my connection to my mother.

I brought the drinks over on a small metal tray. My mother's back was to me and she was kissing Johnny, not noticing me. But he saw me and said, "Set them on the table . . ."

My mother rolled over and reached for her drink.

Nobody Moves, Nobody Gets Hurt

When I was almost seven I attended Rosewood Avenue Elementary School, about twenty blocks from my courtyard home on Burton Way. One day after school, as soon as I saw it was safe to cross the street I ran to my mother's 1947 Plymouth. I loved my mother so much that any chance to be alone with her made me very happy. When Johnny came into our lives, my mother gave him all her attention. She stopped tucking me in and kissing me good night. *Go to bed,* she'd say. I longed for her most of the time.

I pulled the heavy door open, and there was Johnny sitting behind the steering wheel. "Where's Mommy?"

"I told her I'd pick you up. I thought we should get to know each other better." I didn't like Johnny. I didn't want to know him better. I didn't want to know him at all. But my mother told me she was going to marry him and he wasn't going away. I climbed up into the big seat and looked ahead at my feet sticking straight out in front of me.

"Come closer to me," he said. I scooted a tiny bit closer to him. "Closer," he insisted. Again, I obeyed. "That's more like it." When I scooted toward him the second time, I couldn't help noticing a large bulge in his pants.

"I saw you looking at me," he said, and grabbed my wrist forcefully.

"You can touch it," he said, and held my hand down on him. I snapped my arm back. "It's okay, we won't tell your mother or *anyone* that you touched it. It will be our secret."

I felt queasy and speechless. I wondered if my classmates walking by could see me. I wished I were with them. He tried to pull my arm and put my hand on his pants again. I stiffened up and resisted. "Don't you want to touch it again?" I slouched lower in my seat and shook my head *no*. "Maybe another time and don't forget—it's our secret. No one can know." I nodded *yes*, still not looking at him.

We drove away from school and the shade of the street's magnolia tree. The only sound the entire ride home was the ringing in my ears. I felt a yellow light coating around my head, originating from my eyes as if I had been staring at the sun. This was the beginning of a process I would perfect: *checking out*.

When we got home, my mother was at her desk. She never turned around; she kept painting. I wanted to run to her. Instead, I went to my room and closed my door. I looked at my familiar toys—Cootie, checkers, my jar of marbles and pickup sticks. I sat on my bed. *What exactly happened?*

After that day, whenever Johnny tried to get me alone, I pretended I didn't hear him, see him, or understand what he wanted, skipping off as fast as I could. This kept him at some distance for the next few months, but sometimes I would walk by and he would grab me and hoist me up on his lap. I'd squirm to get off, but without a word, he'd hold me in place tighter, locking my arms with his hands.

Six months after Johnny became my predator, we moved to Pacoima. Compared to Burton Way, it was quiet and desolate. The town seemed to stop where the two main streets, Laurel Canyon and Van Nuys Boulevard, met. Past this corner, the small market, the gas station and a few bars was a dirt road that led to the San Fernando mission and a reformatory, El Retiro School for Girls.

Our new two-bedroom tract house was like every house on the five surrounding blocks. Johnny kept setting up errands for my mother in Hollywood; some would take her hours.

"Carole can stay with me," he'd say.

"I wanna come with you, Mommy," I'd call out.

"No, you stay home with Johnny," she'd answer.

"Go to your room," he'd say, after my mother drove off. "I want to show you something."

I hung my head. I went to my room . . . he followed.

"Sit down," he said, pointing to my bed. I sat down on the edge and put my hands on my lap.

"Don't be afraid of me. I'm not going to hurt you. I want to show you something." He sat down next to me in his Fruit of the Loom T-shirt and his loose summer shorts. Like in the car, I stared ahead. I heard his pants unzip.

"Look here, this is my penis, feel how hard it is."

He took my hand and forced me to hold it. I closed my eyes and tried to imagine my bedroom without him in it. He pushed my head down on him from the back of my neck. "Kiss it, kiss it again. Isn't this a great big secret?"

I didn't answer.

One day after school, not seeing Johnny's car in the driveway, I ran into my room to change out of my school clothes. When I stepped through the door, someone grabbed me by my ponytail. It was Johnny, he'd been hiding in my room. He was naked. I froze from head to toe.

"What took you so long? You know I miss you."

By the time I was eight I knew the expression. *If nobody moves, nobody gets hurt.* I continued to hold still. He took my shoulders and pushed me from my room through the hall, into the dark kitchen, where he had drawn the blinds. He pushed my back flat against the refrigerator, placing my mouth level with his penis. He was still holding my ponytail as he shoved himself repeatedly down my throat. My tear-rimmed eyes fixed on a ray of sunshine coming through the blinds from the backyard. I choked and threw up on him.

"What's wrong with you?" he shouted. But before he could start over, we heard my mother's car pull up and he ran off to the shower.

"Get outside and act busy! I'll deal with you later."

And he did.

Later that night, Johnny held me down on the rattan couch in our living room, across his lap, pulled my pants down, and hit me over and over again. I sang in my mind, *Duwopchibop, duwopchibop* and "I Only Have Eyes for You," my favorite song of the Flamingos. With my head hanging over Johnny's knees, I looked at his big feet, which reminded me of my new friend Charlotte's horse. I thought Charlotte was so lucky that she had a horse. I pictured the small wooden stable in her backyard, the old leather bags and bridles on hooks, and hay strewn everywhere. I heard *zist, zist*, the sound of flies frying on the electric flycatcher in her barn, but it was the sound of my butt being hit with the flat side of my mother's hairbrush. I hummed more of *my* song. I could travel so far in my head and out of my body that Johnny couldn't hurt me.

Snowball

I asked my mother if I could stay late and play at Beverly's house after school. Beverly was my best friend. She was an only child like me, which created a bond in itself. We were both nine. We shared an *aloneness* no one else could understand. We changed this by making ourselves like twin sisters. We organized school days with matching outfits, same colors, sweaters and pedal-pushers, or blouses and skirts. I loved Beverly. I wanted to be Beverly. She was beautiful like a young Ava Gardner. She styled her short black hair so it would swoop up in the front and curve into a ducktail to look like the older pachuca chicks. She used her mom's slimy green wave set that dried hard.

Beverly had a big attitude. I admired the way she would speak up for herself. "You're not paying attention," our teacher said to Beverly when she didn't answer. Beverly sassed back, "I was too, I was *thinking* about the answer *first*."

Pacoima's kids were tough, with gangs and clubs. Beverly knew how to survive. She wasn't afraid of authority . . . I could learn by imitating Beverly.

It was easy for her to be independent. Besides being an only child, her dad slept all day because he worked nights as a guard. I saw him only three times, and one of those times was when she made me peek into his room to prove she actually had a father. He looked little and old, and not good looking enough to be Beverly's father. Same for Beverly's mother, an overweight nurse, who wore a white uniform, thick white nylons, and ugly white shoes without any style. She needed earrings or something, I thought. She was older than my mother—more like my grandmother, with short, gray, frizzy hair. She was nice, though. "You and Beverly have a good day at school," she would say, passing me on the porch on her way to her little blue Hillman car and off to her work.

"They're not my real parents."

"What do you mean?"

"I'm adopted."

I had never heard of this, but the possibility of having other *real* parents was thrilling. I told Beverly I wished I were adopted, but I didn't tell her why.

"Today we ditch," Beverly announced when I got to her front door. "I'm going to write a note, like it's from my mother, on her nurse stationery and turn it in tomorrow. I'll change my voice and call the office, like I'm your mother." She saw I was nervous. "Don't be a scaredy-cat, besides, I'm doing all the talking."

Beverly and I shared the bench of her dressing table with the big mirror, playing with makeup she had shoplifted. We took turns with her mother's tweezers, plucking our eyebrows into a high arch until they were almost gone. This way we could draw them back in with a black pencil like the Chicanas. *Overlipping* meant changing our top lip line with a brown pencil and filling it in with red lipstick, also like the Chicana chicks. Makeup was new for us and very tricky, so we practiced, practiced, practiced. It was also a luxury we couldn't afford, so Beverly taught me how to shoplift. How else could we keep up with the neighborhood style pressures?

The first time, it was on a Saturday. Anita's department store was close and, according to Beverly, "There's no way anyone can catch us, there's no guards, and the store people are busy with real customers."

I followed her. We'd measure sweaters by holding them up to our shoulders, and then drop them. Instead of picking them up, we'd look around and stuff them quickly into our bomber jackets zipped almost to the top. The elastic waistband would prevent anything from falling out. Then we'd grab the first sweater on the counter, some silly frou-frou cardigan, and continue to debate which one to purchase. "We have to go," Beverly said loudly, throwing the cardigan aside. "I forgot I have to be at the dentist." And we marched out with our new angora sweaters.

We decided to try it again on this ditch day. Beverly had it all figured out. "Go into the dressing room with two pair of the same pants; put one on under yours. Bring out the extra pair and say you don't like them. I'll be your decoy."

Pushing past my angst, I slipped into the fitting room. *Wow, these are neat, and a perfect fit,* I thought as I admired myself in the long mirror. If Beverly was Ava Gardner, I was on my way to being Lana Turner. I picked up my baggy gray pants and put them on over the tight shocking pink capris.

I stepped out from behind the curtain. I heard, "How were the pants on you?" I looked past her . . . *Oh God, where's Beverly?* "Do you want to try something else?"

"No thanks, I forgot I have to go to the dentist," I said, handing the duplicate pants to her. I spotted Beverly, who'd gotten distracted with scarves.

"Come on, Bev."

"Did you get them?"

"Shhhhh, yes." We scooted out. "See," Beverly said, "wasn't that fun?"

We walked as fast as I could wearing two pair of pants, fueled by adrenaline and laughter. In Beverly's bedroom, our safe cave, I peeled off the new pants.

"They better stay here with you until I figure out what to say about how I got them."

She unrolled some old gym socks. "Today we're going to smoke."

"We are?" Out came two of her dad's Lucky Strikes. We lit up. I coughed and tears rolled out my eyes. We laughed and coughed and coughed and smoked and laughed, blowing the smoke out of her bedroom through the open window behind her closed curtain.

"You want some beer?"

"Beer? Sure!"

She had two large cans of her mom's Olympia beer, hidden underneath a pile of shoes. They weren't cold anymore, but we didn't care. We called boys we had crushes on, giggled, hung up, and listened to her 45-rpm records all day.

I waited until the last second before I went home for dinner, running through shortcuts where unfinished tract homes were being built, loving the smell of fresh lumber and pepper trees, my spirit sinking the closer I got to my house. I knew I might pay for my freedom, but I'd had so much fun at Beverly's, avoiding Johnny was worth the punishment.

I smelled dinner, but I didn't see my mother or Johnny until I came to our small cement deck in the backyard. We didn't eat outside as a rule, but tonight they had set up the card table and covered it with a blue-checkered tablecloth, place mats, even candles. Before I sat down, I dashed to say hello to my pet bunny in his backyard hutch as I did every day, but I couldn't see him in the dark. My grandmother had brought me this bunny two years ago for Easter. I loved my grandmother and my bunny more than anything.

I took my place and began to eat.

"You're late," Johnny growled.

I didn't look up. "Mom said I could be late."

"Why didn't you ask me if you could be late?" Johnny said. "Are you going behind my back? Oh well, it's okay, just eat!"

"Yes, just eat," my mother chimed in. "No arguing, let's enjoy dinner."

"Where's Snowball?" I asked, and I took a bite of my dinner.

I thought about the fun day ditching school. I had to figure out a way to get my own 45-rpm record player like Beverly, so I could listen to my own music—the Penguins and the Platters—not my mother's Sinatra and Satchmo all the time. This day was more than an escape. It was a caper we had won. I loved my new pink pants.

I took another bite.

"Oh, your father, Johnny—" I interrupted her with a squinted glare that Johnny couldn't see, my glare to remind her *I hated when she referred to Johnny as my father.* "He said Snowball's teeth were growing in wrong, that they were interfering with his chewing and he couldn't eat and he was going to die soon, so he had to put him out of his misery before Snowball suffered."

"And no sense in wasting a good meal," Johnny said, almost laughing.

"What???" I said, hoping I wasn't understanding or hearing correctly.

"People cook rabbits all the time," my mother reassured me. "It's like chicken."

I leapt up from the table and ran to puke.

The Big Party

The Renegades were a Pacoima gang that congregated regularly; sometimes they met in houses, yards, but most parties were on dead-end streets with car radios turned up high, all on the same station, lots of beer, sloe-gin, and dancing in between parked cars under the moon and stars. Tonight there was a big party at Manny's house. I told my mother I would spend the night at Beverly's.

She never checked on me. I wasn't even going to be with Beverly. I was going with an older friend, Anna Carone, who was fifteen.

Slow dancing in Pacoima went like this: the girl dropped one or two arms over the guy's shoulder, buried her head in his chest, the guy rested one arm around her waist, the other by his side, and stood as close as possible, each barely shifting a hip, just a slight bounce to the beat . . . until the song ended.

The lights were turned down low. The larger chairs and couches began filling up with older guys and their girlfriends, nineteen and twenty, making out, not coming up for air. It was a game, the touching, first base, second base; hickeys on necks were bragging badges, and then someone ended up pregnant and sometimes got married.

I slipped away into the corner. I didn't have a boyfriend. I didn't want anyone touching me. I did have a million crushes, starting with the Vejar brothers, George and Manuel. They were handsome and smooth dancers.

Some people put on clothes and others wear them like a front-page headline. Manuel Vejar was a headline *styler*. He had on what we called *peggers*—khakis pegged to the ankle and rolled up once—and a sheer nylon shirt over a fresh white T-shirt. His hair was greased back and spiked up on top so it would bounce and drop down to one perfect curl on his forehead.

But Manuel had a girlfriend; he was seventeen and he was never going to be looking at me. I left the kitchen, armed with a six-pack.

Anna was standing by herself near the dimmed floor light in the living room. Tommy, her boyfriend, was out on the porch with the guys talking. Fast songs had been playing and made widows out of girls at parties because the guys would rather talk to each other; only a few were cool fast dancers.

"Why don't we dance?" I said to Anna. Three other girls joined us. We did the Choke and spun pachuco hop circles until I was dizzy and thirsty. I sat down on a footstool and drank another beer. Manny, one of the oldest Renegades, spotted me, raised his bottle of Jack Daniel's, and made an announcement.

"You, little chica Chicana, are going to be our official mascot, and you have a new name . . . *Suki*."

I had been looking for a new name and a new family for a while. This was two for one. I took a big swig of beer.

"Now I have a family I like." Everyone laughed, a few patted my head, and continued where they'd left off. I guzzled my beer down like water.

"That's an honor," Tommy's younger brother Bobby said.

"I know," I said, buzzed from too much beer. "I'm almost a teen-ager."

He walked away, no comment. *Aw, so what . . .* I felt the grandness of my new name—*Suki*. I knew if I told the Renegades about Johnny, they would probably kill him. I liked being a part of something strong.

By 1 AM I had gone to the back room waiting for Anna to say good-bye to Tommy, so we could walk home. I heard a loud commotion, the music stopped, and doors slammed. I heard, "*Hasta mañana,*" and "*pronto esse.*" I wondered if another gang was crashing our party. I was flyin' pretty high and I couldn't have run if my hair was on fire. I decided to have a cigarette when two older girls, Anita and Tina, rushed in to grab their purses.

"You got a match?" They didn't answer and rushed out. Two cops stormed in after them. They found me still searching in a drawer for a light.

"How old are you?" the officer said to me.

"*I'm fine,* how are you?"

He took my beer out of my hand, "You're coming with us."

The policemen led me out. Manny stood by the doorway and glared in the cops' faces. "Good night, Officers," he said. "Don't worry, little Suki, we'll come get you."

I wasn't worried; I was drunk.

Manny's uncle picked me up at the Van Nuys police station. He told the police I lived with his family, and that my parents were on vacation.

"Don't let this happen again," the police warned.

"No problemo," Charlie, my supposed guardian said. "It was an accident."

We snickered on the way out. "Did you bring beer?" I joked. He took me to Anna's house, where I spent the night.

The arrest jarred me. It made me realize that somebody could take my drink away. I needed to be more careful. I couldn't let that happen again.

Charlotte's House

"Mom, can I spend tonight and Sunday night at Charlotte's house?"

My mother was at her desk painting, on the phone with my grand-mother, smoking a cigarette, reaching for her drink. I already had my overnight bag with my Sunday dress packed, my skates over my shoulder, and one foot on the porch.

"Sounds fine," she said, without looking at me.

I ran out before she changed her mind or before Johnny, who was napping, could get wind of my weekend escape. I waited out front for Charlotte and her mom. The second they pulled up, I jumped in so we could get to the skating rink early. Skating was thrilling; it meant freedom from everything that bothered me.

Saturday was the most popular night.

Charlotte's mom looked at the kids waiting to get in; many were rough-looking, others more bookish types. "Girls, we need to think about tomorrow, not just tonight. We want to be fresh for church." *We didn't give a damn about anything but tonight.* "I think eleven is a fair time to pick you up."

"Mom, that's when the fun begins, how about midnight?"

Mrs. Webster spotted some kids smoking on the side of the build-ing, but she had lots of faith her daughter would always make the right choices. She was also fearful of pushing Charlotte to the other side by being too strict. Therefore, Charlotte usually got whatever she wanted. "Okay, be good girls."

"What took you guys so long?" Beverly had been waiting for us at the snack bar.

"We're here now," I said. "Let's go, we only have five skating hours."

"Did you get any cigarettes?" Charlotte asked Beverly. We loved to smoke. I loved the smell of the sulfur from the match. Smoking was intimate. After we got our skates on, we discussed our favorite skaters.

"I pick the Vejar brothers," I said. "You always pick the Vejar brothers," Beverly shot back. We were preparing for a nonstop, Whip, Red Devil–racing, boy-chasing, skating frenzy.

Charlotte was another only child but with real parents, and the lucky girl had no space in the middle of her straight white front teeth, like the annoying one I had. She was twelve and had developed breasts already, large breasts. She wore a real bra. Beverly and I had bras, but they were little AAA trainers. We stuffed them with Kleenex when we wore our angora sweaters.

Charlotte had her own cowgirl style. She always wore cowboy boots, even to school.

"Do you have a cigarette?" Charlotte asked Ronald, who had skated off from the rink. Charlotte liked Ronald. I thought he was real cute too, but Charlotte had first dibs.

"Sure, you wanna smoke out back?"

Boys always had cigarettes, sometimes even beer, that they kept in their bomber jackets in their skate lockers, but Charlotte wanted more than a smoke or a drink; she wanted a kiss. We tagged along on our toe stoppers to the back door.

"Aren't you graduating?" Charlotte asked, twinkling her eyes. Ronald reached into his back pocket for his smokes. Beverly and I peered over Charlotte's shoulder. When he looked up he saw six eyes and three smiles looking back at him. "Oh, you girls want a cigarette too?" We all reached for one. Charlotte got the first light.

"I start Fernando High in September," Ronald answered.

"Don't forget us," Charlotte said, smiling large, so that her dimples accentuated her coyness. He lowered his lids in a shy way, leaning against the stucco wall of the building, and took a big drag. Then he did this weird thing with his jaw and made his mouth pucker. We watched in anticipation, and he blew four smoke rings, following one inside the other.

"That's cool," Beverly spurted out. "Show me how to do that," Charlotte said. I was over this little lovefest. "Come on, we only have four hours to skate."

Back in the rink, Beverly and I even skated together during the couples-only sessions. We didn't want to stop for anything. "I don't see any other two-girl couples," Beverly said. "Who cares? Do you really want to sit down while 'Night Owl' is playing?" The lights went up. Charlotte was skating with Ronald. Chuck Berry's "Nadine" came blasting from the loudspeakers. My prince for the night was the skating floor, and midnight was creeping up my wheels.

The fast songs let us show off. We didn't care about our hair, lipstick, cute guys, or better skaters once we got going. We were flying around the rink for our personal satisfaction. I felt the wind on my sweaty face, the music in my bones. We took turns crashing and falling on our butts.

I was soaking wet, laughing, and never tired of circling the rink. Beverly was skating by my side. Charlotte caught up to us, "Carole, ten minutes before midnight."

"Too soon," I complained.

We skated to the bathroom. It was crowded but we pushed forward to the sinks. Pumping out way too much soap, we scrubbed our smoking fingers, and exited directly to the snack bar.

"One Junior Mints and a Boston Baked Beans," Charlotte said. "I got gum," I told her. "Good, we'll need it after." Charlotte paid for the candy, and poured me a handful. We inhaled the mints. Time was running out. I shoved more mints in my mouth. I felt the mint flavor coming out of my nose. We stuffed the other candy like chipmunks. We still had gum to go. Charlotte's folks didn't drink or smoke. They were real square and assumed Charlotte was too.

I stood in the entry of Charlotte's house, surrounded by hooks on the walls with hats, sweaters, and jackets for all weather needs. I looked at her quaint home and felt the love. Even at this late hour I could smell baked apple pie, not bourbon and stale smoke. My eyes wandered to the family photographs neatly placed on the bookshelves, her mom's embroidery in wooden rings on the dining room table, not overflowing ashtrays of Pall Mall butts. Her dad was still awake, the Papa Bear, sitting in his big personal leather chair, the one that didn't go with any of the other furniture. His wife had connected him to the room with lace doilies on the arms and headrest. There was a tall light behind him so he could read his stack of newspapers. I never saw a newspaper at my house.

Charlotte's mom beckoned from the hall. "Are you coming in or standing there all night?"

Charlotte's mom had tiny happy eyes that always inquired if I needed help, whether she spoke or not. Her mousy grayish hair was so different from my mother's dyed golden brown. She had a perm like Charlotte's, but hers looked like she had left it on too long. Plus, her hair was way too short for her large body. It was hard for me to identify with all this family stuff, but it did feel good.

"Come put your stuff in Charlotte's room. She's putting on her jammies."

"Hi, Mr. Webster." I walked past him to the hallway. I pushed open Charlotte's door with my elbow; the sight of her perfect little girl's room always took my breath away. Quilted blankets were thrown everywhere and a pair of lamps with horses rearing up, one with Roy Rogers, the other Dale Evans, gave the room light.

Charlotte was sitting at her vanity with its large mirror, much like Beverly's, only with a ruffled skirt around it. She was the only child that her parents could have, so she was treated like gold. I was an only child because my mother lost so many babies, they just fell out of her in the toilet or when she reached up to hang clothes on the clothesline. I was a twin, but my twin brother died early in the pregnancy. I'd joked that I told him, "There's only room for one of us."

"Which bed do I sleep on?" I asked Charlotte.

"Which one do you want?" She had bunk beds, expressly for company.

"I always sleep on the ground floor. I'll take the top."

I was putting on my pajamas, and my eyes went to all the dolls on Charlotte's bed and the millions of plastic horses with cowboys and cowgirls on shelves. I never thought of dolls, until I came to Charlotte's house. I had none.

Before Pacoima, I had one doll, my Patty Doll. After my father left, I clung to Patty like a blanket, we were inseparable. I slept with her, ate my cornflakes with her, propped her up next to me when I colored in my coloring books. Patty was my best friend, my sister. The day we moved in our new house, I asked my mother, "Where's Patty?" She must have known, since she took her out of my hands and had me carry a box to the car. She didn't look at me, kept unloading the towels for the new bathroom. "I'll get you another doll. Patty was old, I didn't bring her," she answered with no understanding of my relationship to Patty. It was bad enough she uprooted me from my friends, my school, my home, to move so far away all for Johnny. "I don't want *another* doll." Dolls and I were done.

Charlotte had rows of books too. I had lost interest in books at around six years old, when Johnny moved in, when my mother stopped tucking me in bed, stopped reading to me and kissing me good night. Books made me feel lonely.

"Girls, girls," Charlotte's mom called. "Time for Scripture." Charlotte poked her head out from her bedroom door, "Awww, Mom, do we have to?"

"Charrrrrlotte . . ." her mom called back in a final tone.

We listened to her mom read from the Holy Bible. Bible language was so foreign with its thee's and thou's. When her mom finished, she kissed Charlotte and gave me a hug. "Sweet dreams . . . Jesus loves you and so do I."

I lay in my top bunk for a few minutes, affected by Charlotte's family's kindness toward one another. At my house, I lived on guard, angry and in fear. I pulled the sheets over my head and tried to sleep but Johnny, Johnny, Johnny kept burning through my brain. I felt the ceiling closing down on me. I couldn't stop thinking about the years that this man had been hurting me.

"Charlotte, you awake?"

"Of course. I was thinking about *Ronald*. Isn't he so cute?"

"Yeah." I leaned over the lower bunk. "I have a question for you."

"Shoot."

"Has anyone ever touched you in your private places?"

"What do you mean?" Charlotte asked back too loudly.

"Shhhh!" I continued. "Like a grown-up person . . . putting their hand on you . . . or a finger inside of you where you go to the bathroom?"

"No! Never! Why?"

"If I tell you a *secret,* will you swear to God, hope to die, stick a needle in your eye, that you won't tell anyone? I mean anyone!"

"I swear, come down here."

I slipped into Charlotte's bed and began to tell her about Johnny. Charlotte lay speechless. She didn't interrupt. She put her big arms around me.

"That's so horrible," Charlotte said. "You have to tell the priest at my church tomorrow. Or I will, and I'll tell my mother."

I pulled away. "You promised you wouldn't tell."

"Yeah, but I didn't know it was going to be this bad of a secret."

"Charlotte, you can't say anything to *anyone.*"

"Then *you* tell the priest everything."

The Confession

Charlotte's mom was cracking eggs in a bowl and talking on the phone at the same time, scampering around the kitchen as far as the phone cord allowed her. "Verna, we have to do something about the streetlights, they're just not enough." The house smelled like a busy restaurant, the bacon was already cooked—stacked high on the plate. Wooden shelves held rows of different plates with *Happy Home* sayings from tourist spots across the United States, from Arizona to Minnesota. They denoted time spent together, maybe with relatives, on vacations, or camping.

"Princess . . ." Charlotte's dad was calling from the backyard.

We walked out of the kitchen and through the back door. We jumped from the top of the wood porch to the dirt ground. Charlotte's father stood in front of their red-painted barn. Charlotte's house was set back on a lazy street off Van Nuys Boulevard, in an older undeveloped area, where all the original homes were built by the people who lived in them—homesteaders, citrus and berry people, chicken and cow people. Charlotte's father had lived here since boyhood, a second-generation plowing, bean-picking, weatherbeaten rancher man.

He was bent over picking up the alfalfa strewn all over the ground. Charlotte and I kicked dog toys back and forth with our feet, teasing her collie, Skippy.

"Princess, you need to feed your horse and give him a good brush."

"Could you, Dad? We have to get ready for the church barbecue."

"Oh, okay, sure, but tomorrow, you need to spend time with Sugar."

I had been on the pony rides at Kiddieland (Beverly Park and Playland) near Burton Way when I was younger with my mother or my grandmother, but this was different—who *owns* a pet horse? Sometimes I got to ride Sugar. It was one of the great benefits of being Charlotte's friend! I'd learned how to brush Sugar too. I was glad Charlotte's dad let her pass, because Charlotte would have made me help her, and horse smells lasted longer than cigarettes in your fingernails.

Charlotte's mom came out on the back porch and actually clanged a metal triangle hanging from the porch top. "Does your mom do that for every meal?"

"Yep," Charlotte said, giggling. "Unless it's raining."

In our Sunday best, which for us meant skirts, not pedal pushers, we strolled into the Lutheran Church. It was a pretty white church with a large bell in the steeple. Mrs. Webster was greeted by a flurry of church ladies. Charlotte and I headed for the tetherball court. "Not now, girls!" Mrs. Webster corrected us through her crowd. We turned and went inside.

To the front of the sanctuary, there was a huge organ with tall pipes stretching to the ceiling behind the altar. To the left were bleachers for the choir behind a beautiful wood railing. It was fun to sing along; I didn't know the songs like the others, but I enjoyed the church community. It was nice to hear the positive things said there, like *God is good.*

After the sermon, closing hymn, and the final prayer, and after everyone shook the priest's hand, Charlotte got very serious. "Ready?"

She took my hand. *Ready?* I had hoped Charlotte had forgotten about last night and the agreement we'd made. Daytime didn't feel right for this conversation. It was too bright.

"I don't want to tell anyone else."

"You can't back out." She held my hand tighter. I straightened up. I thought Jesus saved people. He turned water into wine. He told people *Love thy neighbor* and *Thou shalt not kill,* but I had lost faith years ago, when I found out Santa Claus was Johnny and my mother was Santa's helper.

"Charlotte, do you promise the priest won't tell my mother, because I know my mother will tell Johnny, and . . . well, he might beat me to *death.*"

"No, he swears on the Bible, that's what priests are for . . . to help you."

"Okay."

The church had cleared out. She guided me past the altar. "Come on."

She didn't know how threatening it was to expose Johnny, and as dreadful as my life was, there was a big risk that my confession could make things worse, not better.

We walked to a door through the parting of the heavy purple and gold velvet curtains. Charlotte knocked. I stood behind her, hoping no one was there; my throat closed, my blood rushed to my head. I shook my hands for circulation.

"One moment," a voice announced. We heard a swooshing of fabric and footsteps. The door opened slowly.

"Could my friend Carole tell you something?"

"Certainly, Charlotte," answered the old priest in his beautiful white garb. Charlotte moved aside and left us face-to-face at the door. She gave me a little scoot in and said, "You gotta do confessions alone."

I stepped into the room.

"Have a seat, my dear." He stood there in his beautiful white room with light streaming in through stained glass windows. He extended his hands, offering me the seat opposite his. His hands were white, almost pink—not a man who had spent much time outdoors. "What do you want to tell me, Carole?" he said kindly. My words wouldn't come out. He waited patiently. "You can tell me anything."

I felt my breath get short and tight. I felt embarrassed, small as a snapdragon about to snap. With a flood of tears, I blurted out, "The man my mother married makes me do things to him and beats me if I don't."

He opened a drawer and pulled out a Kleenex box. He walked over with a few tissues, put his arm around my shoulder, and tried to comfort me. His touch made me cringe. I pulled away.

"Oh, my dear child," the priest said, somewhat lost for words. He sensed that I didn't like him coming so close, so he moved back slowly to his side. "Would you like a glass of water?"

I lifted my head. "Okay."

He had taken off his priest hat from the church service. He was bald except for a few flyaway wisps on the top. His eyes were hazel, soft looking. Still, I looked at him cautiously as he was walking to me with my water. I reached out for the glass and he noticed my left bicep. A seeping bruise edged out from the sleeve of my lavender blouse. "Did he do that to you?" I sank. I wanted to answer, "I got it roller skating," or "I fell down and bumped myself," or something I usually make up to cover for Johnny. Instead, I told the truth.

"What else did he do to you, dear child?"

I walked out to the parking lot. I saw Charlotte in the distance at the tetherball pole, punching that ball with all her might. The poor faded tan ball didn't have a chance against her. This was our favorite sport. It was an *only child's* favorite sport because it could be played alone. Charlotte saw me and stopped the ball by the rope.

"See, isn't he nice? Don't you feel better now?"

I went to grab the ball from her hand. She pulled back. I wasn't getting to play until I answered her. I didn't know what I felt. The day had softened from the noon sun. The sky was blue. Not a cloud anywhere.

The Arrest

The next day, I did my usual walk home from school, the shortcut off Laurel Canyon, through the mustard field on a dirt path. Construction had started to fill the field, preparing for new tract homes. Walking by the skeletal wood frames, inspecting the floor plans, I imagined the final home, with sofas and rugs and lamps and beds, a basketball hoop if they had a son and frilly curtains, like Charlotte's, if they had a little girl. Probably a dog too. The workers were always gone by the time I came through around four o'clock. When I got to the crossroad of my street, I stopped dead in my tracks.

There were two police cars parked in front of my house.

I stopped at the chain-link fence to catch my breath. I saw Johnny was coming out of my front door, his arms behind his back, followed by a policeman. Following them was another policeman carting a cardboard box. Then my mother came out. She stopped at the porch. No one was speaking.

I waited until the police cars drove off. I walked up our driveway passing the gawking neighbors and their humming chorus: "What did he do, what did he do?"

My next steps to my mother were the longest. She greeted me, with a highball in one hand and a cigarette in the other, ranting, "*There you are. The* police were here; they waited for you. They wanted to ask questions before they took Johnny away. Why didn't you tell me what was going on?"

I wanted to rush and hug her and climb inside her robe, but it was pointless. I dropped my schoolbooks on the porch.

"How could I?" I answered back.

"Did you know about Lowa, the young girl around the corner, and Paula, the woman in the last house down our street? Paula's pregnant with Johnny's child. *What am I supposed to do now?*"

I felt numb. She took two big gulps, and finished her drink. I heard the ice cubes clinking in her glass over her words, until she said, since I was the one who got him arrested, I was the one who had to go to court and testify against him.

Court

The news of Johnny's criminal perversion buzzed like bees through our small community. One thing my mother and I now shared was this gossip. It was in the air like leftover room spray.

"The lawyer is here," my mom called out. "Are you ready?"

I just kept breathing, breathing in, looking around my bedroom, my turquoise plastic 45-rpm record player, paper doll books, boxes of games, hoping I could make the memory of him vanish. I put on my favorite white shirt, crisp like one of Charlotte's, my brown skirt, my matching brown sweater.

My mother was flighty all morning. I was ready to crack, but she was useless, drinking already and preoccupied with talking on the phone to friends.

"I'm coming." I went to the sink to splash my face with cold water. I looked in the mirror, wondering what others could see when they saw me.

My mother called again, "We can't be late."

I was grateful they brought me to a private room until I had to testify. I felt Johnny's fury through the walls, the fury of a caged mad dog.

"Are you ready, dear?" a policewoman asked.

"Do I really have to?"

"You only have to answer a few questions," the lawyer said. "You don't want Johnny to go unpunished, do you?"

"He's right," my mother joined in. "And we'll be right here."

I walked into the room where others had been testifying: Lowa, Paula, and another neighbor lady, named Jean. I was last. The breeze hit my face. I was on the plank, the pirates sitting in rows to my left. The biggest vulture was in the front row at a separate desk with his captain. I felt the ship swaying. *Keep going, keep going.* My chest hurt. I focused on the thick wobbly wooden plank; I couldn't see the end of it, I was towering over a sea of no return. I heard the snapping sharks and whales blowing steam and saw the arms of an octopus about to make its way along the plank to my ankles. There was no light in this sea, it was black as oil and splashed dirt on my clean white shirt and face. I went in the direction I was guided, to what I hoped would be my freedom. I walked to the edge. Before I fell off, someone took my arm and helped me to an oversize hard wood chair like I had seen on television shows, right next to the judge, in a still higher chair, behind his wooden box of law and order. I sat and faced the room. *Don't look at Johnny . . . just don't look at Johnny.*

"Do you know the difference between the truth and a lie?"

"Yes." I lowered my head. Then questions lined up like firing soldiers . . . *What did he make you do? What did he do to you? Where? When?* I was freezing cold, I mumbled my answers . . . I didn't want Johnny to hear me.

"Speak up for the court, please."

Speak up? I was programmed to never speak of this. Now they wanted me to *tell* everything in front of him? This was agony.

"You may step down now."

They found Johnny guilty and gave him the maximum jail time: six months.

The Sound of the Lowrider

Music was the great *amigo.* The deejays on KDAY played music that understood where we were coming from. In Pacoima, it was rhythm and blues. It was Sam Cooke, LaVern Baker, and Jesse Belvin. Pacoima was not Frankie Avalon, Paul Anka, or Connie Francis.

The best place to hear music was in a car, windows up or down, the songs pulsating. By the time I was in seventh grade I had an intense love affair for the low-riders. The loud exhaust pipes popped down the street like a riveting call to adventure. My heart skipped a beat when I saw a candy apple red car that Von Dutch had handpinstriped. The guys stripped the chrome and shaved the door handles off, French-hooded the headlights, chopped the tops, and dropped the cars to the ground, beneath the law's limits.

One night, Beverly and I had her mother drop us off on San Fernando Road. As soon as she was out of sight, we ran across the tracks to the bakery. Cars were beginning the procession in the parking lot. In the back window of each car was a heavy metal car plaque with large raised silver letters that spelled out *Renegades* on a black background.

"Got room for us?" I yelled across the lot to Anna Carone.

"Who's *us*?" Tommy shouted back from his car.

"Just Bev, Charlotte, and me," I answered. Anna gave Tommy her look of love and I knew we were in. We piled into the backseat. Without a word spoken, Tommy's eyes declared, *Caution, girls, you're in my car.* Anna slid in through Tommy's driving side. Tommy's younger brother Bobby got in on the passenger side. I got out my compact and put on another layer of lipstick.

We began the caravan from the San Fernando tracks through Pacoima, music blasting and engines revving, an announcement of independence.

Our classmate Richard Valenzuela had changed his name to Ritchie Valens and was making it big with his song "La Bamba," which was playing on the radio.

Ritchie was Pacoima's star and idol. He put us on the map. Whenever his other hit came on, about his girlfriend, whom we all knew, we yelled in chorus, *Oh Donna!* She broke up with him, broke his heart, and then went back with him.

Cruising turned a good twenty-minute ride into a forty-five-minute ride. Cruising was like slow dancing in Pacoima: *no rush.* Getting there was as important as arriving. We paraded into the preppy white land of Van Nuys, Bob's Big Boy drive-in, invading their space from the first tire rolling up the driveway to the last low exhaust pipe scraping the pavement, all while moving slower than a snail. We peered out the backseat window, giving everyone our hardest looks.

I used music to flood, flush, and control my emotions. I listened to lyrics for clues about life like I watched other people for ways I could be. Fats Domino sang "Ain't That a Shame" . . . Billie Holiday knew about "Good Morning Heartache" . . . and I believed that there were "White Cliffs of Dover."

Disc jockeys Huggy Boy, Art Laboe, and Johnny Otis were my first heroes, over movie stars and comic books. We could actually watch Johnny Otis do his radio show downtown, putting records on the turntable at the radio station in the big picture window on the street corner. He was as handsome as Zorro, wearing all black, greased-back black hair, smiling black eyes, and a little thin mustache with a goatee under his lip in true cholo mode.

Outside on the street, everybody crowded around his triple-thick soundproof glass window, trying to get close to him. I'd use my elbows to make room for myself. I'd come a long way and I wasn't about to be trampled out of a view. Beverly found her way to my side. There was a loudspeaker that let us hear the show. Johnny Otis was very busy with switches and knobs but he lifted his head and flashed a cool smile to his fans. "He's so fine." Beverly and I swooned together. Johnny Otis announced, "Gather round, kiddies, we are gonna do some Hand Jive."

We shrilled.

Johnny Otis sang. He spun his hands and arms into the routine that he made famous. We all followed with our arms in perfect sync. We learned by watching him on his Saturday-night television show. We did the Hand Jive in cars, at lunch, in the shower, and we couldn't believe we got to do it with him looking straight at us.

I loved music and I counted on it. It was consistent, the words never changed, no matter how many times the record was played, and I knew how it was going to make me feel.

Working My Way Through Pacoima

I never did see Johnny again. He must've gone back to Kalamazoo, where he came from. I wished I had known that then, because every day walking home from school, after his six months were up, I would hold my breath in fear.

But he was gone, and so was his contribution of money to our home. The first cutback was my small allowance for chores, like taking out trash and doing dishes. School and books were free, the freezer was filled, but being a pachuca was demanding. How I looked was a social requirement for survival. Money was the conduit for the things that brought happiness: makeup, earrings, the latest records. I had needs. Christmas was coming, which presented me with the perfect idea.

I considered myself an artist. If I convinced my mother I would do a good job, which meant spreading the paint evenly and not going outside the ink lines, there were times she let me paint-in on her celluloids. I got so good at this, she even let me paint the *Mr. Magoo* or *Tom and Jerry* cartoons she worked on. I sat at her desk and painted for hours. She would leave to dye her hair, or take in some sun out back. Before she left, she would line up the correct paint colors that I should use and the correct brushes, for large, small, and tiny spaces. Putting the brush in the paint jar and taking it out with just the right amount of paint was an art.

So I knew I could splash a snowman, a few bells, and a Christmas tree on a neighborhood store window and make some money. I had my own paints, big brushes, rags, and I put them into a cardboard box, pulled on old play clothes, and added a red-and-green knit scarf around my neck to promote the season spirit. Christmas was never cold in the Valley, but still I bundled up and set off on my mission.

I walked one block from my house to Laurel Canyon and I saw pots of gold waiting for me on all four corners. There at Laurel and Van Nuys was Len's Liquor. I'd gone there many times with a note from my mother to buy her Pall Malls and Jim Beam. On the other corner was the Mobil gas station. My mother had actually painted that red winged horse for television commercials, flying off into the sky. I turned to the next corner and I saw the real gold mine: three bars where my mother was well known. I had been in them all, several times, looking for her when I'd misplaced my house key or I wanted to stay over at Beverly's. I figured the old drunks would be the best place to start before I hit the bright lights of Mobil.

The tavern was closest. I stepped up to the big worn wooden door and pulled it open. I was hit in the face with the rancid smell of old cigarettes and beer. It flew up my nose like cat pee. I blew out and took a few steps inside.

It was the land of the forgotten; a few early birds perched on the dilapidated bar stools. They didn't look up, but the bartender did. "Hey, you can't come in here." "I just want to ask you a question," I said. One of the old drunks lifted his head. "Aren't you Gracie's kid? She's not here today."

"Yeah, Gracie's kid," the bartender said. "What can I do ya for?"

"I was hoping I could decorate your windows, you know, paint them with Christmas things, like a snowman and maybe Santa Claus? Only ten dollars."

The bartender barely gave it a thought and shook his head, *no.* "Oh go on, let the kid paint, Mac," one drunk said. "Aww, okay," the bartender said. "But how about for a finsky?" "Give her the *ten!*" the first drunk said. "Aww, okay, 'cause you're Gracie's kid." He handed me a ten. It was as worn out as everything else in the place. "Hey, do you wash the windows after Christmas?" he hollered.

"No!" I shouted back. "Someone else has to do that. I'm an artist."

I painted all four corners successfully. Windows were like big cells; first I'd outline in black, then paint inside the line, filling in with color. My proportions were a little off: a big reindeer head, then I'd run out of room and he'd get a small dog body. Only another artist would have noticed. It took two and a half weeks after school to do it all—the three bars, Len's Liquor, the Mobil gas station, and the local market. I was glad I finished before Christmas.

My gang thought I did a great job.

"Then there's Valentine's Day, St. Patrick's, Easter will be fun, Flag Day, and fireworks for the Fourth. What about Groundhog Day? They look like gophers, I think. Halloween will be a cinch, Thanksgiving: pilgrims and turkeys and then Christmas again."

Still, I needed money in between. I would have to come up with another idea, a regular job, like in January, something before Valentine's Day. . . .

"Hey, Anna, what are you doing after school?"

"I'm working at the bakery, why?"

Anna's family owned the only good bakery in San Fernando, in the big stone building across the tracks.

"Can I come . . . maybe I could help you?"

"Why would you want to do that?"

Anna Carone was a straight-to-the-point Italian girl. I liked hanging with Anna and her family and their good home cooking. Her family moved to Pacoima from Chicago or somewhere far away, and changed one letter in their name: the *r* used to be a *p*. Apparently their real name, Capone, was undesirable. I was oblivious as to why.

"I want to work, and maybe learn how to bake?"

When she stopped laughing, she said, "What're you . . . *Italian* now? Besides, I don't bake. I sell stuff." Anna shrugged her shoulders in disbelief that anyone would *want* to work. "You can come. I'm sure my dad will make you do something if he sees you there."

I loved sweets more than any food. This could be the best job ever.

I worked behind the big counter sorting and boxing for about two weeks. Anna's mom and dad worked in the back where the giant ovens were. Everyone was very nice to me. I could eat anything I wanted, whenever I wanted. I loved the napoleons. Her dad commented, "You-a-sure like-a my cookies, don't you?"

After a few more weeks, Anna came to me late one Saturday.

"My folks love you," Anna said, "but they think you're not cut out for this."

"You mean I'm fired?"

"Well, don't put it like that. They feel you're going to get diabetes working here, that this job isn't good for you."

I did feel nauseous after work from eating so much sugar.

"I got a friend who runs the pizza parlor at the park," Anna said. "You could get a job there if you want to work nights."

I loved pizza.

This could be *the best job ever.*

In the Spotlight

Showcases such as *Al Jarvis Hi-Jinx* and the *Art Laboe Show* were the West Coast's rebuttal to the East Coast's *American Bandstand*. While Dick Clark was all about the Lindy and bubblegum music or cowboy stuff like Jerry Lee Lewis with his *great balls of fire,* we were giving the world a glimpse of pachuco hopping and the party they would never be invited to.

Beverly and I decided we wanted to be on the shows, not just watch them. At the end of every week, an announcer said, "Send in your name and we will put you on our list."

"It's done," Beverly said.

"What's done?"

"We're on the Art Laboe show in two weeks."

Every day after school we went to Beverly's house to prepare. We turned her living room into our dance floor, rolling up the throw rug, pushing back the old brown sofa and matching end tables quietly into her connecting kitchen. We danced without music too, so we wouldn't wake her dad.

We didn't need music—it was in our heads.

"How about 'Shake, Rattle and Roll'?" Beverly sang in a whisper. "Get outta that bed, shake those pots and pans, la dee da dee, la dee da dee. Got it?"

She took my right hand and started twisting me into circles, circling me around her as I spun. One twirl, then again, she almost lost her grip on my wrist, then again, my socks felt slippery, then again until she spun me around her ten times. "Geez, that was so many," I complained.

"Too bad we can't dance together," Beverly said. "We need to be so good it doesn't matter who we dance with."

A few days before the show, I put on my Mexican full skirt with hard thin black velvet flowers and lots of sequins, but it hung limp. I needed more slips. I called Charlotte. Beverly would be wearing hers, but Charlotte wasn't going.

"But my slips are large and you're not." "I can pin them." Charlotte brought three crinoline slips to school in a brown paper bag. "Perfect!"

Saturday afternoon finally arrived and Beverly's mom took us in the ol' blue '51 Hillman. I squeezed into her car with my big skirt and I could hardly see out the window.

"Where's your full skirt?" I asked Beverly.

"I decided we shouldn't look like twins on television."

Instead Beverly wore a tight black skirt, blue angora sweater with snap-on white Peter Pan collar and white Bunny shoes. Still, I felt good the way I looked in my full skirt and Mexican embroidered blouse, and I realized I would be okay without Beverly someday.

It was Valley boiling hot. Her mother started to roll the windows down.

"What are you doing?" Beverly blurted out.

"It's a hundred and five."

"*Mom,* you can't, our hair will blow!"

"We are not driving to Hollywood without a breath of air."

Beverly gritted her teeth. "If you wreck our big day, you'll be so sorry."

Her mom rolled her eyes and compromised with her bossy child, opening her little triangular wing window, which allowed in the slightest breeze to avoid heat stroke. By the time we got there we weren't blown—we were melted like wet rats with carpet for hair.

"Better than blown apart," Beverly affirmed. "They will have air conditioners inside. We'll dry and bounce right back." I loved the way Beverly knew *everything.* We pried ourselves out of the car.

We walked into the studio like we had been there a million times before. Well, Beverly did, and I followed her lead to the door guard. "My name is Beverly Foster and this is Carole Enwright. We're dancers for the *Art Laboe Show.*"

He thumbed through his clipboard and motioned us to go down the hall to Studio B. We walked slowly and curiously, and found the stage door. There it was, the biggest dance space we had ever seen. The lights were dim, except for spotlights hanging over the large wooden dance floor. Crews were gathered around camera equipment on wheels for mobility.

"Wow, Hollywood," I said to Beverly. Empty audience seats were waiting to be filled. Another man with a clipboard came up to us. "You girls, go to the other side, and find a partner if you don't have one." He pointed to a group of kids standing around talking.

"Our whole school could fit in here," I told Bev. "And look . . ." I spotted Johnny Christy, Mickey Morentine, and the Vejar brothers in the crowd. "Come on, Bev." I walked as fast as I could, trying to look casual. "Where's the fire?" she asked. I headed straight for them, then I *accidentally on purpose* bumped into Johnny's back.

"Oh, hi . . . do you have partners yet?" I gave Johnny my best smile, not too big, so my lips would cover the gap in my teeth that I hated. "Not yet, why, you wanna dance with me?"

"Yes," I said calmly, like I was ordering a cheeseburger and fries.

The audience took their seats, people moved onstage with urgency, the lights began blinking, and a stage manager came over to us. "When Art Laboe comes out, give him big applause. When the music starts, rush the dance floor and dance like you're having the best time."

Like? This was my *best* time ever!

Beverly danced with Mickey. I couldn't keep track of anyone else, I had to focus on my dancing and be sure I didn't *fall on live television . . .*

The music took off.

Johnny turned me, twirling me around his whole body, just like I rehearsed with Bev. From one good pull of his strong arm, he brought me into his chest, and as quickly as he rolled me in, he rolled me out into the open space. Next we did the Choke, stiff arms, shoulders turning, twisting back and forth. I was automatically flowing with Johnny.

I had no idea where Beverly was on the dance floor. I had lost sight of her.

It was the last fast song, Little Richard, his fastest song ever . . . we leapt into motion. We were in a pachuco-hoppin' lather. Johnny was twirling me and making my circles tighter, smaller, faster and faster, until I was a sparkling sequined spinning top. The cameraman was following us. I thought I was going to propel through the roof, faster, faster . . . then . . . *Ouch!*

I thought I was stung by a hornet. No, it was the safety pin I was wearing to hold up Charlotte's crinolines—it had popped on my last splash spin. I stopped. Johnny looked like he had seen something horrible crawling on my feet. I looked down. There I stood in a pool of slips at my ankles. The cameraman went swiftly across the dance floor to another couple. Brokenhearted, I picked up Charlotte's slips from the floor like Cinderella after midnight and headed for the bathroom. I turned back to see Johnny still standing in shock. I wanted to spin into the ground. The only thing worse would have been if my stacked pachuca hairdo had come crashing down in my mortified face.

Babe and Virginia

Virginia was my mother's age; they had met working at the MGM Studios inking and painting. They became friends, and my mother asked Virginia and her husband, Babe, to watch me when she went out for a day or three, then I began *asking* to stay at their house, until I was living with them more than with my mother.

They were foster parents; not legal government foster care—they didn't take money—but they brought in stray kids from the neighborhood all the time.

My mother didn't mind. Now that Johnny was gone and she was alone, dating was her main mission. Prior to moving in with Babe and Virginia, I would come home and find an empty house, or my mother in bed with someone, or a house filled with drunken people I didn't know.

Babe ran the local junkyard but kids with troubles came to him for more than cheap batteries and carburetors. Babe gave them lunch and love. The ones who hung out like lost dogs, he brought home to Virginia. They had one child of their own, a six-year-old daughter named Christine. It was one big happy family of interchangeable kids. Some stayed weeks, some stayed months; I had stayed the longest.

Virginia was almost six feet tall, with thick bleached white hair like Jayne Mansfield that she pulled back in a tight ponytail. She was always tan with hot pink lipstick and dressed in pedal-pushers with ballerina flats like Lucille Ball. She was strong in every way: posture, personality, and ideas.

Babe, on the other hand, *looked* like where he worked: the junkyard. He wore thrashed blue coveralls, and his hair was full of axle grease and dust from digging for car parts. He had badly stained yellow teeth and gums so infected he relied on Percodan. He was shorter than Virginia, which may also have accounted for her being the dominating boss. They both had positive outlooks and senses of humor, unless Babe was out of his pain pills. We braced ourselves when we heard, "Where's my goddamn Percodans?"

I loved it there. They talked *to* us kids, not *at* us. They promoted honesty on any subject.

I had been living with Babe and Virginia for more than a year when one afternoon I was hanging out at Babe's junkyard and a guy leapt over the back fence screaming, "Surprise." He was wearing red suede shorts with suspenders, which I found out were common in Southern Germany and called lederhosen. Well, they weren't common in Pacoima.

Billy Grimes was Babe's buddy from the army. He was as eccentric as his outfit. He spoke fast with a thick Oklahoma accent, although sometimes his twang was thicker than at other times. He smoked a long thin brown cigarette called a Sherman. His first words to me were, "How ya' doin,' baby dahl?"

Billy spent a lot of time visiting, and told stories about things I'd never heard of. He told me to count the letters in my name, and that the total count had a particular meaning. If the total wasn't good enough, Billy said, "Change your name, change your numbers and change your life. *Numerology,* baby girl."

I liked his way of thinking.

Virginia decided to give me a birthday party, since my mother wasn't going to. Turning thirteen was a big deal: I was an official teenager. The last birthday celebration I could remember was on Burton Way, before Pacoima—before Johnny. The guest list included my mother; my grandmother; Michelle Carlen, the girl next door; and my Patty Doll. We played Pin the Tail on the Donkey and I wore a white pinafore dress. My mother baked my birthday cake . . . I loved the orange frosting.

My big birthday bash was set for at 7:00 PM. Virginia made her famous Hungarian goulash. We had lots of records and space to dance in the living room without moving the furniture. We kicked back the royal blue shag rug. Babe wasn't much for parties or noise, so he went off to watch television. I turned down the living room lights. I was as free as any teenager could be in a house with parents. Everyone showed up, my gang, Beverly, Judy, Jessica, Linda, Sharon, Marsha and Joe, Charlotte, and some that were unexpected like the Renegades and some of the Igniters. I hoped the Vejar brothers and Ritchie Valens would come.

Also, my mother was coming with my birthday cake. I hadn't seen her in awhile. I was looking forward to her visit and wondered what kind of cake she was bringing.

My party was beginning to jam, Ike and Tina Turner blasting from the record player. Girls were huddled in the bathroom putting on more lipstick and fixing their hair while boys talked about their cars. There was a big pitcher of fresh lemonade in the kitchen. Plenty of Coke, 7UP and root beers all over the counters. Virginia didn't drink alcohol, so none was provided. We could smoke our brains out, but cigarettes only. A few older guys drank in the driveway. I snuck a little sloe gin with Johnny Christy; it tasted like codeine cough syrup.

Jimmy Porter and Ray Schienle walked in together, to my extreme delight. I dashed to greet them. I was high on life, ready to dance. I didn't know who I had a bigger crush on, Jimmy or Ray.

Virginia came out of the kitchen. "Come and get it if you're hungry."

Good timing. After we all ate, it was dance time. I found "Night Owl" and put that on. Tommy's younger brother Bobby asked me to dance. I still had a crush on Bobby, but I really wanted to be available for Jimmy or Ray.

And then somebody said, "Who's got an empty Coke bottle?"

Yahoooo, Spin the Bottle!

Everyone gathered around. I had crushes and I liked kissing. Kissing didn't feel bad to me. I would never let anyone get to second base, though, that creeped me out and reminded me of Johnny's hands.

The boys sat down, Ray sat next to me. Beverly spun the bottle with her eye on Ernie. It landed on Charlotte. Charlotte laughed. "Spin again." Next time it landed on Ernie, but that's because he stuck his hand out.

Then it was Ray's turn to spin the bottle. I felt my temples pound. I crossed my fingers and made a deal with God; I'd stop ditching school with Beverly, even quit smoking, *just let that bottle land on me pleeeeeeeze.*

Yikes! It did. My girlfriends made wisecracks . . . Ray put his lips to mine. Yummy. But before I could die and go to heaven, I had to open my eyes from Jesse yelling, "Hey, where's the cake?" Ray started talking to Jessica, sitting on his other side. I felt invisible.

I got up and went into the kitchen. Virginia was putting on a pot of coffee.

"Have you heard from my mother?"

"She'll be here, she has to come, she has your birthday cake."

I felt reassured. Virginia was always right.

Time passed, my friends were antsy. "Cake is on its way," I promised. I put on fast music to pick up the party. Judy and Charlotte said they had to go. "Don't go, my mother's bringing the cake. Why don't we dance?"

More friends began hanging out front, getting ready to leave. I continued to make excuses but it was useless. Beverly and Ernie were the last ones to leave.

"We gotta go now, it was a great party even without the cake."

Virginia, who tried to console me, shook her head in confusion.

"I'm so sorry, honey, something very important must have happened."
She hugged and kissed me and told me to get some rest.

But I couldn't go to sleep. I stared into the black starless night.
After hours of pressing my nose to the cold glass, waiting and waiting and waiting for her, I decided to go to bed. I realized I had been
waiting for her to be *my mother* since my father left. It was about
3:00 AM. I gave up.

She showed up the next day at noon. I could smell her bourbon
breath through her Fabergé Aphrodisia perfume. She said she'd had
another fight with Kenny, her latest boyfriend, right before she was
going to get my cake, and she met him at Tipsy Turvy to work it
out. "Kenny left at two o'clock, he left me for good, I was crying all
night . . ."

While she made her excuses, I remembered one particular barbecue party at the home of one of her studio friends. I was living at Virginia's, I didn't want to go, but Virginia made me. There were no other
children my age at this gathering, just a few toddlers. I left the main
patio to find a place to pass the evening. I found a small dark area in
the yard, where I sat under the shelter of an old cabana of dried palm
leaves. Two men who had been talking with my mother were coming
my way. I backed up so they wouldn't see me, but I overheard them.
"That Gracie, she's pretty, but what a lush." I wanted to kick them. I
curled up tighter and buried my head in my knees, embarrassed for
her, for myself, for our lives. Everyone knew what a mess she was—
everyone but her.

I stared at my mother expressionless, but my insides were raging.

"That must be sad, breaking up with Kenny *again* . . ."

Next

A few years passed without my mother. I was playing Scrabble with
Virginia one Sunday afternoon. The phone rang. After four rings,
Virginia yelled, "Isn't anyone going to get that?"

Two more rings. Virginia put her letters back in the Scrabble tray and got out of her comfortable position. "Okay, hold your horses, Tonto."

She grabbed the receiver on the wall phone. I was losing by twenty-five points. This gave me more time to find a clever move. I had a Q and a U, potential for a grand slam. Found it . . . double word too . . . *Quack*: forty points! I lit a cigarette and felt so smug. Virginia played to kill, she was going to be so thrown, there were no more big point tiles left.

I looked to see what was taking her so long. She wasn't talking. After a long silence, Virginia motioned me to come to the phone. "It's your mother."

"Why did you tell her I was home?"

Virginia, unflinching, continued stretching the phone out to me. I walked over begrudgingly, annoyed to postpone my Scrabble victory.

Uninterested, I gazed at the Felix the Cat wall clock in the kitchen. The coffee in the metal pot smelled good from the door jamb. I noticed a pile of S&H Green Stamp books filled, ready for retrieving gift items. Virginia and I spent hours licking stamps together. Oranges were spilling out of the ceramic bowl on the kitchen table; I could see the pool was overloaded with plastic water toys. The cookie jar and the matching bread box could barely close because Virginia had them so full of biscuits, Oreos, and Wonder bread. It was a home of abundance and generosity. I grabbed a red licorice from the glass container where others might put straws, and took a big chomp. They were always fresh and soft because we went through them so fast. I took a breath and shrugged. My mother rarely called. I felt the slow motion of boring news about to arrive in my ear.

"Hi, Mom . . ."

"I've decided to move back to Hollywood and you're coming with me."

"*What?* I'm not leaving!"

"I already found an apartment." She hung up.

Virginia wiped her eyes, lit a cigarette, and put her arms around me. I buried my head in her chest.

"I wish I could move to Hollywood," she said. "It will be good for you."

"But I don't want to leave *you*."

I couldn't stop crying, crying for all my time in Pacoima, for the cruising down Van Nuys Boulevard, for the Carone Bakery, for Charlotte and Sugar, for Beverly and our sisterhood, for the dead-end street parties with the Renegades, for smoking and drinking and the pachuco hop. I had transformed myself into the perfect pachuca. I cried because I had gotten to know the soul of this tiny town through my black, Mexican, and Italian friends—even the white kids. I cried for my past pain and uprooting.

Yet underneath I had always felt that Pacoima was a detour, not a destination for me. Although I was miserable about leaving, the reality was that, at fifteen, most of my friends were getting pregnant, then married, and their lives seemed over. I knew this was not for me . . . I felt far from being *over*.

Virginia and I sat on the front steps, with my suitcase, *waiting for my mother.*

Babe came out to the porch in his pajama shorts and a shirt that didn't match. His big beer belly seemed so out of place jutting from an otherwise skinny body. "I'm going to get you a car from the yard, so you can come back soon."

"Really?" I sniffled.

"You betcha."

"I get my driver's license in six months, promise not to forget?"

"He won't," Virginia confirmed.

This time, my mother showed up, but she stayed in the car at the foot of the driveway. "Thanks for all you've done," she called out the car window.

"I'll miss you every day," I sniffled to Virginia as I stood up.

The afternoon was bright and sunny, with that piercing Valley heat I'd come to love that kissed the back of my neck and tired my eyelids like I was under a spell.

It all vanished when I got in my mother's 1955 Studebaker Lark, her square beige boxy car I called a Stupidbaker. She couldn't look at me.

Truth can be so personal. This was a luxury I didn't have with *my* mother. We had so many unspoken issues that it seemed pointless. I had driven through Laurel Canyon with my friends before, going to parties and cruising Hollywood Boulevard. It had never seemed to take this long to drive over the hill.

Perhaps it was the silence.

PART 2

Hollywood

1959–1961

Hollywood High

"Excuse me, but are you a Delta?" a girl asked, talking down to me.

"No, I think I'm a Lutheran."

"Well, you can't sit there if you're not a Delta."

It was my first day at Hollywood High School. I was sitting on a bench in the quad area. I had never heard of a *quad* before this school. Who was she . . . the quad police? And what the hell was a Delta anyway?

Screw her. I didn't see a sign that said *Private Property.* I just wanted to eat my damn lunch.

She looked at me like I was a Christmas decoration at an Easter party. I felt the pencil melting off my arched eyebrows and my red lipstick cracking. No one else was wearing a tight pegged calf-length skirt, a black sweater with a false collar tucked in, a stacked pachuca hairdo adorned with spit curls on each side, and dangling Mexican earrings. I walked over to the other side of the bench around the big tree.

"You can't sit there either," she barked. "That's the Lambdas' bench. And that other tree over there"—she pointed—"that's the Betas' bench. And those benches over there"—she pointed to another and another—"is the Thetas' bench and that one is the Alphas'. So don't sit there either, unless you're an Alpha, a Beta, a Lambda, or a Theta." She looked me up and down. "And I doubt you are."

The social scene at Hollywood High School was harder than Pacoima. They just gave their gangs different names. I had never heard of the word *sorority* or known Greek letters had names. This Delta chick looked very different from Pacoima and *me.* She was polished like an apple, like a picture on a package, like a television commercial. Everything matched, from her white patent leather purse and white patent Mary Jane shoes to her powder blue fuzzy sweater with another tied around her shoulders. Her pleated beige skirt didn't look like me either and her round bubble hairdo didn't move. Her lips were glossy white.

What kind of lipstick was *white*?

I took a deep breath. *She's not going to get me, and neither are all the damn letters of the Greek alphabet.* I remembered the administration building nearby had a large bathroom. Certainly that couldn't be Delta territory. I turned around quickly, and walked without hesitation toward the brick office building, brown paper bag and books in hand. I kept thinking, left or right, which way is the bathroom? *Don't stop to ask anyone.*

I was crushed, trying not to show it, trying not to cry. Not from that bratty bitch, but from what the hell was going to become of me here? It didn't look good. I pulled open the heavy-windowed door, breezed in like I had been there for years, passing students like I was so busy with important things to do. I spotted the sign, Girls' Room. Hold on just a little bit further. I walked faster, got to the door and exhaled the breath I'd been holding.

Inside, there were a few girls fussing with their hair, chatting. They didn't notice me. I saw no feet in the third stall, plowed into it, plunked down on the seat, and locked the door. Safe. I hated to cry. It was a sign of weakness, pointless, and never helped. I took a big breath, stacked my books on my lap like a tray, and unfolded my brown paper bag. I could hardly swallow the dry peanut butter sandwich I had made.

For one week, I sat in that locked toilet cubicle having lunch, constantly wondering about those damn Deltas. Finally bored and annoyed, I figured there was more to this school than classes and a toilet. There must be a Delta in one of my classes. I needed to learn more. I became the Delta detective. Then one day in art class, I heard a new friend, Eve Babitz, talking about the Delta Hell Night coming up. I scooted closer, looking at her drawing. "What's a Hell Night?"

"Well . . . first you have to be rushed."

"What's *rushed*?"

"That's when you are asked by a club to join, then you begin pledging."

"What's *pledging*?"

"That's when you do anything they ask, and I mean anything! It takes a week, and if you pass, you have the final test, Hell Night."

Upon further research, I found the Deltas happened to be the coolest and snobbiest girls. They had privileged backgrounds. Their parents were famous or rich or both. I had none of these qualifications. I liked the challenge. I was determined to be a Delta, if only for vengeance.

Using my survival techniques, I saw that if I had a different walk, different talk, and most important, *different hair,* maybe I could be a girl the Deltas might invite in. As my mother the artist would say after another boyfriend broke up with her, *back to the drawing board.*

First of all, I hated my name, Carole . . . so common. When I complained to my mother that seven girls in my class had the name Carol, she said, "But you have an *e* on the end of your name, you were named after Carole Lombard, your *Carole* is beautiful." "Mom, when the teacher calls *Carol*, she doesn't say, the one with the *e* on the end."

"Carole" had to go. I remembered back in Pacoima Junior High, a new girl in seventh grade announced her name was Carrie, a name I had never heard before. I loved the uniqueness. I had been name-shopping for ages, and I thought of stealing it then, but I had dropped the idea when the Renegades nicknamed me Suki. Outside of Pacoima and a gang party, Suki sounded like a Japanese dog. Entering this new school was the perfect time for me to take this perfect name.

I started telling everyone: "My real name was Carole, but my mother calls me *Carrie* for short." Then I told my mother: "If some-one calls and asks for *Carrie,* that's me."

"You? Why would any one call you *that*?"

"I don't know, Mom, they just do . . . it's a nickname."

So that was that. I was unofficially, officially Carrie, Carrie En-wright. And that was Enwright with a *w*.

Next project was my clothes and hair. I dumped my socks, my bunny shoes, false collars, and full Mexican skirts in the wastebasket. I didn't know where these Hollywood High girls got their looks, but I was sure it wasn't in a store like Anita's off San Fernando Road. They talked about Geistex sweaters and Lanz dresses, *Vogue* and *Harper's Bazaar*. Then there was the world of Max Factor, a makeup store across the street from Hollywood High . . . how convenient.

I listened carefully to the girls in gym chat about Hollywood Boulevard and shopping at The Broadway and Lerner's Dress Shop. I'd never been inside a large department store. I told my mother that none of my clothes fit. I would get a job or help her ink and paint, but I had to have a new wardrobe or I was not going to school.

"Fine," she said, and gave me fifty dollars. That was the most money I had ever seen at one time. I shopped wisely so I could get the most for the money. I even found a cardigan that looked like a Geistex. I think one real Geistex sweater cost *more* than fifty dollars. I bought two knee-length kick-pleat skirts, an angora sweater, and a few blouses. I bought bracelets instead of my usual dangling earrings. Now I had a chance to conquer this new turf. Oh wait, shoes, they tell a lot. I had enough money left over to go to Leeds shoe store, also on Hollywood Boulevard. I bought little flats like that pretty Delta, Rosalind Frank, wore.

But the most important detail was her hair, and I knew I needed to change mine. The Hollywood High hairdo had a name: the Flip. I would study the girls' hair, imagining how they get it to curl up on the bottom. And I needed to cut bangs, smooth bangs that swooped to one side, not like my mother's 1940s movie star bangs. I learned in Pacoima and it held true in Hollywood: *If I could get my hair right, my life would work better.*

Rosalind Frank was in my gym class. I spotted her right away, she reminded me so much of Beverly. She was very pretty and always seemed to have the answer when anyone asked her anything. Rosalind was sharp and assertive and didn't take any crap. She had a Delta friend, Taffy Paul, whom I also admired. I especially liked her name. Taffy would be my new Charlotte. She was smart and sophisticated, rode horses, and studied drama like me. Then there was Louise, Roz's best friend, soon to be her second-best friend, because I was going to be Rosalind's best friend.

I made sure Roz heard me in the locker room, when I would talk about my mother being an artist at MGM and that she had been in films herself.

Finally, Roz said one day, "Do you want to come to Coffee Dan's today?"

I knew this was *the* after-school spot.

"Sure," I answered, not wanting to be too anxious.

"We meet at the *Delta bench* at three-fifteen . . . do you know where that is?"

"I'll find it."

When the final school bell rang, I knew this was it, like a first date: win the Deltas over or end up a dud. Roz was waiting at the Delta bench.

"Hey, everyone," she said. They looked up. "This is Carrie, she's new." They nodded and went back to chatting. Roz said to me, "We're waiting for one other girl, do you know Suzy Sparks?"

"No."

"She's a Delta, her mother played Blondie on television," Roz whispered.

"Oh . . ." I knew the comic strip, but I'd never seen the TV show.

"That's Barbara Parkins over there," Rosalind said. "She's an actress and she's talking to our Delta president, Kathy; her dad is Dana Andrews, famous movie star, you've heard of him, right? You'll meet everyone at Coffee Dan's."

Suzy Sparks came up, talking about getting a *new* car for her birthday.

Another girl rushed over. "Sorry I'm late." She was *that bratty-bitchy girl that booted me off this bench.* Good . . . she didn't recognize me, probably because of my new Flip.

We paraded up Highland and turned at the corner of the Max Factor building to the coffee shop on Hollywood Boulevard. I followed Rosalind. I sat next to Taffy. She was a barrel of laughs, making fun of everything. The conversation settled on the plans for an Easter vacation in Palm Springs.

Rosalind and I were becoming closer. I was dazzled by her. She always had the perfect hairstyle, perfect makeup—from Max Factor Essence of Pearl lipstick to painted eyeliner that curled up at the corner of her eyes—and it seemed she had a new outfit every day, plus many *real* Geistex sweaters. One day she wore a black spaghetti-strap sheath to school. It was shocking.

She said, blasé, "It's *Friday.*"

All the boys were crazy over Rosalind. She dressed older than her age and walked like she was a pageant queen. She had that edge like Beverly. It was confidence and *that* was glamorous.

I was struck by *glamour* since I was four years old, by my one and only grandmother, my mother's mother. She lived in her own world with her movie scrapbooks and vaudeville clippings of herself. She always wore bright red lipstick and had a big dimple in her cheek that she said was just for me. She would constantly tell me, "You're the apple of my eye." As hard as I searched her eyes, I could never quite locate that apple, but I believed her. Sometimes she took me to the fancy Clifton's Cafeteria downtown. We would dress up and she would say, "Order *whatever* you like." Once we went there for her birthday. "Your nana is *fifty* years old, don't I look good for my age?" I had no idea about age, except that it seemed important to look good.

Nana was a manicurist at this point in her multicolored life; her modest apartment was filled with framed autographed photos as if they were art or trophies. The haunting gaze of the magnificent Hedy Lamarr captivated me, along with another woman who had an even more intriguing face. On my tiptoes, I would hang on to Nana's lace-clothed dressing table, studying this woman's huge black eyes and eyebrows. Her name was Joan Crawford. She gave my grandmother her daughter's old clothes to pass on to me. My favorite was a wallaby coat, a fur from Australia.

Nana had run away from home to be in the circus when she was twelve. Later she performed in vaudeville, dressing like a man because women were not allowed onstage at that time. She met and married my grandfather, a magician and xylophonist, when she was seventeen. Through the vaudeville circuit, they became good friends with comedian Stan Laurel. My grandparents had many theatrical connections and as a result they arranged for my mother to act in many *Our Gang* comedies. This led to my mother's aspiring starlet days while attending Beverly Hills High School. My mother and grandmother had parts in the Laurel and Hardy film *Babes in Toyland*. This was their big Hollywood fame. Now Nana was living not too far from my mother and me, in a little apartment, alone, never having remarried after my grandfather left her, before I was born.

Strutting down the hall after first period, Rosalind popped the question: "How would you like to be a Delta?"

"Ummm, I hadn't given it much thought," I said, screaming *whoopee* inside.

"Why not? We do spend so much time together."

Pledge week: I had to wear a paper toilet seat around my neck during lunch and tell everyone I was an ass. I had to come to school without makeup. That was the worst for me, but not as bad as the other two pledges who had to walk around school with a grape up each nostril during lunchtime.

I was well on my way to owning that Delta bench. Then came Hell Night.

We all met at Kathy the president's house. Her father, Dana Andrews, came down the sweeping staircase in his smoking jacket, hair slicked back like I remembered my father's. "Having a little gathering with your friends tonight, darling?" he said to Kathy at the entry, then stepped into his private library and closed the big white door behind him. I was excited to be in this luxurious home in the Hollywood Hills—a movie star home. Kathy hollered through the closed door, "Daddy, you can't come into the kitchen. We're having a ceremony, okay?"

"Okay, dear."

We all went into the den. Pledges were told to sit on the floor.

"This is the most important night of your life," Kathy announced. "Do I hear any objections to any of these nominations?" *I hoped that girl from the first day at the Delta bench didn't make trouble for me.* "Pledges, raise your hand if you are ready to proceed." We slowly raised our hands. Taffy and Roz looked so serious. A few more girls I hadn't met were there. They were *alumnae* Deltas.

"Follow me to the sacred kitchen, one lowly pledge at a time." Kathy directed Ruth to be first.

I heard her scream, "Not me, I'm not going to eat that." Then I heard nothing. After ten long minutes Ruth came out, watery-eyed, with a faint self-preserving smile, and sat back down like a trained pup. Another girl did the same, only she barfed on herself afterward.

"Next . . ." Kathy called from the kitchen.

"That's you," the girls said synchronously. Escorted by Roz, I walked into the kitchen. The lights were off. Little candles were lit on every counter, and on top of the refrigerator with a big one centered on the circular table, like a séance was about to begin. The table had bowls of weird concoctions. One was full of tiny creatures. "Yum, chocolate-covered ants, you'll love them," Roz said, in a deep fake voice. "You take Carrie through," Kathy said to Roz, and walked out.

The next bowl was slimy glass noodles with pickles, sauerkraut, mustard, mayonnaise, and chopped chili peppers. And the last bowl . . .

"What the hell are those?" I said and looked closer.

"It's called Hell Night for a reason. Those *actually* are a delicacy from the Farmer's Market, now eat till I tell you to stop."

I chewed the repugnant rubbery rooster comb, gagging and praying, *Dear Jesus . . . if you're coming back, now's the time.*

It was all worth it, because I passed. *I got in with the in crowd.*

I was cool now and cool was power.

I was settling in, an untouchable Delta! I felt almost invincible. That was, until February 3, 1959.

I was walking up the steps to my next period, when a student rushed by and almost knocked me over. "Sorry," she said. "I'm upset about a terrible plane crash that just happened."

"What plane crash?"

"Buddy Holly, the Big Bopper, and Ritchie Valens died a few hours ago. Their plane crashed in a field somewhere."

My legs gave way and I hit my knees on the next step up and folded up. I felt nauseous and started to cry.

"Are you okay?" She leaned down to me.

"No," I cried. "Ritchie was my friend."

Flipped Out

Just when I'd gotten a handle on making my hair flip, a gorgeous Lambda girl came to school with her hair cut completely straight and smooth as glass. Where had her Flip gone? I was intrigued; the Deltas were too. It was a big day on the quad examining her new do. "Turn around," Roz said. "Again."

This *do* was going to be difficult for me to imitate; it was so exact, so sharp.

"It looks good on you," I said. "But I'm sticking with my Flip."

"Me too . . . *for now,*" Roz said. "Let me see the back again."

Whenever we passed her in the halls, we'd yell, "Great hair!"

We found out that Bonnie was going to quit school and marry the guy who'd cut her hair. He was a *hairdresser.* This was the first time I had ever heard the word *hairdresser.* Bonnie's new boyfriend changed her name as well to Cami and she was going to be a model. She left at the end of eleventh grade.

Her hairdresser boyfriend had a hair salon on Fairfax and Melrose Avenue and it was for men only. His name was Jay Sebring.

Most men's hairstyles were parted, slicked back, or cut with clippers in a flat top or buzzed off in a butch, like a marine. Not with Jay. Cami said. "He cuts hair with scissors to the natural shape of a man's head and he charges twenty-five dollars." The going rate was two bucks.

The Sebring Cut made big news. Jay was going to be in *Time* magazine. Steve McQueen would be on the cover, but the story was going to be more about Jay, for revolutionizing men's hairstyling. She said Jay's customers—Paul Newman, Warren Beatty, and James Coburn— wouldn't go anywhere without their Sebring cut. He was styling Kirk Douglas's hair for *Spartacus.*

I had never been inside a beauty salon. My mother did her own hair with an iron she heated up on our stove's open flame, or she set her hair in pin curls, and Nana set her hair in tiny white rags.

I couldn't imagine running my hands through Paul Newman's hair, or Steve McQueen's or Warren Beatty's. The idea of being a *hair-*

dresser sounded exciting, challenging and artistic, like it could turn my world around.

I was always looking for my world to turn around.

One day, out of the blue, Babe's army pal Billy Grimes called me.

"Billy, what are you doing?"

"As much as they'll let me, baby doll." He laughed.

"I miss you, how's Pacoima?"

I hadn't seen him since I left Babe and Virginia. I always thought of Billy as I'd first seen him, jumping over Babe's junkyard fence in the red lederhosen. He was an ageless spirit that blasted through the universe with no rules. He must have been old enough to be my father, but that was immaterial; our friendship was unique and we connected. I didn't know what he was talking about most of the time—neither did most people—still, *he made me feel* like I was hip enough to understand every word he said.

I was sure he was the second cousin of the Pied Piper.

"How's Hollywood treatin' you?" Billy continued. "That's the sixty-four-dollar question."

"Well . . . I'm a Delta."

"Can I be one, too?" But before I could tell him about my new *quad* life, he interrupted. "Hey, I'm in school myself, beauty school, not that I'm not pretty enough already."

We laughed.

"Yeah, it's all about *hair* . . . in fact I moved to Hollywood too."

"There's a *school* for hair?" The Deltas only talked about the John Robert Powers charm school.

"Sho 'nuff," Billy said. "I met this Beverly Hills hairdresser and he's got it all goin' on."

I had never known what Billy did for a living; it never occurred to me to ask.

"I have to take a test for my hair school and you'd be perfect for me to practice on."

"Me? Sure, Billy, anything with you," I said, not knowing what *practice on me* entailed.

The next day after school, I practically ran the seven blocks to the

Comer and Doran Beauty School on Hollywood Boulevard to meet Billy. Inside, the school was like a long ballroom, with fifty people busy at stations, buzzing around one another, instructors helping kids with mannequin heads screwed on table counters, and another section with real live women getting their hair done by students in white lab coats.

I was immediately enthralled.

"Hey, baby doll, look what they've done to me," Billy said, appearing out of nowhere as he always did, waving his long gangly arms in the air, wearing a white lab coat. Of course he had on all his necklaces with trinkets: bells and medals and beads from an Indian friend in Oklahoma, with an open shirt under his lab coat so they could be noticed. It was funny for me to see Billy in a controlled environment. "I don't think white is my color," he said. "Jewelry helps."

Billy had his own station. He pumped the chair up so I was the right height for him and tied a plastic cape around my neck that covered my whole body.

"This is gonna take a few minutes, maybe hours." Billy laughed.

I looked around. One woman was being taught how to manicure. Another guy was rolling a permanent. It stank like the time my mother gave herself and me that awful Toni home perm.

Billy came closer with a private scoop. "This hair biz is gonna *blow up,* you jus' wait and see."

He began whipping up bowls of bleach powder and peroxide and applied it to my head with a wide paintbrush. Next he jumped in with his hands, smearing my whole head with this blue paste.

"Is this supposed to burn?"

"Jus' a little while, dahlin'."

"Okay. What am I gonna look like?"

"How old are you now?" Billy asked, then before I answered he said, "Time to be a blonde!"

My natural hair color was light brown. I had dyed my hair dark to look more Mexican when I was in Pacoima. This hadn't all grown out yet. When the bleach hit the old dye, it got bright orange.

"Don't worry," Billy said, so professionally. "This is the first process. Now we condition and start over."

He left me lying back in the shampoo bowl to go smoke. He came back with the teacher, who gave him new directions.

"And Billy," she said as she walked off, "night class ends at ten PM."

"Oh, we'll be wailin' outta here by then, sugah," Billy confirmed.

He rinsed me and walked me back to his station. I sat down and opened my math homework, which I hated. He swiveled my chair away from the mirror.

"Don't look till I tell you, m' li'l beauty queen."

He covered my hair with a plastic bag, and six rinses, six applications, six Cokes, a cheeseburger, and six hours later . . .

"Come on, Billy," the teacher called out. Billy was in the final styling stages. She stood at the light switches. He picked up the rubber pump of hair lacquer and squeezed big splashes of sticky crispy spray onto my fried hair.

"Voilà," he said, thrilled with his work, and spun me around to see myself.

"*Yeouwzers.*" My hair was powder pink. Plus he had backcombed it straight up, whipped it around to a point on top of my head, and then stuck in every bobby pin he had. My hair looked like cotton candy on a paper roll.

"It's a *Beehive,*" he announced. "*And* . . . it will last for weeks."

I kept staring at my head.

He packed up.

"We're off . . . like a prom dress," Billy told the teacher. She locked up behind us. "My car's over there." He pointed at the parking lot. "Hey, girl, where are you livin' these days?"

"With my mom, nearby."

"Sorry, baby girl, kinda late for a school night, will she be worried?"

"Nah, she's probably not even home. But you better drive me there, I don't wanna wreck my new do."

"You can't wreck it, in fact, you better call me for help when you wanna take it down."

I kept patting my stiff lacquered cotton candy hair as Billy drove with the radio blasting. I lived five minutes away on Sunset and Mansfield in a small stucco apartment.

Billy dropped me off. I ran upstairs and unlocked the front door.

The bathroom door was open with its light illuminating the living room.

"Mom, Mom?"

No answer. I didn't look in her room, she might have company. I peeled off my clothes and dropped them in a pile. After I put on my pajamas and brushed my teeth, I carefully laid down, making sure my pink Beehive was safe on the pillow.

I slept like a dead person.

The next morning I woke up and dashed to the mirror. Ah, perfect, not one hair out of place.

"Mom, Mom?"

No answer. She'd see my hair later . . . I had to get to school.

I couldn't wait to show off my new Billy do. My hair color was mild compared to the heads in his beauty school yesterday—purple, blue, fuchsia. I was ready to let Billy practice on me again, but maybe I'd wait till he graduated.

I got to school and sure enough everyone noticed my hairstyle, just like Cami's new hairstyle. But, unlike her hair, mine never moved.

Some kids and teachers looked at me oddly. But the Deltas thought I was cool and wanted to know where I got it.

"There is a secret universe . . . on Hollywood Boulevard."

Under the Influence

I was street smart, but I was not book smart. One class had a reputation for drawing the best minds, Harry Major's advanced composition class. Kids rushed to sign up with Harry Major. I went an hour before school started and there was already a line. I stood quietly listening for any clues, in case I was going to be interviewed. When I got to the front of his desk he looked at my hair. I had done it myself this time, henna auburn.

"Are you new to this school?"

"Sort of . . . but I'm a Delta." I smiled big and proud.

"I am concerned with your brain, not your social life, and *if you have a brain,* you should be too." He leaned back in his chair and raised his eyebrow. "Why do you want to be in my class?"

"I want to learn things and I heard you are the best teacher."

"That's not what I hear about me," he said, smirking, signing me in. "You will have to work"—he scanned my list of other classes— "harder than in your modern dance and ceramics classes."

"Oh, I will," I assured him. "And thank you, thank you."

It *was* the hardest class. The pressure to read book after book, week after week, was too much for me. I struggled, leaping from sentence to paragraph then back up to where I left off when I got lost, and finally completed *Jane Eyre* and *Wuthering Heights.* Even though reading was a struggle, I loved writing and reporting my observations.

After the classics, we read radical books, which I loved. Albert Camus's *The Stranger* struck me profoundly with the opening sentence, "My mother died today or was it yesterday?" It captured my relationship with my mother, misplaced, vague, unspoken buried love . . . if any.

I didn't want anyone to know I was so behind, still reading the second chapter of *Walden* when the class was ready for the next book, *The Scarlet Letter.* It was always that way. I was exhausted and frustrated but Harry didn't give up on me. He passed me with a C+.

He knew I worked so hard for that C+.

"How can you stand Harry Major?" Rosalind asked. Kids either hated him or worshipped him. "I heard he's cruel and coldhearted."

"No, he's just kinda sarcastic. I like him."

I studied for his class when I ditched school and went across the street to the Pancake House with friends. I was torn between getting smart and being social. In the end it was good enough to know that Harry appreciated my efforts. I liked how Harry got into the minds of the authors and characters. He sure got into my mind. After his class, I saw the world deeper and differently, through literature as opposed to only from my own experience.

It seemed every girl at Hollywood High wanted to be an actress, including me. I had been good in Shakespeare at Pacoima Junior High.

I even won an award for my rendition of Puck in the Shakespeare Festival at UCLA's Royce Hall.

"If you are serious about your art and craft of acting," John, my acting teacher, told the class, "you should be subscribing to *Theatre Arts,* a magazine from New York, that contains stories and a new play every month."

John made New York come alive. He went on about the famous acting teachers, Stella Adler, Lee Strasberg, method acting, The Actors Studio. He taught us about the musicals *Carousel, Gypsy,* and *Oklahoma!*

We all thought, *Next stop: Broadway.*

John had many students from his class who were professional actors already—Sally Kellerman, Tuesday Weld, Yvette Mimieux, and Ricky Nelson—though they were ahead of me by a few years. And rising in my class, Delta sister Barbara Parkins landed a starring role in the television series *Peyton Place* before she graduated from high school.

The hero of us all was my Delta pal Taffy Paul, who was discovered in our school musical *Annie Get Your Gun* by actress Ann Sothern. The biggest thing to hit Hollywood at this time was the casting cattle call for the film *West Side Story.* I tried out and got nothing. Taffy did score a part, but when production realized she was under eighteen they didn't want to pay for her on-set tutor. Right away, though, Taffy got herself another part in a big film, *Experiment in Terror,* starring Lee Remick and Glenn Ford. Taffy also got a new name: Stefanie Powers.

Spin Cycle

One day in the girls' bathroom, I saw Roz opening a little gold pillbox. She took one pill out and popped it in her mouth. "Hey, watch my purse," she said, talking like she had a sponge for a tongue. "I'm going to the water fountain."

She came back smiling and put on some lip gloss.

"What was that?"

"Want one?"

I didn't ask her what is it for, will I like it, how often do you take them, where did you get them, can I get some more if I like them, are they legal, does your mother know about them, will they make me happy, strong, can I walk, talk, or drive with them, will they make me smarter, prettier, a better dancer, taller, will my hair catch on fire and my eyes light up, how many can I take on the weekend, does everyone in the Deltas know about them, how come you never gave me one before, didn't you like me enough, why are you offering me now, what do we do after the pill, how long do they last, can I have one tomorrow too, are you sick, is it a vitamin, could I die?

"Yeah sure," I said. "I'll try one."

She went back to her little pillbox and handed me a green-and-white capsule. I put it in my mouth.

"We gotta go," Roz said. "Fifth period."

I followed her out the door and went to the water fountain. Roz stayed to make sure I got it down.

"Okay, see ya at the bench," Roz said. "Coffee Dan's today?"

"Sure."

I walked across the quad to Harry Major's class and waited to see what this little pill was about, if anything. It didn't take long. After ten minutes I felt my eyes open wider, like someone had turned the room lights up. My heart pumped up a notch and all of a sudden everything got very interesting. I wanted to get busy, maybe organize Harry's messy papers and the books on his desk, the books on the wall bookshelf, all the wall bookshelves, actually. The whole room seemed to need my attention. I argued with myself, *You can't get up; think of something else.* I quietly took out a Kleenex and began polishing my makeup containers, my tube of lipstick, my eyeliner case; my mascara needed black spots wiped off, and the crumbs in the bottom of my purse from a chocolate chip cookie needed to depart.

Then it hit me. I was full of energy. That's what the pill was about. I'd needed this all my life. I felt connected. This pill was like magic. Maybe I could read faster. Nope, in fact my eyes jumped around on the page more than usual; my new energy was too distracting.

"Excuse me, Carrie," Mr. Major obviously had been calling on me. I was so into my head I didn't hear him. I forgot I was in class. "Can you please tell us what is the significant difference between E. E. Cummings as opposed to Thoreau, who both wrote on the human condition?" Was this a trick question? I repeated Harry's words to myself. "We are waiting," he said.

"Uhhh, E. E. Cummings only used lowercase."

"Is that your best answer?"

My mind flew to other things, back to cleaning my purse, and I'd better clean my closet when I get home. I nodded my head, *Yep, that's my answer*, and smiled. I noticed when I smiled my lips were very dry, about to crack off my face. No wonder Roz went for her lip gloss right away. And my throat was as parched as corrugated cardboard. I needed water.

Mr. Major turned to another classmate. "Ethan, would that be your answer?"

The class genius Ethan, wearing black horn-rimmed glasses, spouted, "Besides *lower case,* they were both at different times. Edward Estlin Cummings liked to distort the syntax and punctuation. Thoreau was very succinct; E. E. Cummings was an artist, Thoreau was not. E. E. Cummings was sarcastic, Thoreau was romantic, a transcendentalist, an abolitionist . . ."

Oh, shut up, Ethan, you big show-off.

Hearing my deficiencies confronted, I slouched in my desk. *Aw, geez, what's this . . . ink from some geek last period left all over my desk?* I sat up, spit on the Kleenex with what little saliva I could muster, and started wiping the ink off. This little pill was incredible. I felt like I had had fifty-seven cups of coffee. I felt like I could climb a mountain. *When's class over already? I might paint my bedroom chartreuse today. I wonder where a paint store is.*

I raised my hand, "May I be excused? I need some water."

At Coffee Dan's that day, I didn't want to seem as enthusiastic as I felt about this pill, but I was very interested in having another one tomorrow. Roz didn't ask me if I liked the pill. I was sure it showed on me, my vibrating cheeks or something. Trying to counteract my boisterous insides, I whispered, "Roz, I feel really alert."

"It wears off . . . I've been taking them for years."

"Years? Can I get one for tomorrow? I have lots of homework and . . ."

"You got the idea, maybe just take half, though, if it feels like too much."

"Half? That doesn't sound like fun."

"Fine, take the whole pill, but watch it if you drink a beer or anything."

"Why?"

"You could get too drunk before you know it."

Roz couldn't understand how I could drink so much, and I didn't understand how she could drink so little. She didn't care if we drank or not. I wasn't happy unless we did.

I didn't tell Roz or the Deltas about my love affair with my mother's bourbon that started in Pacoima or about getting busted for being drunk at age twelve. I never forgot my first sip of my mother's bourbon when I was five; the glow after it hit my body, like a warm blanket. Drinking felt good. And if one was good, wouldn't three be better? Besides, drinking made me feel prettier and smarter.

Roz was more interested in guys than in drinking. I got more interested in guys *when* I drank. I was convinced that if the world drank more, it would be a better place to live in. And I really wanted to try alcohol with this pill.

"So, Roz, where do you get the pills?"

"I got a guy who gets me as many as I want."

They were called Dexedrine. They were diet pills and who wanted to eat when there was so much to do after taking one?

I raced in my mind. I raced in my body. I raced to think of more things to race to. I loved the feeling. I was able to clean my room, do my homework quickly, and expand my thoughts. I picked lint off my sweaters and shined my shoes, hung all my hangers in the same direction; color-coordinated my clothes from white to black, and the same with my shoes. I had my work cut out for me, next maybe I ought to paint my drawers . . .

"What the hell is going on?" my mother said, popping her head in my bedroom around midnight.

"I need to get organized."

"You need to go to bed." She closed the door.

She needed to go to bed, not me.

"I'm not tired," I said through the closed door.

"*Carole,* you have school tomorrow," she hollered back.

"*Okay . . .* but my name is *Carrie.*"

I brushed my teeth and got into bed. My body was tired, but not my mind. *Tomorrow, I will move my mirror to the other side of my room, and my bed should go under the window, more breeze there, and . . . zzzzzzzz.*

The next night, after more organizing, I calculated my needs— better clothes, better acrylics, new shoes, mascara, lipsticks, eye shadows. Which brought me to the main point; I had no money like the other girls I knew.

"I need a job, Roz. I need money. I've worked at a bakery and a pizza parlor. I can paint signs, too. What work do you do?"

"Work?" Roz giggled. "I don't know anything about that." She told me her grandmother and her mom gave her money, each one thinking the other didn't. "And Joe and Mickey and Gary give me money to buy myself presents."

Roz modeled her new black Geistex pullover. *How does she get guys that aren't even her boyfriends to give her money?*

"Hey, you know what?" Roz burst out. "Linda Evans works at the Hollywood Paramount and Ingrid works across the street at Grauman's Chinese Theatre. Maybe you could be an usherette."

The theaters she spoke of were around the corner from school. I wasn't sure what an usherette was, though, I never heard of an usherette at the Van Nuys Drive-In or the Panorama Theatre.

Thanks to Roz's magic pills, I was ready to leap tall buildings in a single bound, and working after school sounded great. I went to the famous Grauman's Chinese Theatre. Outside, Betty Grable had imprinted her legs in the cement, Bob Hope and Jimmy Durante their noses, Groucho Marx and George Burns their hands and cigars. I walked slowly, past the two stone lions guarding the entrance, into the huge pagoda.

It was not busy at 4:00 PM, so I could really see its beauty. The high ceilings towered over me like a cathedral and the gold-trimmed ropes and paintings on the Chinese-printed walls made me feel like I was in China. Even the carpet was a Chinese design.

Asking for a paint job in Pacoima was easy. This was scary. I went to the popcorn girl. "Who do I speak to about a job?"

The man counting the money behind her turned and said, "Try across the street. We don't need anyone here."

Not much I could say after that. "Thank you . . ." I left.

I ran across the street to the Paramount. It wasn't special like the Chinese, no theme, no gold. I asked the girl in the ticket box if the manager was in, because I was looking for a job.

"Come back later, Mr. Katsky will be in around nine."

"Okay, I'll see ya then. What's your name?"

"Stella and I'm quitting, so I know there will be a space."

"Okay, sorry you're leaving, but whoopee for me."

I went home and told my mother, "I think I got a job."

"That's nice," she said, painting at her desk. "How will you get there?"

"I can walk, I'm fine."

My mother liked to ask, but she needed me to be *fine*.

She had no time for me *not* to be fine.

Mr. Katsky greeted me at the snack bar. He was an attractive elderly man in his forties. I got the idea he had only a few minutes for me. It was hardly an interview. "Stella told me about you. I'll need you in two weeks if you want the job. Lots of kids from your school have worked here."

I loved my theater job. I stood at the back and watched *Gone With the Wind* over and over. I decided I wanted *I'll think about that tomorrow* on my gravestone. Next *BUtterfield 8* opened. I had never seen the likes of Elizabeth Taylor's full-screen astonishing beauty, her piercing violet eyes. I had also never seen anything as cool as when her character brushed her teeth first thing in the morning from a leftover glass of scotch sitting on the bathroom sink.

Palm Springs Easter Vacation

"Hey, are you coming?" Roz asked me during lunch at the Delta bench.

"Coming where?"

Roz picked through the lunch her mom made her. "Palm Springs for spring break, for the best time and tan in the whole world, that's where."

I packed my nightgown, my Zizanie cologne in the silver metal spray can, shampoo, Life cream rinse, and Coppertone. I put in my best dress, my black spaghetti-strap sheath, just like Roz's, my black heels, my black fox-collared sweater with the rhinestone clasp at the waist, and my new two-piece Cole bathing suit. I slipped on my sundress and Bernardo sandals and fluffed my Flip. I was ready. Walking out to the living room to wait for Roz, I realized I had forgotten to tell my mother I was off to a desert somewhere . . .

My mother and I lived in the hush of our past and had maintained our distance since we'd moved back to Hollywood. She had her world and I had mine. We had a common courtesy: *Don't get in my way and I won't get in yours.* I loved my mother, but more as a memory, an idea.

She was sitting on the couch in her white cuffed shorts, her skinny little legs too tanned from sunning on the one metal lounge out front on the cement lanai, her skinny little midriff uncovered in a blouse tied under her barely there breasts, with her little too tanned arms sticking out. She was watching television, smoking a Pall Mall, and drinking a beer. It was Saturday, 10:00 AM.

"No work?" I asked.

"No, Bill's coming over, we're going to Marian's, maybe play poker."

Bill, my mom's surveyor boyfriend, and Marian, her best and only friend, loved to play poker. It was their favorite thing to do next to drinking.

"Bill and I are getting married," she told me.

I set my suitcase down.

"Mom, I'm going to Palm Springs with Roz and the Deltas for Easter week. Her grandmother is chaperoning."

"Just like that? *I'm going*? Don't you think you should *ask me* if it's okay? I don't know these girls." She was having her *Good Housekeeping* parenting attack.

"Mom, get real."

She slammed her beer can on the coffee table, that same coffee table that never held coffee.

"Get real?" she mimicked. "Don't you talk to me like I'm one of your kid friends. I'm your mother, that's insulting, I ought to—"

"Mom," I interrupted. "The Deltas do this every year. Besides, don't you have to plan your wedding?"

She lit a cigarette and brushed off old fallen ashes from the last one.

"Okay, but you be careful. And no biggy, we'll probably go to the courthouse. Do you want to come?"

"No thanks, oh, that honking must be Rosalind, 'bye, Mom."

Without looking back, I picked up my little suitcase and pranced out.

"We've been driving over an hour. Where is this Palm Springs desert?"

Rosalind's hair was blowing behind her. The front was held back with a red-and-white polka-dot bandanna that matched her Lanz designer sundress. Her lips were glossed white and she had on big white plastic sunglasses. Gramma Rose was in the backseat like a stuffed cushy Gramma doll. She was silent, staring out the window. Her eyes didn't seem alert to the passing sights. It was more like she was looking inside at days gone by.

"Gramma, you okay?" She didn't respond to Roz and continued to stare out the window. *"Gramma, how're you doing?"* Roz asked louder. Gramma Rose nodded and smiled. She was bundled up in a Mode O'Day housedress and a loose knitted shawl. I smiled back to her.

"Hi, Gramma Rose, you want some root beer?" She tightened her lips and shook her head *no.* I turned back to my side of the world, the front seat.

The car radio was blasting "Jailhouse Rock." All the windows were down. The air conditioner didn't work on Gramma Rose's old Packard.

"Did you see those guys in that big Lincoln? They were looking at us," Roz said. "I bet they're going to Palm Springs."

"Hey, look at that Woody," I said. "Those guys are waving at us."

"Play hard to get, don't smile," Roz said. "What an old clunker, anyway."

We laughed and started singing "Sweet Little Sixteen" with the radio.

Another car passed with girls waving at us. I smiled. When a family drove by and waved, I thought, that was odd, we couldn't be that cute.

"Do you smell something funny?" Roz asked.

I was too busy smoking to be sensitive to any smell. "No."

"Vhat's that smell?" Gramma Rose spurted out in her thick Yiddish accent.

Roz slowed down to 60 mph. Now every car that passed us was frantically waving and pointing at us. Roz and I looked at each other.

Someone pulled close to us and yelled, "Your car is on fire."

We looked at each other and screamed, *"Fire?"*

"Vhat'd he say?"

Roz pulled to the side of the road, we jumped out, and she tried to pull Gramma Rose out of the backseat. "The car's on fire, Gramma, come out."

"Vhat?"

"*Fire,* Gramma Rose, hurry."

"*Fire*? Oh my Gawt," Gramma Rose screamed. "This vaz Poppa's favorite car, *oy vayzmere,* Hoiman, I'm sorry," she ranted, struggling to get out quickly.

"Take Gramma!" Roz practically threw her at me. "I'm getting our suitcases."

"Roz, you're crazy! We need to run *from* the car."

"I'm not losing my best clothes and my new bikinis. Want yours?"

As smoke billowed and red fire shot from the front end, Roz ran to the trunk. People were driving by, looking horrified, but no one stopped.

"Okay, get mine too, but hurry!"

I looked at the huge sprawling sky, blue and beautiful except for our growing black cloud. Gramma Rose and I plunked down on the embankment. Roz ran back with our suitcases. "It'll be okay, Gramma, we'll get it fixed."

"Vhat you mean?" Gramma Rose cried. "Nutting to fix, look, it's gone."

We looked and the car was completely engulfed in flames. I didn't know whether to cry or laugh. This seemed impossible. But lo and behold, to our rescue, two cute guys pulled up followed by fire trucks.

"You obviously need a lift," said the cute driver. "Where to?"

Roz twinkled through her devastation. "Palm Springs."

"We'll take you."

We piled in the backseat, squeezing Gramma Rose in between us.

I let Roz do her flirting. I stared out the window and began to grasp the desert that I had never seen before, calming with its vastness, the random cactus scattered about, hiding all the animals that must be living out there, snakes, rabbits, and lizards.

Then, like an oasis, I saw where we were headed. The glimmer of lights at the threshold meshed with the remains of the day's sunlight. We drove the highway like a river winding through the pass, palm trees bordering both sides of the road, blowing my mind wide open.

I finally relaxed, decompressed. The warmest wind breezed by my face from the open windows. It was a big moment, a moment of recognizing creation and my planet, Earth. I suddenly felt a closeness to a God I wanted to believe in, the kind my grandmother had talked about, the God that knew what was in everybody's heart, even the tiniest sparrow, a God without judgment, punishment, shame, just beauty, welcoming, loving, and all-surrounding. I looked at Roz still flirting; Gramma Rose asleep, the two cute boys still cute. I felt completely at peace in my own body.

The other Deltas were out when we arrived. We plunked onto our king-size bed, our faces frosted like cookies with a fancy cream Roz brought for facials, watching television. Gramma Rose was comfortable in her single bed.

A new day: we popped our Dexedrine with our morning orange juice. "We aren't stopping until next Sunday morning," Roz said.

Suzy banged on our door.

"Time to get out to the pool—cool drinks and hot guys."

"Rosalind, you tell your mother vhat happen t'us? Oy, your Grampa Hoiman, he's rollink ovah in his grave, he loved dat cah. And vhere is da' cah?"

"Don't worry, Gramma, it's being fixed," Roz said, tucking her in her chair in front of the television. "We're going outside." She turned to me. "Put some oil on my back, will ya?"

"Wow, this smells good," I said, slathering her back with her expensive Bain de Soleil tanning lotion. "Can I borrow some?" Roz squeezed out more orange goo in her hand and handed the tube to me.

"Sure, I have three more in my suitcase. It's the best."

She started to walk out.

"Hey, what about my back?"

"Ask a cute guy to rub it on when you get to the pool." Roz laughed. "Come on, let's go before Gramma Rose asks about her damn car again."

We were lying out in the boiling 102 degrees for about an hour. I saw Roz frying in front of my eyes, waves of heat rising off her tummy. It reminded me of summer days in Pacoima, but I was far from Virginia's pool. I wanted to be blasé like Roz, like the other Deltas who were chatting it up with boys, but I felt awkward, half naked, and too shy with them. And I knew I laughed too loudly when Roz told a joke, so I slunk down into a tanning pose, where I could view everyone through my big turquoise framed sunglasses without being noticed.

"Look who's coming in the gate," Roz said. "Joe Montgomery and his friends."

The *Seven Samurai* posse, the best-looking guys from Hollywood High, the Athenians club invaded our pool area. Roger Montgomery, Joe's older brother, was the only one I actually knew. They all strolled in like they owned the place. There was *one* guy in particular who got my attention. Who was he? I felt flush behind my ears. He made my heart jump out of my bathing suit like I was a cartoon character.

For starters, he towered over the other guys, his longish straight brown hair falling over on his forehead like Tarzan, big relaxed lips that showed no emotion, chiseled cheeks, a strong jaw, and big brown eyes that locked onto mine. He was walking over to us with Roger, walking closer and closer.

Oh . . . talk to me, talk to me, not Roz, pick me. Roz had a million guys and she could get a million more. I hoped Roz wouldn't go for him or I wouldn't have a chance. Roz sat up and peeked over her sunglasses at Roger.

"You want to go out with *me* tonight, don't you?" Roger said to Roz, lifting her up off her lounge. She screamed and giggled.

My handsome Adonis stood like a statue taking it all in. Maybe it was his first time here too. He didn't seem as rowdy as the rest. I felt his presence like nothing I had known before. I was paralyzed, hypnotized, mesmerized as I studied him in open view. This must be what "love at first sight" means. I had to do something besides stare at him. I reached for the suntan lotion and unscrewed the top. His big hand swooped down on mine.

"Let me do that for you," he said, with a deep foreign accent.

I couldn't look at him now; he was too close.

He took the tube from me. I thought I was going to faint. Before my next breath, he was on my leg with the Bain de Soleil. We didn't talk. He went up and down my legs with the fancy cream. "How about your back?"

I smiled, hiding my nerves, not wanting to speak, and I rolled over.

The pool area faded, it was just his big hand on my back. Then he undid the hook on my bathing suit top to place the lotion evenly. I was glad I was facedown. He rehooked my top when he finished and said, "Happy tanning session."

"Let's split," Roger said. They walked out as determined as they walked in.

"*Who was that?*" I asked Roz.

"The giant? I don't know. I never saw him before. Why?"

We went out every night that week and all I did was silently search for my tanning-lotion Adonis, but in the whole seven days, I never saw him again.

Sunset Strip

Roz was driving her mom's T-bird. "Mack the Knife" was blaring and we sang every word. We had no particular place in mind but this street, the fabulous Sunset Strip. We thought we owned it.

Roz looked glamorous as usual. She had her super Palm Springs tan and was showing it off in her new white halter cotton dress. Her hair was parted to one side, her vibrant blue cat eyes peeking out, the heavy black eyeliner accentuating their almond shape. Her beauty still captivated me. I loved being with her. She was always self-assured, more girlie than me, more particular than me, more everything than me.

I looked out at the nightclubs, one on every corner, Ciro's, La Rue Nightclub, the Trocadero, the Mocambo, and the ultimate tourist trap, Dino's Lodge, Dean Martin's restaurant, where they filmed the television show *77 Sunset Strip*. Roz told me the whole Strip used to be owned by gangsters. "That's where Bugsy Siegel, Mickey Cohen's flunky, gambled," Roz said, and pointed to the Melody Room.

"Quick, pull into the Interlude parking lot," I shouted. "I see Roger Montgomery."

"Thanks for the warning." Roz screeched over.

Cute parking attendants swarmed us. One guy started to pull his pants down to moon us. "Hey, Goldie, we're not at the beach," Roger said, and turned his butt to us. "Let me do it!"

Roz laughed. "Stop it, you guys."

"What're you girls doin'?" Roger said. "Wanna go in and see the show?"

I wanted to ask about the handsome giant he'd brought to Palm Springs, but Lenny Bruce was performing.

"You can get us in?" Roz asked.

"Don't you know us parking guys got the *real* power on this street?"

"Speaking of power," I said, innocently, "how's your friend?"

"What friend?"

"The guy at the pool with you, the one with all the muscles. He looked like Hercules," I said. "He had an accent."

"Ohhhhhhhh." Goldie flipped his lips like The Three Stooges' Curly. "You mean Big Dan. Why, ya like him, huh? Do ya, do ya?"

I blushed. "I thought he was very nice."

"She *likes* him!" Roger said. "As a matter a fact, he works here sometimes."

I felt all tingly like when he rubbed the lotion on my legs.

Meeting Richard Alcala

Billy Grimes called just as I was about to leave for school.

"Where you been, Billy?" I had called his beauty school for months looking for him. "I had to have *two* friends help me take down that hairdo you made."

He laughed.

"Wanna meet the guy that turned me on to hairdressing and see his Beverly Hills salon?"

I loved hanging out with Billy, especially if he was going to show me something that excited him. Plus this would be my first step inside a beauty salon.

"Yes, when?"

"Today, baby doll, when else is there?'"

That was Billy . . . no tomorrows . . . only *right now.*

I had never been to Beverly Hills.

I was born on Burton Way, a short street referred to as the Gateway to Beverly Hills, but I never got past the gate. I knew my mother went to Beverly Hills High and she had a fiancé when she was seventeen, the track star, but he was killed in a car accident before they graduated. She never talked about it or her childhood.

Burton Way had a plush green bridal path that extended about three miles long, and later was replaced by cable tracks. I remembered the train that brought the Ringling Brothers Circus to town. It would park in front of our Burton Way courtyard home. I heard lions roar in their train cages.

When we moved back from Pacoima, we moved to Hollywood. Beverly Hills and Hollywood were two different worlds.

I ran across the street after school. There was Billy listening to "Great Balls of Fire" and smoking his Nat Sherman. Billy was the first guy, except for a pirate, that I ever saw wearing a pierced earring, one little gold hoop. I jumped into his root beer brown Chevy.

"Babe's gonna get me a car, did I tell you?"

"Groovy, we can race," Billy said. "Wait till you meet this cat Richard Alcala. He's cool like an ocean breeze and got them chicks goin' crazy for him."

I realized, as Billy went on talking, that his hairdressing was a little bit about hair and a lot about getting women.

"Billy, are you going to do hair or chicks?"

"Both, baby doll. You make 'em pretty, then you take 'em out."

Billy could talk the spots off a leopard, sell water to a drowning man and the Bible to the devil, so he was sure to do well in his new venture.

"There it is!" he said. I didn't see any fancy Beverly Hills salon. "And that's Richard Alcala standing out front talking to a woman in a smock."

From across the street I could see a man wearing a black suit and tie—and he was handsome.

"You're gonna love this guy." Billy said.

"Maybeeee," I said. We parked and headed across the street. I felt I was about to meet a celebrity.

"Hey, man," Richard greeted us. The lady walked away.

"Wasn't that Natalie Wood?" Billy said.

"Yeah," Richard said, and watched her go back inside the salon, then turned back to us. "So, how are you, Billy? What's up, man?"

"I brought my li'l friend by"—Billy leaned in—"you changed your name fo' sure, right?"

I couldn't take my teenage eyes off Richard. I was smiling at him way too much. It was easy to see why being near him was captivating. He had an effortless cool and he smelled good. He was Latin, with well-cut jet-black hair, caramel tan skin, and black eyes. I didn't want my fluster to show, and Billy's not remembering my name made me feel more awkward. I nodded *yes* to Billy, still looking at Richard's handsome face. If he wasn't a hairdresser he could be a movie star.

"Meet *Carrie*," Billy continued. "I wanted her to see where I'm gonna work when I get my license."

Richard gave me a wink with fleeting attention. I was no Natalie Wood. "Champagne?" he said, and walked into his salon. We followed.

I'd never had champagne before.

I crossed the threshold of his salon and took a big private gasp. The place was buzzing with activity and loud Latin jazz: Cal Tjader. The phone rang constantly. "Richard, how much longer do I have to leave this conditioner in?" a lady cooed. He acted like he didn't hear her and went to an ingenue sitting in the shampoo area. "I won't be long," he said to her. She smiled. Other ladies were doing needlepoint, chatting, and reading fashion magazines.

Everyone seemed to know one another; the hairdressers and stars looked like best friends. I didn't want to seem starstruck, but that *was* Rita Hayworth getting her nails done. Natalie Wood came out of the bathroom and gave Richard a very long hug and left. Her hair looked beautiful.

This Beverly Hills salon was nothing like Billy's beauty school with white uniforms and an all-sterile environment. There was nothing plastic or white or wipeable in this whole place. Not at the Richard Alcala Salon.

It was small and cozy, with room for three hairdressers, one manicurist, and a reception desk. The furniture was Mexican-style, carved chairs, and tables. I'd never seen Mexican furniture even in Pacoima.

Richard also had a huge heavy Victorian mirror leaning against one corner. It was in an ornate gold-leaf frame about twelve feet high like I'd only seen in pictures of English castles. There was a Kentia palm tree next to the mirror. Maxfield Parrish prints hung on the wall. Louis Icart, too. Billy informed me of the artists' names when he saw me staring at them.

A heavy-set black lady was waving an appointment book, trying to get Richard's attention, the telephone in her other hand.

"Richard, it's Phyllis! Where ya gonna put her?"

"Tell her her hair looks fine," he answered, with a lack of concern, as he walked over with a glass of champagne in his hand. He turned to me. "How 'bout you?" he said, and handed me his glass.

She handed Richard the phone and came over to me.

"Hi, darlin', my name is Mary. You waitin' fo' Richard too?"

"No, she's with me." Billy said. "What's cookin', good-lookin'?"

Richard hung up the phone. "Mary, if she calls back, tell her I love her but I'm doing hair." Richard turned to us. "More champagne?"

"Hell, yeah," Billy said.

"What's that smell, Billy?" I asked.

"Pot, baby girl, lots o' pot smokin' in the alley."

A blind man could see why Billy wanted to jump into this den. The dressing gowns were dropping off the clients' shoulders, and the champagne was flowing.

I knew it would take more than a hair change for me to blend in here.

Richard walked over to the young woman patiently waiting in the chair in front of his massive mirror. She looked up at him without complaint. He moved in to kiss her neck. I overheard him say, "I know what you want."

And he picked up his scissors.

Billy tapped my shoulder. "We gotta split, baby doll," Billy said, lit his Sherman, strummed his hand through his chicken-feathered hair, and put his cowboy hat back on. "I'm late for a date and it's not with you."

The room came back into focus; the private life inside a Beverly Hills beauty salon. I was just visiting but I wanted to be a part of it.

When I said good-bye to Richard I'm sure I stuttered.

I probably tripped too.

My Car, My Danny

"Ready for your car?" the voice on the phone said.

"Babe!" I screamed. "Really?"

"I told you I was getting your first car for you."

The world was opening to me like wings popping out of my back. My first thought, cruise Sunset . . . *find Big Dan.*

"Mom," I said. She was at her desk, drinking and smoking more than painting. *"Mom,"* I said louder. "Babe got me a *car*, I have my own car!"

She looked at me, her eyes watery from years of being soaked in bourbon. They were never again going to sparkle. She still wore the same hairdo from the day I first noticed hair on her head. I felt my life beginning. I saw hers getting smaller and weaker.

"That's great." She looked at me with that glazed smile in front of her sadness. "I wish I could get you a car."

I walked over and put my arm around her.

"When are you and Bill getting married?"

"I don't know, he's surveying in Santa Maria, maybe after you graduate."

I wondered if he loved my mother enough to really marry her. He was such a lush, but then so was she. Who else *could* be with her?

"That's nice, Mom. I'm going to a Delta meeting, see you later."

"Okay . . ." She slowly turned back, taking a last drag from the Pall Mall burned down to nothing in the ashtray, a slug of her highball, picking up her paint brush to go back to work.

The minute the last bell rang, I ran to the auditorium building and stopped on a dime at the sidewalk. Babe's tow truck was parked in front of the steps, and in front of it; a two-door, turquoise '55 Ford with shining chrome bumpers. Babe was sitting behind the wheel with a smile on his face like he'd delivered a baby. I couldn't believe my luck; Babe and Virginia were so good to me. He got out and handed me the keys. I welled up with tears and hugged him.

"Okay, okay," he said, pulling away, uncomfortable with too much love. "Don't get all mushy on me, get in and turn the key." He smiled, jumped into his tow truck, and pulled off. I sat in the driver's seat, stroked the steering wheel, and examined *my car, my two-door turquoise 1955 Ford.*

My first night off work, I got all dolled up in my best red off-the-shoulder ruffled blouse, white tapered pants, my hair almost as perfect as Roz's, eyelashes curled, three applications of Maybelline, a faded Palm Springs tan. I hoped my wish would come true and I could spot Big Dan at the Interlude parking lot.

Roz called. "I can't go with you."

"You have to!"

"I'm meeting you-know-who at Sportsmen's Lodge. Be happy for me."

Awww, crap. Can I do this alone? Yes!

I went out to my *new* best friend, my car, while I still had my nerve and headed toward the Strip. "It's just you and me," I said, and patted the dash.

Awww, crap. What if he isn't there?

Awww, crap. What if he is?

I need a plan, a plan that doesn't look like a plan.

Think think think . . .

I drove on the opposite side of the street to steal a look without being noticed. No one knew my car. I never had one before. I could sit and spy all night.

I couldn't miss Goldie jumping around the driveway, cars lining up, Mario greeting customers. Suddenly *he* appeared! I swooned . . . butterflies. He jumped into a car to park it. I started mine, drove up the Strip, and came back on the right side of the street, and turned into the driveway like a customer.

Quickly I glossed my lips and rolled down my window. Big Dan was coming toward my car. My heart was racing. He didn't look to see who was inside. I watched his big hand grab my door handle to open it.

"I'm not staying. I was looking for Roger?"

"He's not working tonight," he said, still not looking in my window.

Goldie rushed up and poked his head in, "Danny, look who it is."

Danny bent down. I smiled without breathing.

"There you are," Danny said. "I was wondering if I would see you again."

"What a surprise to see *you* again."

"My name is Dan, Dan Zephyros. What's yours?"

"Carrie, Carrie Enwright. *Where* are you from?"

"Monterey Park."

"Your accent is not from Monterey Park."

"Oh, my accent? Do you like it? If you don't, I'll change it."

"It's very interesting." I wanted to say *I love it.*

"I'm Greek and Russian, but I was born in Shanghai."

"I was right. Very interesting."

Cars were starting to pile up and honk behind me. Mario, the boss, was hollering in the background, "Move it, you guys, this ain't no party for you."

"I gotta go, give your number to Goldie."

Danny ran off. Goldie handed me a torn parking stub and a pencil. I wrote my number carefully. Danny ran by with jingling car keys and gave me a look that undressed me without my permission. It was too exciting.

One week past forever.

I got home from work about 10:30 PM, went to the kitchen, and pulled open the fridge door. My mother followed me in to get a beer.

"Someone with a heavy accent called you. He sounded too old for you."

"I've been dying for that call. What did he say? Is he calling back? When did he call? Why didn't you tell me?"

"He just called, and that's another thing; it's too late to be calling."

"Stop it, Mom. I told him I work late."

"Well, here's his number," she said, handing me the paper crumpled in her pocket. I grabbed it, staring at his number with relief but anxious about calling him back. As I charged into my room, my mother called, "Who is he anyway?"

"Just a guy," I said. I closed my door and mentally rehearsed a conversation. I picked up the phone and dialed carefully.

"Hello," a woman answered.

"Do I have the right number for *Danny*?"

The woman called out with an even heavier accent, "Danny! For you."

I heard his footsteps coming to the phone. My heart pounded.

"Hello."

"Hi, it's me, Carrie."

"What are you doing? It's my night off."

"I just got home from work."

"I'm coming that way."

"It's too late. I have school tomorrow."

"You sound wide awake to me."

"My mother would have a fit."

"I live with my mother too. She never gives me any trouble. You should meet her, a nice Russian lady."

"Another night?"

"No."

I froze.

"Just kidding," he said.

I unfroze.

"You *could* sneak out your window."

"Are you kidding?"

"No, it will be fun."

I gave him my address and told him my room was the third rear window.

"What are you doing in there?" my mother said, hearing the noise from me moving my table, so I could climb out from my window.

"Nothing, just bored with my room."

"It's too late to decorate."

"Okay, Mom, good night."

She shuffled off.

I went into the bathroom and never with such great enthusiasm prepared for bed: the best job brushing my teeth ever, putting Pond's cream on my face, and brushing my hair smooth. Back in my room, I put on makeup with my hand mirror, cracked my window to hear his voice, crawled into my bed, nightgown over my clothes, waiting for my first date with Danny.

Midnight. I lay flat on my back; I had ears that could hear a leaf fall.

Tap tap. "Is this you?"

I leapt up. "Shhhhhh, yes, it's me."

"Hurry, I went to the wrong window. I'm afraid the guy might call the police like I'm a Snoopy Sam."

I giggled. "It's Peeping Tom." Danny put his big strong arms under my armpits and pulled me out of my window like I was a feather. We were scurrying down the driveway and Danny said, "Wait, stop." He kissed me. It was the best kiss I ever had.

We walked down my street to Danny's car. It was so nondescript, but when he opened the door for me, it became a Cadillac. We went to Ben Frank's, the all-night restaurant across from the Interlude. He ordered a protein plate and told me why I should have one too. Danny studied acting and competed in karate championships. He was six-four and weighed 240 pounds. He didn't scare me like Johnny, though; I felt protected and madly in love with Danny, and so did my body.

I knew he was *the one* who would take my virginity.

He brought me back home, and like Superman, he hoisted me back through my window. It was 3:00 AM. We dated like this for a month. Ben Frank's, making out hot and heavy in his car, then back into my window, until one night he said, "Tell your mom you're going to stay at Rosalind's house."

We met at the Ben Frank's parking lot and he drove me to the motel around the corner from Hollywood High. "I've never noticed this motel before."

He pulled into the first parking space and turned off the engine. There would be no more conversations about petting and waiting. This was it.

"Are you okay?" he asked. I nodded *yes*. "I will be right back."

He went into the brightly lit office, reached into his pocket, handed cash to the old guy at the desk. Danny came to my side of the car.

"Shall I carry you?"

"There's blood," he said. "This really *was* your first time, wasn't it?" He held me close for a very long time, saying nothing. "I thought you were holding out to be holding out." He kissed me and asked again. "Are you sure you're okay?"

"I'm fine, honest."

"We will have lots of time to make love, more love and better love, because I think I love you."

I knew I loved him.

The dawn cracked way too soon. There was no time to get my car and not be late for school. Good thing school was just across the street.

Danny popped a V-8 juice and handed me the opened can with a little green and white capsule. "This will get you through the day."

I was out of Roz's happy helpers.

"What are these?" I asked.

"A bennie. You know, Benzedrine."

No I didn't know, but hellllllooooo, Bennie, nice to meet you. I popped the pill without hesitation, got dressed, and hoped no one from school saw me leaving the motel. Roz was the only one I'd told about my monumental evening. She was thrilled for me.

I laughed. "I'm glad you're so happy. I thought it was disappointing."

"It's never good the first time, not for the girl. Keep practicing."

So we did, and for a while, things were great for Danny and me. He was very attentive for months, until excuses began to wedge into our visits. He moved to little guest quarters in West Hollywood. Whenever he called I ran to him. But Danny's schedule—karate, body building, parking cars, and bit acting roles—left little time for me.

He took odd jobs too, from being a muscle guy in the *Mae West Revue* in Las Vegas to cleaning pools. My insecurities grew. Everyone knew the pool-cleaning guys were having affairs with the housewives. The joke was: "Did you hear the one about the married lady and the pool guy? . . . And you won't till her husband catches them."

"Am I going to see you tonight?"

"No, I have an appointment."

"With who? For what?"

I hated how jealous I was becoming.

He went into the front room and got on the phone. I got dressed and went there too. He kept talking on the phone.

"I have to go to work," I whispered loudly. "I could use a pickup."

He covered the phone with his hand. "In the bed table drawer."

I walked over and took four pills, putting two in my pocket and swallowing the others. I hoped it would buffer my feelings. I was even suspicious of the actress, Susan Harrison, he was talking to, who lived across his street.

I was losing my title as Danny's Girl. I was losing my mind too.

Our time dwindled to just *sex* time. I kept taking the pills, Roz's or Danny's, and after working nights at the theater and doing homework, I still couldn't sleep, worrying about Danny leaving me. I couldn't eat either. I calmed myself down with my mother's bourbon or vodka and orange juice, which I kept in a thermos in my locker at school. I was a nervous wreck.

I wasn't looking very good either.

I went to work around 5:00 PM.

"You're late," Mr. Katsky said, patiently. "Are you all right?"

"I'm fine . . ."

"Everyone in place," Mr. Katsky called out.

It was a big night for the *Cimarron* premiere. Glenn Ford was coming. All the bigwigs from the executive office were lined up against the wall. Pedestrians lined up on the sidewalk. I forced myself onto the stool in the box office. I'd never felt more tired and nauseous. My *bennies* weren't working.

My workspace started spinning. I was light-headed, my mouth unbearably dry, my lips sticking to my gums. So many people were looking at me, as far as I could see. I lost my balance and fell backward out of the box cage. Except, on my way out, I accidentally hit the ticket button too hard, and saw a hundred movie tickets shoot out of the little ticket window onto Hollywood Boulevard like a long thin snake flying out of a jack-in-the-box.

The next thing I remember, the paramedics were reviving me. I saw poor Mr. Katsky's flustered expression as I lay on the cement of the theater entry. All I wanted was Danny to come rescue me. I had Mr. Katsky call him.

He showed up, wrapped me in a blanket, and carried me to his car parked in front. It wasn't glamorous, but it was dramatic. And it was my last working day at the Hollywood Paramount Theatre.

Danny stayed busy and away from me for weeks after that. I had to talk to him.

"I haven't had my period for a while."

It was fine with me if I was pregnant. It wasn't the way I would have liked it. I wanted to marry Danny first, then have his baby, but the order wasn't all that damn important. He was my man, my first love, and that was all that mattered. I could graduate from high school before I had his baby. That was four months away.

"How late are you?"

"I'm not sure, but it's okay with me—"

"Listen, I have a doctor friend, I'm going to call you back in a minute."

"Okay . . ."

I hung up, confused with his clipped reaction.

I grabbed the phone on the first ring.

"My friend will check you this Sunday," Danny said. "He won't charge anything, he'll be alone, no staff, so okay, that's settled. I have a tae kwon do tournament Sunday morning. Meet me there. I gotta go now."

He must be surprised, he probably won't be excited until we know for sure. I won't tell anyone until we know for sure.

Sunday. I met Danny outside his tae kwon do school. "We got a half hour, hop in," he said. I didn't try to make small talk and big talk was too scary. I didn't look out as we drove over Laurel Canyon to the Valley. I'd seen it all before. I looked in my head and my heart instead. I felt like I had done something wrong.

We parked off Ventura Boulevard. "This won't take long," Danny said, as we walked in the office. "Thanks for seeing us," Danny told the doctor. "This is Carrie."

"Hello," the doctor said. "Undress and put on the gown, down the hall, first door to your left."

"Danny, please come with me."

"Just change, I need to talk to the doctor."

I walked into the bare bright white room with the reclining bed, a metal chair, floor lamplights and a counter with trays, glass jars, swabs, and other implements. I was freezing.

Danny and the doctor came in.

"Sit there, please," the doctor said, pointing to the bed. "Scoot down and put your feet into the stirrups."

They were freezing too. I looked at Danny for support.

"You worry too much," Danny said. "You're going to be fine."

"I'm going to give you an injection to ease the discomfort from the examination," the doctor said.

Easing my discomfort always sounded good to me.

"Make a fist."

The doctor swiped me with a cotton ball of alcohol. I closed my eyes.

When I came to, the doctor was gone. Danny was standing off near a window in the room.

"Hi," I said, hoping we were on our way to a new beginning.

Danny walked over. "See, that was nothing and you were right, you were pregnant."

"*Were?*" I said.

"It's no problem anymore."

I sat up slowly, trying to assimilate Danny's words . . . *no problem anymore.* I felt as white as the sheet on top of me, shocked, speechless, and devastated.

"The doctor said when you came to, you could get dressed," Danny continued. "Good we came in when we did, so he could fix it."

I didn't like Danny's accent with these words. I didn't like his face while he spoke these words. I didn't want an abortion. Danny had more to say.

"You *were* right about something else, I was having an affair with Susan, but that's over too. I'm leaving for Rome to be in a *Hercules* movie . . . Where did you say you parked your car?"

I felt like one of my mother's cartoon characters that swallowed a bomb and its head just got blown off and my heart as well. I figured I was lucky he hadn't taken me to Tijuana to a phony doctor who used a coat hanger.

"Say something," he said.

I just looked at him, holding back tears with a wall of pride. I eased off the bed and got dressed.

"Let's go out the back way." Danny handed me a plastic container. "These pills are for you if you feel any pain, but you shouldn't . . ."

We walked to his car, he went to open the car door for me.

"*I got it*," I snapped, and climbed in.

Graduating

"Hearts will never be practical until they can be made unbreakable."
—FROM *THE WIZARD OF OZ*

As the year closed, the beatniks, their poetry, and jazz were forced to share their stage with folk music. I hated folk music. Burl Ives reminded me of Santa Claus doing a summer singing gig.

Surfers came; the Beach Revolution was the wave that no one could stop. The black tights came off and bikinis went on. The guys started wearing Hawaiian shirts. I started putting bleach in my hair. My new hero: Brigitte Bardot.

I liked boy-watching from a comfortable beach blanket. Since I didn't swim or surf, I ventured north to State Beach with my friend Sheila. She was new to Hollywood High. She wasn't interested in joining any club. I admired her independence. My Delta world could be exhausting, so hanging with Sheila was like having a private life. State Beach had an older college crowd and was very social, with a constant volleyball game going on in front of the parking lot entrance on the sand. It was definitely where the wannabe stars and athletes collided. All bathing suits were accessorized with a *Variety* or *Hollywood Reporter* under the arm.

There was a funny character who kept bumping into us.

"Don't I know you?" he said.

"No," we chimed.

"Well, why not? This is my beach, are you girls enjoying *my* beach?"

The following weekend I bumped into him at the snack bar.

"Are you on vacation?" I asked.

"You don't recognize me? I'm a famous actor," he said with his broad smile and black beady eyes. "My name's Dick Miller, what's yours, and whadda ya wanna be when you grow up?"

"My name's Carrie Enwright. I'm an actress too."

"We have so much in common," Dick said. "Shouldn't we go out?"

I smiled, but not too invitingly. He was old, maybe thirty, and he had an accent like the Dead End Kids, although he couldn't have been funnier or nicer. Besides, I already had my eyes on a cute friend of his.

Our food came and Dick's magic words: "Come meet my friends."

We walked over, me with my Coke and fries, Dick with a box of hot dogs.

"Jack, this is Carrie, and here's your dog."

Jack looked up from his reading, but he seemed more interested in his hot dog than in me. He lifted his left eyebrow as if it spoke for him and said, "Hi."

I gave him my best smile. "Hmmm, somebody's hungry."

He looked up again, squinted a smile out his eyes, and the corners of his mouth, and a "Yeah" fell out of his lips. I did the Roz trick, a lingering five-second stare, as best I could, but Dick interrupted.

"Hey, let's go in the water. Where's your friend?"

"She's at the water, go say hi." Then I turned to Jack. "We've noticed your boys' club . . . here at the wall."

"Oh, have you?" Jack said.

"Okay," Dick said. "I'm going to find Blondie. What's her name again?"

"*Sheila*," I said, then back to Jack. "Are you a comedian too?"

Finally, after more flirting beach days, a real live date with Jack.

He picked me up at our new apartment. My mother had moved us one block away to Sycamore Avenue, for reasons unknown to me. Maybe because Bill would be moving in with us when he came back from Santa Maria. The apartments looked exactly alike. My mother answered the door.

"Someone's here for you, Carole," she hollered.

When would she get that I was *Carrie*?

I had waited through weeks to be alone with Jack, but just before I dashed out the door, my mother pulled me aside. "How do you know him?" Her bourbon breath annoyed my nose. "And he's too old for you . . ."

"Maybe, Mom, but he sounds just like Henry Fonda!"

His name was Jack Nicholson. I was excited to *like* someone besides Danny. I was tired of "Heartbreak Hotel," "Cry Me a River," and *Chet Baker Sings.*

Jack and I made out and within a few weeks I went to his bachelor pad on Fountain Avenue. I hoped to eliminate Danny from my heart by putting someone else there. With Jack's cunning smile and devilish style, I did forget about Danny. All too quickly, Jack would forget about me, but not before he took me to his acting class.

"Okay, your first acting job is to act *eighteen,*" Jack said. "You can't get in unless you're eighteen."

Class began at 10:00 PM. The Los Angeles curfew was still in effect. Jack set up an interview for me with Martin Landau, the teacher. I got accepted. I met Jack's other friends in class, Harry Dean Stanton, Warren Oates, Eric Morris, and Robert Towne, a writer who wanted to learn what actors learn.

Martin Landau was a wonderfully expressive teacher. He was flexible, lanky, and handsome. I could watch his big lips and wide mouth tell stories all night about him and his wife, Barbara Bain; our shared attraction to look at cows and horses on a hill, because they were natural; and I especially loved when he talked about Stella Adler, Brando, and James Dean. I went to this acting class for months but I lost interest after Jack left to do a horror movie.

No Jack, no fun.

Graduation was around the corner. I had been busy living life, not planning ahead. *Ahead* was here. What a shock to find out that many of my friends were moving away. Why? The answer was college. And they were going to colleges in places I had never heard of . . . Boulder, Berkeley, Providence.

"Where are you going to college?" my pal Marc asked.

"I don't know," I said. "Maybe I'll go where you go."

"How did you do with your GPA?"

"GPA?" I asked. "I didn't take GPA."

He explained that it wasn't a class and asked me about my grades in subjects I could barely pronounce, like trigonometry. I told Marc, "I left algebra when the teacher wouldn't tell me what the *x* or *y* was."

Except for Roz, my pretty, fun girlfriends and handsome athlete pals had actually been studying these things, while I was cruising the Strip or painting the marquis signs at the Renaissance Club, so I could hang out after curfew and watch Miles Davis, Les McCann, and Lou Rawls perform.

Even my drama pals were going to *college*. Why hadn't I known to be prepared? I had never even heard the word *academic*.

I was confused and heartbroken. I was going nowhere.

The day had come. It was the tradition for only the summer classes of Hollywood High to graduate from the Hollywood Bowl stage. We students had to meet in the auditorium and then we would be shuttled to the Bowl. Relatives would come later for this grand celebration; even Gramma Rose was coming.

"See you there, Mom," I yelled, and on my way out to school sipped her bourbon coffee she had left on her desk. "Don't be late either . . . you know where!"

She didn't answer but I wasn't concerned; everyone knew the location of the Hollywood Bowl.

In the auditorium, we received our caps and gowns. We all filed onto the shuttle bus.

I looked at Roz, so gorgeous, who looked like she didn't have a care in the world. My quiet Delta friend Ruth, a dark sultry beauty, I knew so little about her, and there was no more time to find out. Did it matter? We were off to our separate plateaus. It was the end of the big high school party. I went to my purse and took out my Max Factor compact to check my eyeliner. I put on my Essence of Pearl lipstick. I looked seriously at my face to see what I could see. I didn't see my future.

All I saw was the big space between my two front teeth.

The bus stopped. We all filed out.

The trees that bordered the Bowl were a protective forest. I felt the excitement of the ceremony. Guided like sheep, we went to our designated positions onstage. The tall kids went to the back and the short ones to the front. And the very, very, smart ones had a special place, upstaging us all near the podium. Being medium height, I was center position, with a perfect view of the dynamic sweeping structure in the magnificent shelled creation by Frank Lloyd Wright. It was a perfect California day . . . I was warm inside and out.

The parents would be arriving in about ten minutes. It would all be over in two hours. The school band sat in front of us. The teachers and speakers lined the first row; friends and relatives would fill the box seats. I began to look for my mother. The speeches were read, some were inspiring, others soooooo boring. I continued to look for my mother.

Pomp and Circumstance played. I still looked for my mother. But, just like my graduation at Pacoima Junior High, just like my thirteenth birthday, I looked for her until it was over, and she never came.

I decided I would never look for her again.

I had graduated from her too.

PART 3

Plan B

1961–1963

Plan B

I needed to get out and do something with my life. I thought of Billy Grimes, who turned my hair into a pink beehive. I called him.

"I want to be a hairdresser."

"Great, dahlin', my pal Al Lapin and his brothers have a beauty school in Reseda."

I wasn't thrilled to go back to the Valley, but I figured I could stay with Virginia and Babe, rent free, and be close to school. I packed up my car and left my mother a note: *Moving back to Virginia and Babe's. You have the number.*

So, while my friends went off to their universities, I went with plan B: Hairdressing.

I drove to the Lapin Brothers' school. It was a simple small one-level building on a small block of other random businesses. I looked at the sign above the entry. It didn't say beauty school, it said Beauty College. Ah-ha, I was going to college after all! I walked in.

"Who's doing your hair?" the girl at the front counter asked.

"No, I'm here to see the Lapin brothers."

She gave me a blank look and walked off, chewing her gum like cud. Beyond her, I saw the students cutting hair and talking. It didn't look as kooky as Billy's beauty school.

"Hello," a man called from a side doorway. He was short, with curly black hair, a big broad smile, and a happy nature. "My name is Itsy Lapin, how can I help you?"

Itsy? I held back a chuckle and shook his hand.

"My name is Carrie. I want to enroll." I didn't tell him hairdressing was my backup plan and that I was going to be a *famous* actress. "I'm a friend of Billy Grimes."

"You don't look like you would be a friend of Billy's."

"I know, but we *are* good friends, didn't he call you about me?"

"Maybe he spoke to one of my brothers, Harold or Sam. Let's go meet them."

As we walked through the school, Itsy explained how I needed a certain amount of hours in the Theory Room and I would need another amount in Practical Work, and I would learn manicuring and facials too.

"All together, it's a total of sixteen hundred hours to graduate."

"Geez, this is complicated, I just want to make hairdos."

"It's comparable to one year of nurses' training. You need to know every nerve and muscle in the head, neck, and arms. Meet John Cusenza. He will be your teacher."

John was a tall handsome Italian man, busy with students, but found a welcoming smile for me. Next stop was a laboratory, where I watched a man mixing potions like a mad scientist. And like Einstein, he had wiry silver hair popping out of his head like an explosion.

"Meet my brother Sam, he's our color expert."

"Hello," Sam said. "A new artist coming our way?"

I signed up. Itsy let me make financial arrangements based on a job I didn't have yet. I spotted a Bob's Big Boy Restaurant near the school and decided I could *act* like a waitress, as research for a future role.

I went for my training at the "original home" of the Bob's Big Boy on Riverside Drive in Toluca Lake. I learned how to stack four plates on one arm, carry two cups of coffee in the other, and fill out an order—all with a big smile.

I passed. My new schedule was: clocking in as cosmetology student from 8:00 AM to 5:00 PM changing in the school bathroom from my white lab uniform to my Bob's Big Boy uniform, a black-and-white shirt and skirt, then dashing to Bob's to be a waitress from 6:00 PM to 10:00 PM, sometimes midnight . . . then drive home.

In between and after cheeseburger orders, I would study. My food was free at Bob's, but I was never too hungry. In order to maintain this nonstop schedule, every morning I popped a Dexedrine, my graduation gift from Roz.

They were called *uppers* for a reason.

I loved doing hair from day one. I wasn't very good from day one, but my desire overruled. Hairdressing gave me a sense of purpose and having a license would give me security.

We students became one another's guinea pigs. My classmates did my hair every color from fuchsia fury to midnight blue. It was all about experimenting. I loved trying to make hair do what I wanted it to do, imitating hairstyles or achieving specific colors. And regardless of the techniques, I was left to make my own decisions based on what kind of hair I was working on: fine, curly, coarse, straight, or just awful.

My first haircut took hours . . . and got *worse* by the minute.

I had convinced one of my Bob's coworkers to come in for a free haircut. I didn't tell her my only experience had been clipping away on mannequins. I put the haircutting cape around her neck with a sanitary paper strip.

"Is that too tight?" I asked professionally.

"It's fine."

She had long, thick, curly black hair. I picked up the biggest comb I had and forced myself in. It was like combing through a mass of steel wool. I gave her my biggest lying smile of confidence and began sectioning her hair as I had been taught.

Whack! It was like I was chopping through the Amazon jungle with a machete. It seemed to grow back where I had just chopped. It was exploding. I couldn't find a way to stop cutting. I began to perspire. I never perspire.

"How's it going?" she said.

"Uh . . . just great, I'm getting my pattern started."

I was lost in this maze.

Why hadn't I asked the girl at Bob's with the thin blond hair?

After two hours dragged by, I walked around to block the mirror. I didn't want her to see what I saw. On the left side, it was a full bushy ball *above* her ear. On the right side, the bushy ball was about two inches *below* her ear. Every time I cut to match one side I overshot my mark and her hair got shorter and shorter. Finally she managed to get a glimpse of herself.

"I didn't know you were going to cut my hair so short!"

I didn't either. I couldn't look at her. I couldn't undo the lopsided-ness. I wanted to shave her head and start all over in a few months. I had to call an instructor for help.

My haircut was lousy, but I learned that hair is like fabric, and I had a lot to learn about the different kinds.

Also lousy was having a coworker who wouldn't speak to me anymore.

After 600 hours, I finally made it to the main floor. Only 1,000 more to go.

Hairdressing had other challenges. Short ladies wanted their hair too high, which only made them look shorter. One lady wanted a big Flip to counteract her big jaw, but it only made her face appear wider. Women with ten hairs would bring pictures of Elizabeth Taylor and expect to leave looking like *Cat on a Hot Tin Roof.* We had a line for this: *I'm a beautician, not a magician.*

Often I would style a lady's hair and if I didn't see a look of delight on her face when I peeked in the mirror, I would change her hair into another style, then another, and another, until finally the lady would say, "What are you doing? I liked the *first* way you did my hair."

"Well, why didn't you tell me?"

To avoid getting a 25-cent tip or stiffed completely, we had hints, such as one of us waving a dollar in front of another's face when we had a new client, then loudly announcing, "This was left for you by your last customer." The best hint was the sign on a station that read *Tipping isn't a place in China.*

I entered small hairstyling competitions with the other students. We *better* hairdressers gravitated to one another and socialized after school. We found the dives and dance spots where we didn't have to show proof of age since some of us were just high school graduates. I didn't have many nights off from Bob's, but when I did I wanted to reward myself like it was New Year's Eve.

One of the *better* hairdressers was a gorgeous green-eyed girl I knew from Pacoima Junior High, Geri Bode. All she wanted to talk about was scissors and the latest style of bangs. I wanted to talk about the latest song and go dancing. She was an advanced student and had a crush on the teacher, John Cusenza. He gave her special attention and she became *the* best haircutter. When she graduated, he quit; they married and later opened a salon on Ventura Boulevard called Cassandra and created a product line named Sebastian.

Another of the *better* hairdressers was a guy named Jordan. We hung out a lot in school and after, when I didn't have to work at Bob's.

Jordan was an attractive, fun student, a few years older than me. He really loved hairdressing too. He said we'd met before in Hollywood, but I didn't remember. He was hipper than most other students.

Jordan was a bit effeminate and admitted to past male sexual encounters, which didn't bother me. We got along great. He said that part of his life was over; he was only interested in *hair*. One night off, Jordan asked me to go out to the Palomino Club. First, we had dinner with his parents. He had moved back with them to go to beauty school just like I had done with Virginia and Babe. We had so much in common.

His parents were very excited that Jordan was bringing a *girl* over. They wanted him to get married and have a nice family like a nice Jewish boy. I wasn't exactly Jordan's girlfriend, but his family liked the idea I might be.

Jordan and I were good dancing partners too, real show stealers. One time Jordan got so fancy with his steps and spins, he split his pants in front of everyone. We laughed and kept dancing. Another night off, I got too stoned after romping around bars with him and his Valley friends and didn't want to drive back to Pacoima.

"Jordan, what if I stay at your place tonight?"

He lived close to school, which was helpful because the next day I would not feel like getting up before noon, let alone going to class.

"Great," he said.

I spent the night in his room . . . in his pajamas . . . in his bed . . . with him in it . . . and oops, we had sex.

We continued to stay close, go to bars, and party. We had sex or we didn't. We thought we were the Fred Astaire and Ginger Rogers of hair. Jordan was quite the fashionista. Or fashionisto? We joked about who overdressed and wore more mascara. He looked more like Elizabeth Taylor than the clients. I nagged him to get his own eyelash curler and stop borrowing mine. Jordan won hair contests when he used me as a model. I was his good-luck charm.

"Hey, my folks think we're so close," Jordan said. "Why don't we get married?"

I thought about it for a minute. We practically lived together anyway these past months, I liked the little poolside guesthouse in his backyard, we looked great together, had fun together, what else was marriage about? By this point, I only went to Virginia and Babe's to change clothes. He came with a big family, and I'd always wanted one. Danny was who I had my heart set on, but Danny was never coming back to me.

"Sure," I said. Jordan adored me and his attention felt good. "Why not?"

We were married under a chuppah.

Three months into our marriage, Jordan didn't come home one night. I figured he was fine and lost track of time. I sat by the pool, drank Mogen David wine, and contemplated how I really felt *out of place with all of this.* Then next day he called.

"Could you pick me up and I'll explain everything."

I picked him up at a crummy little hotel on Hollywood Boulevard. He got into the car and told me he hadn't been with another woman . . . he had been with a man.

Our marriage was annulled before I got my thank-you notes written.

Life Is Full of Surprises

I was glad I hadn't quit Bob's yet. I still had beauty school to complete.

I moved back to Pacoima with Virginia and Babe . . . *again.*

Meanwhile, a client of mine had constantly urged me to try out for *Playboy*'s Playmate of the Month with her photographer husband. I had put her off before, thinking I couldn't do it and, more likely, wouldn't be selected anyway, but when she came in for her regular appointment after this pivotal weekend with Jordan, I blurted, "How much money did you say a Playmate gets?"

"Enough to open your own salon."

I hadn't gone that far into my future, but I straightened up and began to dream. *My own salon?* That did sound good. Still, go naked, nationally, maybe in Europe too?

Playboy was a ten-year-old magazine and it wasn't like it was sleazy. It was tasteful and prestigious. After all, the first Playmate of the Month was Marilyn Monroe. I'd be lucky to get this. I sure needed the damn *three thousand dollars.*

Jordan was all for it and said he'd do my hair.

The day of my *Playboy* audition, Jordan and I went to the photographer's house together. The photographer's wife greeted us at the screen door.

"Hi," she said. "I have a room where you can put your things and get settled."

Jordan carried an armful of my clothes and hair stuff. I had a makeup kit.

"Thanks," I said. I was so anxious, I could barely talk. "You remember Jordan from school?"

"Of course, hi," she said, reaching to help us.

"My husband will be in soon, he's setting up. Do you need anything?"

"A box of tranquilizers." I laughed.

A few minutes later, her husband, Ron Vogel, entered.

"You must be Carrie, don't be nervous."

I shook his hand. "You noticed?"

"This will be easy. I'd like to start with the garments on the chair."

They left. Jordan back-combed my hair. I put on my eye shadow.

We didn't talk much. "Your hair looks great," he said, picking up the can of spray and blasting my Flip. "Thanks," I said, and applied more makeup.

"We're ready for you out here."

I slipped on the sheer nightgown and matching sheer lacy robe and timidly walked into the living room. Bright lights were on stands pointing to a spot on the sofa. Ron was looking into the lens to focus. Heads turned and giggled. Not the reaction I had hoped for. Ron caught himself. "Carrie, you need to be *naked* under the negligee."

I hadn't removed my underwear.

"Oh, already?" I said, embarrassed. "I'll be right back."

I went back to the dressing area, and quickly grabbed the silver flask I had stashed in my makeup kit for an emergency, gulped a giant slug of vodka, which kicked in fast on my empty stomach. I took some peanuts from a dish on the dressing table to mask my breath, unhooked my bra, slid off my underpants, took a deep breath, and glided back in the living room—relaxed and confident. I loved that guarantee from a blast of alcohol.

"How silly of me," I smiled. "Now where shall I stand?"

I followed Ron's posing directions for the next few hours. It *was* fun. A month later, I found out I was selected.

Me, a *Playboy* centerfold. Me, Miss July 1963.

My period was very late, so I couldn't ignore my marriage to Jordan and just move on. I had to tell him I had no interest in working things out and I wasn't going to have another abortion. My heart told me adoption was the best answer for my child. I had been the product of a messed-up home. I did not want to re-create *the scene of the crime.*

It wasn't an easy concept, carrying a baby to full term and then giving it up. Jordan pleaded, his parents pleaded, but my mind was made up. Finally accepting this, they made one request, that our baby be raised Jewish.

"Of course," I agreed. I would find a happily married Jewish couple that wanted to adopt our child.

My pregnancy forced me to quit diet pills. For the next month, I tried to juggle school and waitressing, but I didn't have any energy to handle it. I couldn't burn the candle at both ends without the assistance of my "uppers," and besides, a pregnant waitress wasn't exactly Bob's Big Boy's image either. I didn't quit beer or cigarettes, though—those seemed basic, harmless essentials.

For the following months I kept to myself. I got more involved with competitive hair shows. When I did hair, I didn't think about anything else.

Waiting

I calculated my hours; four weeks left of school. After I had completed my required school hours, I had to wait five or six weeks to take my test. The State Board of Barbering and Cosmetology had a long backlog of students ahead of me. After that, I would still have to wait for the results to come in the mail.

I needed to support myself. I lived free and I could drink Babe's beer and eat Virginia's goulash, but I still needed money for final school payments, gas, cigarettes, and a few progressively larger pregnancy clothes.

Itsy, Harold, and Sam Lapin approached me during the last week of school. "Carrie, we want to help you," Sam said. "We have an offer for you." Itsy stood in his black pinstriped suit and bright white dress shirt, smiling from ear to ear as I first remembered him, and Harold was demure in a gray suit with his lab coat covering it, his hands full of mixing bowls and tint bottles.

"You could work at our Lapin Brothers beauty salon on Sunset. We can't pay you much, but you could work on the wigs. You would get tips and we could give you fifty dollars a week."

I got choked up from their generous offer.

Itsy went on, "You're good at styling and wigs and hairpieces are the same as doing people. You'll work in the back room from five PM to ten PM."

A voice came over the intercom. "Carrie, front desk, please." I plumped up my hair, shook my dress fresh, and walked to the salon entry. "This is Angel," the receptionist said. "She needs her wig cleaned and curled by seven PM. *Tonight.*"

I smiled, took the red wig from her, and examined it. Looked easy enough.

"Sure."

"Don't you need to see it on me?"

"Oh, okay, come with me."

"I usually go to Donnie, but he quit," Angel said, cracking a mouthful of gum between words. I put her wig on over her long black hair.

"Your hair is pretty," I said. "Why do you wear a wig?"

"Thanks, honey," she chomped. "Wigs are good . . . you know, variety, so no one gets bored."

"Okay." I stuck my hands into the wig and mimicked a Flip on both sides, as we looked in the mirror together. "Something like this?"

"You got the idea, see you at seven."

Angel came back like another person. From denims and a cowboy shirt, she had transformed into a Hollywood movie star, wearing a slinky sparkly tight-fitting turquoise dress with high heels to match. She wore dangling rhinestone earrings and enough makeup to perform at the Shrine Auditorium.

"Look at you," I said.

"Frederick's of Hollywood." She smiled, pushing up her push-up bra underneath her dress. She sat in my chair like a queen ready to be crowned.

I brought her my masterpiece.

"What time is it?" she said, ignoring my art and looking at the clock on the wall. "*Aye,* crapola!" She grabbed it out of my hands and pulled it on her head like a sweater, adjusting it evenly. "Got a few pins, honey?"

"Yeah, but how do you like it?" I handed her some long bobby pins.

"Huh? Oh great, just great, honey. Sorry, I'm so damn late."

She reached in her purse and threw down twenty-five dollars.

"This is what I used to give Donnie. The five bucks is for you."

She jumped out of the chair.

"What about hair spray?" I said.

"I won't need it."

She was gone.

The next day . . . "Carrie, could you come to the front desk, please?"

I went quickly, excited to meet my next customer. It was Angel again with her wig, and two girlfriends holding theirs out.

"Hi, honey," Angel said, back in pedal pushers, flat shoes, and no makeup. "This is Stella and Blossom. They loved my wig—can you do theirs too?"

Stella had bleached white hair, chin length, pulled up on one side with a jeweled barrette, and Blossom had a brown ponytail with sharp-cut Betty Paige bangs. All three women were about twenty-five years old and all chewing gum in the same way.

"Do you want to show me how you want them?"

"Just do what you did for me," Angel said. "We like that style."

This was how it went. Stella brought me another girl, and a few days later Blossom brought another, and soon I was up to my belly button in wigs. These clients would pat me on my head, drop off their wigs, and say to their friends, "Isn't she cute? Such a hard worker, and having a baby all by herself in a few months."

"Oh, and honey," Angel said one day, dropping off her wigs, "the red wig was great, but can you make the top of the blond one higher? Actually, honey, a lot higher? It has to last through the night."

I had stopped wearing eye makeup; it was too much trouble. It was exhausting enough just to lift my arms to do my hair. I was happy to work on wigs. Any contact with clients was starting to bug me. I worked hard on those wigs and they always came back to me like they dropped them in the toilet.

"Thanks, honey," Angel said.

"Wow, the red one is trashed, did you get in a fight with someone?"

Angel laughed.

I asked again, "Really, how *did* this wig get so messed up from yesterday?"

"Carrie, excuse me," Frankie urgently interrupted. "I have to talk to you."

I stepped over to his station. He whispered, "Kiddo . . . when *those girls* say, '*last through the night . . . that's all they mean—the night*."

I was working on *working girls,* ladies of the night, hookers and strippers. I stopped complaining about their wig returns. They kept me busy and they confided in me too, like they'd known me all their lives. While I put their wigs on, they would talk about their *johns . . . their pimps . . . this idiot did this and that jerk-off did that.*

I would finish, spray them six times, they'd give me a hug, check themselves in the mirror, turn, and say: "*Somebody's* gonna get *lucky* tonight."

My favorite story was about three notorious prostitutes who lived and worked together successfully, independent of a pimp. One day all three decided to quit and move from their apartment where they ran their business. The day they quit, their clients found only the note they'd left on their front door: *Gone fishing. Go fuck yourself.*

The daily drive from Pacoima and back was getting to me. My belly was bumping the steering wheel. Rosella, the shampoo girl, knew about a rental on this side of the hill. With my small earnings I could afford the single dwelling above a garage on Detroit and De Longpre, only blocks from the salon. It was really an attic with an address. I wondered if I would be able to fit into the place by the end of my pregnancy.

My *Playboy* money hadn't come, so I looked for food deals at the market. My best buys were on cases of canned spinach, Heinz beans, cheap beer, and animal crackers. I was so used to standing while doing hair that I ate that way too. It was more comfortable than sitting down anyway, crunching my oversize stomach into my ribs.

My one window overlooked the backyard. There were two giant sunflowers sprouting and hollyhocks that leaned on the chain-link fence for support as they stretched to the sky with no opinion of where they were, but alive.

My nights were more and more difficult. One unbearable evening, my feelings collided. I lay in my bed and sobbed, desperate for relief. The birth pain. The adoption pain. The alone pain.

It was about 10:00 PM. I got up and walked to the corner liquor store. I needed a candy bar, or a beer—maybe three—cigarettes for sure.

I stood at the back of a small line at the counter. I noticed a guy with his head hung down, in line ahead of me. He had a sharp haircut, too good for this neighborhood. His clothes didn't look like he'd slept in them either. But his energy was that of a homeless person, down and gloomy. I sparked up when I realized I knew him from high school. It was Jay Sebring. He had revolutionized men's hair fashion. He was a big star, his notoriety had surpassed that of Jacqueline Kennedy's hairdresser, Mr. Kenneth. I tapped on his shoulder.

"Hi Jay, I'm a friend of Bonnie's—I mean Cami, I know you changed her name." I stumbled with my words. He lifted his head. "I'm Carrie."

"Oh . . . hi . . ." He looked at my big belly. "What happened to you?"

"It's a long short story," I said. He cracked the corner of his mouth into a smile. He had a bottle of red wine in his hand. He turned back toward the counter, lowering his head again, not extending the conversation. I wondered how he could be so dreary when *he cut Paul Newman's and Steve McQueen's hair.*

He paid and walked out. I paid and caught up with him.

"I live around the corner, wanna come over and have your drink with me?"

"Are you alone?" Jay said.

"Yeah, and it would be nice to have some company."

"Can I leave my car here?"

"Sure, the walk is nothing," I said, and pointed to my building down the block.

It was early December, a cold night, but clear. Jay didn't say a word for the whole walk. I didn't either. We got to the foot of my stairs.

"You live up there?" Jay said. "Isn't this a garage?"

"Uh-huh, it's real cozy."

He was so quiet, I kept checking to see if he was still with me.

We walked in and I started to turn the lamp on in my dimly lit room. "The light's fine," he said. He didn't want more light, and he didn't want to sit in the living room either. He pulled out one of my two red chairs and sat down in the corner of my entry. I looked in my utensil box, rustling past three forks, two knives, the soup spoon, screwdriver, and pliers and handed him the corkscrew. I brought over two glasses.

"How long have you been living here?" he asked without looking up, more interested in pouring the wine.

"Not too long. Hey, guess what? I'm going to be a hairdresser too. Do you know Billy Grimes?"

He didn't answer. He drank his wine. I poured him another. I sipped mine.

"You're going to be a hairdresser?"

"Yep." I took another sip; the wine felt good and so did company. "How's Cami?"

He pulled out some pills from his pants pocket, put two in his mouth, and washed them down with his wine. "Cami and I are divorced."

"Oh, I'm sorry."

"Don't be. It's okay." He stared off into the distance.

"So, do you know my friend Billy Grimes," I asked again, "or Richard Alcala?"

His head popped up like he had been asleep for a moment.

"Yeah, sure . . . cool guys, so what're you doing *these* days?"

"I'm waiting to have a baby, mostly, and waiting to take my state board."

"Hmm," he said, drifting off again. His skin was sallow. Jay was handsome, but not on this night. He poured himself another glass.

After a while he said, "I gotta go . . . meeting someone at midnight." He stood up, scratched the side of his face a few times, and looked at the empty bottle of wine. "I wanna do something for you."

He pulled out a wad of cash from his pocket and put a hundred-dollar bill in my hand. "Why don't you dress up my salon for Christmas and keep the change?"

"Really? Sure, I'm good at that." I smiled at the hundred-dollar bill. "I could go shopping tomorrow, it's my day off."

"My cleaning crew will be there at eight PM . . . do your thing, lock the door when you're done."

The next day, I went to a party store. I waited until evening, then

I drove to Fairfax and Melrose. There was a parking place right in front of his salon with the two big windows that were waiting for my decorations. I looked in the windows like it was a candy store, and wondered, *What chair does Steve McQueen sit in?*

The cleaning lady startled me and opened the door.

I tried my Spanish on her, explaining I was a friend of Jay's, got as far as "Christmas," and searching for the word *decoration* in español.

"*Sí sí,* I know, Mr. Jay told me. Come in, I'm finished, you lock like this," she said, showing me how the knob worked.

My eyes took it all in, each big masculine barber chair with brown leather upholstery, heavy chrome details, and hydraulic pumps. In front of each chair was a large individual mirror, one per chair, not one long wall mirror like the Lapin brothers' salon or at the beauty school where there were too many chairs squeezed in a row. Jay's hairdressers' stations were desks made out of wood, like in a man's den, not Formica stations. Still, it had a strong business tone, not casual like Richard Alcala's salon.

I noticed the clock on the wall . . . 9:30 already? I had a lot to do.

I started pulling out the red crepe paper and streamers of green and little snowmen cutouts. I'd come a long way from Pacoima, painting bars and gas stations. *No window paint. I'm on the inside now.* I had forgotten scissors to cut my paper and wire. Good thing I was in a hair salon—there were scissors in every drawer. I splashed some foaming snow carefully around each mirror, but not too much, so clients could still see themselves perfectly. I tied bows on jars that looked stationary, like the Barbicide sterilizers and comb holders. I was on a roll.

I finished around midnight. The salon looked like a department store professional had decorated it. I did my final touch, silver stars hanging from strings, and smiled. *Excellent job.* I turned the lights off, locked the door, and drove home with a great sense of accomplishment.

The phone rang first thing in the morning. It was Jay.

"What happened in here?"

"Like it?"

"It looks fine, but my hairdressers are flipping out."

"Why? Don't they like it?"

"Actually they don't care, but they want to know what happened to their scissors."

Confused, I thought about it.

"Oh, I forgot scissors. I had to cut a few wires to hang the colored balls and some ribbon. Didn't I put them back in the right drawers?"

"Yeah, they were back, and wrecked, you nicked and dulled all their blades."

Jay went on, using words like *precision, diamond-edged,* and *expensive,* but he knew I couldn't afford to replace them. His generosity cost him new scissors for everyone. It was the end of my decorating career, and I learned how important scissors are.

Time had come to take the state board. I studied harder than all my years in junior high and high school combined. I was losing interest in hookers' wigs and strippers' hairpieces. If things weren't difficult enough, the pressure of the December holiday was upon me. I wasn't feeling merry. I kept forcing myself to look *ahead.*

One afternoon I was driving to the beauty supply store when I saw a guy waving enthusiastically to me out his car window. He was driving a cool blue Corvette. I slowed down to see who it was. I saw an attractive face, a friendly smile, a white T-shirt, light brown hair . . . then I got it—Bucky White, the guy I took to my grad night party to make Danny jealous. Except Danny hadn't cared.

"Hey, where you been? Let's go out! What's your number?" he shouted. "What are you doing December twenty-second? Let's go to a Christmas party! Pull over!" I figured the conversation would end after Bucky took one look at me. I got out of my car and stood by my door. Bucky saw that I wasn't exactly alone. He didn't say a word. His mouth dropped slightly and then he snapped out of his visual evaluation and walked across the street to me, smiling again.

We stood by my car and I told him everything.

"I still want to take you to the Christmas party," he said, and put his arm around me. "If you want to come with me."

"Yes, I'd love to go with you."

"What's your number?" he said. "I'll find out more about the party and call you."

That next morning my phone rang, early, very early, 8:00.

"Miss me?"

I laughed at Bucky's wit and charm.

"Actually . . ."

"I'll pick you up Friday at seven. Do you have a party dress?"

I loved that he had always been funny. I needed humor more than money these days.

We went to the party and he introduced me to his friends. They were whispering in the kitchen, I'm sure. It wasn't like I could disguise my condition. Bucky acted proud of me. He didn't smoke, so I didn't.

"What do you want to drink?" Bucky asked me. I didn't want to be the beer-drinking chick, so I said, "I'll have a champagne cocktail."

"You mean juice cocktail, don't you? You're pregnant."

"My mother drank when she was pregnant. But okay, I'll have an orange juice."

Bucky returned with two glasses of orange juice. We snacked on chips and dip and after a while I felt I had had enough holiday festivity.

"Can we go now?" I asked Bucky. "I feel tired. I'm sorry, if you want to stay longer, maybe you could take me home and come back. I'm just . . ."

"No, fine. Everyone's getting drunk anyway. I hate drinking."

"Really? I never heard of anyone hating drinking before."

Instead of taking me home, he brought me to his place on Hilldale Avenue in West Hollywood. His apartment was a duplex behind a large house. He said the whole property was his parents' but he took care of it. We walked upstairs.

"I should hold you all night. Why go back to your little cold place?"

We talked a lot that night. I was surprised about the strong opinions he had, about how life was supposed to be and his family values. He seemed lighthearted, always joking around, but he was firm, believing in dinner at 6:00—it's the American Way.

I thought that was a little strict, but I found his qualities stabilizing. I had no rules, just instincts, and they dictated my every move.

I leaned over and kissed him. He kissed me back.

We were together every night after that. At Bucky's request, I gave up my place and moved in. It was uncomfortable lying next to him while I was carrying another man's baby, but I tried not to think about that.

I continued to work and participate in hair contests at the encouragement of the Lapin brothers. Each time I won, it placed me in a higher level of competition. I was weeks from delivering my baby when the biggest contest came up, for the title of Southern California Champion.

I prepared my model by making her hair as pink as cotton candy, the way Billy had made mine. I practiced my set and styling on her late into the night. I did my exact creation over and over again, timing myself to finish within the allotted fifteen minutes.

At the Long Beach Convention Center the cheerleading room monitor announced, "Okay, okay, everyone ready. Time is close. The bell will go off in three minutes."

Right before the bell went off, the room monitor announced, "In order to accommodate the unexpectedly large turnout today, we will add a fifth- and sixth-place winner."

That news gave me hope of winning *something*.

Rrrrrring. The bell had power. Like I was a puppet on strings, I felt my arms moving faster and faster, as I had practiced. It was paying off. I completed my creation. I put shimmering silver glitter in my hands and blew it on top of the gallon of hair spray I had applied. I took a fine-tooth comb for the final lift. I saw my model with her powder pink fairy princess hair in perfect form, dipping, waving, and rising to a point in the sky.

When I wasn't called by the time it was third place, I was unbearably disappointed. I held my breath waiting to hear my number, 9, called for second.

"And number fifteen is our second-place winner."

"Okay, that's it, let's go," I said. I stood up and looked for my purse.

Bucky looked at me. "Hey, there's still one more, you can't leave yet."

I stood up. "You stay . . . I'm going to the bathroom."

I headed for the door. I felt the culmination of my whole life as I grabbed the doorknob. I wanted to explode from *all* my disappointments. I felt like a big zero, loser, flop, failure, and I was only nineteen.

"And the number one winner, our first place, is . . ." The emcee's voice rang through the room over the loudspeaker. I stopped listening, turned the doorknob, and as I pushed it open . . .

"Hey, pregnant hairdresser girl," a flaming queen hairdresser hollered at me. I recognized him from the work area. "Didn't you hear? Go get your prize. *You won!*"

I looked toward the stage. The emcee was holding the very large gold trophy high in the air with both hands. I was stunned.

"She's over here," he yelled, waving his scarf in the air, and pushed me forward with his other hand to go the stage. "*Number nine is right here!*"

I Kept My Promise

It was over now.

I could breathe differently.

Not for long . . . it happened again. More massive pain. I was so exhausted I could hardly give another bloodcurdling yelp.

"That's the afterbirth." A nurse patted my forehead. "It feels like another baby."

Don't open your eyes, don't open your eyes, I begged myself. The instinct and the temptation to see my child were unbearable. I squeezed my eyes tighter. I knew one glimpse and I wouldn't be able to go through with the adoption.

Then the worst happened . . . my baby *cried.*

I was not prepared for that.

"You have a healthy baby girl," a nurse called out. I heard whispers. One nurse had stopped the other from bringing me my child. "She doesn't want to see her baby."

They took her away . . . my baby girl . . . February 28, 1963.

I was in my room, recovering.

Blank walls, a blank dresser, no balloons, no cards, no flowers. The windows were open to a view of other buildings, no distance to see, no sky, no trees, no talking, no celebration, no other family, no other visitors. It was horrendous to be in the maternity ward without a baby like the other mothers.

Jordan walked into the room.

"I just saw our baby, she's beautiful."

"Jordan, I don't want to hear that."

"Okay, I won't say any more," he said. "How are you feeling?"

I wanted a stiff drink more than air.

I couldn't wait to get out of there.

PART 4

Headmaster

1963–1968

First Job

My cosmetology license had arrived in my mailbox like a golden egg.

Crazy as timing can be, the next afternoon my phone rang with . . . "Gotcha!"

"*Billy!*" I said. "Where do you disappear?"

"Dahlin', I can't tell you that, or you'd find me, but dig this, I got a deal for my own Bev Hills salon, it's almost in the bag. My backers are sortin' things out and till then . . . remember the Richard Alcala Salon?"

"Yes, and I remember what he was wearing."

"That's funny. So, did ya make it through beauty school?"

"I did."

"See, sugah, like I always say: *it's all fixed* . . . now how'd you like to work for me? Babe gave me yer numba but *where are ya?*"

He pulled up in front of Bucky's place at the crack of noon.

"Nice wheels, where's the Chevy?" I said, looking at his 1960 white convertible Cadillac.

"Upgrade, dahlin'." He tipped his cowboy hat. Billy's hair was askew, but his goatee was trimmed to perfection, matching his groomed mustache and sideburns. He was smoking a brown Sherman like it was his only way to get air.

"Man, I went to a far-out party last night . . . in the Hills of Beverly. We musta drank more champagne than the French in 1944."

He told me about his party pal and client, actress Tuesday Weld, and drove with his seat reclined all the way as if he was lying back on a couch.

"Hey, baby girl," he said, his energy increasing. "I'm cookin' with Crisco, this hairdressing biz is a blast. Girls flock all over you when you tell them you can make them prettier than they are already." He mentioned other clients—actress Barbara Luna and Rona Barrett, the famous West Coast gossip columnist— "And my hottest new chick is Stefanie Powers."

"*Stefanie Powers*? She's one of my best friends from high school! You have to tell her hello for me."

"Tell her yourself, sugah. She'll be in today."

We pulled up to Brighton Way and Bedford Drive.

"You go in an' tell Mary or Richard I'm on my way."

Ah, Richard. I remembered he made hair look smooth as glass and bounce like a ball and women clamored for him to do their hair, but really they just wanted Richard, *period.*

I walked in. Richard was in front of that big gold-leaf mirror that sat on the floor and reached all the way to the ceiling. His long Tyrone Power, Indian/Mexican hair shone like he was in the sun. Mary, his assistant, was sweeping up the fresh-cut hair.

"Hi. I'm with Billy. He's parking his car."

"I remember you, child," Mary said.

Richard swiveled around on his stool and smiled at me but didn't say a word. He went back to brushing his lady, pulling her head close to him.

"See that lady sittin' over there reading that *Vogue* magazine?" Mary said. "Tell *her* Billy's parkin' his car."

Richard stood up from his stool, "Harriet, get washed now, Billy's here."

"Okay," Harriet said. "You're not going to do me today?"

"I'm running late for my house call," Richard said.

Mary leaned over to me as Harriet walked toward us. "I'll wash her this time; you watch."

I nodded *yes.*

"All right, towels here, soap there, get 'em in and out, this ain't the social part of hair."

Mary ran a tight ship. And after all she said about *not* the social part, Mary talked Harriet's ear off the whole time in that shampoo bowl. When she finished, she wrapped Harriet's wet hair in a towel like an African headpiece, twisting and tucking so tight, Harriet looked like she just got a face-lift.

"Harriet, this is"—Mary leaned in—"What's your name again, child?"

"Carrie."

"That's right, *Carrie's* gonna be washin' yo' hair from now on, Harriet."

Billy made his entrance, blowing smoke through his "Helloooo" and swinging a bottle of champagne high in the air. "Who ordered lunch?"

Richard laughed, the ladies giggled, and I took Billy's things; a leather satchel of rollers and scissors, combs, a few brushes, Dep for setting, hair color bottles, and a water sprayer. Richard supplied hair spray labeled Richard Alcala Coiffures. That was a first. Everyone else used regular name brands.

The hair party was on. Pot billowed in from the back door of the salon all day. Richard told a lady who had waited over an hour for her haircut, "Grow it, you look great." He just wanted to leave and smoke pot in the alley.

I met Billy's ladies as they came in and I hollered, "Delta Psi Deltas *rule*," when Stefanie walked in.

"Care, what are you doing here?" I got caught up on Stefanie's life while Billy did her long wavy auburn hair. I wasn't ready to talk about my past.

"See you next time," Stef said to me, and bounced out of the salon, a true star yet still my down-to-earth friend.

"Billy, you're so good," I said. It was amazing that this crazy guy I met in a Pacoima junkyard had turned into such a fancy fashion man.

"Maybe you can do Stef's hair next time," Billy said.

"I don't think I'm ready."

"How ya gonna get ready? Fake it, baby dahl." Billy lit his brown cigarette. Then he gave me my best lesson: "Any chance you get to touch 'em, they could be yours . . . and take 'em if you can!"

In the weeks that followed, I watched. I got past feeling intimidated with the models and starlets that hung on Richard like wallpaper. Hell, I wasn't going to be flirting with the women like the guys did, to be a success, nuzzling down their smocks or kissing them good-bye on the lips. I had to do very good hair if I was going to make my mark on this town.

Billy was buying Gene Shacove's salon on Wilshire Boulevard and Rodeo Drive. Gene had bought a new salon on Rodeo Drive near the Luau restaurant.

Gene was the other hot straight hairdresser in Beverly Hills. He did Steve McQueen's wife, Neile; Janet Leigh; and starlet Jill St. John, so I knew he had to be a good hairdresser too, not just good-looking.

Richard's and Gene's reputations paralleled, before, during, and after work. They drove motorcycles, fast cars, and women *crazy*. I watched the giddiness of having these attractive male strangers in their hair, flirting, fussing, making them feel and look more beautiful. There was the unspoken *potential* of promise, availability, passion after dark, over a martini, in between the sheets.

Women got bitchy and territorial in the name of *appointments*. Catfights were not uncommon with some personalities. One day Mary had to break up two women scrapping right in front of Richard. "My appointment was before her," one said, looking daggers straight into the eyes of the girl next to her. It wasn't about their hair; they didn't want to wait the extra hour to get next to Richard.

Richard, calm and cool, acted as if he had no idea what was going on, and walked outside with *another* girl, pretending he was interested in looking at her hair in the daylight.

Mary would coordinate schedules so that certain ladies wouldn't run into each other, for Richard's sake, of course. The real joke was that so many women thought they were the *only one*. Some men's appointments had to be supervised too, because Richard was having an affair with the guy's wife or girlfriend.

I took in a deep breath of the salon smells wafting from the shampoo bar, from bleach powder to fancy conditioners leaking out of their containers. I could separate the scents like spices and herbs. I reached over and picked up a *Harper's Bazaar*. I turned to the editorials with the young doe-eyed Jean Shrimpton, who was surpassing model Suzy Parker in the fashion world. I looked down at the fine print at the bottom of the page to see who did the photography and who did the hair for each layout. Richard Avedon seemed to always work with the same hairdresser, Ara Gallant. I could see my reflection across the room in Richard's big mirror. The salon was quiet before the morning rush. Richard hadn't arrived yet. The sun beamed in brightly and made shadows with Richard's palm trees like zebra stripes on the floor.

I glanced back to the magazine. Irving Penn worked with Enny of Italy, hairdresser. *Someday my name will be there* with a great photographer, in that small print, in that special space, in *Harper's Bazaar* and *Vogue.*

I wanted all that I could imagine.

Billy Grimes Coiffures

Gene Shacove's popular salon was much different from Richard Alcala's. It was larger, with uniformed assistants, ten hairdressers wearing black, two receptionists, many maids, and no music. The phones were ringing off the hook. It was like Grand Central with clients and hairdressers and staff were bumping into each other as they passed from one area to another. He did need a larger salon. This one was packed like a sardine can.

"Am I dry yet?" a lady asked, interrupting Gene as he leaned over his reception desk for Billy's papers to sign.

"Ask Patty, can't you see I'm busy?"

Gene turned his back, and she walked away.

"They're so annoying," Gene said to Billy. "How do you deal with them?"

"I just love 'em." Billy said, taking the papers from Gene's hand and signing the papers without reading a word.

We went to Gene's private hair room. Ladies sat under dryers. One had her smock draped off her shoulders like a sexy gown; her legs were crossed and her black patent high heel dangled off one foot. I didn't want to seem starstruck, so I looked away. It was Joan Collins.

"Gene, remember Carrie?" Billy said, and handed Gene the pack of papers he signed. "She'll be workin' here with me."

Gene nodded and looked at his watch.

"I got to go, man," Gene said. "Patty will fill you in on the rest."

I watched him walk over to Miss Collins, raise her dryer lid, spread his legs outside of hers, press hers closed, bring her head an inch from his chest, and undo a roller to check if it was dry. "Darling," she said, in her fabulous English accent, pushing him back. "Just do my hair. I have to meet Warren."

I was nineteen, recovering from and covering up the fact I had just had a baby. I was living with Bucky and I tried to give him the impression I was untouched from my overwhelming ordeal.

"Why are you home so late? Have you been drinking?"

Of course I've been drinking . . . I'm a hairdresser in Beverly Hills. I went to the refrigerator to grab something to cover the champagne and avoid a hassle.

"You didn't answer me," Bucky said, and stood in the doorway.

"A client brought Billy some champagne . . . I had a few sips."

"What about *our* dinner?"

"Bucky, I'm pooped! Let's call Ready-Go and get a pizza."

Our problems were surfacing faster than dead fish in an aquarium.

I didn't have the energy for any more life changes, not this week, not next month. I just wanted to do hair and get back to my acting career. Every day, I couldn't wait to escape and be Billy's assistant.

Billy was school. Billy was truth. Billy was wisdom. He was my map for life and hairdressing.

The big day came. The Gene Shacove Salon sign went down, Billy Grimes Coiffures went up. It was a move up for me too. I was now *the* assistant to *the* owner. Not that anyone else was working in Billy's salon yet. Billy gave me my own key, he was always late to work.

"What a party last night in the Hills of Beverly . . ." was his usual opening line. I had his client washed and ready. He sat on his stool, long lanky legs stretched out, and wheeled himself close to her, "How you been, dahlin'? I heard a song that's gonna blow everyone's mind. That Johnny Rivers is a genius." I stood by Billy's side like a toy soldier. "Ricky Nelson better watch out. How's your love life, dahlin', you sexy little thang."

Tracey blushed, she was a quiet married lady who wouldn't utter the word *sex*, but loved when Billy did.

Billy turned to me. "Scissors, please." Then back to Tracey. "You're gonna love this, dahlin', too *avant-garde* for the average gal, but *you* can carry it."

The women loved his attention to detail. The time Billy spent on them was probably more than most husbands gave them all week.

Billy could draw anyone into his web. What helped propel his engaging conversations was a diet pill he took called Ambar, a mixture of phenobarbital and methamphetamine, which he referred to as his vitamins. I started taking one every morning to keep up with him—then we both talked a lot. My chatting kept his clients entertained, so they wouldn't realize how long they'd been waiting for Billy.

Coffee, coffee, coffee. The caffeine pole-vaulted the effects of our *vitamin*. After churning the pill for a few hours, Billy looked at me like I was looking at him, our eyes ready to pop, and we were tired of grinding our teeth and smiling.

"It's about that time," Billy announced. "It's happy hour somewhere."

It was 2:00 PM in Beverly Hills. Time for Billy and me to ease our anxiety from the Ambar. Champagne was the great leveler. It smoothed out the buzz and put us into the perfect pace—up, full speed ahead, with a mellow exterior. If customers didn't bring a bottle in, Billy called a liquor store that delivered. "We need your best bubbles, dahlin', right away . . . it's an emergency!"

Fun was always an emergency for Billy. Five minutes passed and Billy shouted, "Where's that damn li'l delivery boy, is he new? Did he get lost?"

My mouth was watering for the bubbles too, but I acted calm. When the kid came, Billy stopped everything. "Awww right! Who wants a cup of happiness?" *Pop!* Billy sipped off the spewing bubbles. "Carrie, dahlin', get us some glasses."

I came back with glasses on a tray that Billy had decoupaged and poured the Mumm. I skimped on the clients' glasses to make sure there was plenty left for me. I poured a big one to the brim for myself, slowly, so it wouldn't be full of foam. I held the cup to my nose and smelled the sweet and sour champagne like perfume, tiny bubbles popping on my eyelashes. I took a big breath, feeling the salvation that was about to go down my throat to my chest and not stop till it hit my toes, jumped back, and went to the top of my head.

Billy downed his in one gulp and went back to his haircut.

Billy hired a desk girl recommended by Richard Alcala. The two of them walked up the stairs, all giggly and wiggly like they'd just gotten married. I could hear Billy being his charming self, explaining her new job.

"You know, Billy, I've never done this before . . ."

"It's a cinch, honey buns, just tell 'em all to come on in!"

Billy saw me waiting for him at the top of the stairs.

"I bring help," he said, like Caesar.

"Good, we need it. And a maid too." I smiled at Billy and the new girl.

The word was out about Billy being so good and he was always booked. But the more popular Billy got, the later he got, the wilder he got, and the more his social schedule interrupted his work schedule. Sometimes, after doing a cute girl, he'd leave with her. Billy's "I'll be right back" meant *hours*.

"Hi," the new girl said. "My name is Aloma."

"Hi, your name is beautiful."

So was she. Aloma was exotic, with long fine black velvet hair, and she was thin and tall, about five-nine, with high cheekbones and a strong chin with a small dent in the middle of it. On closer examination, inside the dent there was a small ink spot, a tattoo. Her black eyes had the depth of an Egyptian painting. She must have been a panther in her previous life.

"My father is Japanese, from Hawaii. He said my name means *a dream*."

"What about your mom?"

"We don't talk about her," Aloma said. We had one thing in common already. "I'm so nervous about this job."

"Oh, don't be, it's easy and Billy is fun."

Rrring. Rrring. "Billy Grimes Coiffures," I answered. "See? Easy," I whispered to Aloma, holding my hand over the phone. I slid my finger down the appointment column for the following day. "You can have three o'clock tomorrow . . . nope, that's it, unless you want something next Friday . . . okay, 'bye, Rona." I hung up. "That was Rona Barrett, L.A.'s Hedda Hopper. She loves Billy."

It was early morning, ten o'clock.

"After I shampoo two ladies, let's go to the snack bar and get some coffee."

"Billy, your ladies are ready, I'm taking Aloma to fill her in."

"Have fun, girls."

"See . . . it's all about *fun,*" and I whisked Aloma downstairs.

We sat in the back booth of the coffee shop, talking like long-lost friends.

"How do you stay so thin?" I asked.

"Desbutals . . . they curb my appetite."

"I like Ambars. Billy gives me one a day. I hope you like champagne, you'll be ordering it all day."

"I love champagne."

We were gonna get along great.

Billy continued to make his mark in hairdressing. His favorite client and party pal was still the beautiful Tuesday Weld. She was like a baby Marilyn Monroe. Billy and Tuesday together made perfect sense to me. Neither of them cared about public opinion. They were attached in their detachment. Billy's excuse for being later and later to work was, "I was out with Tuesday." Like that made it fine. His clients were getting grumbly.

"Can you set my hair, Carrie?" Rona said, after waiting two hours.

I did.

"Billy's so behind, can you comb me?" Barbara Luna said another day.

I did.

I had watched Billy so carefully I could imitate him perfectly.

Stefanie Powers came in. "Where's Billy?"

"He's got the flu."

"Shit, I talked to him yesterday, he was fine, damn it. I've got an important appointment. Care, can you do my hair?"

I'd been waiting to show her how good I was.

"I never thought my Delta sister would be my first big celebrity."

Billy was best friends with the Lapin brother I never met, the sheep that wandered from the flock, the brother that the other brothers envied but would never allow themselves to be like—Al, with the wild undisciplined lifestyle.

"Baby doll," Billy said, after a hard day's work. "Joinin' us at the Luau?"

"I was hoping you'd ask."

Al came around with many "hairy tales." My favorite was how he created the frosting cap for a man whose hair had been dyed all-black for a film. The guy wanted his own salt-and-pepper hair back. Al improvised with his latest girlfriend's bathing cap and a crochet hook. He bleached the hair he poked and pulled through the cap. The man was Liberace.

Al taught me, "Whatever they ask for, if they want turquoise stripes with pink circles, you tell 'em, *Yes, that's my specialty.*"

They ordered two rounds of Zombies in one hour. I finally understood the Zombie part when I tried to stand up. Good thing we walked back to our cars—those few blocks helped me to get my balance before I drove home to Bucky.

"Why are you so late?" Bucky asked.

"I was with brilliant hairdressers learning brilliant things for my career."

Late one afternoon, Aloma came to the salon area, where I was sitting, looking at the pictures in French *Vogue,* a very expensive magazine Billy bought every now and then.

"A lady named Ketti Frings is out front. She had an appointment with Billy."

Billy was absent. We hadn't heard from him all day. I came out to greet her. "Hi, I'm the other hairdresser, can I help you?"

"Okay," she said, looking me over. She was a middle-aged conservative woman. I could tell she thought I was too young to do hair. "I want *bright* highlights. Do you do the new tinfoil method?"

I recognized her name from drama class and knew that she had written the screenplay for *Come Back, Little Sheba,* and that she won the Pulitzer for her play adaptation of *Look Homeward, Angel.* I also knew her husband, Kurt Frings, was a famous agent.

I looked at her short brown hair. "Oh yes, that's my specialty."

As for the *new tinfoil method,* all I knew was that highlights meant bleach, and my second clue was *tinfoil.*

"I have to be at Scandia Restaurant by eight tonight," she said.

"That shouldn't be a problem," I said. "It's nearby."

I began carefully folding bits of her hair inside the tinfoil until I had wrapped her entire head. After this hourlong process, Ketti said, "What about the bleach?"

Oh, damn, the bleach, I forgot the bleach. Without a flinch I answered, "First I select the hairs I want to highlight, then I put the bleach in the foil, so it all bleaches at the same time."

She looked at me curiously. "Well, that's different."

I went back into the dispensary, mixed up the bleach, then began opening and applying it to the wrapped hair as fast as I could. I looked at the clock on Billy's windowsill—6:16. *Crap!* There was still so much more to do before her fancy dinner. I stared at her head from behind . . . 6:45 . . . she must be done.

I rinsed her, then silently screamed. The bleach had bled through the foil in random patterns, leaving yellow spots throughout her dark hair like a leopard. Her highlights were bright, all right . . . bright *orange.*

"Excuse me one moment," I said calmly, and left her in the bowl to go to the dispensary. *What kills orange? Ah! Blue. Okay. What kills gold? Ah, purple. Okay.* I mixed the appropriate counterbase colors to doctor up my mishaps, including brown dye to hide the leaking bleach-yellowed spots, slapped them on her, said a prayer, and kept her away from the mirrors for the next ten minutes.

"Oh, you're going to love this, so natural, lots of colors like a true sun-streaked blonde," I said. She said nothing.

I kept working and praying and washed it out again. The blue killed the orange. Her hair turned green. Time was running out and I was freaking out.

"Let me cut your hair and get rid of the awful split ends."

"Do I have so many?"

"Oh yes, but don't worry. I'll make it great for you, like Gina Lollobrigida."

My career was on the line. I cut her hair quickly, set her in rollers, standing in front of her the entire time so she couldn't see in the mirror. I put her under the dryer, dimmed the salon lights. When she was dry, I combed her out even faster than I set her. She squinted to get a full view.

"That's fine. I'm late," she said, throwing off her smock and paying me sixty dollars in cash. "Keep the change, and where did the time go?" she said, looking at her big gold watch.

"Thank you, bye-bye, you better hurry."

The next day just as I suspected, she called—she had discovered the green too.

"That's strange. *We* didn't notice it last night, did we? It must have oxidized. Come on in, I can fix it. Color correction . . . *that's my specialty.*"

The months piled up like the unpaid bills at Billy Grimes Coiffures. Unfortunately, Billy's "specialty" was a good evening out, not a good working day. His behavior wasn't unlike that of other hairdressers—George Masters, Gene, Richard—they all had stories.

Hairdressers were *gods* in those days. They could do no wrong. Handsome, talented, in demand, committed bachelors, and somehow that gave them permission to *answer to no one.*

But Billy was losing his inspiration for hair. When he eventually showed up, his work was sloppy. I made it my job to pick him up and drive him to work on time. But this plan wasn't working. He was losing more than his passion; he was losing control.

One morning I drove up Outpost Drive to Mulholland to Billy's little A-frame rental. *"Billy!"* I called out.

No answer. I walked in. There he was still in bed, his mouth open, snoring like Rip Van Winkle. I looked around to see that his fastidious palace was now a pigpen. Every flat surface had an empty champagne glass on it to match the champagne bottles lying on the floor. "Billy, wake up."

"Uhhh, dahlin' . . ." He slowly sat up, putting his hands on his head, his eyes closed, the sheet around his waist. He yawned, leaned over the end table with cigarette butts piled in the ashtray, looking for a long one, then twisted the sheet tighter around his waist and walked off into the bathroom.

"What time is it? I jus' gotta jump in the shower."

"Billy, every day you say you'll be ready. I pick you up so you won't be late. Your backer people are driving Aloma crazy, calling for rent money."

I kept talking to him through his open bathroom door.

"I know, baby doll," Billy shouted back through the shower water. "It'll be okay, don't worry your pretty head."

One morning I arrived at the salon and my key didn't work. A chain and padlock had replaced the lock. A piece of paper was taped to the door.

Public Notice: Billy Grimes Coiffures is permanently closed.

Billy's backers backed out. It had barely been a year. I stood there with Harriet Stuart, Billy's first appointment. She read the fine print, hands on her hips. "I'm going back to Richard Alcala," she said. "What are you going to do?"

"I don't know." The purse on my shoulder had turned into a ton of bricks.

"Call me when you hear from Billy," Harriet said, and left.

I leaned close to the window and pressed my face to the glass. I saw the empty salon that had once been so much fun, so full of life. Poor Billy. How could this be the end? I stepped back.

Not for me . . . this was not going to be my end.

My Way After Billy

Billy was a snake charmer. A heart warmer. A giver and a taker. A player, a faker, and an amazing friend. He was a headmaster, be it with hair or mind. He gave me tools for hair and taught me tricks with style.

Before Billy's salon closed, Aloma insisted that a woman named Mollie Mulligan come to me. She was running Gustave Tassell's couture factory. Mollie's title was Directress. She was a petite freckled tangerine redhead with unique fashion sense and a definite power about her. She had strong opinions and was very vocal. She was also an ex-girlfriend of Richard Alcala. That impressed me most. *What must that have been like?*

I had to cancel Mollie's appointment on the day when I was locked out of Billy's salon.

"I can't do your hair this week. There's no more Billy Grimes Coiffures."

"What? You must call my friend Larry Bowser," Mollie said. "No, I'll call him. You'll work there. He's a refined hairdresser, a lovely man. He's on Rodeo."

I perked up at the sound of *Rodeo.* "Thanks, Mollie."

"You *are* doing my hair this week . . . at Larry's."

It was like a blood transfusion having Mollie take charge. She was my luck of the Irish. She called back in minutes. "You're in. Larry said you could have the back booth that he was using for storage. I'll meet you there tomorrow morning before I go to work. He's next door to the Luau. Don't be late."

"If you're recommended by Mollie, you must be good." Larry smiled at Mollie. "She used to come to me."

"Now, Larry," Mollie said, "you're so difficult to get an appointment with and yes, she *is* good."

"Put your things in there," Larry said, pointing to my new home down the corridor. "I have to get back to work, we can chat later."

I took my paper bag of rollers, brushes, combs, scissors, clippies, hairnets, cutting capes, and bobby pins and walked with Mollie to *my* booth.

"I'm officially a hairdresser, not an assistant. I can't believe it, thank you so much, Mollie."

"Don't mention it. Just do my hair."

"Larry is the hairdresser to the Real Ladies of the Town," Mollie said. "No young starlets—well, one, Marlo Thomas. He does Mrs. Anna Marie Bartlett from Argentina. She's producer Hall Bartlett's wife. And Barbara Marx, she's Mrs. Harpo Marx, and Rhonda Fleming, Jo Stafford, Helen O'Connell, Alice Faye, Fay Wray, Mrs. Jimmy Durante, to name a few."

"Oh," I said.

After I finished Mollie's hair, I investigated my new surroundings. Standing at the front door on Rodeo Drive, I took it all in: the Swiss Café across the street, the fancy dress shops, and two gigantic bookstores opposite each other, Martindale's and Hunter's. Up the street was La Scala. I had heard that the high-powered people had specific tables there and no one else could sit at them.

I couldn't believe I was working on the best street in Beverly Hills on the same block as the Luau, where I had been drinking Zombies and Scorpions with Billy and his friends. Soon I would be a regular on my own.

Larry worked in the front booth. His ladies all seemed to have the same dyed hair that matched a Siamese cat. I watched him create flawless bouffant waved hairdos. He sprayed until they said *stop*. It was common to sleep with toilet paper wrapped around a hairdo so it wouldn't move and would last all week. Larry was a pillar of consistent hair perfection. His soft-spoken personality made him welcoming. He was so professional, so conservative, and so unlike Billy and the other hairdressers I had previously met.

In the months that followed, Aloma, Mollie, and I would meet three or four times a week after work and go to the Swiss Café, the Luau, or La Scala for martinis and hors d'oeuvres; our main course was gossip and complaining about our boyfriends.

On August 25, 1964, owner Jean Leon of La Scala walked into his restaurant and when he saw an early party crowd with a cake and balloons, he asked Miguel, the maître d', "What's going on in here?"

"It's Carrie's twenty-first birthday."

"Her twenty-first birthday?" Jean said. "She's been drinking in here for ages!"

Larry promoted me constantly, even when he wasn't too busy. Soon I was booked with Arlene Dahl, Jo Stafford, Helen O'Connell, Liz Scott, Alice Faye, and Mrs. Jimmy Durante, plus I had my following from Billy's salon: Julie Payne, Rona Barrett, Barbara Luna, and my pal Stefanie when she was in town. Stef recommended George Chakiris to me, and he recommended two Greek debutantes. And so on and on and on.

Larry moved me from the last booth to the first booth behind him, pissing off a few of his older hairdressers. The pressure was on.

I was ready to conquer Beverly Hills.

I was ready to turn in my '55 Ford from Babe.

I was ready for my own assistant, too.

"I love this cut," my last client said.

"Thanks, Donna, sorry to dash," I said, throwing my combs and scissors in the drawer. "I'm supposed to get married tonight."

Larry walked by. "Who's getting married?"

"I'm supposed to, if I get home in time." Larry looked left out. "It's not a big wedding, no one is coming." I grabbed my coat. "See you tomorrow."

"No honeymoon?" Donna yelled.

"Nope," I yelled back.

"Come on, we're so late," Bucky said from the bathroom door.

I sat in the tub, tired and uninspired.

"Do we really have to do this tonight?"

"It's December twenty-second," Bucky said, walking into the bathroom. "We decided to get married on the anniversary of our first date."

That time now seemed light-years away, though it was only a year ago. My tub water was cold. I turned on the hot.

"My folks are probably there already, so come on."

There was a nondenominational church, a block north of Ventura Boulevard, in the Valley. We had never been inside. Bucky had decided on this little brown church. He had also picked out my wardrobe.

"I'll help you get dressed," he said, pulling me out of the tub and wrapping me in a bath towel.

I felt choiceless, obligated. What I needed at this point was a drink, but no chance in this bare house. I had to change that. It didn't matter whether he drank or not. I did. I wanted to, I liked to, I needed to.

"After our wedding, we're going to your favorite place, the Luau."

Ahhhh, a big drink.

"Just you, me, and my folks."

Make that many big drinks.

"Hey, dahlin'," the familiar voice on the phone said.

"Dammit, Billy! I've been calling you, then your phone was disconnected."

I heard him take a big drag off his cigarette and let out an equally big exhale. "Yeah, it got a little crazy, baby girl. Thought I'd call and tell ya sorry about the mix-up."

"Mix-up?" I laughed. I could never be mad at Billy. "Hey, guess what? I'm married. I'm Carrie White now. And I'm so busy I need my own assistant. Mollie got me a great job, *on Rodeo!*"

A few days later, a beautiful black girl about five years older than me showed up at Larry's. "I'm Carol Smith. Billy said we're going to be best friends," she said. "I worked for Richard Alcala and before that, at Lintermans."

"Great, you've worked longer than me. I can't pay much, but my customers are big tippers."

"Can you afford fifty dollars a week?" Carol said.

"Can you start now?"

I was standing by the reception desk when an elegant black lady walked in and said she had been recommended to Carrie White.

"That's me."

"Oh my, you're so young. Do you think you could do my hair?"

"Why not?" I said. "*I do hair.*"

"When are you available?"

"Right now, what's *your* name?"

"Oh, of course, my name is Maria Cole."

As soon as she went into the changing room, Carol pulled me into my booth. "Do you know who that is?"

"Yes, she said her name was Maria Cole."

"No, that's *Mrs. Nat King Cole.*"

Carol washed her hair. I hoped my work would meet my own expectations. I gave her my best imitation of George Masters doing Marilyn Monroe, Larry doing Arlene Dahl, Billy doing Rona Barrett, Richard Alcala doing Natalie Wood, and Gene Shacove doing Janet Leigh.

"This is just what I've been looking for," Maria said.

I handed her the mirror to see the back of her do. "I like to make sure my ladies look great when they're leaving a room too."

"Do you take standing appointments? I like Fridays."

Maria and I became close from weekly hair visits. She shared many stories about her glamorous life with Nat. I wanted to tell Maria something personal too. "Well, guess what?" I said. "I've been married for four months and I'm three months pregnant!"

Maria put her hands up and turned around. "Is it your *first child*?"

I had another flashback to where I did not want to go.

"Ah, yes . . . yes, it is."

I wasn't ready for this pregnancy, but this child could stay in my arms.

"How would you like a baby shower at my home in Malibu?" Maria said.

On the seventh day of the seventh month, Maria gave me a Cinderella baby shower in her charming beach home with friends and clients.

On the ninth day of the ninth month, I gave birth to my son, whom I named Adam after the first man. He was *my* first man.

Going National

Bucky, baby, and me make three. All stuffed into the little one-bedroom West Hollywood duplex. The good news was I had a child I could look at, smell, and hold. I was so crazy over my son that I saved the scab from his umbilical cord and put it into his baby book.

I was loopy from my schedule of a little sleep and a lot of nursing. I had a house to clean and laundry to do and had to figure out how to be a mother and a wife and get back to my hairdressing career.

It had been four weeks.

The Del Nostro family down the street offered to babysit Adam. Every workday I got dressed, dressed Adam, nursed him, dropped him off, went to work, returned to the Del Nostros', nursed him there, went home, and made dinner—one of my famous meals, creamed tuna or meatloaf or Swedish meatballs—or I called Ready-Go for pizza.

After a few months I stopped nursing.

I was booked solid in the salon. Bucky handled all my money, taking my paycheck and letting me keep my tips. They felt good in my pocket.

I started smoking again. Bucky hated cigarettes, so I had to get in as many as possible while I was away from him. Getting a good strong cup of coffee from the little café behind Larry's was my morning inspiration, along with taking my Desbutal diet pills that I got from a Beverly Hills doctor to lose my "baby fat." I rewarded myself with a cigarette after every client while Carol shampooed. Larry didn't have the flow of champagne like Billy, so I learned the true meaning of Happy Hour.

"Bucky, I'm going to be a little late today," my usual line. I needed to unwind. Going home meant more work. I could barely wait to get "happy" across the street at the Swiss Café.

Mollie was already there with her martini. Aloma came dashing in after. "You guys ordered without me?" Mollie lit a cigarette.

"Well, Michael is getting out of the agent business and going to be a producer. In fact, Carrie, he wants you to do the hair for a film he's involved with."

I sat up with renewed energy. "What is it?"

"Remember *A Man and a Woman*?"

Mollie and I leaned in.

"Michael's going to meet with Anouk Aimée at the Beverly Hills Hotel to do a film called *Model Shop*. Michael wants you to do her hair and he's going to get you screen credits!"

We drank, we laughed, we shared our lives and mozzarella marinara.

"Oops, what time is it?" I asked.

Mollie was the only one who wore a watch. She made sure I knew it was a Bulgari, a name I had never heard of. Mollie knew everything and she wanted me to be chic and smart for the caliber of women coming my way. She enlightened me one time with a whisper, "Steak tartare *means* raw, you don't order it medium."

"Carrie, I'm sending a very important person to you," Mollie said over the phone. "From New York. She's the fashion editor for *Glamour* and . . . she goes to *Kenneth* for her hair."

I stood holding the phone like I'd received an Oscar nomination.

"Mollie, *thank you*. I'll do the best job and—" Mollie interrupted. "I know, my dear, that's why I'm sending her to you."

The appointment was booked. I wore my snappiest outfit, navy blue patent flats with chrome heels, navy tights, a dark blue and green herringbone mini A-line dress. I extended my brown hair by adding a fall that draped past my shoulders and had perfect false eyelashes with black baby-doll eye makeup, fashionably current. I was ready to prove that a groovy girl hairdresser can be as good as a man hairdresser.

"Helloooo," she said, with the affectation of New York worldliness. "I'm Amy Greene."

Like I didn't know. All I could think of was that she was a client of Mr. Kenneth, the Godfather of Hair of New York, more accurately, of *America*. If I pleased her, it could mean recommendations from Mr. Kenneth. It would have been nice to have my own salon, but at least I had an assistant.

"Kenneth does my hair like this," she said and proceeded to show me a picture of herself in the famous Jacqueline Kennedy smooth-do, the signature Mr. Kenneth bouffant.

"How about if I add a little Beverly Hills splash to your do?"

"And what might that be?"

"Younger and sexier. I'm a good hairdresser, but I'm a *girl* first. I know what kind of hair females want."

With that zinger, I did her hair like I was on television and Mr. Kenneth was watching. When I finished, she swung her hair around to check how it moved. I stood quietly.

"I'd like to do an article on you," Amy said.

I had to act professional, not scream in her face and hug the life out of her, but *holy crap!* I answered calmly, "That sounds terrific."

"We haven't done anything on California fashion for ages," she said, still looking at her hair. "And I can't wait to tell Kenneth about you."

Amy Greene got back to me. "We will be there in three weeks. My husband, Milton, will be the photographer. It will be a one-page exclusive; *California Carrie,* or something like that, I don't know yet."

Bill, my mother's latest husband, called me at work.

"If you want to see your mother alive, you'd better get to the Hollywood Presbyterian Hospital tonight, she doesn't have much time left."

I felt the blood leave my body. This was the first time I realized that you could die from drinking, as opposed to simply being dead drunk.

I dropped the phone and my brush, said nothing to my client in the chair or Carol, and walked out of the salon. I heard Carol calling from the front door, "Hey, *HEY*," but I kept walking up Rodeo to Santa Monica Boulevard.

My life with my mother passed through my mind like a silent film, flashes when she was young and beautiful, photographs of her holding me when I was an infant on the steps of our courtyard on Burton Way, her too-thin-too-tan body in Pacoima, beer bottles piling up over her head in a trash can, finding her passed out in our Hollywood apartment, back to the old photos etched in my mind of her attending Beverly Hills High School and another of her and my grandmother in costumes from their bit parts in Laurel and Hardy's *Babes in Toyland*.

Then came memories of want and promise, anger and sorrow, disappointment, distaste, and broken pieces of love like a china cup fallen from the highest shelf in the kitchen. I sobbed from an ancient cry waiting to be released. I found myself at the Santa Monica seashore.

I had effortlessly walked to the beach.

I watched the few adults with their children making castles, digging holes with buckets and shovels by the shore. I watched the beginning of the sun's descent and felt the chill coming in. I needed to get back. I felt some resolve. I walked and thought at a fast pace, until I was back close to the shop again. I stopped at the steps of the Good Shepherd Church on the corner and dropped to my knees.

"Please, please, please save my mother's life," I begged a God I hadn't spoken to in a long while. It wasn't Sunday. It was a plain ol' Thursday twilight and my mother wasn't expected to live.

I had needed this time without another voice in my head. I knew my son was fine with the babysitter, but Bucky was probably worried. I walked to a client's house on Doheny Drive and called him.

"Where have you been? You had me worried to death, everyone, Carol, Larry, my folks, and Mrs. Del Nostro."

"I had to disappear."

"Bill called," Bucky said. "Your mother's going to make it, but she has to quit drinking."

My prayer had been answered.

"Can I get you a beer?" my mother said. I was sitting in her turquoise plastic breakfast nook, in her latest Hollywood apartment, on Las Palmas. Bill, the traveling surveyor, was always gone during the week, leaving my mother alone with their toy poodle, Beau. The dog was her best relationship. I was trying to mend ours, but we had little to say.

"Mom, I thought you weren't supposed to drink."

"A beer isn't drinking."

She looked terrible, the wrong shade of Max Factor foundation, deep fuchsia lipstick, and that horrible Fabergé Aphrodisia perfume.

As if it could take her back in time and make her fresh, all new, all right.

"No hard liquor," she said, and set out two beers, Schlitz Malt Liquor. "How are you and Adam and Bucky?"

"Adam's one year old."

"That's nice, honey."

I looked at her face and remembered the day Roz and I walked into the restroom of the Broadway-Hollywood department store on Hollywood and Vine. "Roz," I whispered. "Look at that poor ol' lady going into the last stall." Then she turned. It was my mother. "Oh, Carole . . . hi," she said, nervously. "I was just going to buy some slippers." Roz and I stood with our mouths hanging open, looking at this waif in a raggedy wool coat trying to hide her pint of vodka that was poking its capped nose out of a brown paper sack in her white plastic purse. Now, sitting here across from each other, she couldn't even pretend to be okay.

I finished my beer.

"Ready for another?" my mother said, and shuffled to the refrigerator, returning with two more beers.

"Mom, I'm going to be in a national fashion magazine, *Glamour*."

She never looked at a newspaper, let alone fashion magazines.

"That's nice, honey," she said, closing her eyes and taking a long sip of beer, her bony little elbows perched on the table holding up her chin and tired head. Her once lovely skin was blotchy with broken capillaries on her cheeks and around her nostrils; her eyes weren't even brown anymore . . . fading away like her.

"I gotta pick up Adam."

We stood up.

"Tell him Nana Grace says hi."

I wanted to say, why don't you? He doesn't even know who you are.

"I will, Mom . . . glad you're okay . . . I'll call in a few days."

We finished the last of our beers. We had this in common.

"The phones are ringing off the hook for you," Larry said.

The *Glamour* article was a big hit.

"Thanks, Larry. In fact, I want to talk to you when you have the time."

"Tell me now."

I was Larry's pet. His stunning daughter, Paula, was a heroin addict. She'd broken Larry's heart a million times, because he couldn't help her. He felt he helped me, and he did but I was unprepared to talk to him on the spot.

"Well, I wanted you to be the first to know . . ." I began. Larry's posture became more erect; his eyebrows furled in question.

"I am so busy and the timing seems right . . . and . . . Bucky found a little makeover salon for me around the corner, and I was nervous to tell you but . . ."

"You'll have to leave," he said, and started to walk away.

"*Larry,*" I appealed, "I'm just giving you proper notice."

He turned and his soft-spoken voice became firm. "I don't care, you need to leave *now.*"

He walked out the back door to the alley.

I wasn't prepared for *this,* either. I put all my equipment into brown paper bags the way I'd come in; only I was leaving with more bags and Carol.

"Come on, Carol, I'll ask Gene if I can work for him till my place is ready."

We barged into his salon and went to the reception area. We didn't look like customers or like Gene's girlfriends. "I need to speak to Gene right away."

"One moment." His receptionist walked away. Gene came out.

"Could I work here, just for a month? I told Larry I'm going to open my own salon and he booted me out on the spot."

Gene was disarming in his black tight shirt, cool fitted Levi's, and motorcycle boots.

"I don't have a station for you," he said, unemotional in the face of my distraught neediness.

His receptionist interrupted us. "Gene, Marilyn Simon needs a haircut, can you squeeze her in between Suzanne Pleshette and Jill St. John?"

"Yeah, sure, no, wait, I'm leaving. Cancel everyone next week." Gene turned to me. "Maybe I will let you work in my room, with me."

"That would be *so great*, you'll never know we're here."

I began to do some of Gene's clients when he didn't show up, or would split on a motorcycle ride, or did a house call and never came back. I learned his way and added my flair, something only a girl would notice. I did Steve McQueen's wife, Neile; Jill St. John; even Joan Collins.

I was requested to style the hair of the lead singer of a new band for a new magazine: *Teen*. When she refused to wear the green beret and support the Vietnam War, the photo shoot in progress was canceled, along with my first magazine cover. The band was The Mamas & the Papas. *She* was Michelle Phillips. She liked my hair styling and said she would see me again. She did.

"You're stealing all my clients," Gene said one day.

He was a different ladies' man from Richard and Billy. He played hard to get. One day, he put a lady under the dryer after he cut her, left the room, the salon, and the state, and went to Hawaii with another client. I finished her for him.

I laughed. "Gene, you're never here. Anyway, my salon is ready and I can't thank you enough for all your help."

Gene did have a cute side, and I almost had a crush on him too.

"You *could* stay, you know," he said. "Or come back if it doesn't work."

While I was at Gene's salon, he had brought a hairdresser from London to introduce a new method of cutting. Vidal Sassoon was a wizard to behold, and what he could do with hair showed me there was a lot more art to discover in hairdressing. This was my first exposure to geometric, asymmetric precision technique. Vidal had made his mark in London . . . he was here to conquer America.

I just wanted to conquer Beverly Hills.

Making of Carrie White, Part 1

It was the first day of my first salon, but I really wasn't open yet—no hairdressers, no manicurist, no receptionist. I had Carol and my clients. I knew about hairdressing, and that was all I thought I needed to know.

"Carol, let's put all the dryers by the window so the ladies can watch the sidewalk people parade."

My salon was located around the corner from Rodeo, behind the Luau, on Brighton Way. I looked at my twenty-foot-high picture windows in my main room, where I had two staircases leading to two mezzanines at the back of my salon and back to my entry door. It was beautiful, unbelievable, and exciting as hell.

"I'm so happy for you," Carol said, as we pushed the dryers in a row.

"Where shall we work?" I asked Carol. She didn't answer and went to my car for more things to unload.

I walked to the first booth. It was the largest, and closest to the desk and the front door. I pushed two chairs into this section. I stood behind the one chair in front of the mirror and pretended I had a client. "There you go, Miss Prima Donna," and I picked up the hand mirror from the counter. "Yes, it is perfect on you, isn't it?"

Carol walked in with a box of new leopard cotton smocks.

"Who are you talking to?"

"Isn't this going to be fun?" I said.

"We need to talk, because I won't be able to work for you anymore."

I set the hand mirror down.

"*What?* I thought you were as excited as me about my salon," I said. She remained silent. Carol was more than an assistant; she was my friend.

"I have cancer."

I sank.

"Oh no, Carol."

I hugged her tight.

We stood among the unpacked carts of tints, sponges, brushes, the cases of bobby pins, new rollers, and clippies that needed to be stored. Dep wave set, Aqua Net hair spray, hairnets, and cleaning supplies spilled out of boxes along with shampoo and cream rinses and office supplies for the desk, the calendar, appointment book, pens, pencils, receipt pads, and my new business cards.

"It's in my uterus. When you had Adam, I had a miscarriage, and the doctors figure that's when it started. I have to have surgery."

"I'll wait for you, I won't open till you come back."

"I talked to my family," Carol said. "I *can't* come back."

I looked at her, trying to shut out her words.

"I've had time to think. I can't come back and scrub those Beverly Hills ladies' heads, when there are so many things to clean in my own neighborhood. Life is too short," Carol said. "I'm going to work at a day care in South Central where my daughter went. I have to make a difference while I can."

I understood. I was proud of her. She helped me put the new towels away.

We promised to stay close.

In no time, my salon was filled with sunshine from my new yellow paint. White wicker Kleenex boxes and wastebaskets were my accessories, the latest thing in decorating, to accent my big white wicker chaise for all the waiting ladies. I upholstered the mattress in vinyl leopard, a spoof statement against the overdone serious leopard and red-flocked wallpaper fashionable in so many Beverly Hills salons. I plunked a few palm trees in spots à la the Richard Alcala salon and added fresh flowers, a touch Mollie suggested.

"Oh, and you must subscribe to *WWD*," Mollie said. "*Women's Wear Daily*. That is the fashion Bible."

There were the five fashion magazines in existence: *Glamour, Mademoiselle, Ladies' Home Journal, Vogue,* and *Harper's Bazaar.* No trash allowed in my salon, no *National Enquirer* or *Confidential. Chic* was my goal. I would *outgirl* those guy hairdressers. I would never stop improving until I hit the top: First Lady in Hairdressing . . . then I would compete with myself.

I had everything going for me, except one minor detail—I had room in my fixed-up budget salon for fourteen hairdressers and I had none. Everyone I asked to work for me had the same reply: *Who are you?*

I guess *everyone* hadn't read my *Glamour* article.

"Mollie, I have so much space," I said, early one eve at the Luau.

"Make a boutique."

"A what?"

"That's French for *small store.* That's what you put upstairs," Mollie said.

I took two swigs of my Scorpion.

"Mollie, I was thinking more like I need hairdressers."

"Isn't Don Morrand going to work for you?"

"He said he would, but not for a few months."

"By the way," Mollie said, "I spoke to Amy Greene today and she's sending you her friend Sally, Buck Henry's wife."

Mollie knew from my gaze that I didn't know who Buck Henry was.

"Buck Henry wrote *Get Smart* with Mel Brooks and he's writing a movie called *The Graduate.*"

I never paid attention to *who* wrote things, just the stars and their *hair.*

"Carrie White Beauty Parlour, may I help you?"

"Carrie... are you answering your own phone?" It was Amy Greene from *Glamour.* "Anyway, congratulations on your salon and Kenneth *will be* recommending you, starting with actress Betty Furness."

Was I ready for Mr. Kenneth's clients or a celebrity as famous as Betty Furness, now the Westinghouse-sponsored television star?

"That's fantastic!"

"Gotta run, my dear," Amy said. "Good luck."

I greeted the famed *Magnificent Obsession* film star Betty Furness at my door, extending my arm. "Welcome to Carrie White's Beauty Parlour... I'm Carrie." I had on my best imitation Mary Quant dress, go-go boots, and my long brown hair pulled back, covering over my attached hair fall, coiffed perfectly.

"How long have you been doing hair, since you were twelve?"

"Since high school ... years ago ... well, three ... I have a one-year-old son."

She smiled, looking over my shoulder for someone, anyone.

"My salon is new, no assistant yet, but I give a helluva shampoo."

"You do come highly recommended."

I gave her the shampoo of my life. We walked back to my station.

"Now . . ." she said, picking up the comb off my tray. "May I?"

"Of course." I stood attentively.

"I part my hair here." She sliced a deep side part and pressed her hair flat. "Then"—she combed the sides into two curls at her cheekbones—"and the back goes like this . . ." Without looking she combed and cupped her hair at her neck. "It fits like a cap, and after I dry, you reclip the sides and I will take them out at the studio. How long have you worked with photographer John Engstead? He is the Cecil Beaton of Hollywood . . . I come to California just for him."

"I've never met him."

"Oh." She flinched and returned the comb to me. I finished what she started. When she was dry, I brushed and reclipped her hair the way she suggested.

"Would your receptionist call me a cab?"

"Right away," I said, and went to the desk and made the call. She changed her clothes and walked up to the desk. "Do you do everything, and will that be enough?" and handed me twenty-five dollars.

"Yes to both questions," I said. I felt my newly raised price to ten dollars for a shampoo and set was expensive. I preferred getting *twenty-five.* "Thank you, I hope your hair comes out the way you like it."

"I'm sure it will, my dear." She glided out.

I exhaled as the door closed behind her, then rushed to call Mollie. "I just did *Betty Furness.*"

I felt delirious. I rewarded myself by walking around the corner to the Luau and having a big fancy drink with a gardenia in it.

Making of Carrie White, Part 2

"My hair brushed out perfectly."

Betty Furness was calling me from New York. "John Engstead noticed too, and he will be calling you and . . ." she stretched out the *and* with suspense. "Mr. Kenneth said he was never quite sure whom to recommend in Los Angeles before you." My heart pounded with excitement. "So, my dear, when I return next month to select my photographs, I hope you won't be too busy to do my hair again."

That was how it all started. It was late 1966. I was twenty-three.

Mrs. Buck Henry came in. "Can you follow my Kenneth cut?"

"Absolutely," I said, then zinged her with my power line. "I'm a hairdresser, but I'm a *girl* first. I know what you want from your hair."

It was a line, but I meant it. It did matter that I was a girl first because the male hairdresser's line was: *If you want your hair to look good in the morning, sleep with your hairdresser.*

"Hello, my name is Trudy Owett, fashion editor of *Ladies' Home Journal.* I would like to do an article on you and two other hairdressers: Fred Glaser in Chicago, whose client is a young singer named Barbra Streisand, and Kenneth of New York. Would you be interested?"

I would represent California . . . *me* on the same page with KENNETH.

"Yessssssss, I'd be interested."

"Hello, my name is Nancy Dinsmore. I would like Carrie White to do a layout for *Harper's Bazaar.* I am the West Coast editor."

Packing for this *Harpers' Bazaar* job was an all-night deal. I cleaned brushes and combs and polished bobby pins. I set hairpieces, sharpened scissors, and shined every possible hair clip and accessory. I had to make sure I was prepared.

I got on location at 6:00 AM to find the model was Peggy Moffitt in her perfect Vidal Sassoon bob that needed nothing from me. I was thrilled. I was too exhausted from preparing for work to do any. And anyway, all I wanted was to see my name in small print in the bottom corner of *Harper's Bazaar.*

"Hello, my name is Eleanor Phillips and I would like Carrie White to do my hair if she has time for me . . . I am the West Coast editor of *Vogue* magazine."

"I think something can be worked for you, Miss Phillips."

I was still answering my own phone. It occurred to me that I'd better get an assistant quick, and probably a receptionist too. I was building a clientele that might even expect a maid in the bathroom.

Out of the blue, a guy showed up at my salon.

"Hi, I'm Barry, I used to be George Masters's assistant. Do you need an assistant?" He smiled from ear to ear. "If so . . . I'm your man."

"Okay, Barry, wanna start today?"

"I brought my work apron," he said, and rolled up his sleeves ready to go. "And I know a lot of George's ladies are looking for a hairdresser since he's disappeared. Maybe you can do Betsy Bloomingdale, she's a hairdresser's fashion trophy."

I felt magic in the air.

I felt everything coming into place, *my place.*

I felt Billy's whisper in my ear, "See, sugah' . . . *it's all fixed.*"

"You are going to get a call from someone very important, because James Galanos has recommended you," Mollie said like a proud mama, while I was doing her hair. She picked up the *WWD* from my counter, speaking slowly and precisely. "*Jennifer Jones* needs a new hairdresser."

Barry told me she was one of George Masters's best clients.

George Masters had done another of his disappearing acts from Saks Fifth Avenue in Beverly Hills more than a month ago. George had a reputation for being unreliable and outspoken. My favorite George story was about a lady he was styling who kept changing her mind how she wanted her bangs, this side, that side, back, parted in the middle. George, exasperated trying to please her, picked up his scissors, cut her bangs to her scalp, and handed them to her. *"Here, lady, put 'em where you want them."*

With many important women scrambling to find a replacement for George and tired of waiting for him to reappear, this was a gigantic opportunity for me to win Jennifer and this town.

Barry called me to the phone. "It's her, it's her."

"Hello, this is Carrie White."

"This is Jennifer Jones. Could you come and do my hair *today*?"

I had never done anyone's hair at her house before.

"I'd love to . . ."

"Fine, around five? I have dinner plans at seven."

I rushed through my appointments. I packed everything except the shampoo bowl and threw it all in the basket of my moped. I charged up Benedict Canyon at the swift pace of twenty-five miles per hour, with a mantra in my head: *Jennifer Jones, Jennifer Jones, I'm off to do Jennifer Jones.*

I was on top of the world, the breeze hitting my smiling face. It was my opening night on Broadway. I was winding and winding my way up Benedict, and her street was still not in sight. Oh shit, my heart went on double time, my excitement turning into fear. I'm late! I floored my Honda 50. The steep hill had slowed my moped to about two miles an hour, which made me twenty minutes late, according to the antique gold watch hanging on my neck.

I saw glimpses of the Mulholland ridge, I *was* on top of the world all right, but I still hadn't found her damn street. Finally, a sign: Tower Grove Road.

Once I arrived, the next challenge was pushing my bike up her precipitous driveway to her front door. I parked and rang the bell. The butler answered.

"Hello, I'm here to do Miss Jones's hair," I said, adjusting my composure and summer minidress.

"One moment, I will see if Mrs. Selznick is available."

Jennifer Jones was an Oscar-winning actress and the widow of David O. Selznick, producer of *Gone With the Wind*. I must have watched that film five hundred times when I was working after school at the Paramount Theater.

A maid came to the door in a little black-and-white frilly outfit like a maid in a black-and-white movie.

"Follow me," she said, in a robotic manner. We came to a large dark wood door cracked open a few inches. "The new person is here, madam."

"Send her in."

The maid pushed open the door to a golden-lit room like a stage.

Jennifer Jones was sitting on a handsome padded bench in front of a huge mirror and dressing table, wrapped tightly from her breasts down in a plush white towel. Her hair was slicked back and wet.

"One minute," she said, without looking at me, and she leaned closer to the mirror to dab her cheek with a tiny brush that she dipped in foundation from a tiny pink jar on her tabletop. I stood still.

"It's past five," she said, still examining her face and not looking at me.

"I didn't think you would think I was any good, unless I was late." I giggled, hoping comedy relief would serve and I'd be forgiven.

She smoothed her dark perfectly arched eyebrows with a tiny brush and said in a monotone, "That's why I lost the last one."

"I *am* sorry . . ." I said, with my arms full of my supplies.

"You can put your things over there," she said, pointing to a nearby chair.

Jennifer was breathtakingly beautiful. I didn't want to tell her I'd never seen one of her movies. And I had no idea how George Masters styled her hair. I assumed it was the Marilyn Monroe style that George was famous for.

"I don't use wave set, George says it destroys my natural shine."

I moved in close to her. I saw her fine short brown hair and knew it was going to be limp if I didn't pack it with goop, but oh, well.

"And I don't like hair spray either, George agrees."

This was getting less fun by the minute.

"I will show you how George does the front."

She never looked directly at me. She spoke to me only through her large dressing-room mirror in front of us.

"I want my hair the way George did it for *Tender Is the Night*."

"Ohhhh, like *that*."

Jennifer sat on her throne, her body glistening with expensive lotion. To the far right, still steaming through faded bubbles, was the bath she must have just stepped out of. She had wall-to-wall carpeting right up to the tub. I looked up to see the chandelier's twinkling reflections in the ceiling like stars in the sky.

I was born for this room.

She kept dabbing concealer on her face to perfection with that tiny brush the whole time I was doing her hair, bopping her head back and forth, checking her makeup progress. It was like setting and drying a moving target. I acted like I always did hair with a spinning top for a head.

"Do you do makeup?" she asked.

"I'm a hairdresser, but a girl first, in fact makeup is my specialty."

"Next time you can put on my eyelashes. I'll show you how George does it."

Next time? That was encouraging.

When I finished, she said, "Very close to *George.*" She handed me a fifty-dollar bill. "Is that correct?"

It was more than correct. I nodded *yes.*

"Will you be able to come back? I prefer house calls."

I nodded *yes* again and packed my stuff.

"So . . . tomorrow same time," Jennifer said.

"Tomorrow?"

I tried to be cool, as if she was one of my many movie star clients, but I'm sure I answered loudly, "*Yes, I do* . . . I mean . . . I'd love to."

This was my major turning point in confidence, finance, and fame.

I went back the next day.

And the next day.

And the next. I was there almost every day for three years.

The verdict was out and it spread like brushfire: *Someone named Carrie White was doing Jennifer Jones.* My phone rang off the hook. Within a few weeks I had standing appointments with all the *Wives of.*

Mrs. James Stewart, Mrs. Ray Milland, Mrs. Milton Berle, Mrs. Otto Preminger, Mrs. John Forsythe, Mrs. Edgar Bergen, Mrs. Louis Jourdan, Mrs. James Coburn, Mrs. James Garner, Mrs. Jerry Moss (wife of the M of A&M Records), Mrs. Robert Kerlan (the Lakers' doctor), Mrs. Irwin Winkler, and Mrs. Freddie de Cordova (*Tonight Show* producer). *Then* I got the crème de la crème, two grandes dames of Hollywood royalty: Mrs. William Goetz, daughter of Louis B. Mayer (the second M of MGM) *and next* . . . the queen bee of fashion and the most sought after head in town: Mrs. Alfred Bloomingdale.

If it was 11 AM on Friday, Betsy Bloomingdale was in my chair.

I fondly called her *Mrs. B.* She was all elegance, a brand of sophistication unfamiliar to me. She walked in and her feet barely touched the ground, she peeled a pear before she ate it . . . she said "Divine" a lot.

She asked me to come to her grand home in Holmby Hills, to coif her best friend, Nancy, wife of actor Ronald Reagan. He was running for governor of California. On my next house call to Jennifer, I asked if she would vote for him. She said, "He wasn't a good actor, why would he be a good governor?"

Shear Madness

Opening night at The Factory felt like the biggest night of my life, except for the day my son was born. It definitely was the biggest social event of our town. When I'd told Bucky how excited I was to be offered this privileged membership through Mollie, he wasn't very impressed. But I knew better. This private club in West Hollywood, owned by Sammy Davis Jr., Pierre Salinger (John Kennedy's Senate press secretary), producer Richard Donner, actor Peter Lawford, and other businessmen, would open many opportunities for me, through all the people I'd meet there. This supper club was our taste of New York City glamour, with pool tables and a disco area. The word was that any performer automatically became a club member, so the lineup was from Aretha Franklin to the Byrds. The town was anxiously waiting this opening night. I dressed to impress, with my new hairpiece swinging like a James Bond girl's, my shortest mini, my fluffiest chiffon blouse, black fishnets, and black suede heels. Mollie was going to wear a James Galanos dress. I could hardly stay in my body, wondering what The Factory was going to be like and who was going to be there. I came out of the bathroom beaming in fashion perfection, got Adam ready to take to the babysitter, and I called out, "Bucky, are you ready?"

He was sitting in the living room looking through the mail.

"I've been ready." He looked handsome, but then he said, "And I don't want you to have more than two drinks."

The next Factory outing, my client Janet de Cordova was there with her husband, Freddie, producer of *The Tonight Show*. She was always full of fun and stories. Janet knew everyone. She was this town's social ambassador. She pulled me away from Bucky by one hand, her martini in her other. "Come, my darling, I have a friend who has gorgeous hair, and you should be doing it."

We made our way to the far side of the room. There sat a beautiful black woman, with a mass of long wavy hair. The young woman's husband saw Janet and stood up from his seat. Janet gave him a big hug, and turned to me. "Carrie, meet Bill and Camille Cosby."

Another night, I spotted my Delta sister Barbara Parkins.

"Barbara . . ." I heard she'd been living in London with an older man who ran the Playboy Club, Victor Lownes.

"Hi, Carrie, meet Steve Brandt."

Our town had only two gossip columnists—Rona Barrett, who wrote a syndicated newspaper column, and this skinny little guy, Steve Brandt who wrote a gossip column for *Photoplay* magazine. He was notorious for his ability to demolish people with tongue and pen. Being on Steve's good side was the only side to be on.

"I hear you have a clip joint," Steve said, his dark eyes half-mast, stoned out of his mind. "Are you any good?"

"Come find out for yourself," I said, and gave him my card. "Great to see you, Barbara, you look gorgeous."

I was between the Santa Lucia Mountains and the Pacific Ocean, between Venus and Mars. I was in Big Sur on my first assignment for *Vogue* magazine, only two weeks after I had worked with the famous photographer John Engstead on a *TV Guide* job.

It was my first time on location, and away from Bucky and my son, Adam. I would be working with the celebrated royal photographer Norman Parkinson from London, who lived in Tobago, in the Caribbean. Of course, I had never heard of Tobago in the Caribbean; I had never heard of Big Sur in California.

Norman Parkinson was famous for taking fashion photography

out of rigid studios into the wild outdoors. He loved the Big Sur area ever since he had seen *The Sandpiper* with Elizabeth Taylor and Richard Burton.

He looked like Sir John Gielgud in a beige silk Indian shirt. His fine gray hair popped out of his antique jeweled, embroidered pillbox hat. "It's a Kashmiri wedding hat," his assistant told me. "He wears it whenever he works."

I finished the two models, Norman directed them to their position, and I stood near him both to see what he was looking at and also to make sure no hair got out of place. Norman leaned in to me. "The only thing that gets in the way of a really good photograph is the camera."

We worked on rugged rocky cliffs and sandy trails from sunrise to sunset. Afterward, we ate and drank red wine at Nepenthe, the home Orson Welles bought for his bride Rita Hayworth, although they never spent a night there.

I liked this location business.

I especially treasured a letter I received shortly afterward from Diana Vreeland, the editor in chief of *Vogue*, complimenting my work. Could life get any better?

My popularity increased, making it harder to coordinate my house calls with Jennifer Jones. One day, after shuffling my salon ladies so I could do Jennifer's in the middle of the afternoon. I raced in my car back to my salon clients. My receptionist stopped me on the way in. "Jennifer just called, you have to go back and do her hair."

"I just *did* her hair, what are you talking about?"

"She miscalculated on her bidet, her hair and makeup got all sprayed up, and she said she's having important pictures taken today, so you have to go back and start over."

I laughed and screamed at the same time. My ex-agent's wife, an actress, Louise, had been patiently waiting for me, she laughed and screamed too.

"Just hurry, so I can shoot *Wagon Train* by tomorrow morning."

I floored it back to Jennifer's. I ran past her son Robert Walker Jr. and his friends Peter Fonda and Dennis Hopper on their motorcycles in the driveway.

"Hi," Robert said. "Didn't you just leave here?"

I redid Jennifer. I told her to stay away from all toilets, showers, and yard sprinklers, because I couldn't come back. And those important pictures Jennifer was taking . . . were at the DMV, for her driver's license.

What Edie wants, Edie gets. When Edie Goetz heard I did house calls for Jennifer, she wanted house calls too. I thought she was so clever to never learn how to drive; it justified her required chauffeur. Even before the house calls, she came to my salon in her giant navy blue pinstriped Phantom Rolls-Royce, a special edition created for the queen of England. It was built to such large proportions that the queen could *walk* directly into her car, because the queen bows to no one. This was clearly Mrs. Goetz's motto as well.

"Carrie White here," I said, into the iron gate box at Mrs. Goetz's driveway.

Her butler greeted me at the door and directed me to wait in the library.

"If you are interested, Mrs. Goetz has provided a brochure listing the artists and paintings throughout her home. Please do not touch anything. Her books are first editions and you mustn't touch them either."

I took the three sheets of paper as if I were at a museum and nodded that I understood the importance of his request. The quality and quantity of masterpieces under one private roof was unbelievable: Toulouse-Lautrec, Monet, Manet, Renoir, Picasso. I tiptoed from room to room. One wall held a painting of Degas's ballerinas. On another was a painting by Bonnard. Above the fireplace mantel was the most amazing unfinished piece, a signed self-portrait by van Gogh.

The butler returned. "You may go up now."

I glided up the Lucite-railed staircase. At the top stood a bronze statue. I paged through my brochure. It was the second casting of Degas's *Little Dancer*, the sculpted ballerina, frozen in time with her faded pink silk ribbon in her iron hair ponytail, to match her netted tutu. A maid came out at the top of the stairs. "This way, please," she said. I entered the magnificent waiting area. All walls were presentation areas for masterpieces: Gauguin, Cézanne, Miró, Matisse.

I imagined growing up in this mansion and what a treat it must be for her grandchildren to go to Grandma's house. I thought my nana was fancy because she had a bed in her living room that went into the wall like magic. Twenty years later, I learned it was called a Murphy bed and my nana was actually kinda broke.

"Hello, darling one," Mrs. Goetz said, "So sorry I kept you waiting."

While I combed her hair, she proceeded to tell me another story about her life as a little girl.

"One time, Daddy took my sister Irene and me to spend the night at the Hearst Castle in San Simeon, because Daddy had business with Randolph. He was a clever man, that Randolph," she said. "The chairs that lined both sides of his long dining table were built oversized, all except *Randolph's* chair at the head of the table. This way his guests, like my daddy, all powerful men, would feel small in *Randolph's* presence."

I picked up my can of Elnett hair spray. "Cover your face, here comes the Shellac No. 5."

We giggled as I sprayed. The maid put my cash envelope in my purse and I thought, *I get paid for this fun?*

"Could you do my girlfriend's hair here next week?" Mrs. Goetz asked. "She's visiting from her home in Barbados." Mrs. Goetz was a good press agent.

The following week I charged up her stairs to find Claudette Colbert waiting for me. I picked up my scissors and teased Miss Colbert. "Shall we keep these little bangs of yours or try something new?"

Then came my big treat, Mrs. Goetz's other girlfriend, Rosalind Russell, the great Auntie Mame. I got to do her hair many times close to her final departure. She never once complained of her crippling arthritic pain.

And then . . . my ultimate, ultimate treat in life . . .

Ruth Gordon burst in my salon. "Oh my! You're so cute and *young*."

She walked entirely around me, looking at my interpretation of a well-dressed hippie, bracelets up my arms, scarves at my neck, a sheer pirate shirt and vest, tight lavender flower-print pants, and purple Maud Frizon flats.

"You know, I wore my miniskirt to Edie's dinner party last night and she thought it was my tennis outfit. I told her, 'Edie, get with it, or you're just gonna get *old*.'" Ruth wriggled her little body while she spoke and had a twinkle in her eye that could light up a black night in Egypt.

"So, dollie, all I want is my original hair color back, no fancy do like Edie."

Then with those little quick hands of hers, she undid her braid to show me her roots. "Look at these crazy white wires popping out of my head. I wasn't born with them . . . they need to go."

When her hair was finished, she barely looked at it, braided it back herself soaking wet, slapped some cash down on my station, crunched her shoulders up to her ears, walked out on tiptoes, and said, "*I love it.*"

"Surprise!" Steve Brandt, the gossip columnist, popped in with a woman by his side. I had cut his hair just the week before.

"I want you to do my friend from New York. She's here for a big role with Warren."

"Is that the bathroom?" she said, pointing to the back of my salon.

I nodded yes, she walked off.

"I'm a little busy, Steve," I said, finishing the lady in my chair and not liking his friend's attitude.

She marched back from the ladies' room.

"Steve, why can't California stores catch up to New York and bring clothes to me? Why do I have to schlep all over this town?"

Stores didn't deliver . . . we went to stores . . . what was she talking about and who did she think she was, Joan Crawford?

"Carrie," Steve said. "Meet Faye Dunaway."

"Hello," she said, and looked around. "Where are you doing my hair?"

Steve brought in many young actresses after that. He was good for business and wrote good things about me in his *Photoplay* gossip column.

Mrs. Goetz installed a small refrigerator in her dressing room for Moët champagne splits *just for me.* Little did she know, clients brought bottles of the bubbly into my salon all day and my *happy hour* started hours before I got to her house at 4:00 PM.

New York City, *Hair* I Come

"I won't be gone long," I said to Bucky. "It's just for the opening weekend."

I was doing up a few dishes; Adam was in the bedroom watching cartoons.

Bucky came into the kitchen.

"Why can't she get someone in New York?"

"Because she's *Jennifer Jones and I'm her hairdresser.* Plus, Nancy Dinsmore, the West Coast editor of *Harper's Bazaar,* might have a job for me while I'm there." I stopped with the dishes. "Imagine, a real live *Harper's Bazaar* job in New York, with a New York photographer in a New York studio!"

I mean, what *wasn't* there to understand?

Jennifer was putting herself up at the St. Regis Hotel and paying for me and my airfare, but I wasn't included in the St. Regis package.

"I can get my own place," I told Jennifer. I knew no one in New York, but I knew Mollie. And Mollie always had answers.

"Got a place for you on Second Avenue and Sixty-Third Street." Mollie said, like I knew where she was talking about. "You can walk to the St. Regis Hotel; people walk everywhere in New York."

When I finally got to the corner of Fifth and Fifty-Fifth, I saw the American flag waving proudly over the entrance of the huge gold doors of the St. Regis. The windows at the corner of the building caught my eye. It was that fancy jewelry store where Mollie's bracelet was from. She made me learn how to pronounce the name: Buchchaa-lati.

I would have to find that Tiffany's store also. I love a good window.

I walked through the lobby. The ceiling was so high it hurt my neck to look at it, my calves too. *Walking* was a new concept for me.

"Ready in five, Miss Jones," the stage manager shouted.

Opposite Jennifer in the play *Country Girl* was Rip Torn, whom I met backstage with his wife, the fabulous Geraldine Page.

My eyes welled up when I heard the audience roar for Jennifer as she walked out onstage. Final curtain, more applause, and she returned. I freshened up her hair, and she patted her face and put on new lipstick to greet her friends.

The first two visitors arrived quickly. One was a short, odd, puffy, pale man, the other a woman, grandly posturing, with a sheer cashmere shawl draped around her shoulders over a suit. Very chic. Her eyes were half-mast and she smiled with her mouth closed. When she spoke, she sounded like a man with a deep seductive voice; when he spoke, he shrilled like a Southern belle. Lauren Bacall and Truman Capote.

"Back to the hotel," Jennifer told her driver, as we left the theater. We pulled up in front of the St. Regis, and on her way out, Jennifer said, "Take the car for as long as you like, just remember I need it *and you* back by five PM tomorrow." My jaw dropped with delight. I watched Jennifer vanish into the hotel.

I had cash in my pocket, a driver at my disposal, all of New York, and all of the night. I sat in the back seat and thought, *Stretch out . . . ah, that's why they call it a stretch limo.*

"Where would you like to go, madame?"

I had no clue where to go . . . I had heard of one place.

"Greenwich Village, please."

"Where exactly in Greenwich Village, madame?"

"Isn't there a famous spot?"

"I wouldn't know, madame," he said and drove onward.

"And please, stop calling me *madame,* that word makes me itch."

After a little while, he said, "This is the main entrance to the Village."

We had no villages in California, and it looked like any corner. I noticed three guys and a girl talking loudly, laughing, arguing. I looked again and I knew the girl. She was Myrna, Donald's client from *my* salon.

"Myrna!" I called out. The snobby driver shifted in his seat; not appropriate limo behavior, I suppose. "It's me . . . Carrie White."

"What the hell are you doing here?" she yelled back, and came to my window. I briefed her.

"Hey, come with us," Myrna said. "My boyfriend just played down the street and we're going back to our hotel."

Her boyfriend was Frank Cook, drummer for the band Canned Heat.

"Sure, you all wanna ride in *my* limo?"

They piled in.

"The Chelsea Hotel," Myrna instructed the driver, and gave the address on West Twenty-Third Street.

It was another world, an old, old world . . . a plaque on the wall verified that, *Built in 1884*. We climbed up one floor after another.

"No elevator?"

"I don't know . . . it's the coolest hotel in New York, though," Myrna said.

She obviously hadn't seen the St. Regis.

"Everyone stays here . . . Larry Rivers . . . Bob Dylan . . ," Frank said.

"Fine," I said, huffing behind. "But it's kinda seedy."

We finally got to their room and I sat on the floppy couch. The other two guys lit a joint and passed it to me without talking. I took one hit, but pot wasn't my thing. It slowed me down. I liked being *up*. Alcohol got me going, and I had my little stash of happy diet pills.

Frank disappeared into the bathroom.

Myrna handed me a goblet of red wine.

Back in the limo. We were just off Union Square, on Park Avenue South, between Seventeenth and Eighteenth. I told the driver to park on the opposite side of the street. Limos didn't seem so hip in this area. We walked across the street to a place called Max's Kansas City.

It was packed. Some of the girls were guys, and vice-versa. Myrna pointed that out to me. "There's Nico . . . Andy must be in the back room. All the cool artists come here, and writers . . . look, there's Ginsberg and Burroughs." A guy next to me called out to the tallest girl I'd ever seen in my life, "*Hey, Veruschka . . .*"

I was turned on to a new dimension of outrageous style, and where there's style . . . there's hair. I drank countless Black Russians and listened to Bob Dylan. Max's was a quiet riot, a living room party with intense guests, some throwing chickpeas across the room from small bowls on the table to get another person's attention.

By the time I left, at 4:00 AM, I had dark circles under my eyes and I didn't look like a tourist anymore. I woke up the driver and jumped into the car. While driving home, a carful of drunken girls in a Mustang convertible yelled to my driver, "Where can you get a drink around here?"

He replied, "The East River, ladies."

New York was an electrifying never-ending source of curiosity for me. Every night, it was the same, just more of it: Le Club, Trude Heller's, the Peppermint Lounge, Cheetah, and always ending at Max's Kansas City with Jennifer's limo parked discreetly across the street.

My trip was coming to an end, along with my freedom. I'd had a taste of NYC that filled my head and inspired my heart. I had saved the best for the last. I had to find Mr. Kenneth and introduce myself.

His beautiful brownstone was located on Fifty-Fourth Street. His window display topped them all. It was a mannequin bust, covered with uncooked spiral pasta for hair, glued to form an updo fit for Marie Antoinette. It was so impressive to see a different material used as hair. His salon was a castle to me, and he was the king.

"Excuse me," I told his receptionist. "Could you please let Mr.

Kenneth know that Carrie from California is here and might I be able to meet him?"

She was lovely, very professional, as she stood up and said, "Mr. Kenneth is with a client right now, but I will tell his assistant."

I peeked around. He had a stylish boutique with all sorts of chic accessories and handbags, scarves and services, from waxing to eyelash dying.

Mr. Kenneth walked out to greet me. He was tall and debonair.

"At last, we meet," I said.

He smiled. "Yes, it was bound to happen."

Unlike me, he was reserved to a library tone and probably wondering why I was so animated.

"Your salon is *so great*," I said, nearly jumping. "If you ever come to California, Southern California, you know, Beverly Hills, please call me."

"I have to get back to my client now, but I did want to say hello."

"Of course, and thank you for recommending me, I take the best care of your ladies."

He went back to his private quarters.

I doubted I would ever be so refined as he was, but I certainly aspired to his quality of hairdressing. No one knew who did Mamie Eisenhower's bangs, or who styled Mrs. Abe Lincoln's hair, but the world knew Mrs. John Kennedy had a hairdresser and *his name was Mr. Kenneth.*

Back to my world: L.A. sunshine, my son, Sunset Strip, and Rodeo Drive. I was dying to tell Mollie, Aloma, and all my customers about my trip. My salon felt more like my home than home.

Vogue called *again*. They booked me for a layout with the English beauty who had just finished the film *Camelot*, the stunning Vanessa Redgrave. I made friends with her as one does doing hair, if only for that day. I was also beaming about this *Vogue* layout, because I got to work with another New Yorker, Bert Stern, one of America's *very* important photographers.

This job was instrumental for me. I was moving up and accumulating great credits, and one English beauty brought me another.

Petula Clark requested me for her first television special. It was my first too. Our location was the *Queen Mary,* which had just arrived in Long Beach, and had not been refurbished yet. I swore I smelled Churchill's cigars and hair tonic in the woodwork as I passed his chambers.

Hairdressing was proving to be more than my imagination.

Pregnant Again

"We're out of milk," I told Bucky. "I'm going to run to the market."

I worked hard to meet the demands of my world—my son, my husband, my home—my salon—and I brought in lots of money, which Bucky handled. I had no idea about Bucky's earnings as a carpenter and I didn't care. I just wanted to enjoy life, but I became more successful and *we* became more unsuccessful. New York had given me the idea I could survive and maybe be *better* on my own.

We moved to Elevado Street, right off Doheny Road. It was a house, not a home, a resale thing for Bucky to fix up, so pictures were not allowed to be hung—that would make holes in the wall. And unless we had company, we had no alcohol in the house.

"I'll be right back," I said, running to my car. I drove past Carl's market and headed toward Sunset to Whisky A Go Go.

"Come on in, Carrie," owner Elmer Valentine said.

"Thanks," I twinkled. We became friends because I ran in and out of Whisky A Go Go as often as possible. I loved the house bands and stealing away for a drink and a dance. He ushered me through without a cover charge. I dashed to the bar. "I'll have a double Black Russian."

I took a big swig and made my way to the front of the stage area, gulping down two more huge swallows. They hit down the back of my throat and bounced up to the top of my brain. I closed my eyes and let the music take over, the haunting thumping pumping sexy sound of the new house band, the Doors. I reached out to the lead singer up on the stage, grabbed his ankle and, with my drink in my other hand, started dancing. He smiled down at me and I didn't let go until the song was over. I put my empty glass on the bar and dashed out the front door.

"Thanks, Elmer," I said, leaving as fast as I came. "See you soon." Then I ran across the street to Turner's liquor store, grabbed two quarts of milk, gum to chew immediately, and a box of animal crackers, and raced home, thinking on my short drive, *Damn, that Morrison guy is sexy, and his hair* . . . I pulled up to my house, composed myself, and walked in clutching my brown paper bag.

"What took you so long?" Bucky said.

"Geez, you don't even allow for red lights, and the market was crowded."

A few months later and a year of doing the hair of Bill Cosby's beautiful wife, Camille, I confided in her, "I am *so* late for my period."

"Maybe you're pregnant like me."

"Oh no. I can't be."

I was.

Camille and I grew together over the next months. She was magnificent, conservative, and smart. While I styled her long thick hair, she confessed that she never thought from our first meeting at The Factory that we would become friends because I gave her such a kooky impression. Some nights we ran into each other at gatherings of mutual friends/clients: Jerry and Sandy Moss's or Sammy Davis's house or back at The Factory. I would wave from the dance floor as Camille sat with Bill and friends, smiling back in her reserved way.

Being pregnant never stopped me from dancing the Stroll or the Skate. I danced so much at the Daisy, Jack Hansen's private club, in my A-line daisy print dress, my friends all agreed that if I had a girl, I must name her Daisy.

I was living a hairdresser's dream. I was making my mark in this all-men's field. My appointment book was filled with more and more celebrities: Raquel Welch, Farrah Fawcett, Goldie Hawn, Joey Heatherton, Dorothy Provine, Barbara Rush, and at last . . . Barbara Feldon from *Get Smart*. I was becoming competition for *my* heroes, Gene Shacove and Richard Alcala.

I worked with fashion photographers Steve Horn, Peter Samerjan, William Claxton, and Douglas Kirkland. I did more shoots for *TV Guide* and *Ladies' Home Journal* and continued to do my house calls. I had no time to worry about Bucky or being pregnant. My salon had twelve hairdressers now.

Steve Brandt popped in again, this time with the most beautiful girl I had ever seen. "Meet Sharon Tate," he said. "You've seen *Valley of the Dolls,* haven't you?"

"Sure." I smiled. "And I went to high school with Barbara Parkins."

"Oh, I love Barbara." Sharon said. "She's a good friend."

"Sharon needs her hair done today." Steve said. "Her fiancé is a European director, Roman Polanski. She's doing a vampire movie with him."

"Let me slap a conditioner on my next lady and I can do it."

Sharon's big bedroom eyes and flawless skin stunned me. She stood like an angel with high cheekbones, her fine fawn-blond hair draping her shoulders like a silk veil. She simply demanded the pause that followed the examination of any masterpiece.

Meeting Melvin

It was a late afternoon in April 1967. I was due to have my baby in two or three weeks. I was still working, and busy as ever. Throughout the day, tiny clippings would collect on my dress and I would have a circle of fur that stuck on my tummy. I was completely happy at work. No matter how tired I was, I didn't know it, till I stopped.

"Carrie, can you possibly get away and meet me at the Beverly Wilshire Hotel?" Photographer John Engstead was on the line. "I think I have a good job for you." It was always a good job working with John. He was easygoing and he loved whatever I did.

"If I rush, I could be there by five, what's this for?"

"It's involved. Just come as soon as you can."

I quickly finished Mrs. Irwin Winkler and waddled up Rodeo Drive a few blocks from my salon to the hotel. John greeted me at the suite. The door opened to a room filled with cigar smoke and men and a few women in suits. No one dressed like that in Los Angeles.

Someone called out from the group around a table, "Is this her?"

"Yes," John said, "and we've worked together on several occasions."

I stood in my white A-line minidress, my white Mary Janes, my natural long brown hair in a ribbon like Alice in Wonderland, and false eyelashes.

I smiled, curious that I was on display.

John whispered to me, "It's an enormous New York production for a Burlington campaign."

"Campaign? Is this political?" I asked John.

"Noooo, it's *Burlington*," he repeated, like I would get it the second time around, but I was still clueless. I noticed all the hair still left on my dress. As I was brushing furballs off my tummy, the most peculiar-looking man in the group walked slowly over and looked me up and down.

"And what have you done?"

"I got pregnant," I said. "What have *you* done?"

We locked eyes. With a slight snicker and a raised eyebrow, he turned to the group and said, "I'll take her." I stood on guard. "What's your name?"

This not-so-tall, broad-shouldered, wiry, strawberry blond man with the matching eyebrows, pale freckled skin, and sharp nose with matching attitude pushed my buttons. "Carrie White, and *you*?"

"Melvin Sokolsky."

We locked eyes again, his chest and my belly contesting each other.

"Melvin is a top New York photographer," John intervened. "You would recognize his work."

"When are you due?" Melvin jumped in. "You look like you're going to pop any minute."

One of the ladies walked over to us. She was dressed in a silk kimono jacket with flowing black pants. Her long golden brown hair looked like it was towel-squeezed and air-dried. The wave in her hair reminded me of an antique porcelain doll. Her steady brown eyes looked like they wouldn't flinch under any situation. She had a calmness and beauty that was not screaming *look at me*. She extended her long narrow hand. "Hello," she said, in a gentle English accent.

"This is my wife, Button," Melvin said.

"Button, like a *button*?" I smiled.

"Yes," she said, without further explanation.

"John said you worked with Bert Stern. But I'm not sure I can do this with you, when are you due?"

I decided I wanted this job and I ignored his question again.

"Do you come to L.A. often?"

Melvin Sokolsky let me know he wasn't particularly fond of California; he was only here for this job and very frustrated not to have his preferred New York hairdresser, Enny of Italy, because he wasn't available. His second choice, another New York hairdresser, Ara Gallant, was not available either, and his last choice was L.A.'s George Masters, who was still unlocatable.

"*My* salon is a few blocks away," I said, thanking God I had *my own salon* to impress him. "I can show you *my* work."

He agreed. Button walked with us.

"What college did you go to?" Melvin asked as we strolled up Rodeo Drive.

"Lapin Brothers Beauty College."

"No, what *real* college did you go to?"

"Now, Melvin, stop giving her the third degree," Button said, ever so English.

I laughed. "You New Yorkers think Californians are bubbleheads, don't you? And probably that a girl can't do hair."

We passed an art gallery. Melvin stopped and inspected the painting in the window. He turned to me. "How do you feel about Flemish?"

I gave it some thought, must be a trick question.

"He's fine, I prefer Dalí."

Button and Melvin smiled. "Oh really," Melvin said.

Who is this Flemish guy and what's so funny? We walked the next block to my salon in silence. It felt like a 10K race. Finally, my turf, where I felt the most powerful. Maybe I couldn't fake Art Appreciation 101, but I was good at what I did know: hair.

He looked to see how I had my name displayed out front and checked the size of my salon. "How many hairdressers work for you?"

"Twelve," I answered with a professional air.

He lowered his eyebrows a bit. He noticed my poster-sized *Vogue* photograph of Vanessa Redgrave by Bert Stern on the wall with my hair credits.

"*You* did *this*?" he said, like it was impossible.

"Yes," I said nonchalantly.

"She's good, Melvin," Button affirmed.

"Okay, would you be available next week," Melvin asked, "for five a day?"

Five a day!? He couldn't mean five dollars. Did he mean *FIVE HUNDRED*? My throat closed. I could barely swallow. Keeping my composure, I spoke as slowly as Button. "Well . . . let's see, I think I could work that out, and *five a day* . . . yes, that would be fine."

Man, I liked this New York business. No one ever mentioned the money, the *ENORMOUS MONEY*.

"You must promise you won't have your baby until this job is completed," Melvin said. "I'm taking a tremendous chance with you as it is."

I promised only to deliver good hair.

The next day I told a few of my hairdressers about my exciting new job. Donald had heard of Melvin Sokolsky.

"He's famous for treacherous poses on ledges, girls in bubbles hanging over rivers in Paris, lighting matches in between a model's teeth and getting the perfect flame shot. Girls won't model for Melvin unless they are properly insured. Plus, he's so meticulous, if they are wearing gloves in a shot, he still makes sure they have the right shade of polish on their fingernails."

"This *will* be challenging," I confessed. "But if I'm not ready for this kind of work now, I never will be."

Location was at the Warner Studios, on the set of *Camelot*, which hadn't been torn down yet. Since I wasn't in the Hairdressers Union, I wasn't allowed to do hair on studio property. I would have to work across the street in a motel they rented for preparing the model—hair, makeup, and clothes. This made it even more difficult for me, because

I couldn't be on set to check or correct any hair details. My hair would have to be perfect and *stay perfect.*

Melvin smuggled me onstage to show me what he wanted to capture. "This is incredible," I said, looking at the giant *Camelot* backdrops, the massive medieval décor and soft violet lighting. Melvin spoke to his assistant: "Move those two lights over there; fuse out the clifftops."

"Give me hair that works for *this* . . ." he said, referring to the set. "I'm shooting from every angle; make sure her hair is spectacular from *every angle.*"

I nodded . . . absolutely, piece o' cake, *yes sir, I got it.*

"Can you be done in an hour?"

"One hour it is."

Melvin's assistant drove me back to the motel room. Barry, my assistant, was prepared with clips on his apron, pins in his fingers, combs in his hand, my brush and spray in his pocket, and my accessories laid out on the bed like an artist's palette.

I went at the model's hair as if I was conducting Beethoven's Fifth. I back-combed it, I flung it, I stretched it, I spread it, I sprayed it, I molded it, I stuck flowers and ribbons in it, I curled it, I pushed waves, I combed, I poked, I picked at it, I pinned it, and I sprayed again. I stood back, I looked close, I walked around her with my perfectionist eye, took a deep breath, and sprayed it again.

She proceeded to get dressed. I couldn't take my eyes off my masterpiece.

Melvin's assistant came back, "Ready? Because Melvin's ready."

The model got her final zip by the dresser and she fled out the door. I held my breath.

No one returned for a long time. They must be shooting . . . I had passed.

I could breathe again.

After hours of my staring out of the little motel window, the car returned with Melvin and his entourage: the agent, client, producer, and workers. They entered, all talking to Melvin at the same time.

"I want them all out of here," Melvin snapped. "Now . . . *out,* everyone but my people. I'm not talking anymore, I'm working."

I was dying for his response, his approval of my work. He said nothing to me and walked around the room holding a dress up. "Is she wearing this next?"

"Yes," the stylist answered.

He walked around. Silence. He was thinking. Then Melvin started talking again . . . about everything but my contribution . . . my hair. I was dying. *What about the hair?*

"That set is amazing, isn't it?" Melvin said to his business partner Jordan Kalfus.

"I think we can get one more shot in before lunch," Melvin said. He turned to me. "Oh, and hair . . . *not bad.*"

Not bad? I figured coming from Melvin that was like *almost fantastic.*

I smiled from ear to ear. From that moment on and for the rest of the week, Melvin never suggested one thing to me. All he would say was "I want your best." Melvin tapped a source in me I had never known. It was an artistic rush. That week stirred a new commitment to myself . . . to *push the envelope.*

Also, I kept my word. I didn't deliver my baby. Exactly four days later, on April 20, 1967, I gave birth to my little girl, Daisy. My dream came true—Adam got a baby sister, and I got my baby girl.

It's wonderful being a hairdresser in Beverly Hills on your birthday, on Christmas, and especially when you're having a baby. Daisy received everything a newborn and her mother could desire, including a couture baby dress with infant fishnet tights from Betsy Bloomingdale.

Five weeks later, a gift arrived from the Sokolskys. The note mentioned to expect a call, hinting that I could be up for another job. The thought of working with Melvin again ignited me from head to toe.

When Melvin's call came, Aloma was visiting me.

"*Yes, I want to,* I just don't know how I can work this out."

"Calm down," Melvin said, in his authoritative voice, "I'll call you with more details, you'll need a passport, you know." I hung up and turned to Aloma.

"Melvin just asked me to go to *London—for a week—*and do a television commercial for Yardley with *Jean Shrimpton*."

"You can't miss this! The kids won't miss *you*, husbands just say they'll miss you . . . I'll watch the kids . . . GO . . . this is great!" Aloma's wheels were spinning faster than mine. "We've got lots to do!"

The Trip Was On

"Aloma, you have to be with me when I tell Bucky."

"He's not going to like the idea," Aloma said. "How about we tell him when we go for your passport? That way we have to be somewhere."

"Perfect, come Monday around noon. We'll tell him and run out."

I had Daisy in my arms, feeding her. I couldn't nurse her as long as I nursed Adam. Stress had caused my milk to sour, which created a colic problem for Daisy. She was doing well on bottled formula. This was helpful for my travel plans. She would be cared for, eat, sleep, and be just fine. It was only for one week. I would miss her more than she would miss me.

Bucky was home for lunch. Aloma pulled up in our driveway and came in.

I called, "Martina . . ." I had convinced Bucky after giving birth to our second child that I must have a housemaid, not a live-in, just someone to help with Adam and Daisy and the house. "Would you take Daisy, *por favor*?"

"Bucky, guess what? Melvin Sokolsky called from New York."

Bucky saw Aloma standing behind me.

"Yeah, what'd he want?"

"Well, he has the greatest job for me and I can't *not* do it."

"Yeah . . ."

"In *London*." I bounced up and down. "Isn't that unbelievable? *London!*"

"Isn't it fantastic Bucky?" Aloma said, "Now she needs a passport."

"Wait a minute," Bucky said. "You can't just take off."

"I'm gonna help with the kids," Aloma said. "Don't worry, Bucky."

"And I'll make lots of money," I said, knowing he'd like that part. Martina was holding Daisy in the hallway. I gave Daisy a kiss. "Mommy will be right back." I did the same to Adam, who was playing in the kitchen. He was almost two now. I threw my purse on my shoulder. "It's my only day off . . . I gotta get a passport."

We ran out and got into Aloma's station wagon.

At twenty-three years old, with small children, Aloma and I didn't know we weren't grown-up, except when our older husbands reminded us. We were like Laurel and Hardy for the next three days, getting me organized.

All I had left to do was pack for the job.

My biggest fear was getting to London, getting on set, and not having what I needed. My next fear was *not knowing what I needed*. One more time I packed everything but the shampoo bowl into the new large heavy metal trunk I had bought at the Salvation Army. I wasn't used to working without an assistant. Being alone on the job was a job in itself. This fueled my insecurity.

Melvin called again. "You'll come to New York Saturday night. We all fly to London together, you, me, Button, Jordan, and Jean Shrimpton. Yardley doesn't understand why I want to bring a hairdresser all the way from California. They told me, there are plenty of good hairdressers in London *or* New York. And a *girl* hairdresser?" Melvin chuckled. "So don't let me down."

This would be the second time I had worked with Melvin but the first time he *requested* me. I wore our relationship like a shiny medal of honor.

London '67

Melvin and Button sat together and Jordan and Jean were having an affair. I was holding hands with a double vodka and a cigarette.

The plane was crowded but I felt it was just us. I didn't want Melvin to know how frightened I was of flying, because I wanted to go on more trips. A stewardess came by. "Can I get you anything?" "Another one of these, please." I nodded to my glass. I looked out my window. I could feel the cold outside without touching it. No clouds, no stars, just space. It was all out of my hands for now.

It was a foggy Sunday night when we landed in London town, just like a Frank Sinatra song. Jordan and Jean went their way. Melvin, Button, and I drove to the hotel.

"What an amazing old coach," I said.

"It's just a normal English cab," Button said, unintentionally smashing my awe. I was like their unleashed pup.

"Where's the hot spots, the night life, the dance clubs?" I asked the driver.

"Sorry, madame, there's *no decadence* on Sunday."

We arrived at our hotel, the Dorchester. I loved pronouncing it. I called Bucky. "I landed, safe and sound." I said. "I'm staying in the best hotel in all of London, the DORrrrr . . . CHESss . . . TARrrr. How's Adam and Daisy?" I looked around my room with the satin curtains and unfamiliar pristine English furniture. "Okay, good, I'll call you tomorrow."

I hung up and ran and jumped on my big bed.

I said out loud again, *"The DORrrrr . . . CHESss . . . TARrrr."*

I never got much of a chance to talk to Jean Shrimpton. Jordan took up all her time. But I was excited I would get my chance on the set. She must know everything I wanted to know about London.

Jean was the most famous model since Suzy Parker. She was young, fresh, hip, and gorgeous with her big eyes and lips, broad cheekbones, a strong jawline, and natural long brown hair and bangs. She represented the true sixties girl. We identified with her over the prim and proper previous *women* models, so fifties.

"So . . . where do you go out at night?" I asked her in the dressing room, while her makeup was being applied. "Where are the hot spots?"

"I don't really like to go out at night," she answered.

I thought, why not? You're *Jean Shrimpton.*

"Oh well, how about your favorite clothing stores?"

"I couldn't really tell you. If I'm not working, I like jeans and men's shirts."

"Hmmm, I love your boots, where do they come from?"

"Thanks. I got them in Rome."

Oy vey, that was a dud interview. While the makeup artist did his final touch, I walked out to find Melvin. He was directing the lights and having backdrops and props moved. The pressure and excitement felt like opening night. It was time I got *my* instructions.

"The script calls for a model who must change into many different high fashions, three or four times a day, which means hair changes, and that's where you come in," Melvin said. "Go way out."

I went back to the dressing room and started cutting a cardboard box to pin onto the back of Jean's head to fan her hair out over like a peacock. When I finished my creation, Jean flinched, the clients flinched, but Melvin loved it.

Pleasing Melvin was the only thing that was important.

For the next hairdo I made giant swirls, like Danish pastries, one on each side of her head, adding more hairpieces to spill out of the center of the swirls. Jean looked puzzled, the clients weren't sure, but Melvin loved it.

For my grand finale on the fifth day, I found three toilet paper rolls, removed all the tissue, and attached the paper cylinders to Jean's head, left, center, and right. Then I wrapped false hair around each one, and plugged each hole with a lightbulb from the prop department. Jean saw herself in the mirror.

"I look like a flippin' electric rooster!"

The clients objected. Melvin giggled. I waited for the final verdict.

"I'm shooting it," Melvin said.

One week in the studio cave, shooting morning to night, I was dying to get out. It couldn't have been a more explosive time in London. The Beatles had put England on top musically and fashion-wise, and was there anything else to be on top of? Saturday was my promised walking tour with the Sokolskys.

I thought I was so sharp in my miniskirt and go-go boots, but when we got to King's Road, everyone was in maxi-length antique dresses with pale powdered faces and dark red lipstick—even some guys. Lots of colorful marching band jackets too. "Did you see that, he had on eyeliner and lipstick!"

Melvin and Button smiled and kept walking.

"I forgot this is your first trip here," Button said in her English way.

The latest Beatles album, *Sgt. Pepper's Lonely Hearts Club Band,* was blasting out of every dress shop, gas station, pharmacy, food market, shoe repair, and flower shop—original sounds. I strained my ears to hear more as Button and Melvin moved me along. "With a Little Help from My Friends" was so alive, and so was I.

Alvaro's was the spot for lunch. In Los Angeles I'd never seen a place so packed. This joint was jumping. I couldn't take in enough at one time.

I noticed someone familiar being wheeled in, assisted by a male nurse dressed in all white. They sat two tables away from us. I watched closely. Our waiter told us it was part of this young man's psychiatric therapy. "That's Brian Jones of the Rolling Stones. He never misses Saturday at Alvaro's, and this is *not* his first nervous breakdown."

Lunch was over. Good. Now we could get back to the parade on King's Road. I spotted a wild-looking girl across the street in a wild outfit.

"Carrie White!" she called out. "Is that you?"

We stopped. She took off her crazy flowered hat as she dashed over to us.

"Annie, what are *you* doing here?" I knew Annie Marshall through a group of people in Topanga Canyon, artists and actors, Wallace Berman, Dean Stockwell and Toni Basil, Billy Gray and his belly-dancing actress wife, Helena, George Hermes and . . . well, it was a major hidden world in Topanga. Annie's dad was the famous actor Herbert Marshall.

"I'm staying with Mama Cass," Annie said. "At John Lennon's house."

"That's *so* exciting," I said, and introduced her to Melvin and Button.

They said hello, and then Annie said, "Come to the house tonight. Cass is throwing a party for the guy opening for the Turtles concert."

I looked at Melvin and Button.

"Bring your friends," she said.

We walked by Alvaro's at the end of our day. As we were passing, a girl came running out the café door yelling, "Melvin, Melvin." She was unique looking with her short boyish hair slicked over to one side, big doe eyes, tons of makeup, and thin as a reed. "Say hi to Twiggy," Melvin said. "We're on our way to the Dorchester."

"I'm going there too," Twiggy said. "Let's share a cabbie."

I was speechless the whole ride as I secretly studied her haircut and intricate toy doll eye makeup.

We met Jean and Jordan at an elegant restaurant called Park's, where the elite meet. The chattering crowd was like one big dinner party.

The menu was completely foreign to me, even though it was written in English. Melvin seemed to talk more excessively than usual. He was an accomplished traveler and his knowledge was endless, but not this night, please, no more examples or monologues. I was dying to get to the party. I was drinking wine like water to pass the time. I had been to the bathroom twice to check my new eye makeup. Didn't Jean and Jordan want to get back to their room?

"We should be going, we're leaving for New York in the morning, Jean's got a job Monday." Jordan stood up.

Melvin looked at me. "Do you still want to go to your friend's party?"

Annie greeted us. We walked up a few steps up to the main floor. The room was very smoky and dimly lit. "I Feel Free" by Cream played loudly.

Seated on a cushy brown leather couch with scattered shawls and pillows was a striking black guy. Two blond fairy-like girls were kneeling, serving him tea. He was dressed in a red velvet marching band jacket with gold buttons. Rows of lace spilled out of the large cuffs, like a blouse from another century. His hair was untamed, not processed and greased like James Brown. He wore a multicolored scarf tied around his forehead like a Gypsy, which hung down one side of his face. Annie noticed my fascination and introduced me.

"Carrie, this our guest of honor . . . Jimi Hendrix."

He lifted his head like it weighed a ton. "Hey."

"Hey," I said, back to him, hypnotized by his aura.

"Wait till you hear his music," Annie whispered.

I was already a fan. He dropped his head down, mumbled to the girls, and took a sip of his tea. They all giggled.

Annie looked around. "I don't know where Cass is. Wanna drink?"

"I'd love one," I said. Melvin and Button concurred. "Wine and liquor over there at the bar."

London wasn't the only one on top of the world. The job had gone well. I was solid with Melvin. I was in a Beatle's home . . . *my favorite* Beatle's home.

Too bad for me he was out of town. I milled around. The kitchen was overflowing with people pressed against each other. The corridor was filled with framed photos and art. One childlike drawing caught my attention.

A guy came up to me. "Like that? John wrote a song about that picture."

"*Rrreally?*" I said, sounding ohhhh sooooo English.

"Yeah," he said, with his authentic English accent. "John's son drew that and when he asked what it was, Julian said, 'Daddy, that's Lucy in the sky with diamonds.'"

Another guy walked by and offered his clenched fist. "Have some?"

I couldn't see anything. "Have what?"

"Liquid acid, aren't you in for a lick?"

"Oh, no thanks," I said, trying to hide my squareness. "You have it all."

I had barely smoked marijuana, let alone tried LSD. The crowd in the living room was shouting and singing, the new Beatles album was on the record player. I joined in the dancing. After a few songs, I went to rest on the couch with the guest of honor. He was smoking something from a pipe made out of a small metal film can. He passed it to me.

"Your lips here," Jimi said and pointed to a tiny hole. There was a brown rock on the other edge. "Don't drop the hash."

I took a long slow drag and felt the impact immediately. I liked it. I turned to thank him and he was gone. I couldn't sit either. I got up and danced like I was back at Whisky A Go Go. The hash brought on a dreamy sexy mood.

Like good parents, the Sokolskys tapped my shoulder, "It's time we go."

"Do we have to?"

They reminded me I had just had a baby, it had been a big week, and I might want to wind down. That never sounded like a good idea to me. I found Cass and Annie and thanked them for the best evening and danced down the staircase to the trailing sounds of "With a Little Help From My Friends."

On the way home, I noticed a street sign with a familiar name. I took out a card tucked safely in my purse. I was right, it was Vanessa Redgrave's street.

"Couldn't we just go by and see if her lights are on? She told me she stays up late." They were hesitant. I insisted. I didn't want to go home yet. I was in London. We drove a few blocks. "There's her number, and look, the lights are on."

Melvin and Button stayed in the cab while I walked up to the porch and gave one gentle ring. No answer. I rang again, less timidly. No answer. Disappointed, and about to get into the cab, the most lovely strong English voice projected down from the balcony, "*Whooooooo's* there please?"

I spun around and shouted, "Vanessa, its Carrie!"

"Carrie? Carrie from California?"

"Yes, yes, it's me!"

"I'll be right there straightaway."

She flung open her large door, beaming in a floor-length peignoir that kept slipping off her shoulders, showing her exquisite bones. "Do come in, come in," she said. Anyone would understand the meaning of *star quality* from her beauty.

"I know it's past midnight," I said, and gave her a hug. "I'm with a New York director and his wife."

"Fine, fine. Do bring them in too."

Vanessa brought us into her plush, English country garden living room. It was very white with flowery oversized pillows, billowing curtains, and cashmere throws. Tables and bookcases held thick books of art and theater, and sculptures and porcelain vases were nestled all around. The Sokolskys came in reserved, apologetic for the intrusion. Melvin smiled. "She made us."

"Don't be silly," Vanessa said. "You caught me at the perfect time. I was going crazy about my next film." She threw pillows aside, making room for us to sit. "I don't know how I'm going to pull this off. Oh, what does everyone want to drink?"

I boasted about Melvin and the Yardley commercial we had completed with Jean Shrimpton. "She's a lovely girl, isn't she?" Vanessa said, bringing over a bottle of cognac, and proceeded to tell us about her new role, which made her nervous because "I'm not a dancer, you know . . ."

She thought of herself as too tall, but she loved the woman she would portray, Isadora Duncan. I was mesmerized and I could have listened to Vanessa talk about Isadora forever, but I was fading like bad hair color.

By 4:00 AM the Sokolskys nudged me again to go. Vanessa was whirling an imaginary scarf, imitating ballet moves, and giggling. "How will I ever get this dancing down before shooting time?"

I adored her, and most of all, I adored this night.

Sunday: my last day in London. I could have stayed in my plush Dorchester bed, but I had only a few hours left to cram into this trip of a lifetime.

"We should show you the countryside," the Sokolskys decided after our breakfast of bangers and biscuits.

We jumped in a cab and drove somewhere. I rolled down the window to take in the meadows, the funny little crooked fences in front of funny little cottages with thatched roofs set back from cobblestone and dirt roads. It was like I was breathing in an Impressionist painting. The crisp weather fit perfectly with the vivid and muted mix of colors that only time could paint. It was at this moment I understood the true value of *travel*.

While I was packing, the phone rang. I thought it must be Bucky, but it was Melvin—would I come to their room? They had a gift for me.

"We discussed this and we both decided," Melvin said. "We want to take you to Paris for a few days before we ship you back to California."

I called Aloma from their room. She was as thrilled for me as I was and promised to watch the kids a few more days. Then I called Bucky.

"The Sokolskys want to treat me to two days in Paris, *Paris, France.*"

He didn't get it.

"*Bucky*, I'm minutes from *Paris* and I miss you all, but come on . . . everyone is fine, *it's okay with Aloma*, I already called her."

"Your children miss you."

"Not really, they're too young. Bucky, not only Paris, but we are going to stay at *the Ritz hotel.*"

We hung up the phone. "I can come." I beamed to the Sokolskys.

"I would certainly hope so," Button said.

I ran to my room, *Paris* shouting in my head. The Eiffel Tower and the real Charles Jourdan shoe store and maybe I could see Christian Dior's or Pierre Cardin's store, and what about *Coco Chanel*? Her windows must be the greatest.

I threw the rest of my clothes in my suitcase . . . *the Ritz hotel?*

Is that where puttin' on the Ritz comes from?

Paris '67

I landed at Orly and fell into the arms of Paris.

I got *Vive la différence* the minute the French language hit my ears, a sound of buzzing bees in a honeycomb. The police wore white spats with gloves to match. Little cars honked in French and a few limousines waited with taxis in a queue. The Sokolskys were blasé regulars in this place.

"Carrie," Button called out. "This way . . ."

I had stopped to absorb the French faces, clothes, and hair.

"Coming," I said, pulling myself reluctantly away. England had

Beatlemania. The French were so understated. "Did you see those beautiful scarves?" I asked Button as ladies wearing oversize print silk scarves tied around their shoulders breezed by.

"Normal," she said. "Come along, Melvin is in the cab already."

I took a deep breath, *in France,* another deep breath, *in Paris,* and climbed into the black French taxi.

I couldn't believe where my hairdressing was taking me.

London had basically been gray, from the suits to the fog. Paris seemed brighter, more colorful all around. There was a line of children with a teacher and they were singing. "Singing in the streets? We don't see that in Beverly Hills." I marveled at the way the Parisian children dressed—navy knickers, high kneesocks, white collars, what looked like handmade sweaters with hats to match, sharply pleated skirts. "I've never seen kids dress like that, not even in the movies."

"You'll get used to it," Button said.

I looked at a row of sidewalk cafes. Under umbrellas, people sipped small coffees, smoked, old men and women with attitudes on their faces as if they had been sitting there for a year with nothing to do.

The architecture and the endless window displays were poetry to me, elegant and sophisticated from centuries of practice. Then we were in front of the most impressive building of all.

"This is it," Melvin said.

I leapt out of the taxi in awe. I imagined the secret rendezvous tucked away behind these walls that must be over a hundred years old.

I followed the Sokolskys inside.

"Oh my God," I said. "The St. Regis lobby could fit in this entry."

"There, there, Miss Carrie," Button said. "Try to stay calm."

On our way to our rooms, Melvin bumped into a fellow photographer. It was like they were passing on a New York street.

"Just did a shoot with Donna Mitchell here on the beach," he said. "Guess she's working with you next week."

"That's right," Melvin said, "Morocco."

"Carrie, this is Bob Richardson." We stepped into the elevator.

"Are you sure you don't need me in Morocco?" I said.

"Yes, I'm sure," Melvin said. "All veils, no hair."

Melvin and Button walked me to my room where I used my fancy gold key and let myself in. I gasped at the beauty of it, then dashed for my Instamatic camera. *Aloma and Mollie will flip when they see this!* I clicked at the matching silk moiré curtains, walls and table covers, every pleat hanging to perfection to the floor. Next I took close-up shots of the ties and tassels at every window.

"It's a Jennifer Jones world," I shouted to myself.

Melvin and Button didn't drink as often as I wished they would, and now that I was alone, I could get a big drink and relax in the grandest bathtub I might never get the chance to be in again. I filled the tub with all the French bottles resting on the ledge, the bubbles and fragrances new to my nose.

Off to the famous Maxim's for dinner, where Melvin ran into another stunning model, Wilhelmina, and she joined us. I marveled again at where I had come in my life, far away from the heartache over my adopted child, my nightmare of Johnny, my disdain and sadness for my mother. I had two beautiful babies and two loyal friends, Aloma and Mollie. I was Carrie White, Hairdresser, no worries, no guilt, no fears. I held up my glass and said, *"Merci,"* as the maître d' poured wine around our table. Melvin ordered for me as he had in London. As everyone talked, I smiled, watched, and wondered what I was eating.

Wilhelmina suggested that we go to a disco nearby.

"Great idea," I said.

"Oh, look who just woke up," Melvin said.

We all went to a place called Régine's.

Dancing and drinking too much wine left me with a blur of fun. The next morning I sprung out of bed, and realized one thing, I had a throbbing hangover. *No time for that . . . I'm in Paris.*

How do I cure a hangover? Have another drink. I called room service for a *fast* vodka and tomato juice.

I wanted to see the famous Carita sisters' Maison de Beauté more than the Eiffel Tower. I wanted to see the Alexandre de Paris salon more than the Arc de Triomphe. If someone were to say, "Carrie, you could meet Madame Chanel or the Pope," I'd have to say, "Give my regards to the Pope, and, *Coco, here I come.*"

Button told me I would be happy on Rue du Faubourg Saint-Honoré.

I got delirious from all the fantastic stores. I ate windows with my eyes. I walked into the sweetest children's store and bought two little outfits that cost more and were crafted better than anything I had back home in my own closet.

Boom, there it was, the *real* Charles Jourdan store. I walked in and carefully observed each pair of shoes that could be mine. To select *the right one* was a big decision. I chose apple green heels, four inches high, with a round toe and small platform. Smashing. These would be my one big gift to myself, a very practical, very French, very expensive gift.

I hailed a cab. "The Ritz, *seel vooooo play.*"

I knocked on the Sokolskys' door. "The tourist is back!"

"A war broke out while you were off shopping."

I dropped my packages. The television news was reporting the bombing at a Paris travel agency. "I'm going to be an American tragedy in Paris!"

"Carrie," Button said, in her soft but firm English tone, "it's between the Arabs and the Jews, of which you are neither."

"How would you like to go to India?" Melvin announced.

I returned to my room to pack for my biggest journey yet. The maid was gazing out the window, so I looked. Down below, a small spry older woman was walking in the garden. She wore a navy blue hat with white trim and a matching navy purse and lots of swinging chains that sparkled in the sunlight.

"That's Madame Chanel, she has an apartment here."

My breath hit the glass and blurred my vision as my eyes strained to see every detail. I wiped the glass clear and stood side by side with the maid.

"Isn't she magnificent?" she said softly.

I wanted to holler out the window, *I love you, Coco* . . . I wanted to tell her how she inspired me as a female and an artist, but I didn't. I watched her disappear.

Sometimes we hesitate, where in retrospect, we would have leapt.

The next morning I got the giant shot in my butt for cholera and I was on my way to Bombay. From there to the Lake Palace Hotel in Udaipur.

India '67

"Melvin," I whined, "it's 130 degrees *humidity*." It was also 120 degrees of heat.

We spent one night in the Taj Mahal Hotel in Bombay, then we headed for our final destination, Udaipur. We were rushing to get this Yardley job done before the monsoons arrived. Banners flew on strings across the dirt roads: *Pray for monsoons.* The drought was bad. The monsoons were running late.

This climate problem brought an extraordinary bug epidemic. They fell out of the sky and crawled everywhere, looking for food and water. Our Lake Palace Hotel was supposed to be so elegant. Melvin said *Vogue* had recently done a story about Jacqueline Kennedy staying here. It was hard to imagine, because the hotel was riddled with bugs too.

"Just sweep them away with a broom provided in your quarters," the hotel receptionist told us, as critters crawled across the registration book and he slapped them to the floor. Seeing this, the model Donna Mitchell went into dry heaves.

"Come on," I said to her. "We just need a cold beer."

Melvin wanted an authentic old Indian look, so we spent two days roaming the streets to find Donna's wardrobe. He found books on top of dusty shelves in ramshackle bookstores and pointed out the makeup that I would be doing: red paint on the bottom of women's hands and feet were in every illustration. Some had their breasts painted red too. Melvin wanted the print on Donna's veil to match a picture in one of the antiquated books. Through inquiries, Melvin located an old wood carver to show the picture. The beautiful frail man picked up a block of wood, held it between his feet, and then with two small carving knives whittled away until the design was a perfect match. We left him the white silk fabric to stamp the pattern on with gold paint. The next day, we picked up the veil. Going back to the hotel, Button, Donna, and I sat in the back of the taxi, Melvin sat up front with our guide.

"What stinks?" I asked.

"Probably something on the street," Melvin said.

We drove further and still no break from the stink.

"Check your shoes, I smell shit," Donna said.

"Yeah, shit, that's the smell," I said.

"Didn't you pick up new printed fabric?" Our driver-guide asked. We all murmured *yes*. "Our paint is mixed with cow dung for bulk."

"Oh *shit*." We all laughed. Donna was set to wear this around her face all day tomorrow. Melvin would never give it up just because it smelled like shit.

On the day of the shoot, we set off for an isle gazebo farther out in the water. The light was pale aqua to deep gold, wavy shades of pink sliced through rows of color gradations, like a rainbow spraying out of a hose.

Every day hair and makeup began at 2:00 AM to be camera-ready by 5:15 AM. We worked until the sun was too bright, around 9:00 AM, broke for lunch, napped, and started prep at 2:00 PM to be ready for the sunset shoot at 5:15 PM. We'd break at 7:00 PM, return from location to a spicy dinner, drink as much beer as possible, sleep, and wake up for the 2:00 AM call again. I would have another beer for my hangover and get Donna ready for more sunrise shots. This was my world for four days. In studio terms: *Day for night, night for day* work.

I wanted to make a fantastic creation on Donna for Melvin, but the humidity made back-combing her hair like working with wet noodles. I added a hairpiece for a double drooping hair mess. The perspiration dripped off all of us.

My mother (right), age sixteen, and Nana, when they appeared in the Laurel and Hardy film *Babes in Toyland*. (Personal collection)

My mother, Grace, and my father, George—the only photo I have of the two of them together. (Personal collection)

Me on Burton Way, age four. (Personal collection)

Me in Pacoima, age twelve. (Personal collection)

Me at Hollywood High, age sixteen,
1960. (Courtesy of Marc Robin)

Me modeling in high school,
age seventeen, 1961.
(Personal collection)

Me as Playmate of the Month.
(Courtesy of *Playboy*)

CARRIE ENWRIGHT
Miss July 1963

A job as a salesgirl in a candy store nearly proved Carrie's undoing. "Trouble was, I have this terrible sweet tooth and pretty soon I was eating more candy than I was selling." Fortunately, the job did no harm to her 39"-24"-36" figure. A lifetime Californian, Carrie had lived 11 years in Tinseltown, where her closest link to the movie business was working as a cashier at the Hollywood Paramount Theater. Ron Vogel photographed her for *Playboy* and other magazines.

Me on Rodeo Drive, 1966.
(Personal collection)

OFFICE OF THE
Editor-in-Chief

VOGUE

689-5900

THE CONDÉ NAST PUBLICATIONS INC.
420 LEXINGTON AVENUE, NEW YORK, N. Y. 10017

June 5 1967

Dear Mrs. White,

We want you to know how very very
please we all are with the photographs
taken in California...

You yourself contributed enormously to
the success of these pictures, and we
do appreciate your enormous talent and
the trouble you took...

A million thanks to you from all of us
here at the <u>American Vogue</u>

Very sincerely yours,

Diana Vreeland.

Mrs. Carrie White
9929 Brighton Way
Beverly Hills
California.

Front row: Me, Richard Avedon, Julie Christie, Warren Beatty.
Back row: Richard's assistant, Polly Mellon, and my assistant. (Personal collection)

My assistant Barry and Julie Christie playing hairdresser, doing my hair backstage on a *Vogue* shoot. (Personal collection)

Me and Faye Dunaway, after styling her hair for Oscar night 1968— she was nominated for *Bonnie and Clyde*. (Personal collection)

My hairstyle on Vanessa Redgrave for a *Vogue* shoot.
(Courtesy of Bert Stern)

Me (pregnant with Daisy), Cher, and Pat Crowley, backstage at
The Dean Martin Show. (Personal collection)

My hairstyling and makeup on Donna Mitchell in India, 1967, for Yardley. (Courtesy of Melvin Sokolsky)

Sharon Tate with my hairstyle, on the day of her wedding to Roman Polanski, January 1968. (Courtesy of Getty Images)

Adam and Daisy in front of my 1955 Mercedes, at Richard's house—1969. (Personal collection)

My Valentine's Day wedding ceremony, 1970. (Courtesy of Jim Frank)

Me and Richard. (Courtesy of Jim Frank)

Richard at Joshua Tree.
(Courtesy of Jim Frank)

Billy Grimes in my salon.
(Courtesy of Aloma Ichinose)

Me and Max in my Benedict Canyon kitchen.
(Personal collection)

The Dinah Shore Show, 1971. (Personal collection)

Richard's mirror;
my station.
(Personal collection)

Styling Betsy Bloomingdale while pregnant with Pitita, 1972.
(Courtesy of Aloma Ichinose)

Doing a commercial with Susan Blakely.
(Personal collection)

Making over a boy band. (Courtesy of Julian Wasser from *Time* magazine)

My Snow Queen creation. (Personal collection, courtesy of Jon Ruppert)

Priscilla Presley with my cover hairstyle. (Photograph by Michael Vaccaro)

On the set of a commercial with Melvin Sokolsky. (Courtesy of Chuck White)

On a magazine set with Ulla Andersson (then-wife of Quincy Jones) and Aloma. (Personal collection, courtesy of Jim Britt)

Me and Aloma, 1974.
(Courtesy of Jim Frank)

Aloma and Pitita, my daughters with Richard, 1975.
(Courtesy of Aloma Ichinose)

"It's hard to make a fantastic hairdo in these conditions." I complained.

"That's why I brought *you*," Melvin said, and walked away.

The monsoons finally came, and we finished in time. As we drove back to the airport to leave India, I saw monkeys in trees, wandering wild boars below, and herds of children begging on the streets. Our driver-guide invited us to an auction of the king's elephant's jewelry, but we had no more time. On the last long stretch of the road, I saw how the monsoons had blown roofs off huts, leaving families huddled on tabletops, holding one another, waiting for the heavy rains to pass. But most of all, I saw the piercing black eyes of India, the kohl eyeliner, even on the infants.

We boarded for Paris; from there we would all split up. I didn't know when I'd be called again, but I knew I would never miss a chance to work with Melvin.

I flew directly to California, nineteen hours. I couldn't wait to be with my children, and to tell my stories. God—how I longed for a cheeseburger, fries, and chocolate malt.

But It's My Job

"Mommy, Mommy!" Adam ran into my arms.

Aloma was holding Daisy in the entry. Bucky walked up to me and gave me a half-*welcome home* and half-*I'm mad at you for leaving* hug.

I took Daisy into my arms and squeezed her tight. I had wondered how she had changed in twenty days, but she looked exactly the same, sweet and healthy. Sunday I would take them to Kiddieland—the same one I went to as a child. They probably had the same old ponies! Bucky didn't seem that interested in my trip, just in my return. We viewed life so differently that we didn't have much to share except Adam and Daisy. It was clear I had grown further away from Bucky, further than London, Paris, and India.

It was Friday, 11:00 AM. That meant my standing appointment—

Betsy Bloomingdale—was in my chair. I couldn't wait to tell her about my trip. I felt so worldly now. Of course I had dressed in my new Indian sari, with a halter top, bangles up my arms, gold sandals, and bells on my ankles. I even put a red dot on my third eye and lots of black kohl eyeliner like all the Indian women and children wore.

Mrs. B. smiled. "Oh, Carrie darling, only you could get away with that outfit before lunch."

Not that she would ever be caught dead in my flamboyant attire. Betsy was the fashion queen of Beverly Hills. More ladies requested my Betsy Bloomingdale hairstyle than my Goldie Hawn or my Barbara Feldon do.

"And . . . I got to go to Paris."

"How marvelous," Mrs. B. said. "Did you go to the Louvre?"

"The Louvre? Noooo, I went to Régine's," I proudly announced.

I had lots of "standings." These were ladies I looked forward to every week, relationships turning into families. My clients were my chief source of growth and education, toward goals for personal sophistication.

And the more celebrities I did, the more came. I turned clients away—I only had two hands and there were only so many hours. I raised my prices. No one left. I raised them again!

One day I got a call that outdid them all; it was the representative for United Airlines.

"What can I do for you?" I said.

"We would like you to create a hairdo for all our stewardesses."

I started to laugh. "One hairdo for all of them?"

"That's correct, I'm told *you* can create our new look."

"Sure, just happens . . . that's my *specialty*."

It had been about seven months since my overseas adventures.

"Sharon Tate is on line one," my receptionist, Lori Glick, the daughter of one of my clients, called out. I was just about to do a client for the first time.

"I don't know why I'm coming to you. I have nine beauty salons on my Desilu lot."

Lucille Ball was fluffing her famous red hair in my mirror. "All my friends come to you, so I thought I'd try you out."

"I'm so sorry, could you excuse me one little minute?"

"Do what you have to, honey." Lucy smiled. "As long as I'm out by noon."

I took the phone at my station. Sharon Tate had been in and out of my chair for haircuts and color since the first time Steve Brandt brought her to me.

"Really? When? Fantastic. I can't wait."

Lucy watched my progressive excitement, "What's going on?"

"I was just asked to do my friend's hair for her wedding . . . *in London . . . in January.* What will I wear? It'll be really cold."

"Come to my house, borrow some things from me," she said, batting her false eyelashes over her big blue eyes, speaking through her bright red lipstick. She was surprisingly generous, but it was 1968, not 1958. I couldn't go to London in *I Love Lucy* clothes!

"That is so sweet of you," I said. "I think we are different sizes, though."

I proceeded to do her hair.

"Well, the offer holds. As for my hair, do what you want, as long as this goes here"—Lucy motioned for the sides of her hair to go up— "and the bangs go like this . . ." She pinched in the wave and scooted it to her left. "And the back . . ."

"So, no different?" I interrupted her. We laughed together.

"Well, put your take on it," she said, and we laughed again.

Ladies like Lucy aren't *really* looking for a change. I did her hair exactly how she wanted it—the same, only better.

I couldn't wait to call Aloma with my latest travel news.

Then convince Bucky. *"But, it's my job."*

The airplane was filled with people attending Roman and Sharon's wedding. I sat a few rows in front of model Ann Turkel and Richard Harris, who would stand up and toast periodically. I felt very cool with this hot-shot crowd.

"I love the Chelsea Antique Mart, don't you?" I said to Sharmagne, a girl I knew from L.A. "I'll be staying *with* Sharon and Roman. I can help Sharon get ready and I'm doing her hair, of course . . ." I held my glass high so someone could pass, and someone else walked by and poured champagne into it.

Damn, I was going to have fun. I was having fun already!

Eaton Place: Roman and Sharon's home. Steve Brandt answered the door. He was staying there too. Steve always dressed sharp, always in black to match his dark side, pushing the envelope between life and death. Steve didn't drink, but boy, did he get high. I thought the pills he took made him angry. He worshipped Sharon, though, and never had a grumpy thing to say about her.

"Good *morning,*" Steve called out, no matter what time it was. "Sharon's upstairs with Roman." He dragged my suitcase inside "What the fuck is in here, your salon?"

"I need a shower and a blood transfusion." Sharon came bouncing in.

"Hey, you guys." She gave me a big hug. I worshipped her too. Her presence was staggering. I felt prettier just being around her.

"We're going to Parks for dinner with some friends. Coming?"

"Oh, I just love Parks," I said to Laurence Harvey—*Larry, as they* called him. The table was set with fine wine, delicious food, and wedding bells, and dominated by filmmaking stories. I listened with fascination as they spoke about their experiences with a jaded complacency.

At the end of the dinner, Steve popped a handful of pills and said to me, "Come on, we got places to go."

We jumped from one cab to another, one pad to the next. It was a mad dash as we ran into my pal Gram Parsons from the Byrds, to our last stop, smoking hash with the gorgeous Terence Stamp at his flat.

Rise and shine. Sharon was milling about. Steve was still in a coma.

"Roman's off on business," Sharon said. "Let's go shopping."

Sharon, the natural beauty, was effortlessly dressed in high boots, an underslip she wore like a dress, and a big coat from Afghanistan. For her final touch, she'd grabbed a flower out of a vase and stuck it behind her ear. I decided my entire wardrobe was without flavor or flair. Sharon *wanted* to go shopping. I *needed* to go shopping.

"Let's go to Apple," Sharon said, and shook Steve into this universe.

"What the fuck is Apple?" Steve barked, hungover from his pills.

"It's the new Beatles clothing store, honey." Sharon said, all twinkly.

"I need a glass of water," he said, taking out a black and green pill from his pajama pocket.

The Apple store was packed. The doorknob was carved in the shape of a shaking hand. The floor was wavy like a miniature golf path. Everyone would have to step off this yellow brick road to get to the clothes. The dressing room doors were cutout silhouettes of swinging swans that fit like a puzzle with their body and necks intertwined. The place was a funhouse. I got lost in it.

Steve yelled from the doorway, "We're leaving, we're starved." I dashed out with my purchase: emerald green velvet hip-huggers.

"Alvaro's?" I suggested.

"Yeah," Sharon said.

It was Saturday. And there he was again.

"Look," I said, "no nurse this time."

"What are you talking about?" Steve said.

"Brian Jones from the Rolling Stones." I was a devoted Stones fan. Steve waved to him. "You know him?"

"Oh yeah . . ."

"Can we get some wine?" I asked.

That night, Sharon and Roman left for a private dinner.

"What are we doing tonight?" I asked Steve.

"Dinner show with the Newleys and Paul McCartney."

I concealed my awe.

Steve and I took a taxi to the elegant home of Anthony Newley and his glamorous wife, my client Joan Collins. Samantha Eggar opened the door for us.

"Surprise," she said to me. "I heard you were here."

Samantha stood in the doorway in a beautiful shimmering dress and tiny satin ankle-strap heels. She had the reddest and thickest hair of anyone I had ever done. Samantha introduced me to Tony Newley, and then Joan appeared like Loretta Young making her entrance. "Drinks, everyone?"

Tony called out to a servant, "Bring us the red."

We drank, then Tony announced, "On to the next show." Joan dashed for a final check in the hall mirror, patting her hair.

"Dahling," she said. "You'll keep an eye on me, right?"

"Of course, *dahling*," I said, and we walked out.

"Let's take the Rolls," Joan said to Tony. "Can we all fit?"

I'm fitting in, I thought. I'd never ridden in a Rolls-Royce before.

"Talk of the Town," Tony told the driver, who was the only one *not* crowded. "How about that Diana Ross?"

"What about Diana?" Steve said.

Joan said—*so Joan*—turning to Steve, "I thought you *always* have the scoop, dahling."

"Tell me," Steve said, louder.

"Oh, don't get your knickers in a twist." Tony laughed. "Rumor has it, this might be her last engagement with the Supremes, besides performing at Sharon and Roman's wedding."

We got to the supper club and our table was waiting. It was too dark to see much of anything else. After our first round of drinks, the late guest appeared. I tried to not look like a Beatles stalker but I had an empty seat to my right. Inside I was screaming, *Paul, sit here, sit here, sit here.* He did. Unfortunately, following him was his girlfriend Jane Asher, who sat to his right.

Ehhh, who cares, I didn't like his skinny black tie anyway.

Diana sang like she had already left the Supremes and was on her own. And Joan told her *that* when we went backstage.

January 20, 1968

The Wedding.

I prepared Sharon's hair so that her beautiful face, doe eyes, and flawless complexion would be the main attraction. I added a fall and put tiny white flowers and ribbons throughout her do. She looked like an Arthur Rackham fairy princess.

The actual wedding ceremony was at the Chelsea Register Office in the Old Town Hall. There were only about six of us, and amazingly, one of the six was my Delta sister Barbara Parkins. A few hundred scrambling photographers greeted us on the courthouse steps, where we slipped off in waiting limos to London's Playboy Club for the big party.

People had come from all over the world for this event: Leslie Caron, Ursula Andress, Jeanne Moreau, Jacqueline Bisset, and I think these were just Warren Beatty's dates! Mick Jagger, Keith Richards, Marianne Faithfull, Anita Pallenberg, James Fox, Peter Sellers, Joanna Pettet, Candice Bergen, and Michael Caine were there amidst a thousand other guests. The Supremes sang.

I was dazzled with the grandness of the party, breathing in the Beautiful People. Constant champagne in hand, I stopped on every floor to look around. My last stop was the penthouse, where an ultraprivate group was draped on sofas like shawls. Built-in televisions, stacked one above the other, featured erotic films that no one paid attention to, nobody but me. I felt a hand clutch my shoulder and I turned. It was Steve.

"Come on," he said, loaded on his pills, weaving, his eyes rolling around in his head like they had nothing to do with vision. "We can't stay here all night. I told Brian Jones we'd come to his studio. He's recording a French singer."

We found Sharon and Roman. "You have your key?" she said to Steve. "We're leaving for Paris early in the morning." Roman's film *The Fearless Vampire Killers,* starring Sharon, was about to open.

I hugged her and thanked her for the amazing whirlwind, "See you back in Los Angeles, Mrs. Polanski."

I had almost forgotten I had another life back in L.A. Going solo felt good.

"Drink, please," I said the next morning, stumbling through the kitchen, looking for anything in the fridge and cupboards, which were bare. "My head is pounding like Uncle Ben."

"It's Big Ben," Steve grumbled. "I told Brian we'd stop by."

"Oh, no, is he still recording?" I remembered the previous night, meeting the Rolling Stone Brian Jones, a true space cadet, who was in the middle of recording a song with the infamous transsexual performer Coccinelle.

"No, at his house."

"Oh, good . . ."

"Who are you?" A wacked-out chick answered Brian's door the next night.

Steve squeezed by her. "Brian's expecting us."

"Right then, well, he's in the bathroom. I'm sure he'll be awhile. Would you like Guinness, Jack, or LSD?"

"Thanks, beer for me," I said. "He'll have water."

Covering one entire wall of the living room was the original artwork for the Rolling Stones' new album cover, *Their Satanic Majesties Request,* in 3-D! The band was dressed like sorcerers, with Mick in the middle. I kept walking back and forth so Mick's 3-D eyes followed me.

"You're making me fucking nuts," Steve said, on the couch with a passed-out couple nearby who didn't even know Steve was there.

"Try it," I said. "It's fun."

Steve rolled his eyes.

Brian was coming up from the dark hallway with his girlfriend stabilizing his walk. He was fumbling, mumbling how the door got jammed and he couldn't get out of the bathroom. He was flicking his Zippo, trying to light his cigarette, when he caught his hair on fire. I screamed. No one else seemed alarmed, including Brian. "I think me 'ead's on fire."

His girlfriend calmly patted his flames down to smoke with her hands.

The last night of madness.

Steve and I went to a few clubs and ended at Bag O'Nails. Michael Caine was there and Steve introduced us. Michael had been at the wedding but we hadn't met. Michael was alone. I hadn't seen *Alfie* yet, but I *acted* like I had. We all drank and smoked and laughed in a booth. Steve wandered off, Michael and I drank and smoked and laughed some more.

"Do you want to come to my flat for a nightcap? We'll have to be quiet, though, me mum's probably sleeping."

"What about Steve?"

Morning came. I met Michael's sweet little mother for five seconds. Michael and I kissed *tah-tah,* like our encounter had been an afternoon of tea and crumpets, and he stood at his door until I popped into the cab he had ordered for me.

I returned to Eaton Place. Steve was furious that I left him alone all night. But then, Steve was always furious. "So, did you sleep with Michael?"

I went for a cookie in the cupboard. "It'll be strange to go back in my world again, after all this freedom."

I had flown to London in a ponytail and gaucho pants and I was coming home in a slinky brown jersey dress, hair frizzed, with two black beauty marks painted under each eye like Charlie Chaplin's daughter Geraldine.

"*I said . . .* did you sleep with Michael?"

"Shit, I gotta pack." I leapt up. "What time is our plane, anyway?"

There was a major art opening at the Pasadena Museum for our Venice hero John Altoon. It was a big art night for California.

"It's good for my business, lots of chic people, and besides, you know how much I love the art world," I said to Bucky.

All my friends, from The Factory to Topanga Canyon artists, would be there. I knew Bucky would object to my having cocktails at the party, so I thought I'd better get them in at work. I didn't want to lose my buzz.

He left to take the kids to the babysitter. I fixed myself a vodka on the rocks and threw in a green olive for looks. I got into my hot bath à la Jennifer Jones.

I jumped out of the tub with a plan. I put on my slinky little Biba dress, waved my hair like Veronica Lake, and did my makeup like I was going to have a close-up photo shoot. But most important was maintaining my perfect level of intoxication. *Perfect* wears off.

"Ready?" Bucky said, walking in.

I picked up my jacket and followed him into the car. I sat for a second, then, "Oh, wait, I forgot my purse."

"I'll get it," he said.

"*No.*" I pushed the car door open. "I'm not sure where I left it."

As soon as I was out of his sight, I made a mad dash for the broom closet, grabbed the bottle of Smirnoff by the neck, and tilted it upside down, letting it flood nonstop down my throat. It burned like gasoline, some spilled out of the corners of my mouth, but I couldn't think about that; *get it in* was my only thought. I chuggalugged more before Bucky could get suspicious. I got nauseous; I never drank like that. *My plan* was that this would hold me through the night and kick off at intervals like a time-release Contac. I ate the olive I'd left in my earlier drink, ran to the front door, and walked outside casually, swinging my purse.

"That took a while," Bucky said and started the car engine.

I couldn't look at him. I was hysterical inside with my successful caper, my bomb of stored drinks. Bucky was trying to make conversation, but I was angry. Why should I have to throw a bottle of vodka down me instead of being able to drink and socialize the way I wanted to? I glared at him. When he returned the glance, I'd turn away.

"You okay?" he said.

"Yeah, how much farther?" I said.

"Twenty minutes," he said.

I was exploding from vodka and resentment. Another plan brewed in my head: *Escape.* I saw a little corner market at the next red light. A split second before the light was to turn green, forcing Bucky to go, I jumped out of the car.

"Where are you going?" he yelled, and tried to grab my arm but missed. I ran as fast as I could to the unsuspecting cashier behind the counter.

"There's a man who might come in here," I said, frantically. "He'll say he's my husband but he isn't. Don't tell him you saw me."

I ran down an isle of canned corn and Campbell's soup, and squatted down to hide. My plan of downing a bottle of vodka hadn't been such a good idea after all. I looked up. There was Bucky at the counter.

I heard him say, "Did you see a young girl . . ." I got up to run out. Bucky caught my arm this time. "What the hell is wrong with you?"

"He's not my husband," I said, and tried to squeeze away.

"I *am* her husband," he said, and pulled me outside. "Are you crazy?"

I burst into laughter.

"Look at you," he said. "What do you want to do now?"

"I want to go," I said. "And I want a drink when I get there."

"Fine," he said, "but fix your makeup."

Penny, whose husband owned Somper Furs, told me, "In this town, husbands don't buy their wives furs to keep them warm . . . they buy them to keep them quiet."

My other client—Ruth, Milton Berle's wife—said, "In this town, it's not how well you marry that counts, it's how *well* you divorce."

The best was from Jolene, wife of George Schlatter, when she talked about women who kept divorcing for richer men, "Yeah . . . she keeps screwing *up*."

I wasn't looking for a fur coat or profit . . . I just wanted *out*.

Bucky was a few feet away, pacing the hall with his lawyer. I was in the Los Angeles courthouse with mine.

"Are you sure you want to do this?" asked Jack, the lawyer husband of my client, culture queen Joan Agajanian Quinn. Everything I did or had was taken care of through clients: my accountant, my travel agent, my clothes, my sheets, my dishes, and now my divorce. Jack had the papers with Bucky's demands: a quit claim for our home and my promise not to ask for any child support.

In exchange I got all I wanted: my kids and my salon. I had my hairdressing license and I knew with this, I would always be able to support my children, keep a roof over their heads and food in their mouths. My mother had raised me with no child support. The only difference was that Bucky would get visitation rights on weekends. I never saw my father once after he left.

"Where do I sign?"

Will the Real Carrie White Please Stand

"Randy, got my spray? William, you have all my pins? Jere, the Styro-foam?" I asked my assistants as we scurried around backstage.

It was 10:00 AM at the Hollywood Palladium and I was about to perform my one-woman hair show. As in my previous Clairol shows, Dolly, my other assistant, doubled as my model. This show was for Revlon. They hired me to motivate Southern California hairdressers to use their color line.

"Who has my hairpieces?" I shuffled through my kit. "And who's got the champagne? I need an upper. I need to take this Desbutal."

Randy dashed over with a glass and I threw the diet pill down with one gulp of champagne. It splashed in my eye. "Damn it! Did I wreck my makeup?"

Randy inspected me. "No, you look perfect, oh, wait, your cheek is smeared, more blush."

"Mirror, quick!" I yelled. "Somebody . . ."

"Five minutes, everyone," a stagehand called. The Revlon people walked in wearing conservative gray outfits, very boring, very professional. "Are you prepared?" someone asked, as she curiously scanned my supplies.

"We do this all the time," William said.

Speed in chemical form was the best thing in my life. I had so much to do in such a little time, *all the time.* I took another swig and refreshed my lipstick.

I walked onstage like I was going to perform at a rock concert. I had on my pink boa flung over my neck, my London slinky maxi dress, a look that hadn't hit L.A. yet, my two Geraldine Chaplin beauty marks in place under each eye, my hair waved, and no idea what was going to come out of my mouth—possibly champagne bubbles. I looked out from the brightly lit stage and a room full of *my* people . . . *hairdressers,* hundreds of them, as far as I could see.

"Ready to have some fun and watch the fur fly?"

The crowd hailed, *Yeah!* Dolly sat down center stage.

"Hair is *our* material, *our* fabric, what do you want to do with it?" I tossed Dolly's hair from side to side, scooped it up in my hands, then flung it around, making my first hairdo in one minute. "The answer: whatever we *can* do with it!"

I spun Dolly around. The crowd was fueled by my energy. My pill kicked in. "It's architecture, building a house, making a dress . . ." I twisted and turned Dolly's head, to show the audience my next construction. "How much fun is hair?" I shouted.

My boys were sharp in their suits. Everything was in their hands: combs, brushes, accessories, clips, pins, and spray.

"Take a hairpiece and throw it on here." I put a big clump of curls on Dolly's head. "Cone, please," I poked pins into a Styrofoam cone and put it on top of her head. "Lacquer, please." Jere handed me spray; William held the second hairpiece up. I grabbed it and stacked it on Dolly's head.

I knew Revlon was waiting for their promotion. "And where there's hair, there's opportunity to *color* hair." I pitched like Elmer Gantry. "So get out the Revlon, make your own masterpiece, experiment, enjoy your art, tell your client . . . whatever they want, *it's your specialty*!"

I started another hairdo. I went into my zone, just me, the spotlight, and Dolly's head. I was a surgeon at the operating table. I tore down her hair and did five crazy mile-high creations, one after another, without taking a beat until I was done. The audience was screaming; all the budding hair-babies fresh out of beauty school, salon owners from Corona to Bakersfield, and hairdressing friends.

"Let's hear it for Carrie White and her staff," the master of ceremonies said. I bowed and rose up with the peace sign on both my hands. Dolly stood up, trying to balance her towering hairstyle, and we all trotted off.

"Thanks, everyone," I said to my gang backstage. "That was a blast."

A man from Revlon came in. "Congratulations, I'm not sure what just happened out there, but the crowd enjoyed you."

"I have to get back to the salon," said William, who was now one of my busiest hairdressers. "Not me, I booked out for the day," Randy said. "Let's go get a drink."

"Good idea," I said.

I was twenty-four years old; divorced again, this time with two little children and a booming business.

I found a Craftsman two-story rental in Hollywood. At the dead end of my short street was the gorgeous Huntington Hartford estate. The real estate lady announced, "And Ozzie and Harriet Nelson live across the street!"

"Great, I'll take it."

I was baffled about how gas, lights, and phones got connected, how dishes got into cupboards, how curtains got on windows—and where did towels come from? I could run my salon, but common household functions overwhelmed me.

Decorating, on the other hand, was going to be fun. Mollie, Aloma, and I were thrift-shop queens. I found a store that had children's furniture, toys, and patchwork blankets, and they delivered. I bought anything that caught my eye—lamps, baskets, salt and pepper shakers, pots and pans. I bought antique shawls that reminded me of London to drape over cheap chairs. For my bedroom, I wanted *exotic* on a low budget. Pier 1 was the answer. I bought a Moroccan bedspread with tiny mirrors sewn on it, oversize Indian pillows, inlaid abalone shell end tables, wall statues, mirrors in mosaic wooden frames, goddess paintings, as many things as possible to hang on walls. This was my rebellion against the restrictive Bucky days, and the bigger the nail to bang in the wall, the better.

Now that I was single, I was another babe on Steve Brandt's asexual arm. I was his date for the premiere of *2001: A Space Odyssey.* "I hear this is incredible," Steve said, and took out a pill. "You need to try one of these. It will make the movie even better."

He seemed so adamant. I never tried his pills.

"Okay, but just one."

Steve popped a handful and I popped one.

I dressed to the max, my best hair and clothes, ready to bump elbows and have a good time. It was my first big premiere, an industry event at the Cinerama Dome on Sunset and Vine. We breezed through the crowd and found our seats.

"Did I tell you this movie is *long*?" Steve laughed. "Long like . . . what time do you have to be to work tomorrow?"

"Steve, is my mouth supposed to be so dry?"

"It'll pass."

"My tongue feels like cardboard."

"Okay," Steve said bitchily. He got up and went for drinks. I felt extremely tired all of a sudden.

Steve returned. The lights went low, the opening score: *Dun Dun Dun Dun dun dun dun da dunnnnnnnnnn DA DUNNNNNNNNNN-NNNNNNNNN.*

"Wow," I whispered to Steve. "That was *heavy.*"

Steve was focused straight ahead, "I told you this was going to be good."

The sun slowly rose and filled the screen, like the first sun ever, day one, and then two monkeys appeared, squatting on a small mound of dirt. *Dun da dun da DAHHHHHHHHH.* One monkey finds a bone, *DA DA DA DAHHH.* The monkey throws the bone in the air, it flies high in the sky, higher, higher, it spins in the big blue sky, the white bone, then in slow motion, falling down, turning over and over and over . . .

"Hey, wake up, wake up." It was Steve.

Dry drool was on the corner of my mouth; many people were walking up the aisle. I sat up straighter and slowly came to. "Is it over?"

"No, just intermission," Steve said. "Lots of people on acid in here, we could get a contact high if we sat in the front rows."

"Forget them, what did you give me?"

"A Tuinal."

Downers weren't for me. I took serious note when Dorothy Kilgallen died of barbiturates and drinking; I didn't want that to happen to me, and I knew I wasn't going to give up alcohol.

At the end the film, I ran into Stefanie Powers, who was married to the film's lead actor, Gary Lockwood. I hadn't seen him in the movie, though. As far as I knew the film was about monkeys.

I was doing Mama Cass's hair for *The Julie Andrews Hour.* Judy Garland was also a guest. She was full of energy, but she would have to start over and over because she would forget a lyric or mess up a dance step. "Could we do that again, please?" Judy said apologetically and sipped her drink from a table nearby.

"Of course," the director said. "We know you've been traveling, take your time, you must be exhausted." She took another big gulp. I felt queasy; there was a familiar sadness I saw on Judy's face. It was my mother, frail, out of focus, unstable, and that amber glass of booze. I went back to Cass's dressing room and my own drink.

Cut and Run

Hairdressing was filling the vacancy I had had all my life. I felt unstoppable. I became as comfortable at the studios as I was in my own salon. I drank beer with the crew guys, champagne with the guests, and of course I always kept a flask of Bloody Marys stashed in my kit.

I worked all day, played with my babies until they went to sleep, then played all night with my friends. I was trying to date, but that was as foreign to me as Budapest. I had flings.

One guy I really liked was Sonny Bono. He was funny and sexy, the best combination. He gave me a gold watch with a solid gold coin face that was worth more than my house. A few weeks later, his assistant-driver-bodyguard came over and told me that Sonny and I were *finito*. And I shouldn't call him.

Johnny Rivers. Very cute, too close to Billy, though Billy set it up. Johnny went on tour and canceled our future dates.

My next fling was with the lead singer of Steppenwolf. He was a god, with long blond wavy hair. One night after they played Whisky A Go Go, he gave me the gold chain from around his neck and spent the weekend with me. I thought it must be love. Later I realized that he probably had a trunkfull of gold chains for *tour time*. I would have to go to a record store and look up his name on an album cover . . . Nick something.

I was about to turn twenty-five.

"I'm giving myself a birthday party," I told everyone in my salon and my special clients. "Here's my address."

I made sure I had a birthday cake. I made sure I had lots of champagne. I made sure I was going to have fun. I took an upper and started getting dressed. Aloma came early. We loved dolling up and getting high.

"I have an Ambar," I said, "if you want one."

"I already took a Desbutal."

"Oh, good, well, have some champagne. And pace yourself out, you know how crazy you get."

I put on my sheer chiffon floral with the off-the-shoulder ruffle straps and a train like a calypso dress. It slid on like a slip. The doorbell rang.

"Aloma, could you get that and just leave the door open, okay, sweetheart? I'm almost ready."

By the time I came downstairs my house was full of friends.

The crowd dwindled around 1:00 AM. Then the after-party, *the never say die* crowd, decided we should go out. Gene Shacove had just opened his private club, The Candy Store, on Rodeo Drive, directly underneath his beauty salon. He had done well for a hairdresser.

We parked in the Luau lot and like a band of wild Gypsies marched up Rodeo. We got to the Candy Store and there was a crowd outside, waiting to get in. "We don't do lines," I said, and walked up to the bouncer.

"Hi." I batted my false eyelashes and tossed my hair. "Is Gene here?" He looked at me, his arms across his chest. "Maybe," he said. "Aw come on." I smiled. "It's my birthday, Gene knows me, tell him Carrie White's here."

The guy came back within minutes and motioned us in. The room was dark, the dance floor packed.

"Order me a drink," I screamed to whoever heard me, and ran to the floor. For the next hour, I did the Hustle, the Skate, the Watusi, and the Crazy Chicken. I threw my head back and forth, I shook my ass, I waved my hands in the air, doing the *boogie oogie oogie till ya just can't boogie no more.*

Randy walked up. "Wanna red?"

"Wine?" I said.

"No, a Seconal," he said.

I shook my head. Why the hell would I want a sleeping pill now?

Meanwhile, back at the salon, some of my hairdressers were stealing, by way of clients who paid them directly and skipped the front desk, which skipped my percentage. I knew this because my supply bills were higher than my revenue. I guess everyone thought I was so popular and had so much money, that they could cheat me. The truth was, editorials paid nothing, and I worked hard to cover my expenses. But I figured as long as my salon doors were open, food was on my table, clothes were on my kids, and my liquor store charges were in good standing, I would look the other way. I didn't have time or energy to *police.* I was never interested in the business of hair . . . I was interested in the art and fun of hair.

Hairdressing was my way of life. I measured money in one way: How many haircuts it would take for me to get what I needed.

"You gotta come over," Steve said.

"As soon as I put my kids to sleep."

I rushed Adam and Daisy into their pajamas and put them to bed. I sensed they felt my rush, but I couldn't explain to them my urgency to reward myself with a party invitation. I was so discontented to just stay home. I told myself that they would be fine. They would be sleeping anyway. "Sweet dreams, close your eyes, Mommy loves you so much . . ." I kissed their foreheads, took in a big breath of their baby scents, and continued to rush out of the house.

Thank God for live-in housekeepers.

"Here," Steve said when he opened the door to me. "Someone just gave me this drink . . . don't they know I only drink water?"

I took a taste, we walked into his living room, and I plunked down on his purple sofa. Then *he* walked in Steve's front door.

If I felt that much chemistry for someone on sight, after Danny,

I should've known to run. He had the face of every guy I had ever fallen for, including Bob Dylan. Just the way he sashayed in the door was so sexy, so smooth. Steve must have seen my mouth drop and came over.

"Antonio, come over here, say hello to Carrie." Steve walked away.

"Hi," I said to Antonio . . . the greatest name I'd ever heard.

"Hi," he said. "I'm going to get a drink, do you want one?" At last, a guy who drinks. I smiled and nodded yes and finished the one I had.

When Antonio strolled back with two drinks, he sat right down next to me.

"So, what's your name again?"

"Carrie."

Antonio lit a cigarette. Steve glided back.

"Lean over, the both of you, actually, stand up, that will be better."

I wanted to do anything with Antonio. Curious, we complied. "Face each other," Steve said, cracking something in his hand and shoving it in our noses. The fumes made me close my eyes, a rush of blood flowed to my head, my heart, I left my body, euphoria hit, smack down to my underpants, and stayed. It was fast. It was sexy. It was tingly. *What the hell was it?*

I opened my eyes. Antonio moved right into my mouth and gave me the most perfect mad kiss. I wanted him to swallow me up and keep me in this state forever. As I came down, back to my feet, back on the ground, our kiss dissolved into laughter.

"That was good," I said to Steve, then looked at Antonio.

"Where'd you get the popper?" Antonio asked Steve.

"Charlie," Steve said, his stoned eyes at half-mast. "Want another?"

"What was that again?" I said.

"Amyl nitrate," Antonio said.

Steve threw a handful of tiny glass tubes wrapped in yellow gauze on the table and walked off. And that's how *that* started.

"You got a telegram," William said, waving an envelope as I walked into my salon. "From *New York*."

I had promoted William from assistant to doing Ann-Margret's hairpieces. I told him, "If you can do these, you're ready for the floor."

He continued to look after me like he was my first assistant or *my boss*.

"Oh, my God . . ." I read the letter over again.

He snapped it out of my hands and read it. "Oh, my God!"

It was a request to be the guest on *To Tell the Truth*. I had grown up watching this television program. "It says you can bring someone."

William beamed, but I knew this was my chance to take Antonio away.

I called Aloma. "Guess what?"

"You're going away?" Aloma was always happy with whatever made me happy.

"New York! Will you check in with Bucky about the kids? I'll just be gone for the weekend."

"I've heard that before," Aloma said.

"No, seriously."

I called Antonio. "Guess what?"

I told him my great idea, and he answered, "I'll see if I can get away."

I went back to my client. It looked like I was doing hair, but all I was thinking about was Antonio's answer.

"Are you crazy?" Joan screamed at me.

Joan and Marvin Worth had become my friends through Aloma. I had been doing Joan's hair for more than three years. I guess I drifted off to Antonio-land while I trimmed her bangs. Joan, like all of us, wanted her bangs covering her eyes like curtain shades.

"What the *fuck* did you just do?" she snapped.

I had miscalculated and cut her bangs above her eyebrows.

"Joan, calm down, *short bangs* are the latest thing."

"If *short bangs* are the latest *fucking thing*, how come your *fucking* bangs are so *fucking* long?" She got up and stomped out. I had never heard *fuck* so many times in one sentence, but then her husband did manage Lenny Bruce. By the time I reached Aloma on the phone, Joan had already called her.

"Joan wants to sue you," Aloma said. "But she'll get over it. Her bangs will grow back before she can get a court date."

Antonio called. We were on.

Betsy Bloomingdale got me my first credit card at a time when few people had them. Her husband, Alfred, owned Diners Club.

"Alfred and I didn't do anything," she said. "You were approved."

All I knew was that this little plastic card was going to come in real handy for my trip to New York.

We landed late at night, made our way to the Americana Hotel, enjoyed some wine and snacks, made love, and passed out.

The hotel phone rang.

"You requested a call at nine AM, Miss White."

"Morning? Already? Okay. Thank you."

Leaving Antonio asleep, I dressed in my most untrendy outfit, so the panelists wouldn't guess I was the hotshot hairdresser. I grabbed my invitation, went downstairs, and hailed a cab.

"Lady, that's around the corner," the cabbie barked. "You can walk."

I zoomed to the studio.

"You know how this works, don't you?" the director said. "The panelists will question you and you *tell the truth*."

"Yes," I said, but more excited to get back to the hotel bed with Antonio.

"You stand here." He positioned me in between the Carrie White imposters. I was called on. Peggy Cass drilled me with her high-pitched voice. "You serve *champagne*? How old are you?"

"Yes, I serve champagne and I just turned twenty-five."

"Well, you don't look it." She checked her notes. "Your celebrity list is *humongous*," she shrilled. "Do you *really* do *all* these people, Jennifer Jones, Betsy Bloomingdale, Raquel Welch, *and* you charge a lot of money, fifty dollars for a haircut? Again she looked down. "*You're* the mother of two small children?"

"Yes, it's all true." I laughed. Peggy shook her head, looked at Kitty Carlisle, and said, "I don't believe it, do you?" Kitty shrugged and smiled. "Orson?" "Doesn't seem possible," he said. Peggy called out, "Where's the next contestant?"

It was difficult to keep a straight face while the last girl stepped forward.

The host, Gary Moore, said, "We're out of time, so now..." Drum roll, silence, simmer. "Will the real... Carrie White... please stand up."

We all stood still, playing the game, each one of us edging out, then back, looking at one another, waiting another long moment, and *voilà*, I stepped out.

Peggy screamed, "I don't believe it!"

Not one person guessed me. I raced back to the hotel.

Antonio was lounging, watching television.

"I won," I said, and walked over to the bed and gave him a big kiss. He undressed me and I still had my purse in my hand.

Dusk swooped in like a velvet blanket. I wasn't interested in dancing or gallivanting all over town. In bed, in Antonio's arms, in love was all I wanted.

"A friend of mine has something I need to pick up," he said.

"You have to leave?" I poured us more wine.

"I'll be right back. Do you have fifty bucks cash till we get back to L.A.?"

"Sure."

He returned with nothing in his hands. Then from his pocket he pulled out the tiniest brown glass bottle and tapped it on the bedside table three times.

"Better than poppers." Antonio smiled.

"*That's impossible.*"

He dumped some of the contents onto the glass top of the bedside table. It was a white powder. He took a business card, diced it up, scooped it together, and placed a small portion onto the soft spot of his clenched fist. He put his nose to it, held his other nostril, and took a big snort in.

"Your turn," he said, and put more on his fist and passed it to me.

I never asked him what the powder was; I just pinched my nostril, and snorted it all up with my other like he did. My eyes watered immediately.

"It kinda burns, but it's kinda sexy."

He did the other side of his nose and then my other side.

"I'm going to take a quick shower," he said.

I opened a new wine bottle, poured us each a glass, and stretched out on the bed like a Persian cat. I looked over at the little brown bottle on the table and thought: *More*. So I took a little more. Then I sipped my wine, looked at the little bottle again, and thought: *More*. I did more. Another taste of wine, another look at the little bottle, and another thought, last time: *More*. I did it.

My handsome Antonio came out of the bathroom with a fresh white towel wrapped at his hips, his perfect light brown waved Michelangelo hair. He walked over and gave me a tingling kiss on my neck and didn't stop until he had his tongue in my ear. I was racing, from him, our rendezvous, and the white powder.

He reached for the bottle, turned it over, and tapped it out on the glass tabletop. "Fuck! Where is it?"

I recoiled. "Is that all there was?"

Antonio got up, pissed off, and stomped around the room swearing.

"Can't we get more of it?" I said.

"I guess," he said, and put on his pants. "And *it* has a name: cocaine."

I gave him a hundred-dollar bill.

We made up, stayed up, and I got that there was never enough of this stuff called cocaine. When I woke up, I wanted to lick the glass tabletop.

How do I cure a hangover? I called room service for breakfast: Bloody Marys. Antonio looked through one of the hotel's travel magazines. "Wouldn't it be cool if we could go here?" He showed me pictures of paradise: Puerto Rico.

"Why can't we?" I reached into my robe pocket for my secret weapon, the Diners Club card. "All I have to do is sign this."

I loved this new plastic card concept: Fly now, pay later.

This would be the honeymoon I never had with Bucky. We flew to San Juan for a romantic holiday. No more white powder, just margaritas and sex.

We walked down cobblestone roads, passing wooden wagons filled with mantillas, colorful blankets, peasant blouses, and painted flutes. I bought shirts for Adam and Daisy. The food was great and endless sights, but I stared at Antonio's beauty more than at the city's.

The next day we walked from the beach to the little city area, and I was rushed by two *federales.* "Your papers, *por favor,* just the señorita."

I smiled, a bit tipsy from lunch and happy we didn't have cocaine on us.

"What's the problem, Officer?" Antonio said.

They escorted me to a paddy wagon with two drunken Puerto Rican bums for company. I was half laughing, half concerned. They handed Antonio a paper.

"You can make her arrangements here."

I was put into a barred cell until Antonio returned.

"Where's that Diners Club card? You need to pay a fine."

"What the hell was I arrested for?"

"Indecent exposure." He laughed. "No one is allowed to wear only a bathing suit in town."

I returned to Los Angeles. Broke. Tan. Happy.

I was called to do another major show for Clairol, this time at the Miramar in Palm Springs, and the following day, to do hair for some beauty pageant, also in Palm Springs. My team would meet me there.

I talked Antonio and Aloma into coming with me. "Antonio, try to get more of that white powder."

I got so buzzed before the Clairol platform show the next day, I remember very little. I could do outrageous hairdos on automatic pilot, but the room was spinning as words flew out of my mouth. Clairol found me wild, but Aloma and Antonio found me passed out backstage after the show.

I came to on the couch to the sound of their voices.

"I was just resting," I said. "We need champagne and to get back to our hotel."

"You can't go," Aloma reminded me. "I just saw William, he's on his way with the pageant contestants for you to do."

The producer and director of the pageant arrived backstage, along with more people, carrying mikes and television cameras. I worked in a blackout. I remember nothing until I heard, "It's a wrap; we're done here." I knew I was done. And from the way Antonio's eyes refused to meet mine and how his lips remained sealed, I could tell he was done with me too.

It was a quiet, sad ride back to L.A. We were out of pills, poppers, and the small amount of cocaine we'd brought. I wanted more alcohol, but no one else seemed to bring it up, so I didn't either. I was crushed to lose Antonio and mortified by my messy behavior. Up until then, no one person had seen me all the time, so no one knew that most of the time I was speeded up on diet pills and drinking to come down. At times I would cut out the diet pills, but I could never do a whole day without a drink.

I had immersed myself in Dylan's music, but maybe I did need a weatherman to know which way the wind was blowin' . . .

I had a reputation for being wild and energetic. In my salon, I would tease, "The hair's free . . . but the personality is expensive."

It cost me plenty.

PART 5

Reenter
Richard Alcala

1969–1979

Running with the Pretty

It was the beginning of 1969.

It was the end of the sixties.

It was the beginning of the end.

Hair was still big in 1969. No ladies left home without their false eyelashes and add-on hairpieces unless they were on their way to the beauty salon. Hairdressers thrived on their dependency on false hair and professional needs for back-combing. Vidal Sassoon had made his mark with his geometric bobs, yet the majority of ladies still wanted a set look and a big poof on their crown. I had some clients for whom I did natural cuts—May Britt, Judy Carne, and Jean Seberg—but for most it was *the more hair, the better*.

Changes came with the dawning of the seventies.

Our patchwork jeans, fringed jackets, peasant dresses, and hip-huggers needed an overhaul and so did our hair. I had been wearing an Afro wig with scarves tied around my head like Jimi Hendrix to kick it up. Then along came the Shag to reshape us all . . . guys and chicks. It started with Jim Morrison and got better with Mick Jagger. The rock stars had become as important to fashion as designers and movie stars. The Beatles proved that. But the Beatles looked like bankers compared to the new rock hair. The musical *Hair* proved that.

"Is that Ursula Andress on my books?"

"Is that Mrs. Horst Buchholz on my books?"

"Is that *Capucine* on my books?"

Word of me had traveled across the ocean and had reached Paris.

Melvin Sokolsky requested me often, and I dropped everything when he called. "Bring four assistants, you'll need them," Melvin said. "We'll prepare one day in New York, then we go to Philly."

The next day I told my clients I was going to New York. A lady waiting for me said, "Oh, I hear it's freezing there right now." I was cutting Margo Winkler; she turned to the other lady and said, "My dear, it's never cold in Bergdorf's."

I took my hairdressers—Donald, Barry, Randy, and William. Donald and I stayed with the Sokolskys', while the rest stayed in a hotel. The Sokolskys had a beautiful two-story brownstone on East Thirty-Ninth Street—living quarters upstairs and Melvin's studio downstairs.

"Here's your key," Button said. "Don't forget you have to work tomorrow."

"I won't forget, but, tonight . . . *I'm in New York!!!*"

"The Salvation," I told the cabbie. "It's in the Village."

I lit a cigarette and turned to Donald and Barry and William and smiled. Randy sat up front. "After, we have to go to the Electric Circus."

We hit the club, and I went straight for the bar. "Double martini, please, and just wave the vermouth cap over my glass." I threw it down like a shot of water. "Ahhhh," I said, chills running from head to toe as the vodka hit. "What's more refreshing than that?"

"Isn't that the wacky hairdresser Monti Rock over there?" Randy said.

"Yes and it's Monti Rock . . . *the Third.*"

Monti was wearing a tight white satin shirt, pants to match, tons of beads, rings on every finger, a hat and boa, and had more eye makeup on than I did. "Knock on Wood," blasted from the speakers larger than cars.

"I gotta dance," I said, and ran to the floor. We danced and danced and drank and drank.

"Electric Circus," I told the cabbie.

We danced and danced and drank and drank.

"Arthur's," I told the cabbie. We were low on cash, so I signed Natalie Wood on the tab and skipped out.

⌣

"Max's Kansas City," I told the cabbie.

We got home at 5:00 AM.

"Donald, we gotta work in two hours." I giggled. "And sssshhhh, don't wake Melvin and Button." I dropped to the couch and pulled the blankets over my head.

"Why ya goin' to bed with yer clothes on?" Donald slurred.

"So I won't have to get dressed in the morning," I slurred back.

"Honey chil', what *is* wrong with you . . . still in bed?" A voice entered my dream world. "Mr. Melvin's callin' for you downstairs."

I could tell someone was talking to me, but who and where was I? I peeked out through squinted eyes. It was Marion, Melvin's housekeeper.

"Mornin', Marion, and not so loud, I got a terrible headache."

"Mr. Melvin's got a bigger headache looking for you." She tried to sit me up. "He's downstairs for an hour already."

"Donald," I groaned to the dead person in the living room. "Come on, we're late." Donald rolled over. "For what?" I laughed. "The reason we're here . . . *to work.*"

I pulled on my boots, pulled my hair into a ponytail, and met Donald's cracked eyes with mine. "You look like I feel."

"I made y'll some breakfus'," Marion said.

"Thanks Marion, but it's too early to chew."

Downstairs: Melvin lifted his left eyebrow so high that his forehead seemed to arch. I stared at the light on three long hairs from his right eyebrow that seemed to reprimand me.

Next stop Philadelphia. The Arboretum. There were five models for the job. I instructed my assistants to set the girls in electric rollers and went to Melvin to see the storyboard for our job.

"You must make each hairdo more beautiful than the flowers in the greenhouse where we are filming."

"Oh, is that all?" I said.

We worked long hours for days. Then my favorite sentence was hollered out—"It's a wrap!"

"Who's in for going out?" I said.

"I'm in," scattered voices announced. "Me too," another model said.

Civil riots had been going on all over the country since the mid-sixties—New York, New Jersey, Chicago, the Watts riots—and more fuel was added when Martin Luther King Jr. was assassinated. Nearby us, there had been fighting in the streets for the past two days in a town called York. Some areas were banned while others had curfews. Martial Law they called it. This revolution *was* televised.

"I'm not going out," Melvin said. "You all are *crazy.*"

One day, a few months later, Donald called me aside at work.

"I have a great offer in the brand new Century City area," he said. "I know you're doing all you can, but it's a functioning salon with a bigger commission."

Functioning was the key word. Next, Randy left me to work at Gene Shacove's. David Matheson decided to open a salon above his brother's flower shop on Melrose. Two other hairdressers left to do the same and another two moved to Arizona. Last, Carl Vasta, my color specialist, left to travel with the Fermodyl product line.

It was a mass exodus in more ways than one. I didn't know how I was going to carry all of it, the salon, the career, the financial burdens, by myself. I felt like I was spinning five plates on three sticks.

My best friend from Hollywood High blasted into my salon one day, speaking gibberish. "I'm going to kill myself," Rosalind said, crying.

I excused myself in the middle of a haircut and walked her to the bathroom. A large prescription bottle of Dexedrine fell from her purse. "This is your problem, Roz, these make you crazy!" I threw her pills down the toilet. She flipped and ran out. Two months later I got a call: Rosalind was dead. Her family said she died of complications from a miscarriage and pain pills.

After that heartbreak, I received another call: my *first* best friend from Pacoima had picked up a gun and blown her brains out. Beverly had become a prostitute so she could support her two little girls and her heroin addiction. Marsha said, "She couldn't do it one more day." Beverly was only twenty-three.

And of course, bad things always happen in threes.

On July 3, 1969, the headline read: *Dead Rolling Stone. Brian Jones Found Facedown in Swimming Pool.*

But it didn't end there. One day Billy walked into my salon—a surprise visit—clutching the neck of a bottle of vodka in one hand, a lit Sherman in the other. I was thrilled to see him, but he was pasty white, and unshaven, and looked as frail as my mother.

"Excuse me," I said to my client, and then to Barry, "Big rollers. When she's dry, brush and spray."

I walked into the back and pulled the curtain shut. I'd never seen Billy cry. I put my arms around him. "What is it?"

"Michael's dead," he said.

I jumped back. Michael was Billy's son. He had recently come back from Oklahoma to live with Billy again.

"He was shipped off to Vietnam, wherever the fuck that is . . ."

I felt hollow. I looked around my small dispensary, a beat-up sink, a hot plate, Billy sitting on a stool next to my cheap refrigerator, the old wooden shelves jammed with tint, peroxide, bleach, and mixing bowls.

"I got a letter my boy's head was blown off on his third day and I'm waiting for them to send me his body."

We hugged. Billy pulled out a familiar little brown glass bottle, stuck in a miniature gold spoon, and leveled off the powder with the lip of the bottle.

"This shit'll fix anythang," he said, and took two big snorts. Billy already lived in free fall without a net. I feared what would become of him without his son. He took more scoops of the white powder and said, "Well . . . almost anythang."

"Your turn," he said, and put the spoon up to my nose. I took a deep inhale. I felt the blast of cocaine, a high-voltage spike that brightened up my head like lights were turned on. My gums got numb and then my face. It was like breathing in food, food to fill a hole wherever that hunger needed to be plugged.

"This came from Bolivia," he said. "It's the finest, like Dom Pérignon."

I could taste it in the back of my throat.

"I had it once before, I like it."

"Like it? You're gonna *love it*. Wanna another toot?"

"Toot? That's funny, but you better save the rest for later."

"Don't worry, baby doll, plenty more where this came from."

Cut To—

"Is Billy there?"

"Maybe," a guy answered. "Who wants to know?"

"Carrie White."

"Hey, how've you been?"

"Who is this?"

"Richard."

"Richard Alcala?" I lit up.

"You got a good memory."

"You remember me?"

"Of course I do."

"That's nice to hear." I blushed through the phone.

"Billy's supposed to meet me at the Aware Inn, why don't you join us?"

"I can do that."

"See you at nine."

I put the phone down and shook my hands to get the tingle out. Richard Alcala for dinner! I had longed for this since I met him in high school. His invitation was like a blood transfusion.

I darted out of my salon. I had only two hours to get ready. It was Friday night; no kiddies and no distractions. I hit my driveway, dashed straight to the kitchen, and poured a chilled glass of Pouilly Fuissé. I put on Paul Butterfield's *East Meets West*, pulled off my clothes, plugged in my electric rollers, lit a Sherman, took a big gulp of my wine, and turned up the music, screaming, *Richard Alcala!*

I flopped naked on my bed. *Hi, Richard, great to see you again, did you ever marry? Are you engaged? Have a girlfriend?*

I stepped into the shower. Shaved. Scrubbed, Polished. Got out, turned on the bath, poured in oils, bubbles, and salts. While the tub filled, I pushed back the cuticles on my fingernails with the towel like my nana taught me years ago: "Let your moons come through."

I sank into the tub, my body let go of the day and the years. I thought about my world.

I realized I was tired of showing up to every hot spot like it was my night job. Except of course when the Troubadour had that new comedian Richard Pryor, or the guy from London, Elton John, but not out every night. Watching television by my own fireplace in slippers with a man I loved sounded like the *real* glamorous life.

From now on, I'd just go dancing *once* a week . . . for *soul* reasons.

I spotted Richard sitting alone and walked over to his table.

"Hi," I said. Richard was ten years older and made me feel like an innocent schoolgirl.

He stood up. "Sit next to me—who knows when Billy will get here?"

"Isn't that Jim Morrison over there?" I said. He was sitting three tables away. But the Jim Morrison I knew for years, rockin' it at the Whiskey, was missing. He looked bloated and more out of it than ever.

"Too much sauce," Richard said. "He's moving to Paris, I hear. But forget about him, what made you call tonight?"

"I was homesick for Billy. He told me about Michael's death in Vietnam and gave me his number, I didn't know it was *your* number."

"Yeah, he's staying with me for a while," Richard said, looking too deeply into my eyes. I felt stripped to my bones. "Wine?"

Richard had a way about him.

He was a pound of Valentino, a cup of Clark Gable, and a pinch of Brando.

Time passed.

No Billy. More wine.

We ordered dinner. More delicious conversation about how our lives had paralleled for years, yet we never knew each other.

No Billy. We ate.

"How was it that we met ten years ago and never had a private conversation or an evening together?"

"You were too popular to notice me." I smiled.

"Look who's talking."

"That's for my hairdressing—you're popular after the spray can goes down."

He laughed. "I've almost quit hair."

"No, you're too good to ever do that."

"I dig hair, but I've been decorating some clients' homes . . . I like it."

A pretty blond lady came up. Richard smiled. I felt a jealous tinge.

"Elaine, this is Carrie White, the best hairdresser in Beverly Hills."

"I thought you were," she said.

"Carrie's wearing the crown these days." Richard turned to me. "Come to my place for an after-dinner drink, I live around the corner. Billy's gotta come home sometime . . . he lives there."

3:30 AM

"I gotta go. This is crazy. I have to work tomorrow."

"Stay here. You can sleep in my bed with me, in case Billy comes home with someone. I won't bite."

I might, I thought.

Richard gave me one of his big T-shirts to wear. I slipped into it and his bed. I was trying to match Richard's calm, but I could barely sleep.

Dawn arrived. Richard reached over and in one smooth move kissed my neck. We made love without hesitation, without a word. But I couldn't linger and savor the morning; I had to get to work.

I felt like a mess from the night before; add bad breath, smeared makeup, and what could my hair look like? I tiptoed off for a private shower.

I stood under the water hoping to wash away my guilty feelings. *Now look what you did! You made it through the whole night like a lady, then you lose it in the morning.*

It was the longest shower of my life. I couldn't bear to face Richard, especially stone cold sober. But I was going to have to come out sometime. I put on last evening's clothes, used his dryer to fix my hair, and thanked God for long bangs.

When I finally exited, Richard was standing in the hallway wearing a big white terry-cloth robe. I could smell the fresh coffee coming from the kitchen.

"Good morning *again* . . . cream and sugar?"

"I can't," I said, looking at his sweet smile. "I gotta get to my salon."

He put both his hands on my face and gently kissed my mouth.

"I'll call you later," he said, from his front door. "Have a beautiful day, beautiful."

I left with pins and needles pulsing in every cell of my body. His call was the only thing on my mind, plus my hangover, but a screwdriver could cure that.

That day, I heard every phone ring from my desk downstairs, but it was never the right one. No Richard. I was not enthusiastic about doing Lola Falana's wig or Melba Franklin's updo. I was diving into remorse. The day was almost over. I gave up. Minutes later, a girl with a big floral arrangement walked into my salon. My receptionist pointed in my direction.

"Excuse me," I said to my client, and went to the top of the staircase.

"These are for you," the girl said.

I had never seen such an elaborate arrangement. It was a miniature forest scene with toy-feathered birds in a nest, twigs forming bridges amid moss and ferns, wildflowers and heather.

"I almost forgot," the girl said, and pulled out a small white card. My waiting clients froze while I opened it, except Melba, who said, "Are you in love?"

I reread the card a thousand times in one second.

"Ten years out the window. I Love You, Richard."

"I think so," I answered.

"HOLD EVERYTHING!" the bartender shouted when we walked into the little saloon, Slater Hawkins, on Fillmore Street. "IT'S RICH-

ARD ALCALA FROM HOLLYWOOD!" Then he threw a bucket of ice cubes into the air from behind the bar. "SNOW CONES FOR EVERYONE!!!"

Richard and I were officially together for a month. We flew to his hometown, San Francisco. He wanted me to meet his friends and family. His very best friends were Tommy and Betty Tucker. Tommy was the bartender.

"When Tommy Tucker moves from one bar to another, his clientele follows him like a hairdresser's."

"HOW LONG ARE YOU HERE? HOW MUCH TIME DO WE HAVE?"

Richard was a big celebrity with his friends and family in San Francisco. He had broken away and made it in Hollywood. They all saved his press and bragged about his affair with Rita Hayworth, and clients Natalie Wood and Anne Baxter.

"BETTY'S GOING TO BE UPSET IF SHE MISSES YOU."

"Betty is Tommy's better half," Richard said.

"YOU GOT THAT RIGHT!"

I couldn't help laughing from Tommy's energy.

"HEY LOOK, WE BOTH GOT A SPACE IN OUR TEETH." He pointed to me, then turned to Richard, "*I LIKE HER ALREADY.*"

I closed my mouth and covered my space with my lips.

"Thanks but I hate my space. It's okay on guys."

"I love your space," Richard said.

Tommy set down two shots of tequila and Richard and Tommy slammed them down together.

"I LIKE *HIS* STYLE," Tommy said, leaning in close to me over the bar. "CAN YOU HANDLE THIS CRAZY GUY?"

Tommy made me feel so welcome.

"WATCH THIS," Tommy said, after making a potion in a silver container.

"SHAKE THIS UP FOR ME," Tommy told a flashy chick sitting next to us. "AND IF YOU DO A GOOD JOB, I'LL GIVE YA A FREE DRINK."

He put the shaker in her hands and lifted her arms high, "OKAY, NOW SHAKE IT GOOD." He winked at us as her boobies jiggled with every shake. "I GOT A FUN JOB, DON'T I? BUT DON'T TELL BETTY."

Tommy turned to me. "DID THAT LUG TELL ME YOUR NAME YET?"

"This is Carrie, my competition," Richard said.

I looked at Richard, glowing from his compliment.

"PLEASURE TO MEET YOU."

Someone asked Tommy for a drink. "BE RIGHT BACK . . . DON'T MOVE."

Richard put his arm around me and whispered, "How you doing?"

"I'm so fine."

He pushed my hair back and kissed my neck.

"I've waited ten years for that move," I said.

Tommy returned and yelled to the other bartender, "TURN THAT UP."

It was Creedence Clearwater Revival, "Proud Mary."

"I love them," I said.

"I GOT A GIRL THAT WILL BLOW YOUR MIND, TOMORROW NIGHT, THE FILLMORE, JANIS JOPLIN."

"REALLY?" I screamed back. "I LOVE HER."

Richard smiled, watching Tommy and me get along.

At 2:30 AM, we pulled into the driveway of Richard's childhood home on a dead-end street in the small town of San Bruno. The biggest and only thing in San Bruno was the San Francisco airport. His mom's little white house had a huge hydrangea plant that covered half of the front of the house.

We walked in. A plane zoomed over the house, sounding way too low for my comfort zone. "Come on, it's okay," Richard said. "You'll get used to that."

The light was on in the kitchen. I smelled beans cooking. Another fragrance overlapped, fresh coffee. Richard's bubbly mother popped out from the kitchen doorway.

"Hi," she said, sparkling. "I'm Richard's mother, Mary, they call me Mary Ma."

"Mom, this is Carrie."

I was surprised she was awake.

"Hi, Richard tells me you have children," Mary chattered. "That's so nice, what are their names, how old are they?"

"Mom, we just got here," Richard interrupted. "Too many questions."

"Oh, sorry." She giggled and crunched her shoulders like Ruth Gordon. "I get excited to know what my baby boy is up to, you know, you're a mother."

Mary was a petite Mexican-Indian lady with a light in her eyes that could torch a cornfield. She was petite except for her enormous bosom.

"You should have my beans with fresh salsa before you go to bed, and Richard's grandma made tortillas. You'll feel good when you wake up. Coffee?"

She held up a small old-fashioned metal coffeepot.

"No coffee," Richard and I said in unison, smiling at our synchronicity.

We sat and Mary served us homemade treats, showing me newspaper clippings of Richard in Europe with Rita Hayworth, his graduation picture from beauty college, and a few of herself when she was a hot tamale. She told me that Richard's father had been killed by a train on the tracks, around the corner from this home. Mary was a cashier at the Lucky Market and said she would retire in ten years at sixty-five.

"Mom, we can't keep up with you." Richard stood up.

I started to pick up our plates but Mary stopped me.

"Leave those, dear, it will give me something to do."

I followed Richard up the bright red enamel painted staircase behind the kitchen to his secret add-on quarters, a room above the garage that Richard and his brother Bob had built as teenagers. Pictures hung in every possible space, from Mexican drawings to scenes of mountains and rivers from the 1930s, obvious thrift-shop finds. Crammed along one wall were two extra portable clothes closets that couldn't shut from being so jam-packed. The whole room was a closet with two beds, probably unchanged since her boys had moved out twenty years ago.

"My mom's a packrat," Richard said from the double bed. "Now, take your clothes off and get over here."

This night was it. I knew I wanted to be with Richard for the rest of my life.

We came downstairs in the morning, and Mary Ma greeted us like she had been waiting for us since last night. "Now you want coffee, I bet."

It was the strongest cup of coffee I'd ever had.

"I'm going to take a shower," Richard said.

Mary giggled. "Oh good, no interruptions." She wanted to know everything about me, and could I teach her the latest dance, the Latin Hustle? "You must be very smart and organized to have your own salon and raise a family. Richard needs someone like that around him."

After a day of San Fran sightseeing, we headed off to the Tuckers'.

"Hi, you must be Carrie." Tommy's wife, Betty, stood with open arms at the front door of their apartment in the city. She was a tall beautiful blonde, cat blue eyes, a broad smile, and a golden tan, which brought out her highlighted hair and freckled skin. "I just got back from Hawaii, I'm a stewardess. What did I miss?"

"EVERYONE READY?" Tommy bolted out into the living room.

I was stunned through every second of Janis Joplin's performance at the Fillmore. No singer ever touched me like that . . . I more than loved her. Janis was earth-shattering and gut-wrenching. She melted the enamel off my teeth, made my skin shed, and I purged an ancient buried cry.

Back to L.A. "Come by work," Richard said. "We can go to dinner after my last cut."

I drove to Sunset Plaza, found a spot right out front, and walked in. It was a small space Richard had taken over, but the ornate gold mirror still leaned against a wall like I remembered from ten years ago. He was cutting a client. Richard stopped, spun around on his stool, and greeted me. "Hey, baby. Phyllis, meet Carrie White." I smiled.

"Mary," Richard called out. "Get Carrie a glass of wine."

Mary came barreling out of the dressing room with an armful of smocks.

"Jus' a minute, chil', I can't do five things at once. Smocks come first."

There she was, beautiful big Mary, just like I remembered her from his salon when I was in high school, except her temples had gray streaks in her processed upsweep hairdo.

"*Mary,* drop the smocks. Carrie's wine, then smocks. How 'bout you, Phyllis?"

She shook her head no.

"Richard, you always be in such a big hurry o'er nuthin'. Carrie can wait one minute fo' her glass of wine, can't you, honey?"

I smiled and nodded. I sat down on the bench with an Indian serape thrown over it, exposing its carved armrests and legs. It was easy to see why ladies wanted Richard to decorate their homes. He had transformed this area with Mexican artifacts, Indian blankets, old Mexican furniture, trunks, tapestries, cathedral paintings, and vanity dressers for stations. Miniature and large cactus plants were his final touch.

"You done come a long way since workin' fo' that crazy ol' Billy," Mary said. "Richard tells me you gotcho' self yo' own salon, and two li'l children." Mary picked up scattered towels as she talked with me. "Richard never had no girlfriend with children, that's *good* fo' him."

Richard caught my eye in his big mirror and gave me a wink.

"You mus' have a good business head on yo' shoulders."

I thought that was funny, but compared to Richard, I guessed I did.

A hairdresser came up to us. "We're out of Arctic Blonde, Mary."

"Chil', jus' use some Flaxen, she won't know the difference," she said. "And say hello to Carrie. Carrie, Vern Pingatore."

"I know you," I said. "I asked you to work for me and you couldn't be bothered . . . didn't you work at the Hair Place or Hair Palace?"

"I should've come with you," Vern said.

"Stop flirting with my girlfriend." Richard said. "Let's get out of here."

Richard spent that night with me. And the next night, and the next week and the month after that.

"We're going to see the blooming cactus gardens at the Huntington Library." Richard had brought me breakfast on a tray. Adam and Daisy followed him up onto the bed with me.

Richard was wonderful with my children. I loved that we were one big happy family. He loved taking us for rides out of the city—Santa Barbara for vegetables, or sightseeing, from Vedanta temples and Catholic churches to the Descanso Gardens with massive camellia trees.

"I thought cactus were prickly desert weeds," I said. "They bloom?"

We all held hands, and the creaturelike cactus plants along the dirt path hedged us on each side. Some were giant towers; others were short and oddly shaped with muted color. Flowers burst from them, hot pink, white, yellow, and lavender. The displays arching out of succulents and balls of thorns and were fifty, sixty, even a hundred years old.

"Look at this one, Mommy," Adam said. "And this one . . ."

Further down, I watched Richard with Daisy on his shoulders, as Adam ran to his side, as he explained a particular cactus to them. I was enthralled with these gardens, but mostly by Richard's presence. I held my breath for this moment to last, then exhaled. I had never felt so much hope before. Or love.

Richard always seemed to have a fun plan or place in mind. He took me to new spots, the Catalina Club in Hollywood and the Strand in Hermosa. We experienced a whirlwind of live jazz, from Horace Silver, Carmen McRae, and Ray Brown to Latin jazz with Willie Bobo and Tito Puente.

Richard opened my mind to P. D. Ouspensky's *Tertium Organum* and the remarkable teacher Gurdjieff. He loved Krishnamurti, especially his book *The Art of Seeing*. Richard's quest for higher consciousness seemed to underline his motives for getting high. He introduced me to *The Urantia Book* and Richard Alpert, newly renamed Ram Dass, and his book *Be Here Now*. It looked like a big coloring book to me. I would smoke pot and paint the drawings and barely read a thing. My favorite was Madame Blavatsky's book *The*

Secret Doctrine with her epigraph, *There is no Religion higher than Truth,* on the first page.

Richard stashed his pot in a shoe box in my bedroom closet. His cleaning ritual was like looking for gold in a screen, shaking and separating the seeds from the dried leaves. It smelled better than fresh-ground coffee. He was very particular about the quality of pot he smoked. Good pot was as religious as Richard ever needed to be. "You can't roll it too loose or too tight," he would say, looking at his excellent job, smelling it, and striking the match, waiting for the sulfur to vanish. Then he would fire the joint evenly, turning it like a rare cigar, like tasting the first sip of fine wine, then pass it to me.

The process took way too long. I preferred grabbing a drink and that fun quick hit of cocaine. I didn't have the passion or patience for marijuana. I smoked it with him when it was ready, but it wasn't meaningful to me, whereas for Richard it was part of a culture surrounding American Indian ceremonies, peyote, and mescaline. "When you're ready, we'll take a trip."

"Where to, Richard?"

"Who knows, maybe we won't even leave the house."

The change I had prayed for had come . . . it was *Richard.* He was inspiring and comforting, and he had a great sense of humor. He loved life and took it lightly. Richard wasn't critical by nature. I knew he wouldn't judge or complain about my past, my flamboyant style, my professional involvement, or my drinking. Life was loving and exciting with Richard by my side.

In the Mix

Rita was the new assistant Richard recommended. She was a pretty little Mexican girl with a sexy Mexican style, sheer embroidered Mexican peasant blouses, hip-huggers, gold bracelets, hoop earrings, and a backstreet sense of humor. She was an experienced shampoo girl and not interested in anything but being a shampoo girl.

"I think I just made one of those social faux pas when I was putting the perm solution on your customer," Rita said once.

I jumped in, "Neil Diamond?"

"Yeah. He asked me, 'Am I going to make it for the *Glenn Campbell Show*?' I told him, '*If Glenn Campbell can make it, you can make it.*' He seemed annoyed, and said, '*No*, will I be out of here by three o'clock?'"

She blundered innocently like this many times. I had just put highlights in Bobbie Gentry's hair for her TV special. When Rita met Bobbie, she remarked in passing, "I hope my gray hair comes in as pretty as yours."

I gave Rita the stink-eye.

Regardless, Rita quickly became my confidante. Her athletic résumé read like mine: dancing and jumping to conclusions. She liked to drink too, and kept a strong Bloody Mary, screwdriver, or Salty Dog in my coffee cup at all times, my requirement for a good assistant. She could open a bottle of champagne quietly and she did a good job of covering for me when I was running late, which was always.

Champagne was my glue and peacemaker. I had so much to think about all the time—my kids, their school, their health, their play, groceries, my business, my clients, training receptionists that came and went, *my new big romance,* and my financial responsibilities. I couldn't imagine life without the buffer of bubbles.

My brain and numbers did not click. I was the classic example of *I can't be overdrawn—I still have checks left.*

My accountant called me. "You're short for your income tax payment."

"How is that possible? I bring in so much money."

"Your supply bills were astronomical this month," Leo said.

"Again? I'll make it, I have a big job next week."

It was difficult to digest. Even as my success grew, nothing around me stayed. I caught my latest receptionist stealing. I discovered my tickets torn up in the trash and money missing from the drawer. I had to let her go. I quickly hired my client's daughter, Joanie Glick.

"Your son had to be corrected four times today for his white shirt being outside of his pants," his teacher said when I picked Adam up curbside after school. "We cannot have that at Buckley."

I looked at her and the preppy wealthy kids behind her who probably had two parents with shirts tucked in. We drove off.

"Mommy's going to find another school for you, honey," I told Adam, remembering a client telling me about a new progressive school called the Center for Early Education.

"Good, I don't like it there."

We stopped at the market. I did minimal shopping, dragging my son, who wanted everything on the shelves, and then went home.

I put some Bob Dylan on the stereo.

While Adam and Daisy played, I began to make spaghetti dinner. My housekeeper came into the kitchen. "Sorry, miss, I have a new job next week with more money and one child."

I blew out my last wind and said, *"Bueno para usted, Teresa. Adiós."*

I put down my wooden spoon, lowered the heat on the sauce, went to the freezer, grabbed the Aquavit, poured a double shot and slammed it back, and Bob Dylan's lyrics filtered in. *She's an artist, She don't look back . . .*

One evening Richard brought Billy and me over to Rita Hayworth's home for drinks. "It's time she meets you," Richard said. He pushed the buzzer. "It's me."

Rita opened the door all smiles, but it quickly changed when she saw Billy and me. "You know Billy," Richard said as we walked in. "And this is Carrie . . . are those new rugs, babe?"

It got colder than Siberia in five seconds.

"Has it been that long since I've seen you, Richard?"

Billy interrupted like a Washington diplomat. "Soooo, Rita, dah-lin' . . . what're you workin' on these days?"

Rita's eyes were on Richard.

"I'm filming in Italy next week," she said, then to Richard, "I thought *we* were going to have an evening together before I left."

A housekeeper brought us wine.

"We are. Right now. But we can't stay long."

We toasted. Drank. Richard walked to the bathroom. Rita followed.

"This is crazy," I said to Billy, commenting on the vibe.

"Don't worry yer pretty little head, Richard knows what he's doin'."

"You guys change girlfriends like underwear."

They returned; Richard looked fine, Rita looked pissed.

"You must have a lot to do," Richard said. "And we have dinner reservations."

Billy jumped up. "'Bye for now, you gorgeous *thang.*" Billy took her hand and kissed it. Richard kissed her cheek and walked out and I followed. "It was so nice to meet you," I said, exiting. Rita slammed the door before my heels left her threshold, nearly knocking me out of her house.

Richard caught me before I tripped, and I said, "What did you say?"

"I told her I wasn't going to be seeing anyone but you from now on."

Richard said all the right things to me, but I began to doubt my sanity attaching myself to this roving confirmed bachelor. I knew I had a jealous trigger that I kept well hidden, but it seemed incurable. I thought if Richard and I worked together, he'd remember he was in love with me.

Richard and I sat by my fireplace after the kids were asleep. We were having some Châteauneuf-du-Pape.

"Why not move into my salon?"

"I can't leave poor ol' Mickey and Eddie, and Gloria and Vern. We're good friends, and I could never work without Mary."

I snuggled into the comfort of his arms. I *was* his girlfriend, he practically lived at my house. Billy had taken over Richard's bachelor pad.

"I have room for everyone."

Richard paused. *Sketches of Spain* played on my turntable.

A few weeks later, Richard brought over all his people. I needed Mary as much as Richard did. While I worked on one side of my balcony, Richard worked on the other. He found me a new receptionist named Irit. It was a little weird, though, she was an ex-girlfriend of Richard's, Rita's close friend, and she was dating Bucky. Oh well. She was sweet and gorgeous and I needed her.

We took another trip to San Francisco. I met more of his family—his brother and his brother's family. It was a big night. We went upstairs.

"Come here," Richard said. "I want to show you something."

I walked over to where he sat on a trunk, looking out the window that he had built, to see the sparkling evening star and a cloud traveling by. He patted his leg for me to sit on, put his arms around me, and looked me in my left eye . . . Richard always told me *it's the eye of truth*.

"See that star?" he said. "I want to be with you until it drops from the sky."

I looked at him.

"Will you be my first, one-and-only Mrs. Richard Alcala?"

I thought of the first time Richard drove me, Adam, and Daisy to Olvera Street for tacos. He made sure we all noticed the silhouettes of the palm trees lining the freeway as we drove. "See how some are tall and skinny and some are fat and full?" he asked the children. "They were brought to California from Mexico long ago." It was never about the destination with Richard, always the journey. I loved how he honored his Latin heritage. I loved how he took us on trips, to Santa Paula for fresh fruit or a remote place downtown for Armenian food. We would eat lahmejun, a small thin pizza, from the special stand where he knew the owner. Richard hoisted Adam up on a stool and sat next to him. "I have a big family now," Richard told the owner. I climbed onto the next stool and put Daisy on my lap. We each ate one, and took a dozen fresh ones home.

I had never seen my L.A. like I did through the eyes of this San Franciscan.

I thought about what a delicious cook Richard was, what a fun dancer, a beautiful lover, and my hair hero. Although he had lost interest in hair, he was sparking back since he was working with me.

Most important, I loved that Richard loved my children and they liked him. Richard was the first man, other than their father, that I

had let around them. Because of Johnny, I was skeptical and protective. I watched his behavior. He was never overly involved with Daisy,
talking to her in a way I would find suspicious, nor did he insist she sit
on his lap. And Richard had a wonderful family and that was always
a missing limb in my life.

I touched his cheeks with my hands and looked deep into his
black eyes, ancient as Mexico, wise as the owl, and beautiful as Korla
Pandit. I felt weightless. I gave him my best kiss and melted into his
body. I answered his question: "I am Mrs. Richard Alcala . . . since the
first day I met you."

Richard planned another trip. "It's time we go to the Joshua Tree
Monument. Teddy Markland has a house there, but more important,
he has a *mountain.*"

Richard's friends Marsia and Yipi met us at my house about midnight. Marsia wore tight hip hugger jeans, a sheer T-shirt, and a
paper-thin leather jacket she had made, along with a rhinestone glitter belt that had a sheriff's star for the buckle.

"Will you be warm enough? Richard told me it gets freezing there
at night."

Marsia Trinder was *the* hippest chick I ever met. Her parents
were Lord and Lady Mayor of London and she was a full-on rebel
artist. Before I met her, I saw a picture of her with a small *Vogue*
write-up, because she designed the clothes for *Hair* in London at
producer Michael Butler's request. I showed Richard the picture.
"This is the coolest haircut." "She does it herself," Richard said. "How
could you know that?" "Because she goes with my friend Yipi." I
laughed. "Is that a name?" "Yeah, and they will be here in a week.
Yipi was the star of *Hair* in Acapulco. The president of Mexico shut
it down."

Marsia answered my question, "I'm always hot."

"She sure is," Yipi agreed, with charisma that would make a nun
strip.

Richard walked in from our bedroom, dressed in Levi's, tan cowboy boots, a black V-neck sweater pulled over a white T-shirt, and
his turquoise necklace with coral pieces in between each turquoise

chunk. He had a vintage Pendleton jacket in one hand and a big Indian blanket in the other.

"Hey, man, I brought peyote pills," Richard said. "And peyote tea to wash them down."

"It's three-thirty AM here on KFWB and . . ."

We pulled off the highway to the sparsely lit road. Richard reached into his pocket and took out the magic pills, wrapped carefully in Kleenex. Marsia unscrewed the jar of peyote tea. Richard gave one to Marsia and Yipi, then turned to me. "Open up."

I looked at Richard.

"You're going to love this," he said. "Don't worry."

Richard reassured me that psychedelics were a spiritual experience, a ritual with God and nature. It was the first time I ever trusted anyone so much in my life.

I took the capsule of beige powder and reached for the peyote juice.

"How long does this take? And how long does it last?"

"Too late for that question," Marsia laughed. "And you'll wish it lasted longer."

"The moon is full," Richard said and turned off the headlights. The desert was a pool of private luminosity. I saw weird trees that looked like furry ballet dancers out of a Dr. Seuss book. The further in we drove in, piles of stones turned into bigger piles forming sculptures. Hendrix played softly on the radio.

"There's Teddy's parked car." Richard pulled over.

Teddy got out of his car and sauntered over like a highway patrol cop. "You kids all good in here?" he said, peering into the car.

Teddy was an actor friend of Richard's. He was an extra in *Easy Rider* and hung out with Peter Fonda, Dennis Hopper, and John Phillip Law. This was just another night for him.

"Yeah, man," Richard said. "We're cool."

"So, just one *virgin* tonight?" Teddy squinted his eyes at me like an evil ruler.

"Teddy!" I said. "You're freaking me out."

Richard helped me out of the car. We looked at this giant mountain off the road in the middle of nowhere.

"There it is, Teddy's mountain. He brings people here twice a week. He brought Timothy Leary a few times."

The walk up the mountain was rocky and steep.

"Walk in my footsteps," Richard said, "and you'll be fine."

I put my foot where he had just stepped, solid ground, no crumbling earth. I thought I saw a diamond on the ground but I kept moving, blinking and squinting. I wanted to stop but I didn't want to lose Richard, I didn't want to slip. I looked down and I saw two more diamonds.

"Wow," I said. "Did you see that?"

"What?" Richard said, climbing ahead of me with our picnic basket.

"Someone dropped a diamond, I think," I said. "Two, actually."

Richard looked back to me. "You'll find lots of things here."

His voice echoed like it was coming from another mountain. I took another step and looked on the ground again. A big sapphire was shining by a small cactus to my left. Another step and three sapphires hid behind a bigger cactus, another step and a cluster of amethysts appeared by my foot. I moved to the side not to crush them, but I stepped on a bigger group of topaz stones. My mouth dropped. I took another step and I found myself in a bed of rubies.

"Jesus God, this place is unbelievable." But Richard had gone too far up the mountain to hear me. I was on my own. I couldn't figure out where he stepped anymore, and it didn't matter. I knew . . . keep walking *up*.

The black sky was full of pinholes with light streaming through from the other side. The bright moon had rainbow rings around it and was moving in the slowest motion. I looked at the face in the moon, a perfect old man smiling down on me. I felt I had done everything right all my life to deserve this honored night. I took one last big step onto the flat plateau where everyone was standing still at different edges looking out to the surrounding vastness.

This was the *highest* I had ever been . . . in every way.

I wandered over to Richard. He looked like an Indian chief wrapped in the Indian blanket he brought for us to sit on. He unwrapped and laid out the blanket.

We sat down.

"We will watch the moon go down . . . and the sun come up," Richard said.

I snuggled close to him. I wrapped my arms around him and held on.

Richard and I worked together all day and enjoyed each other all night. Business was good. My children were good. Life was good.

"Put the suitcases here for now," I told Richard, who had just returned from picking up Melvin and Button at the L.A. airport. "You guys are so late."

"The traffic is dreadful," Button said, in her authoritative English manner.

"It's Saturday night, Button," Melvin jumped in. "Californians have to go out on Saturday night."

"Guess what, I'm not drinking," I said so proudly. "And I quit smoking." This was huge for me. I had never tried to *not* drink before. Many of our friends were becoming vegetarians, involved with Yogi Bhajan and yoga, so I thought it would be fashionable and interesting. And yes, I knew it was a healthy idea, not that that had ever appealed to me before. But being so happy and in love with Richard made it the perfect time to try this. "I've been drinking since I was six and smoking since ten."

Melvin laughed. "So," he said, "you're on a health kick now?"

Not drinking and being healthy was not new for Melvin. He had worked out in a gym since he was a kid.

"How 'bout some healthy pot, Melvin?" Richard hollered from the kitchen.

"I'll lock up," I said.

I turned out the lights in each room, with my clear head and eyes devouring my special belongings in my new life: my needlepoint pillows that took me years to make, my paintings, one of Alice B. Toklas and Gertrude Stein, the other of all my rock and roll heroes—Hendrix, Morrison, Janis, Gracie Slick, and James Brown—standing together in one painting, and another sad and humorous painting of an old man and an obvious hooker at opposite ends of a Cooper's doughnut counter in the wee hours of the night. I checked that the side doors were locked and I brushed my hand over the detailed hand-carved Chinese trunk my grandmother gave me. I blew a kiss to my camel like saying good night to my child.

Last, I went to the dining room and stashed my purse with $500 in cash, which I would need for taking the Sokolskys to the Rose Bowl swap meet tomorrow. I didn't need my purse . . . no cigarettes.

I locked the front door and jumped into the car with everyone.

We arrived at the home of Elaine Baker, owner of the Aware Inn restaurant. We all took off our shoes, ate an Indian vegetarian meal, and listened to Ravi Shankar music. Johnny Rivers and Billy were there. Kundalini yoga had hit Hollywood. I liked the Indian dress and jewels, but head wraps weren't for me, not good for my business.

Yogi Bhajan stood tall in the middle of the living room in his white robe and turban with the large amethyst jewel above his third eye. He was here to tell us how to live a better, glowing life. Los Angeles was glowing already, mostly from doing Owsley acid aka Orange Sunshine.

"You need to change your ring from that finger," he said, pointing to the antique sapphire ring my grandmother gave me, her mother's ring, which I wore on my middle finger. "That is your Saturn finger of Destiny . . . it must never be strangled."

We excused ourselves and dashed to a private midnight screening at the Westwood Theater of Papa John Phillips's film-producing debut: *Monterey Pop.*

I felt surprisingly invigorated at this late hour without drinks or drugs, the abstinence high I had heard people talk about.

It was after 2:00 AM. Now I was fading fast and it was *three hours later* for our New York guests. When we pulled up my driveway, I noticed a flood of water.

"Richard, did you leave the hose on?"

We got out and Richard went to check the faucet on the side of the house.

"It's so dark," Button said. "I think the porch is wet too."

"Sorry," I said. "I was sure I put the light on."

I got out my key and Richard hollered, "We've been robbed."

I turned the key, pushed the door and it fell down to the ground. I saw the black hollow cave of my living room and smelled the vestiges of an inferno.

"Oh, God, there's been a fire!"

I felt the floor go out from under me.

Richard ran over and wrapped his arms around me, but I couldn't stand to be touched.

"Thank God Adam and Daisy weren't here." I rocked, standing in place. Everything flashed by; my new beginnings were my latest endings. I couldn't imagine how to pick up these pieces. I was tired before I got home, now I felt buried alive. The smoldering charred wood smell was wrapping itself around every hair in my nose. I was nauseous and couldn't stop sobbing. I heard Button say, "Melvin, it's burnt to a crisp here." Melvin was silently assessing the situation.

Richard said, "There's a note. It says to report to the fire station."

"I need a minute alone." I walked out into the front yard, my feet sinking into the water on the lawn. My home looked fine on the outside. It was too much to absorb. I walked up the street—no lights on in the other homes, no neighbors waiting to tell us what happened. Finally I had a thought worth having: I need ten cigarettes. I need a triple vodka. I need ether.

Richard met me with the note. "We should go to the fire station, it's close by."

"Richard, I just want a drink and a cigarette."

"Okay, but right now we just need to get to the fire station."

As we drove, I started being grateful I hadn't come home to the flames and tried to jump in to save baby pictures or stupid jewelry or God knows what.

There was one fireman on the graveyard shift. "It happened near eleven PM. We couldn't find the fire's origin. It wasn't electrical."

"No one was smoking," I said, through sniffles.

"One of our firemen picked up the table, threw it through the French doors, and found this sitting underneath." He handed me my purse. Nothing else was saved. I flashed on how *I really had* said good-bye to my belongings.

"Let's check into a hotel," Richard said. "We can figure this out tomorrow."

Richard drove with his arm around me, trying to shift and hold me at the same time. We went to the Continental, otherwise known as the Rock and Roll Hotel, on Sunset. We stormed into the lobby, full of soot and tears. I stood at the polished wood counter.

"We need two rooms," I said.

The receptionist responded, "Do you have reservations?"

"*RESERVATIONS?*" I screamed. "My house just burned down. What do you think? I planned a fire at midnight and a room at *FOUR AM*??"

No vacancies. We went down the Strip. No vacancies. We went to La Cienega and Santa Monica. No vacancies.

Finally a motor hotel on Beverly near Fairfax took us. I wanted to crawl inside of Richard and sleep for a year. The walls were paper-thin. The couple in the room next to us was either on a cheap honeymoon or making a porn film. The banging of their headboard never stopped. Not that I could have slept if I was in silence, but this *fucking* noise made the time double hell.

It was 5:30 AM. Where was my drink . . . and the cigarette? How much upheaval could I take in one lifetime?

Tick tick tick tick tick . . .

Get Set, Go

Starting over. A lot of shampoo sets and haircuts went up in smoke, along with the tragic loss of all my children's photographs.

Richard took us to the Malibu Inn Hotel for a few days. We needed fresh air. Billy was still living at Richard's, but the phone was disconnected. We found Billy, booted him out, and Adam, Daisy, and I moved into the bachelor pad with nothing but new toothbrushes— that was it. My kids were confused.

"Mommy, what happened, how come our house burned down?" Adam asked.

I didn't have an answer. I was depressed and devastated, with no time to stay that way. "This is our home for a while, sweetheart, we're gonna to be fine."

Richard's place wasn't fine, though, it had turned into a slum with Billy at the helm. He had let the electricity lapse, so dusty melted candles dripped off the mock fireplace and in every ledge and table in every room. Billy hadn't noticed since he was always stoned, slept all day, and there were no lights at night to reveal the filth.

Mary Williams came over to help us and bring motherly love. We put new sheets on Richard's bed and Mary said, "Sumpthin' good always comes out o' every tragedy."

"Well, I can't find it, Mary!"

"Honey chil' . . . now you're in *Richard's home!*"

I loved being in Richard's home, but it was too small for all of us. Again I was saved by a client.

"My sister's husband is Helmut Dantine," my client Marty Stevens said. "He has a place for rent in Benedict Canyon."

It was four acres and five hundred dollars a month, which was a huge financial stretch.

Rows of avocado trees flanked the steep driveway.

"Kids, be careful," I said, as they jumped out of the car. "No running."

There was a forty-foot drop off the embankment at the side of the garage and driveway. Richard held my hand and we looked inside the little two-story farmhouse. It was perfect. My children would have their own large space in a loftlike room above ours. We walked into the living room.

"A fireplace!" Richard said. "Let's take it."

I looked at the kitchen with its big window facing the huge backyard. The kids raced back and forth chasing each other, in one room and out the other. I was thrilled for them. In their short little lives, they had been moving so fast alongside me. All I wanted was to be still and build a real life for my babies and myself with Richard.

"Hey," I said, "we even have a guest room."

There was an add-on room with sliding glass windows, overlooking a garden of roses with heads the size of cabbages. It was a real country home only minutes from the hustle and bustle of Beverly Hills.

Richard said. "We will be married *here*."

"Wake up, wake up, Carrie," Richard said. "What's going on?"

It was the morning of August 6, 1969. I was in a sweat. It was just getting light and I had been tossing and turning from a horrifying nightmare. "It was so real," I said, on the verge of tears. "I was coming out of a bathroom, walking down a long hall. I passed a den and overheard two men talking about murder: a small dark man was folded up on a couch in lotus position, giving orders. He was dark; dark hair, dark eyes, dark aura, and gave deliberate orders through his bearded mouth—'You must kill everyone in the house.' I sensed myself in the hall eavesdropping. I was naked. I know, weird."

Richard held me and listened to my tale full of panic.

"The other guy taking the orders questioned, 'Everyone? Do we have to kill everyone?' '*They must all die*,' the dark one answered. I ran to find you and said, 'Richard, we have to get out of here, now.' We ran out to the driveway, through big iron gates, and when I looked back at the house, bombs burst through the windows. I was screaming and crying. That's when you woke me. We were at a party at Roman and Sharon's house."

"It was just a bad dream," Richard said, and he got out of bed. "I'm going to make us some hobo coffee and eggs, we gotta get to the salon."

"I can't eat," I said, realizing what I needed, the one thing that would comfort me. "But I'll have a screwdriver."

Later, Billy sauntered into my salon. "Hey, baby dahlin'." He looked thin and so did his hair.

"Billy you need a trim," I said, laughing. "You look like a crazy person."

Richard and I were at the desk. Billy leaned in. "You need *wake-up*?"

"Oh yeah," Richard said, and we all walked into the dispensary and pulled the curtain closed.

"Just a little sumpthin' sumpthin' in from Peru." Billy said. "I call it the Inca Message." We each had a big hit from Billy's long-nailed pinky finger.

"Ummm," I said, "I needed that."

"Yeah," Richard said. "How much of that message you got, my friend?"

"I can score whatever you need."

"Let's get some of our own," I said. I really liked cocaine. It was better than the grinding effect of the diet pill. It gave me a creative brain spurt.

"Hey, I'm waiting on a big job, and it would be groovy if I could stay with you guys for a little bit," Billy said. "You know, just till my first paycheck. I'm hookin' up with a new friend, Jimmy Ford, another big music deal, and—"

Richard stopped him. "We always got room for you."

"And the kids love their uncle Billy around."

Billy was fantastic with Adam and Daisy. He got them gluing things, decorating stuff, making pictures, or beading hippie neck-laces. Billy was still nothing but fun.

"I gotta go," I said. "I'm late."

"Whar you off to?" Billy said.

"Beverly Wilshire Hotel . . . to cut Warren."

"He still lives in that penthouse?" Billy turned to Richard. "And I thought you cut Warren's hair."

"I gave him to Carrie." Richard smiled. "I think he likes her better."

Two days later I did Julie Christie's hair for a *Vogue* layout. Warren was dating Julie and he popped in on the shoot. Knowing Warren made it easier to get close to Julie. I wanted to capture her as a client after the shoot.

I was *thrilled* to work for the great Richard Avedon. I also got to work with the great style editor Polly Mellen. She would hold up three garments, look at them, then throw two on the ground. "This is it," Polly would exclaim, like she discovered gold. "This is the shot, don't you agree, Richard?" Polly and Richard worked off of each other like two artists creating the same painting.

AUGUST 9, 1969

Saturday morning. Richard and I were driving the picturesque Benedict Canyon road to work. He pulled out a joint. I turned on the radio. *"Sharon Tate and friends have been found in a bloody massacre at her Beverly Hills home."* I froze. *"All have been murdered."*

Richard slowed down the car and looked at me, remembering my recent nightmare.

". . . a massacre with the word Pig written in blood across the front door."

I was in shock and started sobbing.

We got to the salon and clients rushed us at the door. My phones were ringing off the hook: *was I the hairdresser that was killed with Sharon?*

"What hairdresser?

Slowly more news came in. It was my friend Jay Sebring. And my client Abigail Folger. I got sicker from every new phone call.

AUGUST 10, 1969

The next night, more people were massacred in the same way. It was baffling and horrifying. Our town changed forever. Overnight, gates were built; alarms were installed in homes. No more opened or unlocked doors.

And definitely no more picking up hitchhikers.

Peace and Love had been betrayed.

AUGUST 20, 1969

Eleven days after Sharon's murder, Richard; Ann-Margret; her husband, Roger Smith, and I gratefully took off to the Hollywood Bowl. Our box seats for Janis Joplin were practically onstage.

"I performed on that stage," I said, happy to be talking about something other than the murders, as we settled in for Janis's opening act with our picnic dinner and wine.

"You did?" Ann-Margret said.

"I sure did—Hollywood High classes graduate here."

"That's a good one," Roger laughed.

The lights flashed and the opening act came onstage.

"Tommy Tucker talks about this band playing in Golden Gate Park all the time," Richard said, and nodded to the stage. The first strums of the guitar got our undivided attention. "They call themselves Santana."

It was a volcano of Latin music meets rock and roll. I loved their revolutionary sounds but still I couldn't wait for Janis to fill the universe. I knew she would hit every star in the sky with her voice. This would be better than the Fillmore, no lid, no roof to shrink her blast. Pot was the only fragrance in the air. The buzz in the audience was higher than the surrounding trees.

"And now . . . *Janis Joplin* . . . and the Holding Company."

AUGUST 25, 1969

My twenty-sixth birthday. Still no answers regarding Sharon's murderers.

A month later, Warren and Julie, Robert Towne, and his wife, my dear Julie Payne, Richard, and I met at Dominick's to discuss ideas for Robert's new film that I would be technical adviser for. We all knew Robert from back in the day, when he walked around Beverly Hills with scripts under his arms, trying to meet the right people at Jack Hansen's tennis parties every Sunday.

"This was one of my first screenplays." Robert said. "I wrote it in your shop, Richard, and Gene Shacove's salon, too. But it's all your characters, your wealthy married girlfriend and her husband that you cut. I even put in your maid, Mary, and your ex-girlfriend Mollie as the receptionist."

No one had wanted Robert's hairdresser story until he'd established himself with Jack in *The Last Detail* and helped Warren with *Bonnie and Clyde*.

"The working title is *Shampoo*," Robert said.

Warren was producing *Shampoo*. He was also perfect for playing the woman-charmer lead. When he sat in my chair and I cut his hair, he would tease me with sexy remarks, or slyly drop his arm and grab my leg to see me jump. He knew I was loyal to Richard but he couldn't help himself. The rumor about Warren was that he gave a lot of girls self-worth, if only for one night.

"And Carrie," Robert promised, "you'll have screen credits and money."

"I can't believe they haven't found the killers yet," Julie blurted, off the subject. We stopped in our tracks. We all shared friendships with Roman, Sharon, and Jay.

Warren said, "Peter Sellers offered a ten-thousand-dollar reward for any information leading to the killers."

I finished my drink. "Richard, I'll have another martini."

Home on the Hill

Richard and I married on Valentine's Day 1970, in our backyard, under a big tree branch that years ago had broken in half and formed a perfect arch. Family and friends and special clients joined us.

Our wedding present from the Sokolskys was one of Melvin's prized treasures, a 150-pound Newfoundland. He was the grandson of Newton, the top-winning Newfoundland in American Kennel Club history. Melvin had been raising pedigreed Newfoundlands for years in Upstate New York. I named our beautiful gift Max, after Maxfield Parrish. Adam and Daisy would ride Max like a horse.

We all nested in, including Billy, who had temporarily moved into our glass guest room, off our rose garden. Every day I would tell the children, "Shhh, don't wake Billy, he got in late last night." It was pretty hopeless, though; Adam and Daisy didn't know how to play quietly. Neither did Max, who bumped furniture as he swaggered through the house wagging his tail. Then there was the sunshine streaming into his curtainless room, and add the morning *cock-a-doodle-do*, because Richard decided to bring home a pet rooster and a hen one Sunday.

"I think Mama Hen has a crush on me," Billy said, shuffling into the kitchen looking for coffee. "I got up to take a leak, and when I came back, she left me a gift."

I walked into Billy's room and there was a fresh chicken egg in the center of his pillow. After that, Mama Hen laid one egg on Billy's pillow every morning, and a few times right next to his head, because he hadn't gotten up yet.

APRIL 4, 1970

Richard's birthday. He turned thirty-seven. What could I give my newly married, no longer confirmed bachelor?

I wrapped up an empty box of my Enovid birth control pills and made him a card that read: *Happy Birthday but you'll have to wait.*

It took him awhile, but then he got it. "Really?"

"Yes, you're old, we need to get started."

OCTOBER 1970

"Carrie, it's me, Bill." Bill Cosby was calling from Massachusetts. "Camille's birthday is coming up, I don't know what to get her. I know she likes you, could you come to Tahoe in a week and do her hair?"

We flew to San Fran to get the Tuckers, and all drove to Tahoe in a rented red Cadillac convertible.

I was seven and a half months pregnant.

DECEMBER 31, 1970

Michelle Phillips was engaged to *my* second boyfriend, Jack Nicholson. They invited us and a hundred other friends over to Jack's house for a New Year's Eve bash. I came in and found the biggest, most comfortable seat for myself. I was afraid to move all evening, let alone tap my toe to the party music. I was due with Richard's first child any minute. I'm sure I knew everyone there, I just don't remember much except trying *not* to have my baby. I was the elephant in the living room that people walked around.

9, 8, 7, 6, 5, 4, 3, 2, 1, Happy New Year!

Richard gave me a big kiss and said, "I better get my young beautiful bride home now."

King Richard, I called him, because he treated me like a queen. I loved a line in the play *The Heiress,* when she was asked, "Why do you love him over the others?" And she answers, "Because he loved me for all those who did not."

⌒

JANUARY 4, 1971

Exactly nine months to the *day* from Richard's birthday, his first child was born: Aloma Alcala.

I had told my best friend, Aloma, "Richard said if we have a baby girl that I could name her after you." And she said, "If you give your child my name, I better clean up the name."

My friend Aloma had crazy out-of-control bouts with drinking and drug using. I thought she should just pace herself better, but I found out she was shooting morphine and doing hard drugs with another group of friends that I had never met. She ended up in the psychiatric ward at Cedars-Sinai after a few suicide attempts. I would visit her and cut all her inmate friends' hair. When she got out of the hospital, she started going to AA meetings. She wanted me to join her, but it sounded awful and boring.

For our Valentine's anniversary, I got Richard new white Gucci loafers. He got me a Gucci scarf, rings, and bag. Gucci was a new store that had just moved around the corner from my salon on Rodeo Drive. Before that I didn't know what a Gucci was. This store changed Rodeo Drive forever, and not just fashion-wise. I was informed that my rent was going to be raised from five hundred to eight hundred dollars a month.

This was going to be difficult because, even though I was getting busier, Richard's hairdressing business was slow. He had become the domesticated cat: not flirting and dating his clients. He was a good hairdresser and he had his stable of ladies, but without the Casanova incentive, he lacked ambition.

One night, Hugh Masekela brought over Charlie Smalls. Hughie brought a small brown paper bag full of ganja pot. He twisted the open end of the bag, lit the other, and said in his deep African accent, "Who needs rolling papers?"

After we stopped laughing, he passed the bag around, until the kitchen floor was a mess of pot and ashes. The guys talked about old African ceremonies and tribal dances with rubber boots making sounds of thunder, and the never-ending political trouble in Johannesburg. Then they cycled back to music.

"A *black* Dorothy?" Billy said to Charlie.

"You gotta do it, man," Hughie said.

"I'm serious, I'm thinkin' Broadway," Charlie said. "Maybe call it *The Wiz*."

Every night was a party at our house. I couldn't wait to get the kids to sleep, fix my hair, put on a fabulous Marsia Trinder outfit, and get ready for whoever the evening's guest might be. The fireplace crackled, sounds of John Coltrane or Dr. John streamed, drinks flowed, an abundance of party pot, and on good nights, the dessert of cocaine . . .

Cocaine was the perfect picker-upper from a long day of hair. It was perfect in between doing hair. Basically, I found it perfect for all occasions.

"I'll get it." I pulled my short chamois leather dress into place and then walked casually to the screen door, my heart pounding with excitement. I knew who was expected this night.

"Carrie, this is Sly," Jimmy Ford said, and walked into the living room to see Billy and Richard. I was at my door, alone with Sly Stone. He was a freeze frame of cool, big lips without a smile, all eyes and gorgeous. He was dressed for a concert performance, wild Afro under his glittery cowboy hat, tight white leather pants and a fringed jacket with his shirt open, making room for his jewelry to sparkle on his chocolate skin.

"Welcome," I said, like a good hostess. "What can I get you?"

Sly answered in his deep slow sexy voice, "I'll have . . . *the rest*."

Our house was definitely the fun house. Some just drank, some smoked pot, some did coke, some did not . . . and some did *the rest*.

I did as much as I could. After the salon, after dark, after dinner, after clubs, after dancing, after the dishes. I was so wired up most of the time, I never wanted the night to end. And usually, an unsuspecting guest would get one of my "kitchen" haircuts before the night was through.

Back at the salon, I was about to set Priscilla Presley's hair for a new look when she popped the big question. "Do you think you could cut my husband's hair? His hairdresser got married and left town."

I covered my extreme delight, while the hot roller was burning my hand, and answered casually, "Sure, I'd love to."

I would cut Elvis's hair at his house in Holmby Hills and sometimes at his old bachelor pad that he still maintained in Trousdale. I cut wigs for him too, for disguises.

Elvis told me, "Sometimes girls crash into my car if they spot me and say, 'I know it's my fault, but would you sign an autograph for me?'"

"That's horrible," I said.

When I was with Elvis, it was my *King and I* time.

Once he asked me, "Could I wear my hair like Ricky Nelson?"

I laughed. "Elvis, let's not mess with your success."

Even Elvis wanted to look like someone else sometimes. I knew he dyed his light hair black because he loved Roy Orbison. I thought, *Hairdressing will never be obsolete.*

Elvis called out to his bodyguard, "Go get Carrie a gun."

"El, I don't want a gun, I don't like guns, I don't need a gun."

Elvis had collections of guns on every wall, all sizes and styles.

"*Yes* you do," Elvis said. "You'll sleep so much better tonight."

"*Charlie*, get her that lady's Derringer, the one that fits in an evening bag."

"An evening bag? And what kind of evening would that be?"

"And get her a box of bullets too," Elvis hollered.

"Richard," I said, one morning a little after our second wedding anniversary, when our daughter Aloma had just turned one. "I think I'm pregnant."

"We just had a baby," Richard said.

"I know, but I think we're going to have another one."

We had just moved to a smaller salon that Richard found. It was one block east of Doheny, on Burton Way and Wetherly, on a corner with full window views, keeping the place bright and cheery. The first thing to get installed were the big speakers that hooked up to my radio. Next we painted everything. I had no time or money to build anything to hide the big pipes and vents, so I painted them all chrome silver.

Quincy Jones's wife, Ulla, sent her girlfriend Joanna Shimkus to me, an astounding beauty, natural, sexy, with a quiet presence, unlike most of us chicks. "You're not going to have a baby before you finish my highlights, are you?" Joanna smiled.

"I'm always pregnant." I laughed. "Don't worry, no baby today."

I wasn't doing any drugs, because I was pregnant, so no Mother's little helpers, but I almost drank the Windex in a plastic cup thinking it was champagne. I asked Richard, "Should I put a new sign out, Mrs. Richard Alcala, or Richard and Carrie Alcala, or Richard Alcala and—" Richard interrupted. "Just put Carrie White, in neon lights," he said. "Everyone knows *your* name."

He insisted I have his giant gilded mirror, the mirror I first saw him in, the mirror he took to Sunset Plaza, the mirror he brought to my Brighton Way salon . . . that mirror was now mine.

I gave Joanna a headful of highlights, cut and styled her hair. She was pleased, which made me even more pleased. Her boyfriend walked in to pick her up.

I took a private gasp. I had been in love with him since I'd seen *Blackboard Jungle* in Pacoima. Her boyfriend was the handsome Sidney Poitier.

Life Grows On

A very hot August and hotter for me. I was due to have my fifth child any day. I was twenty-eight.

AUGUST 14, 1972

It was the crack of dawn and I hadn't been comfortable all night. My last resort was a chair off to the side of our bed. I buried my head in the seat, arching my back, creating a hammock for my baby, and at last I fell asleep.

Richard woke me. "You're upside-down and moaning."

"I'm fine, just gas pains."

"Are you sure you're not having the baby?"

"Richard, after all the babies I've had, I think I'd know if I was having a baby."

I walked into the bathroom and lay down in a ball on the cool soothing tile. It was better than standing on my head in the chair. I was almost asleep when my gas pains started getting more frequent and my moans woke me up.

"Carrie," Richard yelled. "Where are you having our baby now?"

"I'm here." I kicked the door open with my leg. "No, I'm not having a—" Another violent gas pain with no time in between. "*YES . . . I AM HAVING A BABY, HURRY, CALL THE DOCTOR!*"

"I knew it, I told you so." He grabbed my overnight bag and started to leave.

"What is it . . . what is it?" I cried out.

"Another princess," Richard said proudly.

Richard got to name this child, because I had named our firstborn.

Months earlier, Richard brought me a copy of *Women's Wear Daily,* with the photo of a royal beauty from Greece on the front page. "How do you like this name if it's a girl?" and pointed to her name. "P, I-dot, T-cross, I-dot, T-cross, A. See, two dots and two crosses: Pitita. And her middle name will be Carita, after you."

"Pitita Carita." I giggled. "Certainly an artist's signature . . . I love it."

Months after Pitita's birth, I received a call from Glemby International to come to New York regarding a business proposal they had for me. I heard: free trip to New York for Richard and me.

At my request, we met at Sardi's. I had heard it was a chic hot spot.

"I love all the drawings," I said, looking at the walls over the distant bar. "Hirschfeld, right?" The Glemby people weren't interested.

They wanted to get to business. I perked up when the waiter came. "Champagne for me."

"Yes," the lead man said. "Let's have a bottle of Dom."

"I've always wanted to come here," I said.

"Let's talk about why you are *really* here," the lead man said. "We want to talk to you about *syndication*."

I had no idea what that word meant, but I didn't want to sound dumb, so I stayed *dumb* and didn't ask any questions. He went on.

"We have big plans for you . . ." I had enough plates spinning in the air already, to add one more thing just sounded like more pressure. In fact, the Glemby men sounded like a Peanuts cartoon, "wah wah wah," talking of *big things, big money,* and their *big factory.* "So, Carrie . . ."

The waiter came and poured our drinks. Mine went down quickly.

"Someone was thirsty," one Glemby guy said.

"I *was.*" I smiled. "Now I'll have one to sip," and I held up my glass.

"We at Glemby International are interested in creating Carrie White salons all over the country."

"A franchise?" Richard said.

"Yes," another said, and directed his conversation to Richard, as if Richard might be the brains behind the Carrie White Salon. I felt relief and I could actually listen better. They chattered about how great it would be for *me*, about *me* traveling, *me* teaching in schools, promoting my many salons. "One day you'll make an appearance in Philadelphia and another day in Texas and—"

"Whoa," I said, picking up my champagne. "How do I know if I'll feel like going to Philly and Texas?" I took a big swallow. "I'm used to *one* key, one salon, and if I want to go away, I leave a note, *Gone fishing, do your own hair.*"

They laughed and asked how I could have such a successful reputation and think like that.

I smiled. "Are we going to order more champagne?"

After Glemby, we went to visit Aloma's friend, artist Joe Eula, at his studio apartment across from Carnegie Hall. Joe was famous for his illustrations of couture collections for *Vogue* and *Harper's Bazaar.*

Joe was occupied with his work for a new designer, Halston, who was the rage, designing sexy clingy comfortable fashions made out of silk jersey that went on a women's body like something for the bedroom. "It's fashion as revolution," Joe said. Halston was dressing everyone from Elizabeth Taylor to Liza Minnelli.

I never heard back from Glemby Enterprises. Not that I really cared.

Joe Eula came for an L.A. visit and called me to pick up his jewelry designer friend, Elsa, because Joe was already at my house with Richard.

"Elsa *Peretti*, who designed the famous silver belt for Halston?" I said.

"She just got a gig with Tiffany," Joe said. "I want you to cut her hair."

I was leaving my salon to pick up Elsa just as Billy glided in. "Hey, pretty little thang." He leaned in. "Thought you might like a little zip in your doo-dah."

"I do love the sparkle." We ducked into the back. "Pass the rest to Rich."

"Maybe I will"—I laughed—"and maybe I won't."

I drove to the Beverly Wilshire Hotel and went to the room number Joe told me. A tall, stunning woman opened the door. "Hi," she said. "You must be Carrie." She turned and said good-bye to a woman with sketches on drawing papers strewn all over one of the beds. "Why don't you come too?" I asked. She looked up for a brief second, smiled, then went back to her drawings.

"Thanks, I can't, I'm on a deadline."

"This is my friend Donna Karan," Elsa said. "She's up for a major position at Anne Klein and has to turn in her designs tomorrow."

Elsa and I arrived to find that my housekeeper, Maria, had made a big Mexican dinner for our East Coast guests. We ate and drank Richard's fantastic margaritas. I put the kids to bed. Joe walked over to Elsa and grabbed a handful of her short hair like fabric, "Cut it off," Joe said. "She's an artist, she doesn't need hair." Richard sat back smoking a joint. "Great idea," I said, and excused myself to finish off my coke stashed in the bathroom. I came back fresh and excited, and in my kitchen cut Elsa's hair shorter than Mia Farrow's. The next morning, I hoped my haircut was as fantastic as I had thought it was the night before.

"What's a limo doing in our driveway?" Richard said.

"It's Diahann's fiancé, David Frost," I said. Diahann Carroll was my client and she had bought the home next door to us. I'd tease her when I was late for a house call that the traffic was terrible. David was delivering a case of wigs for me to style for Diahann's television special I was working on.

Peter Sellers was one of my very favorite guests. Warren had me cut Peter's hair for *Being There.* Peter told me he had a trunk of assorted eyeglasses that he'd dig in to find his character's identity before he thought of anything else for his roles. Peter was always knocking things over accidentally. Very Inspector Clouseau.

"Carrie, it's Toby." Bob Rafelson's wife was on the phone. "I want to bring my friend Ellen Burstyn over for a haircut. She needs you, and can we be private?" "Sure, what's it for?" I said. "She has the lead in a film, *Alice Doesn't Live Here Anymore.*"

Every day was something or someone exciting for me to work on. My secret weapons were alcohol and cocaine. I never felt I wasted a drop or a line. It made me so happy all day and I relaxed with it at night.

At my salon, I made tea rinses for fragrance and stains for color benefits, like a cinnamon reddish rinse to counteract hair that was too ash green. I made parsley rinses and mint rinses to neutralize hair that was too red and made it smell great. I made conditioners with everything from olive oil to vinegar with lemon and vanilla. I made hair treatment packs of mayonnaise combined with whipped-up avocados.

I talked up the avocado treatment so much, the news spread to the National Avocado Committee, and a representative asked me to do a radio talk show and plug avocados. "Sure, I'd love to," I said. "That's my specialty."

After that, my client Dinah Shore said, "Come be a guest on my show," she said. "Let's give a demonstration."

The night before I was to be on the *Dinah Shore Show,* there was another party in my living room. It was about 11:00 PM. The phone rang.

"Mom, what're you doing up this late?"

We rarely spoke. I was still pissed off at her for showing up drunk at my wedding to Richard, after I begged her to not drink until she arrived.

"Your father died today."

I froze. I had only resentments for him too, not that I knew him. After he left, I saw his face only once, when he showed up at my house on El Camino, a few years back. He had the nerve to come over with a girlfriend and nothing else in his hand. We shared *my* wine. I told him off. They left. A few weeks later he called me at my salon. "Never a birthday card, Christmas call all my life, and now you want money from me? My house just burned down, ask someone else." I hung up on him. His death was the ultimate insult, leaving for a final time with no chance of ever being a father to me.

"I wish I cared," I told my mother.

"Don't you want to know how he died? He had an asthma attack—"

"Asthma?" I laughed. "That's a joke, Mom. He was a big drunk. Thanks for the call, but I gotta go, I have company."

I walked into the living room, "Richard, can you call for more champagne and get us more coke too?"

Dealers delivered.

At 3:00 AM, everyone had left except Rita. I'd finally told Richard about my phone call. He asked if I was okay, then went to bed. I stayed up all night, drinking, smoking, playing music, and talking to Rita until she passed out on the couch. I went into my den and puttered with my workbag, wondering what I was going to wear on TV.

Richard and the kids awoke around 7:00 AM. I woke Rita. "Shake, rattle, and roll."

Rita answered, puffy and groggy, "Any coke left?"

I did Dinah's show on no sleep, still stoned and full of champagne. I was careful to avoid breathing directly toward her when I spoke.

I set up my bowl of avocados, fresh parsley, cinnamon sticks, mint, and baby powder to demonstrate my emergency dry shampoo rescue; an egg to whip with mayonnaise and a can of beer for setting hair. "I don't know if we're going to do hair or have a picnic," Dinah said to her audience.

I laughed and did my thing like a robot. I was so far from my feelings I could've had my tonsils removed without anesthesia.

"Girl, I know what a music junkie you are, I'm working with Roberta tonight and thought you might like to come over."

Richard was on the bed watching TV. "Quincy called, he invited us over to meet Roberta Flack."

"I'll stay here with the kids."

"But why? Maria's here and they're asleep."

"You go, have fun, sweetheart."

I sat with a big glass of red wine in Quincy's den, where he recorded, rehearsed, and wrote music. It was always nighttime there. I chatted with Q's wife, Ulla, but mostly I eavesdropped on Q and Roberta, singing, talking, joking, getting ideas, humming up a storm. It was heaven for me to witness this process. Hours passed and Ulla wanted Quincy to come to bed.

"I can give Roberta a ride home," I said.

"You don't mind?" they said.

"Are you kidding?"

I told Roberta how much "The First Time Ever I Saw Your Face" moved me, especially the part about the captive bird. She generously sang the song for me . . . all the way to her house. I could've driven her to New York.

Quincy called again. I was at his front door before he could say Ray's last name.

"Where's Richard?" Quincy asked.

"He was in bed already."

"Okay, girl, come meet *the man*."

"Ray," Quincy said, "this is our friendly neighbor, Carrie."

"I feel your happiness," Ray said, smiling.

I'd been feelin' my *happiness* all day. Once I got wound up for work with bubbles and cocaine, I could go all night. I moved to the piano bench and told Ray about my days in Pacoima, how rhythm and blues saved my life, and especially "What'd I Say?" I had no shyness with Ray, so I flung my leg up for him to feel my new platform leather patchwork boots like Braille. "Far out," he said. I laughed. "No, you are!"

Ray swayed on the piano bench like he was getting ready to take off.

"Q, what do you say we try this?" and he began singing. It was a concert for one as far as I was concerned. Ray got stuck for a line and I belted it out, "For amber waves . . ." "You go head-on, girl," Ray chimed in.

I couldn't get the smile off my face for weeks. I told everyone, "I sang with Ray Charles and he loved my boots." A few weeks later, Quincy brought me a cassette labeled, *To our favorite White Lady*. It was Ray Charles and me singing "America the Beautiful." Quincy had been recording.

Quincy called me again. "How'd you like to do the Duke Ellington special?"

"I'll keep everyone perfect."

Day 1. I arrived and looked for my rock, Quincy. He was with the Duke. I poked my head in the dressing room door. "Thank you so much for this."

"Come on in," Quincy said. The Duke didn't need me for hair. He wore a cute captain's hat and unfortunately he was sick with a high fever. Quincy was very concerned about his friend's health. We bid the Duke good-bye and Quincy took me across the hall. "You might as well come meet someone else, there's not much for you to do today, we're still rehearsing, we film tomorrow." He opened the door and there was the spry, cool Count Basie, full of joy. Later that day I passed by to say hi again. The Count had visitors, and he insisted I come in with the magic word: "Champagne?"

Day 2. I made it a point to bring the Count a bottle of champagne. "Mumm's the word," I said. "Girl o' my own heart, let's open it right after lunch." Bud Yorkin came in.

"Roberta's waiting for you," Bud said.

"Oh, I'm sorry," I said, and dashed to Roberta's dressing room.

Roberta and I had planned her hairstyle a few days prior, at Quincy's house. She had sat for ten hours with hairdresser Omar, getting cornrow braids in a deco pattern on her head. All I had to do was *my specialty*, attach an Afro wig at the nape of her neck like a chignon. I was so proud to have been written up in *Jet* magazine for this new style and silhouette I had created for the album cover of Letta Mbulu. Roberta sat majestically at her dressing table.

"You probably should hurry," Roberta said politely. "Quincy's waiting . . . onstage."

It was a closed set. I couldn't bring Rita for assistance and I wasn't used to working alone.

"That's great," she said, and looked at the full view with a handheld mirror. "I have some changes, so don't get lost."

"I'm right here for you." I packed up my spray, combs, brushes and pins.

I went to the restroom down the hall, locked myself into the stall, and took a few extra hits of cocaine.

I went to Paula Kelly's dressing room; she was next on set. "Hi, I'm Carrie, Quincy's friend, I'm here for your hair."

Everyone in her room stopped talking.

"I don't think I need anything," Paula said. Her hair was cropped close like a bathing cap. She was a chiseled beauty.

"Oh, okay," I said, feeling out of place. "I'm here if you need me."

"Miss Kelly has to change now," someone said. I stepped out into the hall. He closed her door behind me. I was getting thirsty anyway. I went into the bathroom and repeated the drill. It was after lunch. Maybe Mr. Basie was ready for bubbles. I went to visit. Another show guest, Joe Williams, was in the Count's dressing room.

"The Duke doesn't look so good," Joe was saying. "Q's real worried."

"Hi, I'm Quincy's friend Carrie. I'm here for hair."

Joe reached out to shake. "No hair for me, maybe my wife would like something." He introduced me to his petite white schoolteacher-like wife, not what I'd expect with this jazz singer. "She's not in the show, though." Joe smiled and his wife smiled and walked out.

"Later, man," the Count said as they left, then turned to me. "Shall we have that champagne?"

"Well, sure, if you're having some . . ."

I went back to do more hair for Roberta. I stood by. We broke for dinner. I wasn't hungry. Roberta left. The Count was on stage. I watched him and Quincy work. At 10:00 PM I drove home. My kids were asleep. I joined Richard in the living room with Jimmy Ford, Billy, and our friend JD, who invented the Deering, a coke grinder.

Day 3. That morning, I took four lines before brushing my teeth.

Day 4. There was nothing for me to do until Roberta's finale. I walked down the hall to my new friend, the Count. He offered me a shot of cognac.

"There you are! I been looking for you *again*," Bud Yorkin said, finding me drinking in Mr. Basie's dressing room.

"Oh, hi, you need me?"

"One of the guys in *Chicago* needs a haircut before he goes on," Bud said. "Can you do that?"

I stopped off in the bathroom quickly to freshen up with a hit of Inca Message. I walked down the hallway peeking in doors, looking for the only white boys in the show. I heard guys laughing through a half-opened door. "Somebody need *hair*?" The guys were all kicked back on the sofas.

"I do," Robert Lamm said.

Ah. Robert Lamm. The cute one. I wanted to keep him for a client, so I let him know I cut Elvis, Joe Namath, and Warren Beatty.

"You want a drink or anything?"

I wanted to say, like Sly, *I'll take the rest.* I answered, "Sure, whatever you got there, just not Scotch, though, it tastes like soapy dishwater."

Knock, knock, knock.

"Is the hairdresser in there with you?"

"Yeah, I'm here."

"They need you on set."

I went out and fixed wigs for two dancers.

"We need you to be out here," Bud said.

"I was cutting Robert's hair."

"That was two hours ago."

"I need to go to the ladies' room," I said. "I promise I'll be *right back*."

I darted into the restroom, flushed, snorted, wiped my nose, and was back on set. A production assistant came up to me. "Could you fix a curl—"

"Oh crap, I left my workbag in the bathroom," I interrupted him and ran off.

And as long as I was in the bathroom again, and might not be back for a while, feeling the pressure from Bud, I took another hit and slugged some warm vodka from my flask. It made me ill. I held back vomit. I shouldn't mix drinks. I looked in the mirror and saw anything but a *beauty representative*. I washed my face, got out the brush for my greasy hair, and shook my head upside-down to give it volume, then threw it back and almost fainted. I collected myself and charged out the door and almost bumped into Quincy's chest.

"Oh, hi," I said. "Geez, this is amazing, I just love working with you . . ."

Quincy gave me a polite smile. It wasn't his usual smile, or his usual look into my eyes. "Yeah, and you've been fine, but . . ."

"But what?" I interrupted, afraid of his next words.

"Well, it's been called to my attention that we got it all covered from here."

I froze. "I thought we had two more days?"

Quincy put his arm around me, "It's a good thing . . . you can go home."

"Not even finish the day?"

"Girl, you get to go have dinner with your family, say hi to Richard for me, okay? I gotta get back to the set." He kissed my forehead and he walked off.

It wasn't a *good thing* to me. I felt like my mother caught with a bottle of vodka in her bag at the Broadway department store, exposed and sad. I went to the bathroom and scraped the remaining coke for a hit. I didn't flush to cover the sound and I didn't check my nose on the way out. I licked the remains from my white folded paper and tossed it in the trash. This could never happen to me again.

I had to do a better job of camouflaging my drinking and using. I had children's birthday parties to give, school events to show up for, new jobs booked from Melvin's recommendations: Michael Cimino, Bill Helburn, and Ridley Scott.

I tried to keep a wiser pace by drinking and doing blow later in the day, using less, controlling myself, unless I was at home or on the dance floor . . . then I did *the rest.*

Richard hinted about my amount of drinking and using, and I was sneaking more than what he saw. I justified my intake for *our* survival. How else could I coif fifteen clients a day? I had to be entertaining and creative and on a schedule . . . that was always late. "I'm only tired when I stop," I told everyone.

I was doing practically all the hair for any advertising that had a girl in it, from Virginia Slims to toothpaste commercials. I just said, yes— to work, to play, to drinks and drugs.

"Somebody important must be guesting . . . Carrie White's backstage," the *Tonight Show* producer Freddie de Cordova would joke, seeing me in the greenroom having a drink. At the annual SHARE (Share Happily And Reap Endlessly) charity-show-party, I worked backstage, then joined a table for dinner with Sandra Moss and Candy and Aaron Spelling. Aaron said, "Here's Carrie White, she takes care of all my *Angels.*"

I was receiving the kind of validation I'd wanted all my life. Richard remained content behind the scenes encouraging me. I wished he could bring in more money but I accepted other qualities about him as more important: his character, loyalty, and his love for me. He would introduce me in this way, "Did you meet my young beautiful wife?"

"This is neat, Mom," Adam said one morning, walking into the kitchen wearing the tie-dyed T-shirt I had made for him around 4:00 AM. I had placed it on the foot of his bed and a dress for Daisy. He looked at the kitchen at the array of spilled colors in the sink, in the pots and pans. "Did you stay up all night?"

This wasn't the first time the family would find me with rainbows of dye dripping off the stove. I had a whole private life while my family slept, especially if I had stashed cocaine. I never planned to stay up all night, but I always did. I would start with one T-shirt, and not want to stop until the cocaine and Galliano was finished, or whatever the drink of the week was.

I would twist, knot, dunk, and dip everything from baby clothes to dishtowels. It was more fun than Easter eggs. When I ran out of clothes, I'd tiptoe into someone's room for more. During these times, I drank and inhaled cocaine and cigarettes deeply, to hold the moment and embrace the quiet time, *my* time, trying to beat the morning from coming before I was ready and the damn birds started chirping. Their song meant my party was over.

Adam stood in the doorway.

"It looks great on you, honey," I said, rushing to him for a morning hug. "*I love it*, don't you?"

Richard walked in holding his shorts. "Not my underwear too? Did you stay up all night?"

"I'll be fine at work today, don't worry," I said, still buzzed. "Billy's coming by the salon with a surprise for us."

"I'm giving you first option," our landlord, Helmut Dantine, said on the phone. "I'm selling the property you're living on."

"Oh no," I said, not ready for this. "For how much?"

"One hundred thousand."

"*A HUNDRED THOUSAND? DOLLARS?* That's a lot of shampoos and sets."

I had no idea about the real world, buying a home, the cost of living. We lived month to month. If I needed extra money, I did extra hair. I'd never saved anything but Green Stamps as a child and cocaine for my morning wake-up as an adult.

I felt panicked, hopeless for a split second, then realized hairdress-ing had been my source for problem solving since the day I discov-ered it. I called my client Lenore, the real estate agent. She found us a place just around the bend on Mulholland Drive. No school changes and plenty of room for Max to romp.

Still, I hated leaving the home where Richard and I were married.

My mother called for the first time since she phoned about my fa-ther's death, asking me to take her to the Hollywood Presbyterian Hospital. I picked her up at her Hollywood apartment and waited for her in the driveway. She weighed eighty-nine pounds. Her legs were like toothpicks stuck into marshmallows, her ankles swollen like elephantiasis. Her once pretty face was now covered in broken red and purple capillaries and her black eyes were enlarged glazed gray-brown circles in pools of yellow bloodshot sadness. Bill had left my mother for her best friend, Marion. She drowned her sorrows and lived alone with her toy poodle, Beau. I left her there.

The hospital called a day later. She had suffered a stroke. There was nothing more they could do for her; she needed a nursing home.

"A nursing home? She's only fifty-three years old," I balked. She couldn't stay with me; my kids didn't even know her. I couldn't quit work and take care of her, not that I had the money or the time. "She walked in. Why can't she walk out?"

"You need to come get her today."

I found a nursing home willing to accept her meager health insur-ance.

"Adam, I wrote your name on these boxes, so put your books, games, and Hot Wheels in them." I turned to Daisy, who was playing with Aloma and a toy kitchen set. "We need to move to our new house *today.* Just like your brother, you need to put your toys inside the boxes with your name, okay, sweetie? I'll be back to help in a few minutes."

I took Aloma with me and walked downstairs.

"Maria," I said, *"donde està Richard?"*

"Yo no se." Maria was packing my collection of Perrier-Jouët painted champagne bottles that filled our bookshelves instead of books.

I looked at the dusty bottles. "Maria, maybe *no màs las botillas.*"
"*Sí?*"
"*Sí, Maria, es tiempo, la vasuda . . .*"
"*Bueno . . . muy bueno.*"
I went outside to look for Richard.

"You sure collected a lotta stuff since your fire," Yipi said, packing Indian rugs and quilts into a box. I put Aloma in her crib. Marsia was taking down our curtains.

"Have you seen Richard?" I said.

"Yeah, he was loading the truck."

As I looked that way, I saw Richard run across the grass, bound over the side of our driveway, off the cliff and out of sight.

"What happened?" I yelled, running out the screen door. A mover loading the large van said, "I told him his truck was rolling, he ran after it, then the truck flipped over the cliff—"

Maria was outside and cried, *"Pitita es entro!"*

"*PITITA?!*" I screamed, running and screaming down the hill, watching Vern's truck roll sideways, over and over, down the mountain.

In another place of my mind, while all this was going on, calmness was brewing. I imagined my return back up the mountain with Pitita in my arms, limp, in fact, dead. And for all the horror of this thought, without question, I knew I would run into my house, set her down, get the biggest butcher knife I had, and before anyone could stop me, stab it into my heart, pick Pitita up in my arms, and die with her. I was so clear about this. Richard would have little Aloma; Daisy and Adam would go with their father, and I would go with Pitita.

I saw the truck take its last roll over a giant patch of pampas grass that stopped it, wheels spinning in the air. I ran for my baby. Richard was standing with her buried in his arms. "Pitita," I sobbed, and she turned her little head to me. I pulled her away from Richard, looking at her face, examining her body. She wasn't crying. She wasn't bleeding. No bones poking out anywhere. I glared at Richard, then looked away and held Pitita tighter.

Yipi had followed me down the hill. "What happened, man?" he asked. "I put Pitita in the truck and went for more boxes," Richard said. "She must have bumped the emergency brake."

I walked away, deeper down the hill, to collect myself and be alone with Pitita. I wiped my tears from her little face. She only had a few scratches on her face from flying through the pampas grass blades while coming out of the window. Other than that, she was fine. She even had a look in her eye like *that was fun; if I give you a quarter, can I go on that ride again?*

Richard walked up to put his arms around me but I stiffened up. I had trusted Richard with *my* life. That was over. I couldn't trust him with his own child.

He was the one person I'd thought I could count on. *Wrong.*

I'm Doing Hair as Fast as I Can

"Carrie," Helena said on the phone, "can you do a house call now?"

"Helena, I'm done for the day. It's seven-thirty. I'm fixing dinner."

"It's for Marlon, he starts *Missouri Breaks* tomorrow."

"I'll be as fast as I can walk across the street!"

I handed Richard the spoon for the spaghetti sauce, slugged down the rest of my white wine, and grabbed my scissors from the bathroom. "Be right back, Helena wants me to cut *Marlon Brando!*"

While our new home was small, we were living directly across the street from three homes behind large electric gates: one was Jack Nicholson's, one was my belly dancer roller queen friend Helena's, and the other belonged to Marlon Brando. Helena greeted me at Marlon's front door and introduced us. I hadn't touched him yet and I was unglued by his chemistry.

After I cut his hair, I wanted him to see my fine styling job, but there was no hand mirror in the whole house, so I couldn't show off. I suggested treatments for his thinning hair with my high-frequency ultraviolet glass rake. He laughed, asked me if I wanted more wine, and said, "Hell . . . it's the process of getting old, who cares?"

I did . . . I wanted to come back.

Marlon picked up twenty strands of Tahitian seashell necklaces sitting in a pile on his counter, and placed them over my head. "They look good on you."

He walked me out to his driveway and asked if I wanted him to walk me across the street to my door. It was dark. He stood too close. I was already in shambles from his sexual presence. "No, thanks, I'm fine."

"But Liz," I said. "It's nine o'clock, Saturday night."

"I know, but I just remembered I have to catch a plane to Baltimore in the morning, and well . . . you are *my hairdresser.*"

I hung up with Elizabeth Taylor. I had done her hair a few times before at my salon and at her home in Bel Air. She was a National Treasure.

"I feel like a doctor delivering babies." I wearily got out of bed, got dressed, and grabbed a bottle of Amaretto to share with Liz. I kissed Richard and the kids, who were piled on the bed watching television.

Richard took a hit of his joint and smiled. "We'll be here."

"You have to do my hair before Monday," Louise said. "I leave for Oregon."

Louise, Jerry Bick's wife, had remained my client all these years. Jerry was producing these days, and got me screen credits for my work with Elliot Gould for *The Long Goodbye.* Louise had just gone up for the role of a nurse working in an insane asylum. Michael Douglas was producing it and at his and Brenda Vaccaro's Christmas party, I had heard that another Louise got the part. I decided I should be the one to tell her she didn't get it. After all, who better to let her down gently than her friend and hairdresser?

"I'm sorry, sweetheart, but a Louise Fletcher got your part," I said, while repinning the towel around her neck. "I'm sure there will be other—"

Louise interrupted, "*I am* Louise Fletcher, you dummy."

"What?"

"Fletcher is my stage name, Bick is my married name."

We screamed and howled.

Saturday night at my house, Louise told me about the character she would play, a stubborn rigid nurse. She had no change of hair or wardrobe. "Ah, I got it . . . I'll do you like my mother, a woman trapped in the forties." I recorded Louise's hairstyle with my new Polaroid camera for her to show Michael and the on-set hairdresser.

Buzzzzzz. Buzzzzz.

"Bette Midler on line two," my receptionist said. I grabbed the phone. "Why aren't you here?" "Where are you?" Bette said. "Where are you? I'll pick you up," and I left for the Westwood Marquis Hotel to bring her back to my salon.

We had never met before.

"Carrie White here," I said into the phone box at the Copa D'Oro gates of Peter Bogdanovich. I had been cutting Peter's hair since he saw the haircut I gave his girlfriend Cybill Shepherd, just before she did her next film, *Taxi Driver.*

Rita and I were in the dispensary, supposedly mixing up hair color.

"Hey, where's the *Klute* photo that Jane just gave me?"

"In the trash," Rita whispered.

I handed Rita a spoonful of coke.

"How the hell did it get there?"

"Mrs. Bloomingdale . . . I saw her tear it into a bunch of little pieces, as soon as you and Jane walked up front."

"Wow, must be about Vietnam," I said, reaching into a little brown bottle for two quick hits, then holding my head up for Rita to check me before I went back out to my station. "How's my nose?"

Mrs. B. sat patiently waiting in my chair. On one side of the room was band boy Eddie James waiting for a new look to go with his new name, Edward James Olmos. A chair away was my new client Bette Midler, behind me under another dryer sat my darling Vanessa Redgrave. I had on Elizabeth's big rock from Richard Burton while she was drying and having her nails done. Raquel Welch came barreling in unexpectedly with her arm in a cast from her *Kansas City Bomber* roller-skating accident and when a "nobody" client asked

Raquel what happened and she told her, "Buzz off," I tried not to laugh. Cathy, my receptionist, walked up. "Wilt Chamberlain's at the jewelry case inquiring about a turquoise necklace—oh, and Dusty Springfield called . . . she's running late, and wants you to come with her to Century City when she sings tonight. Where can I put Stockard Channing?"

I was doing the ex–Mrs. Johnny Carson and the new Mrs. Johnny Carson and trying not to get them confused, plus trying to keep a few of Dean Martin's girlfriends separated. From Governor Jerry Brown and Senator John Tunney to Rick Springfield and Iggy Pop, celebrities were bumping elbows in my salon. The music blared and the bubbles flowed. If it was holiday time, it was spiked eggnog. Some clients would have to wait for hours while others would slip me a gram of coke and they were definitely next in my chair. Some never saw any of this and had no idea about the party that was happening.

The nursing home called. Due to lack of funds, they couldn't keep my mother any longer. This would be my third move down for her. The bureaucracy overwhelmed me and finally I got Medi-Cal for her, which got me to a dingy little last-call nursing home in Baldwin Hills, an all-black neighborhood, that accepted her. It was death's waiting room, dark, cold, and grim. The average person was eighty. My mother just looked eighty, at fifty-three.

On days I decided I had to visit her, out of respect and the piece of my heart that loved her, I armored up with plenty of vodka and took someone with me, an assistant, a manicurist to clip her toenails . . . anyone I could talk into coming.

Carol, my first assistant whom I'd remained close to, accompanied me this time. All my drugs and alcohol couldn't defuse this frightening picture as my mother lay paralyzed on the single metal cot with sheets as rough as sandpaper, blankets thinner than her skin, and the odor of stale breath hovering like a veil. She stared at the ceiling, a skeleton with eyeballs. Her hair had grown out with a six-inch band of gray roots next to the brassy badly dyed hair she always did herself.

I pushed her hair back and kissed her forehead. No response. I flinched from the rotting smell of her parted mouth.

"Hi, Mom, you remember Carol?" No response.

"Your mom's too thin," Carol said. "Don't they feed her?"

She was right. I left to find a nurse. It was 9:00 PM but no one was around. I rang a little tin bell twice. A lady that looked as old as the patients came out.

"Shhh," she said, in a loud whisper. "People are trying to sleep."

"My mother looks terrible." I pointed to my mom. "She's too thin."

"Your mother won't eat. She just grits her teeth."

"Well, you *have to make her eat*," I said.

"We've been trying for four days, she won't."

I walked back. "Mom, you have to eat," I said, and took a pair of tweezers from my purse and plucked eight long neglected hairs on her chin. She didn't flinch.

"We have to go now, Mom." I put my tweezers away and turned to Carol. "Promise you'll do the same for me when hairs pop out of my chin."

Carol was rubbing her cold feet. "She needs socks."

I went to the rickety cardboard dresser and fanned through some underpants, brassieres, and a few flimsy nightgowns.

"I'll bring her some tomorrow."

I looked around. No pictures. No flowers. No music. I kissed my mother good-bye. I was itchy for a drink. It had been hours.

Carol lived nearby. Her husband, Warren, greeted us at their front door.

"You'll be seeing a lot more of me—my mother's in an old folks' home a few blocks away."

"I'm sorry 'bout that," Warren said.

"I know, it's unbelievable what the human body can take."

"Warren," Carol interrupted, "get us a drink, we've jus' come from Hell."

Carol pulled out a joint and lit it. It had a funny chemical smell.

"Angel dust?"

"*Yes* . . . Warren doesn't like me to smoke it, though," Carol said, holding a big mouthful of smoke. She passed it to me. I didn't like angel dust, I wouldn't buy it, but I never said no to anything, so I took a big drag.

"This is all I do now," Carol said. "And drink, of course."

"I thought you were giving that up," Warren said, coming in with three glasses of wine. Carol took a last toke.

"That shit is brain damage!" he said, handing me my wine. "It's elephant tranquilizer."

Carol grumbled, "I like it, so let's talk about something else."

I looked at them bickering over drugs and felt grateful Richard never bugged me to quit what I did—well, he was doing it too, so that helped.

"Warren, can we talk about how Carrie's mom hasn't eaten in four days?"

"You can't leave her there," Warren said. "She needs a *hospital* and fast."

"He's right," Carol said. "We gotta move her now."

"*Tonight?*" I asked, feeling the effects of the angel dust more than I wanted. It was like bad pot and weird acid, my body feeling rubberized, slow motion, but my mind on full speed ahead.

"Call the paramedics, Carol," Warren said.

Carol grabbed the phone and dialed.

"I better tell Richard what we're doing," I said, not up for all this commotion.

"There's no time," Carol said. "They're on the way, they know the place."

"I'll follow in our car," Warren said, and Carol and I flew over in mine.

The paramedics were there, waiting for us. "Whose mother is she?"

"Mine."

The little house was completely dark. We banged on the door like a police raid. The peekhole cover opened. "Yes?"

"Open up, Ma'am, it's the paramedics."

We heard *click, click, click.* The caretaker lady stood behind the chain-latched door. "No one here called you."

"We have an emergency request for Grace Jeffries."

She unlatched the chains, and we busted in past her like James Bond. I rushed to my mother's side while they set up the transfer bed on wheels. Her eyes opened wide, terror and confusion screaming out of them.

I thought it was a good sign, a response.

"I'm getting you to a hospital, Mom, for some real medical help." Her jaw locked tight, her neck was stiff. She clutched for my arm as they moved her onto the stretcher. She was cold, the peach fuzz on her arms was standing up, a last rising fight for life through her bruised skin.

"I'm going to ride with you, Mom, don't worry."

They got her into the ambulance. She didn't talk and she didn't take her eyes off me until they gave her an IV and put her to sleep. I held her bony little hand the whole ride.

At County General we were ushered into a very brightly lit waiting room, where they placed my mom on a temporary bed. I was in my own haze coming down from the alcohol, and angel dust and standing on my feet all day. I wanted to be in my bed. I gazed over at my mother. All of a sudden, she sat straight up from her hips, and her eyes looked directly into mine.

"Carole . . . you know I've always loved you, don't you?"

My vision got sharp, my ears got keen from my mother calling me by my born name, saying the words I'd longed for since my father walked out and her boyfriends walked in. I pressed flat to the wall. My mouth dropped open. My heart spoke. "Yes, Mom . . . I do know that."

She fell back down as fast as she came up and closed her eyes again. Like it never happened. But it did.

I was in bed, in Richard's arms, trying to sleep. My mind wouldn't shut down. I kept hearing that sound in my mother's throat, a sound I had never heard before. It had been days since I had taken her to County General. She was in a nice room with open windows and five beds lined up next to each other. She kept making a sound, a loud raspy gargle. "Excuse me," I asked the hospital housekeeper. "Have you ever heard a noise like this before?" She shrugged her shoulders,

"No speak English, Miss, you find nurse." I pulled the blanket closer to my mother's neck and tucked it around her. The disturbing noise continued with her every breath. The man in the next bed told me, "That sound is called the *death rattle*."

Midnight. The phone rang. I answered it quickly, not to wake Richard.

"Hello," I whispered.

"This is County General Hospital. Is this Carrie White Alcala?"

"Yes," I sat up and gripped the phone.

"Is your mother Grace Jeffries?"

"Yes."

"I'm sorry to inform you, but your mother has expired."

"Expired?"

Like a warranty?

Like a membership?

Like a library card?

Like a date on a milk carton?

Like a driver's license?

Like a parking meter?

Richard awoke from my sobbing and put his arms around me. He took the phone and said, "Thank you," and hung up.

It was over. The end. My sorrow transformed to ether and put me to sleep.

My clientele continued to flourish in diversity, from Mrs. Bing Crosby to Mr. and Mrs. Kenny Loggins. I did Mouseketeers Annette Funicello and Cheryl Holdridge and icons Sandra Dee, Karen Carpenter, and Lee Remick.

I was a television guest for Vidal Sassoon on his beauty show. I still worked with Melvin in New York and California, and I did Candace Bergen's hair for the cover of *Vogue*. I got to do the hair for Zandra Rhodes's fashion show at the opening of Mr. Chow's in Beverly Hills. Marilyn McCoo got married in my hairdo and Phyllis George and Kelly Lange did the news in my haircuts for Channel 2, or was it Channel 4 or 7?

Details bored or baffled me.

Advertising got *wild*, literally. I did a series of cat commercials: Cheryl Tiegs, with a live cougar for a Cougar car commercial. Another job with Melvin featured a lion, and then I did a model with a panther for Clairol shampoo. I declined when Tippi Hedren called, asking me to curl the mane of her trained lion that she promised to tranquilize. I told her to get a curly wig and snap it on his head.

Life moved into the faster lane as friends dropped by with surprises of champagne and cocaine to outnumber clients. Billy's visits were always uplifting.

"What time is Barbara coming in?" I asked Rita.

"Barbra Bain? Barbara Feldon? Barbara Eden? Barbara Parkins? Barbra Streisand? Barbara Luna? Barbara Barrie? Or Barbara McNair?" Rita asked.

"No," I said. "Barbara Bach."

I loved that I was cutting everyone who was anyone—at my salon, on location, or in my kitchen. I was having the greatest time of my life. I gave my kids birthday parties at the zoo and took them to clients' homes to go swimming. On Sundays, Richard packed us up and we went to the Beverly Hills Hotel coffee shop for breakfast (Ramos Gin Fizzes for me), and a long drive anywhere afterward, to relax and smoke Acapulco Gold or Ice Pack or Thai stick or Panama Red.

I drank like a lady in the day and a sailor at night. In between: cocaine.

Because of cocaine, I was able to drink more and burn the candle at both ends. It was written into some jobs as a lunch expense, never listed as cocaine of course, but that was the seventies, powdered sugar heaven. "Is it snowing? Are you holding? Who's got the blow?" Cocaine became a basic staple for me, alongside music and air. At one Sunset Strip restaurant, we could pull up to parking attendants, give our keys and a hundred bucks, and when we came out after dinner, we got our cars and a gram of coke was in the glove compartment.

It made me more alive, creative, taller, thinner, smarter, careless, and care more. And there were different kinds that brought out different qualities. Some bit. Some were smooth like wines, vodkas, and tequilas. Some were pure and psychedelic. One time I heard Billy tell Jimmy, *"That last batch smelled like pussy."* Jimmy said, "That's because some chicks smuggled it in from Bolivia in plastic bags up their vaginas."

In the beginning a few hits lasted me all day. After that I needed a gram. As time went on, there was never enough. If I had one gram, I wanted two.

Mrs. Goetz began to ask me to wait until I was finished with her hair before I had my champagne split.

"Wake up, wake up, Carrie. What do I have to do to get you to work on time?"

I cracked my eyes, then sat up in shock. I couldn't remember a thing; then I realized the man waking me was director Bill Helburn from New York.

"Oh shit," I said. Richard was still asleep. I was due on set hours ago to do hair for his commercial. "Okay, give me five minutes, I'll be right out."

I couldn't move or drink or think without coke anymore. I became an awake drunk, which was much better than a passing-out one.

My real estate lady called. "Your lease is up, but I found a perfect house for you if you can raise the down payment."

I was in the kitchen; my meat loaf in the oven, Daisy was folding napkins, helping me set the table. "Not already? I was just starting to relax here." I picked up my martini.

"This home is it," Lenore said, "Brand new A-frame, half an acre, you'll still be on Mulholland, four bedrooms, a fireplace, great kitchen, den, room for Max . . ."

It seemed like a minute, not eighteen months, since we'd last moved. I had no money saved and Richard didn't even know where we banked.

"How many haircuts is it?" Lenore laughed. I was serious.

"It's only one hundred and twenty-five thousand, can you come up with twenty-five?"

There was never a good time to talk about finances with Richard, He either felt pressured or offended or he was too stoned to care.

Richard was barely supporting himself, Bucky wasn't giving me financial support for Adam and Daisy, and I was supporting my other children Aloma and Pitita. Of course, I ignored my pressures with more work, more champagne, and the cocaine push.

I was sick of Richard's freeloader friends hanging around the salon, because they knew he was a soft touch and there was always cash in the desk. My resentment toward Richard was building again—subtle, pissed-off anger.

I was already doing hair as fast as I could.

Highlights

My daily cocaine use went from want to need. I needed it like other people needed gas for their cars. And I needed extra money to afford my escalated habit.

I tried to get a few of my hair product ideas to Clairol. I thought if American hair dryers could have a flip switch for travel in Europe, it would solve the current problem. The Clairol rep said they were already working on that. They said that about all my inventions.

I managed to borrow a big chunk of money and we moved into our new perfect home. I finally had my first dishwasher and garbage disposal. I felt like Betsy Bloomingdale. We had giant picture windows and on a clear day we could see all the way to the ocean.

"Where you going?" I said to Richard, who was standing at the front desk, a newspaper under his arm.

"I'm done."

"Already?" I said. "Maybe a customer will drop in."

It wasn't unusual for Richard to leave midday. He wasn't helping his business either, by telling ladies who wanted a haircut, "Let it grow."

"Don't be too late," he'd say after we kissed good-bye at the door.

I mumbled, "If you made more money I wouldn't have to be late." Then I called out to Rita, "Order more champagne."

⟿

"Michael Crichton on line one."

Michael was my favorite male client. I would take an extra long time cutting him, just to hear what he had to say about current events, science, art, or politics. He'd always duck at my doorway with his six-foot-ten, so he wouldn't bump his head, and his opening line would be: "Got any jokes?" Besides being very tall, Michael was very handsome in that clean-cut college guy way. I had a *giant* crush on him, but all he called me was *kid*. He was too Harvard smart for me anyway, and besides . . . I was married. Michael had been through a few marriages, many dates and girlfriends, but I was his only hairdresser. That made me very happy.

"Michael." I beamed. "What can I do for you?"

"Is there such a thing as cutting hair and that's it? No setting, no drying, no fussing?"

"Sure, that's my specialty . . . why?"

"I'm tired of waiting for the set hairdresser to fix the actresses' hair. If I get you two thousand dollars and screen credits on *Coma*, can you do Geneviève Bujold right now?"

I did.

Jon Peters, a rising Romeo hairdresser, followed the rule *If you want your hair great in the morning, sleep with your hairdresser at night,* and took Barbra Streisand from me, then brought her back when he became her producer-boyfriend. I traipsed behind the two of them after doing her hair for premiere night of *A Star Is Born.* Time passed, Jon called again. "You'll get hair credits on the *Streisand Superman* album if you make Barbra's hair red and give her a perm."

I did.

Melinda Dillon said, "I told Julia Phillips I wouldn't do *Close Encounters of the Third Kind* unless you did my highlights."

Costume designer Anthea Sylbert brought Mike Nichols and Robert De Niro into my salon for a film called *Bogart Slept Here*. The film got canned, but I got to cut De Niro.

⟿

"They messed up on your screen credits for *Beau Geste*," Roger Smith said, "I'm calling Universal and if they don't pay you double, I'm going to tell them Ann-Margret will never work for them again."

They paid double.

"What time is Peter coming in?" I asked Rita. She answered, "Which Peter? Allen, Fonda, Bogdanovich, or Sellers?"

I took mescaline every few months whether I needed it or not. It was a *real* trip to take acid and do hair. I would travel from my head through the back of my clients' head to the mirror, see what she wanted, and then travel back to the front of her forehead, back into mine, and give her what look I thought was best.

I could see that I saw my clients prettier than they saw themselves.

One time at the Bumbles Club, a friend gave me a tab of Orange Sunshine, the strongest acid at the time.

Nothing happened . . . until the morning. I woke up and the walls in my bedroom were throbbing with color. Richard looked like an animated Walt Disney king in his castle.

I had promised my first client to do her hair and makeup for her wedding that day by noon. I drove to my salon and felt stable until I tried to do her eyelashes. They turned into butterflies and flew away. I started to chase after them.

"Where are you going?" she called.

I turned back to her. "Oh . . . there you are."

David Steinberg generously invited me to be a guest on his live audience television show to talk hair and do a makeover demonstration. Right before I was about to go on camera, I snuck in an extra hit of cocaine in the bathroom. Big mistake. I was onstage with my dry lips stuck on my gums, and I could barely speak, sit still, or keep my left leg from falling asleep. The worst part, I kept interrupting David's questions like it was my show.

I met with Mark Rydell to discuss Bette's hair and clothes for *The Rose*.

I cut Richard Mulligan's and Robert Altman's ponytails off.

I cut Hal Ashby and Conrad Hall.

I cut Shaun Cassidy and Joanna Cassidy.

I had the world by their hair.

I went to Halston's first L.A. fashion show with Joe Eula. Everyone came up to our house later, including Halston with Pat Ast, Andy Warhol's *Heat* star.

I was wearing my one and only Gustave Tassell long dress. Joe said, "Get me some scissors, your dress is too long. Don't you agree, Richard?"

I turned to Richard for backup.

"It's Joe Eula," Richard said. "Let him do what he wants."

I looked at the handsome man I married. He was getting a big belly and a puffy face. That damn marijuana made him lazy and crash out. Meanwhile, I was on coke, all zippy and ready to rock and roll. I was ten years younger than Richard. We had been together nine years, and I thought, *He's getting too old for me.*

I went into the kitchen and poured a full goblet of red wine and got the scissors. Joe picked up the hem of my Tassell and in one swoop cut half the dress off. Even Halston gasped at Joe's bold madness. "And your hair's too long, too," Joe said.

Everyone was cheering on this deconstruction of me. I stood like a mannequin. He cut my hair off above my ears.

"Its all about the shape," Joe said, "not the craftsmanship. I love it."

"Lookin' goooood," Richard said. "Who else can say they got a Joe Eula on their *head*? Now, how about you get the gun Elvis gave you and show everyone?"

It was another 2:00 AM, another night. I was blasting the soundtrack from *Eyes of Laura Mars.* Daisy came out from her bedroom as spokesperson, Aloma trailing beside. "Mommy, could you turn that down?"

"Oh, sure, honey, I'm sorry. Sometimes Mommy forgets how late it is. You girls get back in bed, okay?"

"Carrie, come to bed." Richard would call me from our new bedroom. Richard and I rarely had a night alone. When we did, I would go to bed after him and he would be asleep. I preferred to reward myself after a hard working day with coke and alcohol, rather than go to sleep. I enjoyed my self-containment in the wee small hours.

"I got a sick friend," John Phillips said on the phone one afternoon. "Do you know who I can call for smack?"

"*Smack?*" I said. "I don't know anyone who does heroin, that's a dead-end trip. I mean, really, why would anyone even try it . . . to see if they liked it?"

"Let me talk to Richard," John said.

I called Richard to the phone, fixed myself a Bloody Mary, and went outside with the kids. I had a machete from the garage and I was giving my century cactus a haircut. Daisy was trying to convince Aloma and Pitita to play school. They didn't want to because Daisy always got to be the teacher. Adam saw me hacking away at the cactus. "What're you doing, Mom?"

"See . . . I'm giving him a David Bowie haircut."

"You told us the birds of paradise were the David Bowie haircuts."

"Well, I'm making the cactus like that too."

Adam tilted his head, eyeing the shape on the cactus head. "Okay, Mom, I can see it now."

I finished my Bloody Mary and needed another one.

"Stay out of the driveway," I said, and went upstairs to Richard. "Why would John call *you* for *heroin*?"

"I know a guy who knows a guy . . . it's nothing, don't worry 'bout it."

The phone rang again.

"I'm quitting," Rita said.

"What? You can't quit, I need you."

"You'll still have me. You can buy coke from me."

"What the hell are you saying?" I couldn't digest that Rita was leaving me.

"I get more money and more coke by selling it."

"Rita, your timing is awful."

"See *me* everyday, you'll get more for your money."

"Rita, wait, please, I'll pay you extra. I am too busy to start over with someone right now."

"Okay, a few weeks, but no more."

Bob Banner on line three. "Carrie, we have a great opportunity for you," Bob said. "*To Russia with Love,* Peggy Fleming's second television special."

I did Peggy's first one, but I thought, *Me in Russia with all that vodka and no cocaine?* I would fall on my face. I declined the great opportunity. I knew this was bad, but I chalked it up to *oh well . . .* I was just being smart, protecting myself.

I had to be clever about my using, pacing myself, and not missing work because of it. I didn't mix pills and drinks. And I would never go so far as to do heroin. I considered myself a functioning artist–party girl. I drank and did cocaine every day, but carefully. I didn't want to die, I was a mother, I had so much to live for, I was the hairdresser to the stars and a wife . . .

I decided to reignite with Richard, put the spark back into our marriage, not that he ever commented that our spark was dull.

"Richard, let's do Pilates," I said one night. He kept watching television. "Richard," I said, a little louder. "We need to get in physical shape."

I was thin but not fit and Richard was getting rounder by the month—even his nose looked fatter. He smiled. "What's Pilates?"

"I don't know, but let's try it. It's the latest rage. They use special machines . . . hey . . . *Richard . . .* " My voice was a lullaby that put Richard to sleep. He rolled over, propped himself up on a pillow, took a sip of his B&B.

"You go ahead," he said, laughing. "I just wanna get fat and roll down the hill."

"Well," I said, pissed, "I'm not rollin' down with you."

I walked out and poured some vodka into a small amount of orange juice. "*More bourbon than 7UP,*" I could hear in my mother's voice.

With my family at the Ann-Margret show, after cutting Elvis's hair
at the Las Vegas Hilton. (Personal collection)

Me, Adam, and the artist Erté. (Courtesy of Aloma Ichinose)

On location with Melvin Sokolsky, wearing my Marsia leather patchwork dress, my Beatles Apple boutique pants, and my necklace of paintbrushes. (Personal collection)

My hairstyle design used for Nurse Ratched in the film *One Flew Over the Cuckoo's Nest*. (Courtesy of Peter Sorel)

Carrie darling,
Couldn't have
happened
without you!
My love
Louise Fletcher
April 15. 1976

Taking Billy to New York City for his first time—he thought the buildings would be taller. (Personal collection)

Styling Bruce Dern for *Silent Running*. (Courtesy of Aloma Ichinose)

My sketch of David Bowie, which he signed in 1975. (Personal collection)

leave me along
or leave me a bit at least
love

Bowie ——— 73

Me styling David Bowie for promo shots on the set of *The Man Who Fell to Earth*. (Courtesy of Chuck White)

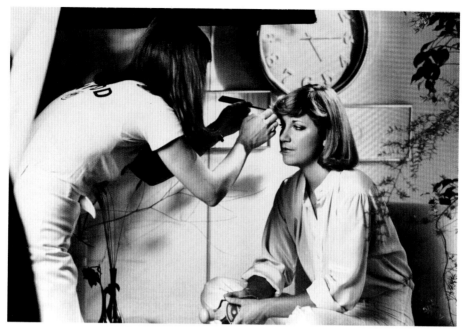

Styling Chris Evert for a commercial. (Personal collection)

Creating the hairstyle for *The Last Remake of Beau Geste* with Ann-Margret.
(Courtesy of Aloma Ichinose)

Me and Stanley Marcus on
the opening night of the
Beverly Hills Neiman Marcus.
(Personal collection)

Me and Michael Crichton at Chasen's premiere party for
The Great Train Robbery. (Personal collection)

Me, backstage with models at James Reva fashion show.
(Courtesy of Jim Frank)

My MINI Cooper, which I painted with intentions of being invisible while
driving to the drug dealer, 1980. (Personal collection)

Me in my beach living room that I turned into a sandbox, 1983. (Personal collection)

Billy Grimes and Aloma celebrating at my first year of sobriety party, 1985. (Personal collection)

Me and Betty Ford. (Personal collection)

Me, Michelle Phillips, Aloma, and Joan Agajanian Quinn.
(Personal collection)

Me preparing for QVC, 1989.
(Courtesy of Aloma Ichinose)

After styling Anne Archer on Oscar night 1988—she was nominated for *Fatal Attraction*. (Personal collection)

Me and honoree Quincy Jones at Friendly House awards luncheon. (Personal collection)

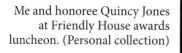

Me and Michael Crichton at one of his book signings. (Personal collection)

Button, Melvin, and me at the opening of Tova Salon. (Personal collection)

Polo games with Stefanie Powers,
1994. (Personal collection)

Me and Sydney Guilaroff, the iconic film hairstylist of the 1940s and 1950s. (Personal collection)

My fifty-fifth birthday party at Spago with my client Wolfgang Puck. (Personal collection)

My sixty-fifth birthday with
Mollie Mulligan, 2008.
(Courtesy of Aloma Ichinose)

Me and Naomi Campbell at
the Grand Prix in Monaco,
2004. (Personal collection)

Me and Amber
Valletta, 2009.
(Personal collection)

My red carpet 'do for
Sandra Bullock, at the
2004 Oscars. (Courtesy of
Getty Images)

Styling my granddaughter Olive before her
first ballet recital. (Personal collection)

Ten years after uniting with my first child, Tyler, and
my first husband, Jordan (top row). (Personal collection)

Me and Peggy Albrecht, 2006. (Personal collection)

With my children: Daisy, Adam, (me), Pitita, Tyler, and Aloma.
(Courtesy of Johannes Gamble)

I went to our record player and I put on the blue record Jerry Moss gave me to check out, The Police, a new band he had just signed. I cranked it up like I was alone.

We were behind in our mortgage from catching up on our taxes. I had paid back Mrs. Goetz when she helped me buy our house. I couldn't ask her for more money. Besides, she had stopped coming to me. Mrs. Bloomingdale and a few other charter clients dropped out too. I knew they didn't like all the drinking, my crazier than chic outfits, my dancing around in the salon, and mostly, not being so available for them. I rationalized I had a younger, snappier clientele now. Margo Winkler kindly loaned me a thousand bucks. A month later, I borrowed another thousand from my friend Judy, the wife of Gil Friesen (of A&M Records). I hadn't paid Margo back yet.

Then Richard committed the ultimate sin. And how many had I missed?

Walking past his station, I saw he was nestled too close to a young cute platinum blonde. Also I saw his hand go down inside the front of her smock, and then he saw me. I felt fire shoot out of my eyes. I charged away, he chased after me. I went to the bathroom, slammed the door, and locked it.

"Let me in, let me in," Richard said. "I'm sorry."

"How long has this shit been going on?" I shouted through the door, shaking so much I could hardly get my little brown cocaine bottle open.

Richard pounded on the door, rattled the doorknob while I sat on the toilet, scooping all the coke up my nose as fast as I could. I did the last scraps, licked the paper, and threw it in the trash. I opened the door, Richard tried to hug me, but I pushed past him.

I walked over to my waiting client, the no-talk zone for Richard.

"Sorry, Lindsay, more *Bionic* highlights today?"

Hairpin Turn

The process began. My criteria for hiring a new assistant: one who could mix a drink, help disguise my cocaine use, and cover for me being late. I'd been through three useless assistants already.

"There's someone here who wants a job assisting." My reception-ist called me to come up front. There stood a lanky, androgynous boy-god. He had a beautiful face with high cheekbones and silky, shoulder-length, dark henna hair, slightly hanging over one eye. I was glad I had been doing *my* Pilates.

"My name's Scott," he said, never taking his eyes off mine. "I just moved here from San Francisco. I wondered if anyone needed an as-sistant. I have a Sassoon background and—"

"Do you have a license?" I was connecting to his brown eyes and his flawless olive skin more than to his words.

"Yes, you can check my references."

"If you can get soap out of their hair after you shampoo, the job is yours."

When he left, Richard came up to me.

"You're not hiring *him*, are you?"

"I just did."

On day two, I followed him into the dispensary when he went to mix color. "Do you like champagne, wine, and vodka . . . and cocaine?"

"I love it all," he said.

I was having a midlife crisis at thirty-five. I was drawn to Scott, while Richard and I were failing. Scott and I had crazy chemistry. One morning in my dispensary Mary said, "I see what's goin' on with this young Scott *boy*. Richard must too, what're you doin', chil'?"

I pulled away. "It's nothing, Mary, he just works for me."

I fixed a Salty Dog in my coffee cup and went out to do Joanna Cassidy.

I had caught Richard with his hands in a few girls' smocks, so I was going for Scott's attention. We kissed in my car coming back from a house call. We made up house calls after that and kissed often.

"I told Richard we had to separate."

"Why?" Scott said.

"I thought you'd be happy about that."

"I don't think you should've done that," Scott said, completely unmoved.

"Well, don't worry, it wasn't over you . . . this has been brewing."

Richard moved his station to the very front booth to get away from me. Richard couldn't talk me out of our separation. And I couldn't talk Scott into *me*.

Scott Free

"I will always love you, Richard," I said, trying to break up with peace. "But we are on different paths."

Richard moved out. Our lifetime friend Aloma took him under her wing. She had high hopes that Richard would join her and her nondrinking friends. Richard and Aloma were alike, they couldn't hold their liquor, they needed to quit. My hands didn't shake like Richard's when he cut hair; besides, I couldn't imagine a day without a drink. I thought people who waited for Happy Hour could've been happier earlier.

My friend Dana married Jerry Magnin. They bought a fantastic house off Hollywood Boulevard and it was the new Party Central.

"Come over," Dana said. "I'm giving a party for Governor Jerry Brown."

"Come over," Dana said. "Jackson Browne's here with his son."

"Come over," Dana said. "Mick Jagger's in the bushes with *some girl*."

"Come over," Dana said. "Joel Tornabene wants you to fly to San Fran to cut Todd Rundgren and put crazy colors in his hair."

Bucky had started taking Adam and Daisy every weekend again. Richard was also taking his little girls. And I was left free to run.

I arrived at Joel Tornabene's apartment Saturday night wearing five pairs of fluorescent spandex pants on top of one another. I couldn't decide which color to wear. I thought I'd be an ever-changing clever art piece, peeling off one pair at time as the night went on. I left each zipper slightly unzipped at different levels to show off all the colors at once, hot fuchsia, vibrant turquoise, purple, acid orange, and flesh tone for the final underpair. I was so thin, it made layering easy.

Joel managed a group called the Ramones, who were milling around his living room. Todd came out of the guest bedroom.

"This is the girl I flew in for you," Joel told Todd. "She did Elvis."

"Just his hair," I laughed.

I came home too late for dinner. My children were standing at the foyer.

"Are you going to tell Mom?" Daisy said to Adam.

"No, you."

"What's going on?" I said, through my daze of hair and alcohol, just walking in my front door after work.

"We're going to move in with Dad," Daisy said.

"Why would you want to do that?" I said, shocked. I stared at my fourteen-year-old son and twelve-year-old daughter.

"You're never home, Mom," Daisy said.

"I am too . . . sometimes I have to work late."

"*Mom*," Adam said, "you go out all the time and Dad wants us."

"*I want you too*," I said, defending myself. "I only go out after you're asleep."

"That's not true," Adam and Daisy harmonized.

"And my dad said my teeth need braces," Daisy said.

"And you never come to my Little League games, Mom," Adam said.

"What? I just went a few weeks ago!"

Aloma and Pitita stood together in their nightgowns watching, holding hands.

Aloma started crying. "Are they going to leave us like Daddy?"

I dropped my purse and went over to Aloma. Maria looked sad holding Pitita. I picked up Aloma, but I suddenly felt a pain, like my heart contracting. I set her down and kissed her. I pressed my chest with my right hand.

"Daisy, Adam . . . I'm doing the best I can, and you know how much I love you."

"Well, how come you're never with us?"

Their disappointed eyes stabbed me in the heart like a dull, rusty sword. I walked into the kitchen and poured a glass of vodka to calm myself down. They were right. I had failed as a mother on so many levels, but I never thought it would come to this.

"I don't like it, but maybe *it is* your dad's turn to have you. Let me think about it." I saw their bags already in the corner by the front door. "So this is final? You've decided behind my back? When are you planning on leaving?"

"Dad's coming for us tomorrow," Adam said, hugging me. Daisy followed.

"Let's all be together tonight." I forced my tears down. "Come upstairs."

All snuggled up on my bed, we watched the ridiculous *Partridge Family.*

"Why doesn't Richard come back?" Adam said. Daisy and Aloma looked to me for an answer. I covered Pitita with a quilt. "We could all be a family again," Adam said. "When Richard comes back . . ."

"I guess I'm the one who comes to get you on weekends now, huh?"

"Mom," Daisy said, "you're busy on the weekends too."

"Yeah," Adam said. "*When are* you going to see us?"

I stared at the television, but I was deeper into the dark hole in my head. Maybe I could be a better mother for Aloma and Pitita. They were still young and their lives weren't so demanding.

I got another Olympus camera job with Cheryl Tiegs, but I woke up so late from spinning myself into the ground on the disco floor at the Pips Club, I shined it off. I looked like hell, I was still in a stupor, and I was having trouble breathing. I could hardly inhale my cigarette. After almost ten years, the coke had taken a toll on me, but I couldn't be without it. I needed coke to get me moving, a drink to calm me down from the coke, and by the time I had the right combination and felt *normal*, it was evening . . . so I went out.

"No màs para mi."

"Maria, *no*, you can't leave me!"

Sometimes Richard drove the girls to San Francisco to be with his mother, his brother, their children, and, well . . . it was a whole big family. I couldn't compete with that. More failure on my side, but I was happy my girls had this *family experience*. I knew they were happy like Adam and Daisy.

But the more my children were away, the more my life disintegrated.

One morning I woke up, squinted my eyes, and saw a painting on the wall that I didn't recognize. *I don't remember hanging that picture in my room.* I looked next to me and realized nothing else looked familiar, including the redheaded guy passed out next to me.

I had had sex with my last customer of the day, a new guy, on the back table in my dispensary.

I had one week before my girls returned from San Francisco.

I would change then.

"You need highlights," I would tell clients, but I was the one who needed the extra money for coke and alcohol.

"Hi, Frances," I said, walking into Roy's restaurant. Frances was Miles Davis's ex-wife. She was the most powerful lady in this celebrity-filled restaurant; she was the hostess. No one got anywhere in Roy's without her approval. She was more fun than a summer vacation and she always greeted me with a warm welcome even when I was falling apart.

"I'll have a drink with you at the bar." Frances was taking a reservation. "And let me tell Roy you're here."

Roy Silver was a bigwig in the music world who had opened the best restaurant in town. I saw Cher sitting with Diana Ross at a booth, lots of rockers and executives. Roy was always good to me. He'd cash my checks, hold my checks, buy me drinks, pick up my dinner tabs sometimes, and kept my credit line open.

I walked over to the bar. "Hi, Carrie," the bartender said. "What'll it be?"

Frances dashed over. "You better get to Roy's office fast. Richard's walking up the stairs and he looks mad and crazy. I thought you said he quit drinking."

There was no time. I ran to the ladies' room. Richard busted in after me.

"You should be home with our girls," said Richard, grabbing my arm to pull me outside. Frances came over.

"Richard, come on, you're a nice guy, Carrie's getting food to go. I don't want to call the police. Richard, please . . . you gotta leave."

Richard hollered louder. *"Tell her to go home and take care of her kids."* He was shaking his fist at me.

I looked at my face in the bathroom mirror.

I saw a broken bride and a ghost of a groom in my shadow.

I remembered Richard and me standing in the driveway of our Benedict Canyon home, where we were about to begin our life with his words, *"This is where we will get married."*

I remembered Aloma and me chopping up Black Beauty diet pills to fine powder and snorting them, so we could finish gluing lace doilies to the old-fashioned vintage Valentine's cards and handwriting the seventy-five wedding invitations with the words: *We will be honored with your presence at our wedding.*

I remembered the wonderful Zen Buddhist priest that Richard found to marry us, who wore his traditional outfit, a purple-and-white silk robe with his pleated obi (belt), swinging incense in a brass pot in one hand, in the other holding a prayer book. I remembered my darling little Adam, the ring bearer, standing proudly by Richard's side, holding the handmade pillow with our rings; Daisy, my little flower angel, clutching my hand and holding the rose-petal-filled basket with her other hand; Aloma, my maid of honor; me wearing a blue garter belt and underpants borrowed from Rita because the ones I planned on showed through my skintight white velvet vintage wedding dress; and my nana all gussied up, including her mink stole, accented by a subtle mothball scent.

I remembered my mother's huge effort to show up, in her freeze-frame hairdo from the forties, glassy-eyed, propped up with her husband Bill and his broken-blood-vessel face. I saw big proud Mary Williams, and Richard's mother, Mary. I saw Ann-Margret and Roger Smith, Johnny Rivers, Diahann Carroll, my incredible Sokolskys, who flew in from New York, Marsia and Yipi tending to every detail for us and our guests, and of course, the best man that started it all for me, who introduced me to hairdressing and to Richard and Aloma . . . the great Billy Grimes.

I had been thrilled to be the first, the one and the only, Mrs. Richard Alcala. It was so far away from this night at Roy's, in another universe far away.

I looked into my eyes and I saw two black tunnels leading to two destroyed hearts—mine and Richard's.

I needed a drink now more than ever.

A Flip Isn't Always a Hairstyle

"Rita, it's me, come by or send someone, okay? I'll pay you at the end of the day, you know I'm good for it."

I'd drag my weary ass down the stairs, through my house of missing limbs from the family tree, no Richard, no Adam, no Daisy, only Pitita and Aloma greeting me . . . *"Hi, Mommy . . . 'Bye, Mommy."*

That was all my little girls knew about me these days.

Sometimes I could manage to pour cereal and milk into a bowl for them.

Then came a private club for skating: Flipper's Roller Boogie Palace.

Flipper's was on La Cienega, only a couple of miles away from my house, which made it very convenient. I started wearing tube tops, spandex pants, and roller skates all the time. Driving to work was challenging wearing my four-wheel skates, operating the clutch, the brake, and the gas pedal. Not spilling my drinks or falling on my scissors in the salon was challenging too. Clients marveled.

Flipper's was *the* place, a roller-skating nightclub. It was glamorous and it was open every night. I didn't need a date or friend to go there. I knew everyone and I skated alone.

Social groups mixed like drinks at Flipper's. Speaking of mixing—try adding skates, alcohol, cocaine, opium, mushrooms, and Quaaludes all together—a dangerous proposition. We had to sign an injury waiver before we were let in. Every night the paramedics carried out at least one person on a stretcher.

You could build your own skates at Flipper's: speed wheels or wood, knee-high shoe skate, covered socks, or Day-Glo laces and matching colored wheels and brake stoppers. The clothes racks sported leopard silk and satin hot pants and Flipper's painted T-shirts for girls and guys. I took all my children and got them fancy skates and decked them out from a new stash of cash.

"And we want the rainbow wristbands," Adam said, speaking for all.

They loved going to Flipper's *almost* as much as I did. I thought we were all having equal fun. I had a reputation for not being the greatest skater but taking the corners like a Porsche. I was just skating low to the ground so I wouldn't have far to fall.

My business was crumbling . . . along with me. More loyal clients were dropping out or hanging on by a hair, while the more recently introduced clients didn't know yet how much of a wreck I was.

I continued to put on my skates at work and reel around my salon in my spandex pants, a cowboy hat, Porsche sunglasses, a drink in one hand and scissors in the other. Sometimes I left clients under the hair dryer and went to Flipper's for a few laps around the rink and came back to comb them. Sometimes I didn't come back.

One night I stopped off at Roy's just to get Chinese chicken salad for my little girls, who were with their new French au pair that my friend Dana Magnin had recommended. I planned to go right home and have dinner with them. I sat at the bar and had a martini. The bartender put my drink on a napkin and scooted the bowl of cocktail mix my way.

"Oh, no thanks, I'm waiting for food to go, my kids are at home, but I'll take a handful of the miniature Snickers, they love these."

My food came. And so did some buddies from Carlos 'n Charlie's restaurant. They ordered champagne and I had a glass. They asked me if I wanted a toot.

"I have to go home."

Benny passed me a folded dollar bill. "Have a toot, *then* go home."

I smiled. "Yeah. Sure."

His friend Judy followed me into a bathroom stall. I opened the folded bill and almost gave myself a heart attack with two big hits. "That is strong," I said. Judy took her gold straw and scooted her nose up and down the dollar bill, snorting two more fat lines full. I had another. "God," I said. "What time is it?"

"Nine-thirty."

"Oh shit! It was so early when I got here. Dammit. I missed the kids' dinner again. They're probably in bed by now. Damn, damn, dammit."

"So have another drink," Judy said.

Around midnight I started home, up Sunset, and when I got to Doheny Drive I thought I'd better take the back road. I got to the gates of Trousdale and I had another thought, *Maybe I'd better pull over, so I don't get pulled over . . . I'll just park and rest a minute till the liquor wears off a little more . . . I should've taken one more hit . . . I'm so wiped out . . .*

I woke up from the light in my eyes. I didn't know where I was. My head was on tin and plastic crinkly paper. I smelled stinky chicken salad. It was in my hair and stuck to the side of my face. I lifted my head slowly and looked at the clock on my burl-veneer dash. It read 5:45 AM.

I barreled home through the hills, trying to get back before the children woke up and found me missing. I would tell no one about this. I rolled the window down to slowly ease some fresh air into my lungs. I had to get the drool and salad juices off my face before I walked into my front door. I could barely conjure up enough spit on a Kleenex to wipe my face. Good thing my neighbors' houses weren't that close to mine.

I pulled up, and with my last ounce of *the show must go on*, I opened my front door. There stood Aloma and Pitita in their night-gowns. They were growing so fast. Aloma was almost nine now, Pitita already seven. "Mommy," they said, "where were you?"

It was Halloween of 1979, my favorite day of the year—costumes and candy. I usually entered parties saying *Trick or Drink,* but this night, no party. I would just take the children trick-or-treating. I marked myself off work early and only drank a little wine all day. No cocaine, though I really wanted some.

"Mommy, Mommy, you made it!" Aloma said, jumping up and down, as I pulled up the driveway. "Are Adam and Daisy coming too?"

I pushed the heavy door of my Mercedes open and picked her up.

"Yes, but they won't be spending the night. Where's Pitita, sweetheart?"

"Getting ready."

"Lets catch up with her. How about if you're a Gypsy?"

"What about Daddy? Can Daddy come?"

"No, he's not coming, honey."

We dressed up and jumped in my car and I drove to Bucky's house. He was divorced again. We were an even three marriages each.

He was reluctant to let me take Adam and Daisy. "Bucky, *relax,* I'll have them back in an hour. We're only going to my friends on Roxbury, after we'll go to the Witch House on Walden Drive."

The Witch House looked identical to the witch's house from "Hansel and Gretel." A set designer had originally built it. On Halloween, the owners played scary music and sheets billowed out of the attic windows. A lady dressed like a witch stood at the gate of the rickety picket fence handing out candy. My kids went there every year, as did droves of children from bordering cities in buses, vans, and station wagons.

My friend Bob and his wife were having drinks on the porch of their Roxbury estate.

"Why aren't you at Flipper's?"

"Why?" I said, taking a glass of wine.

"I thought you went to Flipper's every night," Bob said.

The kids were rolling down their front lawn and playing with the eighteen giant cutout pumpkin heads that bordered their walkway. Yeah, *why aren't I going?* I thought. I could get the kids home, get dressed, and be there by 10:00.

Finally I got everyone home. I had run out of money for fancy nannies and begged Maria to let her daughter Aurora work for me. The girls knew her and loved her and I was very grateful.

"*Aurora, yo via para la fiesta.*"

"I speak English." Aurora smiled. "We'll be fine."

I dressed to the max: white cat rhinestone shades for my mask, white spandex pants, Harriet Selwyn white silk see-through gossamer shirt over sequined silver tube top, white and silver wristbands, white and silver shoe skate covers, rhinestone disco-ball earrings, a white Afro wig, and a full feathered boa wrapped around me. I looked like Big Bird in white. I spit out the feathers that kept sticking onto my bunny pink lipstick and raced to Flipper's.

The place was rockin' with the Leroy Jones live band in the center of the rink, and all the booths filled. I smiled to the impeccable James Galanos in his Nehru suit and Gustave Tassell in his Brioni, at the bar. I sat down and quickly laced up my skates, fluffing up my silver and white pompoms, then went down the rabbit hole.

I began my laps, the wind in my face, blinking disco prisms in my eyes. Oh yeah, I felt it, the freedom. I dodged the bad skaters, drifted through the crowd, a race to the finish line. I saw friends, cute guys, clients, and a few of the lesbian chicks from the salon around the corner from mine. The song changed, so I slowed down and got off the rink. Candy Clark, a pal and client, was talking to her new boyfriend at the guardrail.

I took out my Nat Shermans and opened the box. "Want one?"

"No thanks," Candy said. Her boyfriend lit my cigarette. I stood with my arm stretched behind me, cigarette in hand.

A deep annoyed voice spoke from behind my back. "*You burrrned me!*"

I turned around.

I saw a pair of unusually black eyes glaring at me, not a hint of a smile in them anywhere. Without asking, I took her by the shoulders and turned her around to inspect what damage I had done.

"No blood," I said in my flippant manner. "Guess you'll be okay."

"What you think . . . I am *silly* like you?"

"Hey, I didn't see you. Your shirt's fine, or I'd buy you a new one."

She made me nervous, not a flinch in her expression. It was like she was lookin' for a rumble but I wasn't in a *West Side Story* mood. Her accent was from another country. She looked like Steven Tyler or maybe Patti Smith. And Patti Smith looked like Bob Dylan and Freddie Mercury's child. I turned back to Candy to avoid further confrontation. Out of the corner of my eye I watched her sulk off until she sat down at the prestige front-row booth.

"Who *is she*?" Candy snickered.

"I have no idea," I said, taking another peek. "Kinda fascinating with that androgynous rocker-boy hair and the diamond watch hanging on her necklace."

A minute later, a chick I knew came skating off the rink to me.

"I saw that," Zan said seriously. "Be cool, you know who she is, don't you?"

"No." I laughed. "But I like her anyway."

I looked up again; she was looking toward us. I smiled. She didn't. Her booth was filled with attractive girls. So who was this revered mystery person with a bad attitude—another hairdresser?

"Well, be cool, she's *the Princess*."

"Everyone's a princess in Beverly Hills," I said. Zan dashed off.

Ahhhh, Fffffreeeeeeak out, le freak, c'est chic, freak out . . .

"Candy, I love this song, I gotta skate." I dashed off.

I kept thinking, *Princess?* I'd heard of the queen of England, and Grace Kelly *became* a princess, but that was all I knew of this subject. Maybe that was just her nickname. I buzzed around the rink, letting Earth, Wind & Fire push me, as we all shouted *Dance!* to "Boogie Wonderland," swinging and swaying. Then my favorite song came on, Bowie's "African Night Flight," but I was exhausted. I slid into the rail for a landing. Boom. Crash.

With my wig almost off, boa feathers in my mouth, I busted out laughing at myself, spitting out feathers, and there was Zan again, standing in front of me.

"The Princess thinks you're a 'silly one,' but she wants you to join her."

"Really? I said, looking at her booth. "Because she seemed pretty pissed off and accused me of burning her."

"*She* sent me over to get you."

"Okay, I could use a drink."

Zan went ahead and whispered something in the Princess's ear. The girl sitting next to the Princess got up, making room for me.

"Hello," the Princess said, somewhat dismissive. "You sit here."

"Hi, how's your invisible burn?"

"You like champagne?" She poured me a glass of Cristal.

"This is Carrie," Zan said to the girls. The hip, sexy girls, dressed in black, open shirts with gold chains like guys, cool short hair on some, long hair on the more feminine girls, checked me out and smiled.

"You know my name," I said to the Princess. "What's yours?"

"It's too long," she said in her unfamiliar accent. "Call me K."

"Where're you from?"

"That's too long too," she said.

She filled my glass again.

"They tell me you have famous hair salon in Beverly Hills," she said changing to a more seductive tone of voice. "You want to do *my* hair?"

"Call me, I'll make sure you get in."

"Is this the latest Piaget, K?" a girl on the other side of the Princess said, picking up the dangling necklace with the watch hanging from it. "It goes so well with your Ted Lapidus suit." I thought I knew so much, but I'd never heard of Piaget and never dared enter the Ted Lapidus store on Rodeo Drive, it was beyond expensive.

"You like drugs?" the Princess said, slowly and hypnotically rolling the *d* and *r* together when she spoke.

"Sometimes . . ." I said.

The bathroom was packed. It was *snowing* in Hollywood, wherever you went.

"There . . ." she pointed to two empty stalls next to each.

I went in, sat on the toilet, and saw her feet sitting next to mine. Again, her slow deep voice came through the wall. "You would like cocaine or heroin?"

"Oh, just cocaine for me," I whispered, shocked with the proximity of heroin. I reached under the partition and took the little brown bottle, flicked the glass a few times, then gave myself a bump of cocaine. The bottle was full, so I took a double hit, screwed the top on, and passed it back to her under the partition.

"Keep it, I have more."

K's secretary told me, "K wants you to ride with her." I had a queasy feeling in my gut. K was so dominating. But the voyeurism and the underground ladies tempted me, as well as more drinks and drugs. I'll just be social, play a game of pool . . . just this night, it's harmless, my little girls are sleeping, Aurora's with them, I'll get home no later than 5:00 AM.

I threw my boa and skates in my trunk and put on my high heels.

A brand-new sexy silver Jaguar XJS, a rarity in L.A., pulled up to the curb. The Princess leaned over the driver's seat and pushed open the car door. Nancy and her girlfriend got in the backseat. I followed.

She squealed off and floored it.

"I like to drrrive fast," she said, rolling the *drrr* like when she said "drrrugs."

"No shit," I mumbled, clutched the door, and braced myself.

PART 6

Never Say Never

1979–2000

Crossing Lines

"Stef?" I said, "I need help."

"Care?" my high school chum Stefanie Powers said. "What's going on? I called your salon months ago, they said they didn't know where you were or when you'd be back."

"Things got bad, then really bad . . . could I stay with you for a few days?"

"Sure. Where are your children?"

"Adam and Daisy live with Bucky now and my little girls live with me, but they're in San Fran with Richard for a week."

"Where are you?"

"Down the street from you, but I need to know if I can come over or if I have to figure something else out."

I pulled up at Stefanie's driveway in my Mercedes, which was stuffed with my best things: the lamp designer Paul Ferrante made for me from the 1964 Château Latour jeroboam Peter Sellers gave me, a Tibetan scroll from Richard Rutowski, my personally signed Erté serigraphs, a small box of jewelry, patchwork quilts off my daughters' beds, a bag of clothes, and a rare copy of the book *The Art and Craft of Hairdressing* from Richard. Stef was at her opened garage door waiting to put my car out of sight.

"Care, are you running from the KGB?" Stef said, as I got out of my car.

"Only the Girl from U.N.C.L.E. would say that," I said, grateful to smile. "It feels worse than that."

"You look worse than that, what's going on?"

Stef's radiant mom came to greet me. "Hi, Mama Powers." She had changed her name to match Stefanie's.

"What the hell are you doing to yourself?" She put her arms around me. "You need food, you're wasting away, I know you girls like to be thin, but—"

Stef interrupted. "Mom, let me settle her in, then we'll have tea with you."

I was dying for a drink to settle my nerves, but I swore to myself that I would postpone a drink for as long as I could.

"Care, you're shaking, how come?"

My nose was running. I hadn't slept in ages, and never for longer than two or three hours. My hair was greasy; my skin was dry as a brittle leaf. I never drank water. There was nothing in water to get me high. My teeth showed decay spots and were yellow from smoking, my pants were wrinkled from not changing clothes for days on end, until I bought new ones. My sweater was too warm for the hot afternoon, but I was freezing.

"I'm fine."

I plunked myself down on her guest bed with a sigh. "How can I thank you?"

"By being okay . . . what are you running from or who? Richard?"

"Oh, God no, Richard has his own multitude of problems."

I *wished* Richard was my problem, and that I could turn the clock back to Halloween 1979 and say *no thanks* instead of getting into that fancy Jaguar that night. I also wished that my head wasn't banging in pain, and my body wasn't cramping like the worst flu.

"Could we turn the light down a little?"

"Okay." Stef adjusted the dimmer. "*Now* what is this all about?"

I held the throbbing vessels at my temples, sure they were going to pop.

"One night after Flipper's I went home with a princess," I said. "She wrote *I love you* on a mirror in cocaine and passed it to me. I thought *well, I guess I love you too* and I spent the night with her."

"Whoa, wait, a *princess* . . . from where?"

"It doesn't matter," I said. "Anyway, after that first night, she kept sending her secretary into my salon with envelopes of ten thousand dollars in cash and notes that read: *Do you really have to work today?*

"Do you know how many haircuts that is? I was scrambling to make a hundred bucks, but I sent it back to her each time, until one day I didn't." I explained how I took the envelope, and in my hot pink spandex pants and roller skates, I wheeled out of my salon and never looked back, leaving Candice Bergen, Margo Winkler, and God-knows-who-else on my appointment books. I had been on a runaway train since Richard and I broke up, running out of money, out of answers. And out of time. I needed to love her. I put my home with Richard up for sale and moved in with her.

"But Care," Stef interrupted. "You're not gay."

"I know, but I convinced myself I *could* love her, she liked me so much. She had tons of money and drugs and I thought that could save me and I could save my kids. It backfired. Money and drugs just trapped me, all we do is get high, 24/7, and we do it just to feel normal . . . so it's not even like we're high."

I scratched my face, cracked my neck, and tried to get comfortable.

"It makes me sick, but I can't figure how to change things, so I pretend we're having a great life. I lost Adam and Daisy to their dad, that was bad enough, well, it's good for them, I couldn't keep up with their school and after-school stuff . . . and . . . oh, shit, my head is killing me."

"You need to rest. Do you want an aspirin?"

"I'd really love a drink."

"Oh, like what?"

"Whatever's open, like vodka?"

"You want vodka this early?"

"Or wine," I said trying to play down my need for hard liquor.

"I'll get you vodka if you want it." She headed out.

I lay on the bed. I had been isolated from my friends for over a year, except Rita when we bought coke from her. I'd snorted heroin a few times, actually the day before, maybe that's why I was so ill. Oh God, where's Stef with that drink?

I got up and walked to the bathroom and puked. I hoped she didn't hear me. I cleaned the toilet seat like a maid, lumbered back to my flower-printed guest room, wallpaper, and fluffy matching bedspread with lots of pillows—very chic, very grown-up—nothing I could identify with, only admire.

Stef came back with my drink on a painted tray with a linen

napkin, vodka with too much ice and a thin lemon rind hugging the glass.

"Sorry, Hon, I had to take a work call."

I sipped the vodka. It tasted gritty, hard to get down without cocaine; my face curled up. I took a bigger sip of vodka, this time it soothed.

"So, go on . . ."

"The first time she kissed me was, I don't know, it was shocking . . . it was so different. I knew from all her attention, she expected me to kiss her and I had postponed it, because, well . . . because of every reason. But anyway, everyone had left her house, I sat on the edge of her couch, and she leaned in and kissed me like any man had ever kissed me. Passionately."

I stopped and tried to see Stefanie's reaction. She didn't flinch. I went on.

"I stayed in for her kiss, then I stood up and walked into another room. I knew I had crossed a line. She came in and said, 'What is the matter with you?' She spoke in an angry tone. When she saw my watery eyes, she stomped into her bedroom. I felt guilty. It was all just weird. I followed her and tried to explain, but it was more than language, we were worlds apart. I could come over to her side, but she could never realize mine—a mother, a wife, a career that I had trashed—so I surrendered to her and said, "I'm sorry, I never kissed a woman before." I guess that was good enough for her because she relaxed. She said, 'Oh.' So then I moved in with her shortly after and tried to act like it was all normal. The friends were just different, only women. I was mesmerized by this whole world, this . . . this luxurious *high*. That was for a few months, then it all changed. She became jealous and she cut everyone out of our lives. That's when the fun turned to fear and my survival was in flux. I catered to her to keep peace. She became irrational if she got too high. God, we lived like hermits, ordering from Chalet Gourmet every night, Cristal champagne, tons of beluga caviar, chocolate éclairs, that was dinner, except when she would call a belly dancer to bring us Moroccan food and dance for us—well, for her. I have my girls with me, so she hired a limo to take them to school every day, because she never wants me out of her sight. I have to tell her when I go from one room to another."

"Care, this is crazy!"

"You don't know crazy. One time she accused me of crawling through her air-conditioner duct to screw the old man who lives next door."

Stef starred at me with her jaw dropped. I knew I did not sound like the girl she had known all her life.

"Like I said, at first it was fun, we went to concerts—oh, *The Wall* was fantastic, ever see Pink Floyd and the floating pig? But the worst was when we went to see Stevie Nicks at the Forum and forgot where we parked our car, can you imagine, searching for our car on foot in that huge parking lot? We had to wait till every car was gone to find ours."

I started laughing so hard I couldn't finish the story.

"Are you okay?"

"Yeah, so get this . . . the *worst* of the worst part." I collected myself. "All our stash was in the trunk of that damn car, all our drugs, and *we needed them* . . . coming down is awful."

I took a sip of vodka, shivered, and began again.

"We never went to a concert without a driver after that. Oh, and then there was the time I talked her into seeing Jackson Browne, who she never heard of, at the Cow Palace, near San Fran, in a limo. My two little girls came and we headed north, with lots of cocaine and smack, she likes heroin . . . I snorted it a few times but mostly we smoke coke together, it's called free-basing."

"Geez, Care . . . I can't believe all this."

"I know, I know, but I got her off pills. I threw her Tuinals and Quaaludes down the toilet like I did with Rosalind's diet pills, re-member?"

I didn't tell Stef that I heard K's pills scream *Noooooo* as they went swirling down the toilet like tiny drowning people.

"We took the girls to Richard's mom's house, the driver took us to San Jose, and after the concert, the limo driver was holding K's briefcase. He wanted to blackmail her for the drugs he found or he was going to call the police. She said she would have the five thousand bucks he wanted in the morning, but to hand over her stuff now. He refused. She told him she'd be very ill if he didn't, so he let her take some. He drove us back to Richard's mom, who welcomed us, for the girls' sake, I'm sure. Can you imagine my being in Richard's house with K?"

"Uh, no, I can't."

"She immediately called someone to get money and a new driver for us. At nine AM, another limo pulled up and the new driver came to the door and handed K an envelope." I sat up, excited to deliver the punch line: "Here comes the good part—"

"Care, what could be *good*?"

I leaned forward. "When she gave that creep driver his lousy five thousand, she told him, 'You fool . . . I would've *tipped* ten.' Great story, huh?"

I sat back, exhausted, looking at Stef, an accomplished talented woman of the world. I knew she wasn't judging me.

"Yes. Now just get some rest." She gave me a hug, turned off the light, and closed the door.

I lay there in the dark thinking how I'd painted K's entire house, from her mailbox to her swimming pool, using twelve cans of new colors my friend Don Kaufman had created for Dutch Boy and had dropped off one day. I had nothing to do but get high, nowhere to go, except to the dealer, so I painted, drank endless bottles of champagne, did endless lines of cocaine, and painted.

I'd painted K's mailbox, which led to my painting her partition outside the garage. I did this in all pastel colors like Easter eggs. Parked in the driveway was K's MINI Cooper. I painted the body sky lavender and the tires white for clouds. I figured when we went to the dealer, the car would be invisible and we'd never get busted.

Then I began on the house, swirling the walls with rags, pressing sponges, and socks tied into balls for other effects. I painted our bedroom purple for royalty and glued copper pennies and broken mirror pieces to the walls like mosaics. Mirrors broke all the time there from our throwing or dropping them, big ones and little ones.

My next masterpiece would be my little girls' room. I'd make them a happy new space; maybe they could be distracted. I painted their room sky blue with clouds like the crib scene from Bertolucci's *The Conformist*. I took a pillowcase and wrapped it around a broom and dunked it into the paint and did all the ceilings like sky. I had new wall-to-wall carpet put in their room, green as grass to substitute for all the cement at K's house. There was no yard to play in, just the pool.

A week or a month passed, I still had paint, I still had coke. Time to redo the faded chipped swimming pool! I found a hardware store that delivered special pool paint. I painted in my roller skates and a bathing suit, with a giant paint roller. Zoom to the deep end, painting the sides. Zoom, splat, swipe, charge to the shallow end, get momentum, skate to the deep end, up the center wall, grip the edge of the pool with my elbows, take drags off my cigarette, slug down some champagne, take a few toots of cocaine, then dip back down to the drain into the toxic pool paint to refurbish the mermaid painting.

Billy would have been proud of my artwork.

Many days, when my girls were at school, I sat outside in K's backyard with pen and pad, looking at the view that stretched over the Benedict Canyon hills with telephone poles in between the trees. The poles had five wires. Birds sat on the wires in all different positions; four in a row sat on one wire, one sat by itself on the very bottom wire, and three more sat down on the middle wire. Since sheet music has five lines, I was convinced God was writing songs with the birds on the wires. After I copied their positions, I would stand up and holler at them, and they'd flutter off, return, and land in new configurations . . . next stanza. Unfortunately, I didn't read music, so I didn't know their songs. I filled pads and pads with bird music, thinking, *Someday I'll learn and I'll play God's birdsongs . . . someday . . .*

I must have finally drifted off to sleep when I heard my name being called, but I couldn't figure out from where.

"You okay? It's five o'clock in the afternoon."

It was Stefanie's mom. I had slept through yesterday and almost all of today. I lifted my heavy head. "Come in."

Mama Powers sat beside me on the bed. "You're burning up."

"Just bad dreams . . . where's Stef?"

"Stefanie's still filming, come eat something. I'll be in the kitchen."

The thought of food was impossible. It took everything I had to get out of bed. Taking my clothes off and letting water touch my bare skin was a terrorizing thought. I splashed water on my face without looking at myself.

Walking past the bar, I found the vodka. Vodka had always worked for me, even if I had the flu. I poured a sneaky shot and threw it down. It hit like a lightning bolt. Yes . . . it still worked.

I walked into the kitchen. Mama Powers said, "It's evening, you missed breakfast and lunch." She opened the big refrigerator door and I was reminded of what a real fridge looks like, green and red things called vegetables, fruit and yogurt and cheeses, juices . . .

I ate some cereal and felt chills again. "I think I need more sleep, I should be better by tomorrow. Tell Stef she can wake me when she gets home."

I passed the bar and took another two shots of vodka before I went back to my dark haven under all the luxurious comforters.

Knock, knock, knock.

"Powers Wellness Center." Stef laughed. "How you feeling?"

"Much better, and you're the best friend ever."

"Thanks, but let's hope you don't have to do this again. Hey, do you want to do my hair tomorrow for the *Hart to Hart* title promo?"

Staggered at the thought of doing hair, I bluffed, "I'd love to."

"Are you sure you're up for it?"

"Sure, but I don't have hair stuff with me."

"I have everything. I told RJ I'd pick him up, then we'll go to the *Hart to Hart* house." RJ was her nickname for Robert Wagner. "It's just pickup shots, I wasn't going to have anyone do my hair, but hey . . . you're here, lucky me."

"Like the good ol' days." I smiled. "Hey, Stef, is it okay if I get a nightcap?"

"Help yourself to anything, Care . . ." and she left.

I tiptoed to the bar, took some cashews from a bowl, and fixed another vodka, a big one this time. I went back to my little guest room and called collect to San Francisco, no answer. I had a cigarette, my drink, and looked at Stef's bedside books. I thought about *doing hair* in the morning. I could use the cash, but I wouldn't take it. I turned off the light.

"Rise and shine."

"Okay, Stef," I said, through a banging hangover. I hoped she wouldn't notice how much vodka was missing until I could replace it. I went to the bathroom and made myself take a fast shower. I didn't want to get my hair wet; it would be too much to do my hair too. I brushed my teeth, trying not to gag, and put on the spare outfit I had brought. I was sicker than the day before, *not better*. I needed to put vodka in the orange juice Mama Powers had brought me. But then Stef would smell it on me, so I didn't.

"I'm washed, let's do something quick," Stef said, undoing her wrapped towel of wet hair. "We can fuss on set, after the run-through."

I picked up her dryer; it felt like a ton. Stef's hair was always my favorite, but not this day; it was a struggle to pull smooth and blow-dry. I tugged away at her, trying to appear professional. She sensed my difficulty.

"Looks great, Care . . . we gotta go, we'll finish later."

We pulled up to Robert Wagner's house. It didn't take Robert any time to notice I wasn't myself. We knew each other from my years of doing Natalie's hair.

"Kid, you look like you could use some Fernet-Branca." He went to his bar and poured me a jigger. "What's that?" I said. He handed me a drink that smelled like licorice. "You've got a hangover, don't you?"

I somehow managed to get through the day, and we returned to Stef's place. She had a date, and while she was out all I could think about was K, who I knew was home with heroin, coke, and plenty of champagne. I knew she wanted me with her, so why was I running away? My body was my boss, not my brain nor my heart. And I hadn't done Stef's hair very well either.

I wrote Stef and her mom a thank-you note, resigned to my destiny.

I would try harder to make things more normal with K. I had what I needed with her, a roof over my head and my girls, my medication, and money if I asked for it. I would get healthier food in the house, and I would cook for my girls. I just needed to get organized. I could manage this life if I got smarter: at least, until I got stronger so I could change myself.

Because one thing I knew: Nothing would change until I did.

I drank Stefanie's remaining vodka and filled the decanter with water. I would get her a new bottle of Stoli soon. I headed back down Benedict Canyon to K's. I pulled up to the newly repaired electric gates and saw two armed security guards pacing behind them.

"Who are you?" one demanded through the gate.

"I live here," I said.

"Just a minute." He walked to the house.

K came out, hands on hips, barefoot, wearing a man's shirt and tight pants. She saw me, nodded to the guard, and walked back into the house.

"Sympathy for the Devil" played in my brain.

The gate opened, I pulled in. It clanged shut behind me.

I Have No Brakes

"Let's buy this one—my girls can walk to school."

I hoped our personal dynamics might get better if we bought a house together and moved to the beach, not that K was interested in changing.

We had seen a real castle up a steep winding mountain road, but I knew we would crash off the driveway the first month living there, so that one wasn't good. We had looked at another Malibu house that had a swimming pool in the living room, and I knew that was dangerous too. Then we looked at a house that was too close to the Malibu Sheriff's Department, and that was *really not good.*

"Fine," K said. "Get it . . . I don't care."

I'd taken my half of the Mulholland home money and added it to K's money, so we would own the house equally and I wouldn't feel like a prisoner anymore. But by this time, I was a prisoner to something bigger than K, bigger than alcohol and cocaine: heroin. It started when K wanted me to slow down instead of buzzing around day and night on cocaine. I thought, *Oh, a snort here and there won't hurt.* At first I didn't feel much, except a bit dizzy and nauseous. "Try this way," K said. She sprinkled some brown powder on a small piece of tinfoil, then lit a match underneath, and the powder melted into smoke. She inhaled the smoke, following it with a straw. "It's called *chasing the dragon.*" I followed her lead. It gave me a mellow feeling. I liked it. I used it with caution, not that often, once in a while, once a day, and at night we smoked together often. It *was* what we did together. My dabbling had progressed to a need and the fact is, it didn't matter if someone shoots heroin, snorts it, or smokes it on tinfoil, there's only one result . . . a *junkie.*

I couldn't breathe, think, walk, talk, drive, eat, or sleep without it.

Lenore, who sold Richard and me our Mulholland home, had found us the perfect house. It was down the street from a grammar school, a junior high, and a night school. My girls would be free to enjoy a walk to school, and *maybe I would go to school too, take photography or ceramics.* I felt hopeful for us all.

We walked up the porch and Lenore opened the front door to a big kitchen with a Wolf stove, the kind I had admired in so many clients' homes. Directly off the all-wood kitchen were steps to a sunken living room with a marble fireplace and box seat at a large bay window. K focused on the spiral staircase. Lenore said, "It's called a captain's ship staircase."

"Lets go up there," K said.

Clunk, clunk, clunk . . . the metal steps echoed as we walked up the hollow turret that led to the second-floor master bedroom.

"Look at that view of the ocean," Lenore said.

"If you're standing," I said. "Those windows are pretty high up."

"Yes," K said, looking at Lenore with her hands on her hips. "How can we see that view from a bed?"

"I can stack four or five mattresses," I said.

The girls' bedroom was directly below ours, with a built-in bunk bed and a beautiful handmade wooden ladder that hooked onto the top railing. They would have a play area, their own bathroom, and a big backyard. I would make sure they got lots of toys and books and dolls and a television—whatever they wanted. It would be the ideal setup. Upstairs I could be with K and downstairs, with my girls. I didn't have to read Dr. Spock's child care book to get that this wasn't good parenting, but I knew my girls would be safe and *with me*.

"There's room for horses, if you want," Lenore said.

"Maybe later," I said. That was too much to think about. I saw that K was getting impatient and I knew why. My heroin was wearing off too.

We signed the papers and moved to Malibu. My girls started a new school, but nothing was changed for us . . . K and I just got loaded. Every day. The only thing new was that we had to drive farther to our connections—one on Burbank Boulevard, one in Laurel Canyon, one in Beverly Hills, one in Hollywood, and one in West Hollywood.

We needed furniture—more than just mattresses. I had put all of my Mulholland home in storage, my armoires, beds, quilts, tables, chairs, paintings, photographs of my children, scraps of mine, and years of vintage shopping with Richard.

I wasn't ready to look through my life with him yet, so I kept it in storage. Maybe I would open my own thrift shop in the winter of my life. Then I recalled someone saying, "You never see *old* junkies . . . they don't live that long."

On our daily trips to and from the dealers, slowly we furnished the house: a table here, a television, chairs, towels, plates, and the four essential mattresses for the bed.

K told me she spent over a million dollars the first year we were together; grams and ounces were a few thousand a day, and that didn't count gas or pizza. But now K's trust fund had significantly dropped, limiting her to only $10,000 a month. We would have to pace our intake and ration our cash, so we wouldn't run out of drugs, alcohol, gas, phone, lights, or McDonald's . . . and in that order.

One day my daughter Aloma said, "Mommy, I need new shoes."

I was downstairs grabbing a beer; I couldn't drink vodka anymore; it broke down the effects of the heroin.

"Honey, I only have five hundred dollars today," I said, desperate for her to be okay, because I really needed that money. "Can you wait just a few days?"

Aloma looked let down, but she knew what came first. "Okay, Mom." My daughter, now eleven, turned stiff as stone when I hugged her.

"I promise I will get you shoes real soon." I headed back up the captain's staircase. "We'll check out the Cross Creek stores after the bank on Friday."

It was always the same—first of the month, we were flush with money, and by the end of the month, we were fighting withdrawal, and just fighting, period.

"You have the flame too high," I said. "You're cooking the coke too fast." I turned down the gas flow of the propane torch, put a nice-size rock on the tiny screen, and fired it up until the coke crackled and melted. I took a big hit, slowly, evenly, pulling the fire back as the rock got smaller, letting the base of the glass fill with the pure white smoke. I loved that big cloud in my head. I forgot everything at that moment.

K pulled out a gram of smack from her back pocket. She took the lighter and heated the heroin from beneath the tinfoil until the smoke appeared. Cautious not to let a molecule of smoke escape, she quickly sucked it up with a cut straw (from McDonald's). We chased that dragon of Persian brown powder all night, passing the tinfoil back and forth until there were only scrapes for the morning.

K got a bonus check from her trust, which meant doubling up on drugs, some new clothes for everyone, and more Tower Records pit stops. K hated being anywhere but at the dealer's or at home. Stopping for gas and oil took too much time.

"Your tires are low," an attendant told me.

"Next time," I said, handing him twenty dollars for gas for my Mercedes.

Next time came. "Check under the hood?"

Next time.

"What's that smell?" I asked the attendant.

"Your carburetor, lady," he said, looking under the hood.

"Can it wait?"

"Not long or you'll blow it up."

"Tomorrow," K said. "Let's go."

"Tomorrow," I shouted. He slammed down the hood. Off we went to the dealer.

Next day, K followed me in her Jag to leave my car at a Mercedes mechanic. A month later the Jag started acting up. No oil. We had cracked the engine. We had it towed and took a limo to buy a brand-new Volkswagen Rabbit.

"Now, no more fucking car problems." We let the limo go and drove from the car dealer to the drug dealer.

"I want to make lunch for my girls," I said one night. K was my other child, the demanding sick one. "Will you be all right?"

I missed my girls in the morning or I saw them for minutes here and there. They dressed, fed, and took care of themselves and got to school without me. Making a fun lunch for them occasionally was my way to prove my motherly love.

"Go ahead." K said, stoned out, supine on the four mattresses, with the television on, not really watching it.

We had smoked the coke until it was gone and the smack was down to scrapings. It was 3:00 AM. This was our sleepless coma time, every night passing out, coming to, nodding off, looking at each other, my head screaming to let me out of here but my paralyzed body and brain doing nothing. K and I had nothing in common but the drugs. She usually passed out first and I would stare at the black-and-white *Felix the Cat* cartoons, interrupted by the inspired commercials that the hilarious speed-talking Shadoe Stevens created for Federated Group. I looked forward to him; he was a beacon of life for me. Then I would pass out and we would come to around 5:00 AM, ill, and like robots begin the routine of struggling to get our bodies out of the house and the drive to any dealer who would see us at 6:00 AM. I was back to serious thinking once again . . . how can I change this, how can I get out of here peacefully? I never had an answer.

"Okay, I'll be in the kitchen."

The kitchen was a ghost town. All that was sitting on my Wolf stove was a burned saucepan from boiling glass bottles to make free-base rocks to smoke. I looked at the dirty dishes piled in the sink, scuffled over to the refrigerator, and pulled open the door. Inside, a carton of milk, a can of whipped cream, a package of cheese slices, dilapidated celery, a plate of green grapes in a torn plastic bag, and a large box of baking soda for cooking the cocaine.

I grabbed the grapes and cheese and went to the cupboard for saltine crackers and the ever-abundant box of tinfoil. I cut squares and made cheese and cracker sandwiches. I wrapped three sets for Aloma and three sets for Pitita and put them in little brown lunch bags. Then I cut twelve little squares of tinfoil and wrapped each grape individually and dropped them in their bags. I thought, *They'll have so much fun opening these. And they'll be so happy.* I smiled. *Job well done.*

I scuffed back upstairs, reopened a bottle of flat warm Mickey's Big Mouth, as we called it, and took a big swig. It was awful, but I took another gulp and finished it. I reached to the table for a More cigarette, the poor man's Sherman. I couldn't get to stores that sold Shermans anymore. I sat on the toilet. I reflected on the vacuum I was in, my dormant life. It had to change, I wasn't sure how, and . . . well, not today. I took a deep drag off my cigarette. I was starting to feel dope-sick. I waited for K to wake up and the girls to find their happy lunch surprise.

"Bad news," K said. "There's a notice in my check, my trust is cut in half."

"We have to quit this," I said. "We leave good jewelry at stupid gas stations for five bucks of gas, forget where the gas station is after we get some money . . . it's ridiculous how we live." K looked at me like she was actually listening to me, and for one moment I thought there was a light of consideration.

"I tried to quit before," she said. "And look . . . it didn't work."

"What's that fucking smell?" K said, walking down to the kitchen from upstairs. I was cooking the coke on the stove; the girls were watching television in the living room.

"It's the toilet," Pitita said.

"Again?" K said, and kept walking toward me.

"We have to take care of that," I said. "I'm sorry, girls."

"It's been over a week, Mom," Aloma said, disgusted, coming into the kitchen to look for something to eat. "We've been telling you the sewer's backed up and it's horrible. Why do you think the maid left?"

"I'm *really* sorry, girls," I said. "We've been strapped for cash."

"What you mean, *sorry, girls*?" K said. "What about *my* nose?"

I turned the stove off and moved the pan to the table, burning the wood. "Oh shit, I scorched the table."

"Bring it upstairs when it's done . . . it smells like shit down here . . . I want some mint tea too."

She sauntered back up the staircase making her point. I was on my third Mickey's. It was early morning, but what day, I didn't know. Pitita walked into the kitchen and asked Aloma, "What did you find?"

Aloma held up a box of cereal. "But there's not much milk."

I was dressed in my gray flannel jumpsuit that I hadn't managed to jump out of for over a month. I poured Evian water into the teapot and turned on the flame. "Aloma, honey, did you see any mint in the fridge?"

"No, Mom."

I walked out on the porch where I'd planted mint but saw only dry twigs.

"We're out of mint leaves," I called up to K.

"*What?*" she yelled. "After all I give you and your kids and I can't get mint tea?"

The girls sat at the table eating cereal, pretending they weren't listening, always prepared to take off like little soldiers in this cold war. It was the *unsayable* that spoke the loudest. The words they didn't speak or couldn't speak.

The teapot whistled. I took the large glass vial from the saucepan with the coagulated free-base floating around like honey in water, my mouth watering for it, and I headed upstairs to K.

"I'll be *right back down*, girls."

I could feel *those eyes* on me as I disappeared from their view.

"Hi, is my car done yet?" I had finally found the garage number. "It's the 1955 classic black Mercedes convertible, the four-door 300 SLD?"

"Where you been, lady?" the guy on the line said. "We put a lien on that car a month ago, it's been here for six."

"A *lien*? What's that?"

K bought a 1982 Pininfarina Fiat Spider to replace the car she'd sold to buy coke the previous month. She insisted it be custom-painted purple. We barreled back and forth every day, dealer—home, dealer—home, dealer—home. Sometimes K drove, sometimes I drove—whoever was the least sick that morning. We stopped only when absolutely necessary for gas.

"The brake pads are down."

"Next time."

"Lady, you need new brakes."

"It'll have to wait."

The day came when my foot went to the floor. I pumped and pumped the brake pedal, nothing. "The brakes are gone."

"Well, I'm too sick," K said. "We have to get to the dealer."

"We have no brakes."

"So?" she said. "I'm too sick to wait for a limo."

"Girls, out of the car, stay here and play, okay? We'll be back in an hour."

I started up the purple sports car, sick as a dog myself from no morning line to smoke. A Mickey's Big Mouth helped me a little, but it made K sicker. She lit a Gauloise cigarette. "Uhh, shit . . ." She smashed it out in the ashtray and folded over in her seat. "Hurry, dammit."

We hadn't left yet.

"We have *no brakes*," I said, coasting down our long driveway, holding my hand tight to the hand brake. She was silent through the Pacific Coast Highway, my winding across Kanan Drive to the 101 Freeway to Laurel Canyon.

Honk. Honk. Honk.

"Go around!" I motioned with my left arm to all the complaining drivers. "Cyrus better front us after this."

We couldn't call him to make sure he was even home, because our phone had been turned off for nonpayment. We used that money for drugs like we did with the water bill. We juggled bills all the time. Drugs first. K's monthly income was lowered again. It was impossible to make ends meet. Four hundred dollars was a regular day for us, two hundred just kept us from being terribly ill. We borrowed money and hocked all the jewelry K had given me in the beginning of 1979. It was the end of 1982.

Cyrus said he'd be home Sunday, and we were counting on it. We were his best customers. We saw him every day. We couldn't buy for two days anymore, it wouldn't last; whatever we purchased, we did. If we had a gram, it would last one day. If we had an ounce . . . it would last one day.

I clutched the wheel and kept my eyes on the road, praying that a cop wouldn't spot me on the freeway. I was always petrified that I'd be arrested and lose my girls. "Thank God it's Sunday," I said. K was still not speaking. I saw the Laurel Canyon off-ramp, downshifted, and pulled on the hand brake at the foot of the exit. I looked left; no on-coming cars, so I could continue my roll, making a right onto Laurel. "And thank God for green lights."

I crossed Ventura Boulevard, put my foot on the gas, and started up Laurel Canyon. It looked so normal out the car window, this street I'd known all my life from Pacoima through Hollywood. I hadn't looked at it so carefully in a while, the trees, the little homes lining the street where probably happy families lived behind little wooden fences. Not my world, I thought; seems I would rather die from no brakes in a car crash than *not* get to the dealer. I looked down at the blackened fingers on my left hand, the hand that used to cut Elvis Presley's hair. I saw dried blood between my middle and index fingers. I had nodded off last night with a cigarette and had burned myself to the bone. I didn't feel anything.

That wasn't the first time.

"We need to get off this shit, maybe just do methadone, or just coke and drink, but we gotta get rid of this fuckin' heroin, what do you think?"

K turned her head in her folded-over position, her eyes almost shut, nose running, her mouth dry and cracked, thinner than a reed, a mirror of myself. "Not today," she grunted. "And turn off the fuckin' Bonnie Raitt."

A few more blocks up Lookout Mountain and we would be saved from our physical agony. I drove faster, and eased onto the dealer's street. He was watering his yard. I hit his fence, though not hard. We piled out of the car like two bums from Skid Row, not from two gorgeous acres in Malibu.

"What the hell?" he said, dropping the hose and scooting us into his house. "You can't come here and park like that . . . *my neighbors.*"

"I have no brakes," I said, proud of my accomplishment. "I downshifted the whole way like a race-car driver."

"Fucking get us something, will you?" K said. "Talk later."

And I Cannot Stop

"What's this?" I asked Aloma. She was twelve years old and Pitita was ten. "Is there going to be a parents' night?"

"No, Mom," she said. She came over to the table and grabbed her school papers. "It's nothing, the teacher's parents are coming . . ."

I had had a mother who never showed up at my school events. I realized I was the mother whom my kids *didn't want to show up.* I glossed over the unspoken and tried again.

"Honey," I said, "I want to come."

"It's okay, Mom."

I came up and hugged her. I felt her body stiffen from my offending alcohol smell, cigarettes, and the unsightliness I had become.

"I'll look nice," I said. Aloma looked at my hands. I was still burning my fingers from nodding out. "I'll wear a Band-Aid, and by the way, we're going to quit heroin."

"I don't want to talk about it," Aloma said. "It makes me sick."

"No, really, both of us are going to quit."

"I thought you *couldn't* quit."

"We're going to do a detox program . . . soon, anyway, K won't come to school and I want to meet your teacher."

K did come to the open house, but she stayed in the car. I walked onto the school grounds with Pitita and Aloma. "Slow down, girls," I said, following them into Aloma's classroom. The teacher was busy talking to the parents one by one. I stood in the greeting line. I had on a black felt hat and some busy black-and-gold outfit I'd bought on Melrose Avenue. The other mothers were in beachy white or beige or powder blue. I smiled at their glances and avoided eye contact. I wondered if there were ladies in the room who knew me, ladies whose hair I had once done.

Aloma and Pitita wandered away, then came back. "Let's go," Aloma said.

"It's my turn to meet your teacher." She was finishing with a couple. "Hi, I'm Aloma's mother."

"Aloma is such a fine student, you must be very proud of her."

"Yes, I'm so proud of her."

"Aloma tells me you are a popular hairdresser like her father."

I flashed on a whole life gone.

"Well, I'm retired now," I said. "But I wrote a children's book about hair. I'd love to see how the children like it."

"We have sharing day on Fridays."

"My children love it, they can recite it by heart," I said. "Right, sweethearts?" They looked down and nodded their heads.

"We need to go now, Mom . . . before K comes looking for you," Aloma said.

"Should I come next Friday?"

"That will be fine," the teacher said. "Around eleven."

"Great," I said, knowing I'd be back from the dealer by then.

We walked to the car. The engine was on.

"What took so long?" K said.

Nighttime was unstable time, when K could flip into a tantrum without a warning. Right now she was like a restless shark. I didn't want a scene in front of the school.

"It was crowded," I said.

"I'm hungry," she said. "McDonald's or Kentucky Chicken?"

We were all quiet. It wasn't a good idea to be driving the Pacific Coast Highway at night with K at the wheel.

"Whatever's closest," I said. "Or whatever you want."

We made it home. The girls went to their room. We went to ours. They went to bed. We got high.

"My book is called *Why a Hairy Me?*"

I looked out to the children sitting at their little desks. It wasn't the audience at the Palladium for Revlon or the Century City Hotel for Clairol, but I was just as thrilled to be doing something that felt honorable. I saw Aloma brace for my performance. I smiled at her . . . like I was normal.

"And," I said to the group. "I did the illustrations."

The kids looked with wide eyes. I had layers of clothes on to cover my filth. I wore a hat. I had brushed my teeth, covered my beer breath with Listerine. I had taken a smidge of heroin that morning, so I wouldn't be sick but not be stoned. This was an important day for me. I wanted to make Aloma proud.

I had written this children's book over ten years ago, when I was with Richard but before we were married. It was amazing I hadn't lost it. It was like it had followed me for this very moment. Maybe the book could be my way out.

"*I saw a hairy caterpillar . . . I saw a hairy dog . . . I saw a hairy kitty . . . I saw a hairy bug . . . I saw a hairy rabbit . . . I saw a hairy bee . . . but still I always wonder . . . why a hairy me?*" I looked up and I had the kids' attention. Aloma looked okay. I went on. "*Whatzit there for? . . . Whatzit do? . . . This thought confuses me . . . Do you suppose I have it . . . just for you to see?*" They laughed and so did the teacher. I went on. "*Yes that's a good idea . . . it could be just for fun . . . I think I'll brush it gently . . . and take it in the sun.*"

I held up each page so everyone could see my drawings. The cartoon character was modeled after my son, Adam. I finished all thirty-two pages. "*And when I give thanks . . . I must be aware . . . to say how much . . . I love my hair.*"

The teacher said, "Let's give Aloma's mother a big thank-you."

They applauded. I looked at Aloma. She wasn't applauding; she was looking around the room at the other children looking at me. "Thank you," I said to the teacher.

A little girl had her hand up waving urgently. "Do you think his hair is good?" she said, pointing to a little boy next to her. "I like my hair," he said, and pulled away from her. "I think he should cut it, don't you?" the little girl continued.

"I have an idea," the teacher said, "You can all draw yourselves and your hair, and Aloma will bring the pictures home for our thank-you to her mom."

I was getting clammy, the craving was raving, I needed a fix. I shook the teacher's hand, and walked over to my daughter. "See, I didn't embarrass you."

"No, Mom."

I hugged her, over her natural resistance to me these days, and rushed home. At 4:00 PM I heard the front door and went to greet her. She'd brought back a drawing from each student. I looked through the self-portraits, so simple and innocent. "These are fantastic, where's yours?"

"It's in there . . ."

K came down the stairs ready to freebase. "What's all that?" she said, and rustled in the cupboard for a saucepan to boil water. My attention immediately went to the new batch of coke.

Between Rocks and Hard Places

"Mom . . . are you home?"

I put the pipe down and looked out the window. It was Adam.

"Who is that?" K said.

"My son."

It was early afternoon, the girls were in school, and K was in her silk pajamas. I was afraid of her reaction to unexpected company. He'd come a long way to see me. I couldn't tell him he wasn't welcome where his mother was living.

Adam had known about cocaine since Richard and I were using together, and he knew about K because we talked when I moved into her place. He knew about Malibu, because I'd given him my phone number.

"Your phone isn't working, Mom."

"Yeah, I know, honey, I'll be right down."

I pushed my stash underneath some blank notebooks and put the used tinfoil in the drawer with the roll of foil. I picked up the propane torch to put it away. "I'll take that," K said, so I handed it over and she started in on the pipe.

"Try to pace yourself. You know how you get when you have too much." She gave me a dirty look, and took a big spiteful hit.

"Bring your son up, maybe he wants to try some."

Freebase with my son?

I went to the door, tucking my hair behind my ears and licking my lips—they were so dry. I opened the door and hugged him before he could look at me too carefully. I hugged him so tight.

"Mom," he said, "what's wrong?"

My eyes welled up. I missed everything that was good. I missed *me*. I kissed Adam's forehead.

"Nothing's wrong, honey, come in."

"Where's the pool table?"

"Upstairs with the foosball. K bought a pinball machine too."

"Did I interrupt you . . . what are you doing?"

"You know . . . what we do," I said, and moved some plates around as we passed through the kitchen. "What are you doing out here? Are you all right?"

"Well, I could use a few bucks, Mom."

I looked at my little boy growing up, thin, sweet, and neglected. I knew he'd dropped out of high school, stopped playing tennis. He didn't get along with his dad, so he'd moved in with friends. He lived with Richard at one point, and with our friend Seymour Cassell and his family for a while, and he'd lived with people I didn't know.

"You're almost seventeen," I said. "What are you doing with yourself?"

"Come here," K called out.

"I'll find you some money, but don't say anything."

We got to the top of the captain's staircase and went into the shipwrecked bedroom. I was past explaining my mess. This was how it was.

"Hi, K," Adam said.

"Hi, you want some?" and she reached out with the pipe.

"Hey, wait a minute," I said. Adam and I had never done drugs together. I knew he smoked pot with Richard and we had shared beers, but nothing like this. He reached out for it. I was surprised. "Do you know what *this* is?"

"Of course, Mom, I've done this a few times."

"I don't think it's a good idea for you to get started with this."

I gave in. I figured I'm doing it; heroin is the real problem, and we wouldn't be sharing that.

He took a big hit and then another.

"Hey," I said, "pass it back to K, don't be greedy." K took it and he sat waiting for another round. I took a quick hit as an example of drug courtesy and passed it to him. Again, he kept the pipe for a long time.

"Okay, that's enough," I said. K watched. She seemed amused by the family dynamics. It wasn't funny to me.

Bottoms Up

K and I got to the Pacific Coast Highway about 1:00 PM. This day was especially beautiful with airbrushed clouds swiping across the blue sky. I flashed on the few times I'd taken Aloma and Pitita to the beach. I'd made picnic baskets and couldn't eat with them. I'd get chills and pretend I was okay. It had been a year since my feet touched the sand. K had never. I pulled over at the Zuma Beach sign.

"What you doing?" K said, scratching her face. "I want to go home, now."

"Wait, I have an idea."

"You and your ideas . . ." I got out, popped open the trunk, took out an old shoe box, and walked quickly to the sand. "Where you going?"

I filled the shoe box full of sand, came back to the car, set the box in backseat, and got behind the wheel.

"What was that?" K said.

"You'll see."

Another *same* day.

"Not again," K complained.

"One minute." I pulled over to the side of PCH and pulled out the shoe box from the trunk. On the way home from the dealer, every day for several months, even if we were in the limo, I pulled over so I could fill my shoe box with sand.

The sun was blazing, the breeze felt good, I felt good, I wasn't freezing, I wasn't in pain. We were living on a bonus and I didn't know how long the money would last, so I was enjoying not being dope-sick. And I liked my shoe box project.

I walked back, put the shoe box in the trunk, and drove to our house; it looked so wholesome on the outside. I walked in and dumped another box of sand onto the living room floor. I was a junkie and I knew that I would never spend time on the beach, so I brought the beach home.

"Girls, we can use the umbrella now."

We had an elaborate Moroccan patchwork umbrella. It was for outdoor furniture, but I had never gotten around to buying the rest of the patio set. I stacked throw pillows over the big rocks that I placed to support the opened umbrella, and spread more sand around. I threw a few rugs over thin sand areas.

"I think I have a chiffon dress that matches this umbrella," I said to the girls. "Get the Polaroid, we'll all take a picture." The girls watched my burst of coke-induced energy. I changed clothes and sat under the umbrella. "K, come look," I yelled up the staircase. She came down and sat on one of big stuffed pillows.

"Aloma, honey, would you get Mommy and K two beers?"

I put my Virginia Slim out in the sand on the living room floor. Aloma returned. I took the big bottles from her little hands.

"Girls, isn't this fun? All we need are seashells."

K pulled out her straw and tinfoil with the smack. The girls got right up.

"It's okay, don't leave."

"Let them," K said. "They probably have homework."

The money evaporated. I was scrambling through every corner of the house.

"What are you looking for?" K asked.

"The fucking storage receipt for all my stuff from Mulholland. I can't remember the name of the damn place. I could sell some of my things."

Jimi Hendrix buzzed in my mind's ear like a radio hum. I felt like the joker asking the thief how we were going to get outta here.

I reached for the last purse in the closet; there it was, folded like a secret will. I rushed to make the call. Our phone was working this week, so I didn't have to run to the Trancas Market phone booth.

"Hello, a while back I put my whole house in storage with you, my name is Carrie White."

"Just a minute," a man said. "I'll check." I sat on the windowsill and thought of those happy times long gone when Richard and I purchased our treasures. "Okay, I found your papers."

"Good . . . I'd like it all delivered to—" I was interrupted. "Ma'am, the paper here says we auctioned everything a year ago—don't you open your mail?"

I hung up the phone.

"What happened?" K said.

"Nothing, just fucking nothing."

I stepped out on the porch. The sun was like a gash of acid on my zombie face. I was already dead; my body just hadn't dropped yet.

"I can't drive today," I said.

"I'm sicker than you," K said.

"Fuck . . . okay." I drove us down PCH to the Venice methadone clinic.

"We want to be on the twenty-one-day methadone detox," I said, to our very own Nurse Ratched. It took us forever just to get to her window with the line that had been ahead of us. I wasn't going to be able to wait much longer before I would start screaming. K was turning green leaning on the wall.

"Have you ever had treatment or been in a hospital program?" she asked.

"No, a friend sent us here," I whined. "If this doesn't work we'll go into a hospital." I stood shaking and freezing and about to heave my raw empty guts up. "Please, we need something now, it's for the two of us."

"The doctor will be right out." She peered out for another inspection. "I'm sure you qualify."

"Hurry the *fuck* up," a guy in line behind us said.

The doctor came out with two little paper pill cups filled with liquid. "This is for you girls."

K grabbed one and threw it down her throat . . . I took the other.

"You have to be here between six and eleven AM. We close after that," he said. "Each day we drop your dose down until you are withdrawn from heroin."

That sounded so good to me. K said nothing.

"Don't forget," he said. "No methadone after eleven AM."

My neck was a frayed electric wire in a pool of water. I wanted to claw my flesh off.

"How long does this take?" I said. He took our papers and handed them to the nurse. "You'll feel better soon," he said. "Good luck."

I looked across the street and saw the Rose Café.

"Let's get a beer."

"I'm not walking," K said.

We drove across the street and I went in and grabbed two Coronas. When I got back, K said, "There's a phone booth, go call Jimmy."

"I thought we were going to quit."

"What d'you think . . . I can quit so easy?"

Unfortunately, as our detox dose was lowered, our sickness got worse. We ended up using the methadone as a means to tide us over from the beach until we got to one of our dealers in town. Finally, K got her family to help us into a hospital. My girls stayed with my friend Jeannie. We got extra high before we were admitted.

We'd been there two days.

"I hate this place," K said.

"Sure, but it's the only way we can get better." I needed her to stay, so I could stay. "Tell them you need more meds."

"I'm calling Jimmy," she said. "I know what kind of meds I need."

She went to the office. I stayed in bed. She came back.

"He's coming here."

The Klonopin I was on left me with no energy and no blood pressure, but this got a rise out of me. "What? He can't bring anything here."

"He can and he will." She picked up the remote for the television.

We walked into the house after walking out of rehab. The electricity was off. We lit candles and got high all night, passing out, coming to, passing out. The next day we were fine, fine meaning *not sick*. Jimmy had given K two grams and we didn't have to go anywhere but to the bank. I guessed K knew that a bonus was coming, so why quit now? We got the cash and paid the electricity and phone bill. I called Jeannie.

She brought the girls back and let them out in the driveway. I waved hello and good-bye. I was high, not to be confused with high and happy. I just wasn't puking my guts out. My demon was fed and resting but I was aware of my failure.

"Why didn't you stay, Mom?" Aloma said.

"I couldn't. K didn't want to stay."

Aloma gave me a dirty look. She was growing up. She saw through everything and hated what she was seeing. Pitita ran and gave me a hug. I bent over her and kissed her. "I missed you so much. Aloma, come here . . . please."

I sat on the porch and she reluctantly came over.

"Honey, I'm disappointed too, but I'll try again, I promise."

"Okay," she said pulling away from me. "Can I go? I have homework."

"What kind of homework? Can I help you?"

"Don't you have to get *upstairs*?"

The time with K had turned into three years. In drug years that was a blink. In child years, it was an eternity.

One day I realized that if I was ever going to get out again and support my daughters and myself, I needed to practice doing hair.

Aloma wouldn't let me work on her. I had cut bangs on her and she hated them. I came home after scoring one morning and saw Aloma coming out of the bathroom. "Where are your bangs?" I asked. She had had Pitita recut them to the scalp line. Aloma answered, "I didn't want them anymore."

Pitita let me practice on her, though. I washed her hair in the kitchen sink and prepared her for a brand-new style. I had found some scissors and bought some bleach and film at the Malibu pharmacy. Of course, I cleared the time and space with K.

I cut Pitita's long hair into a short cute style. She was a perfect little model. I photographed her by my half-painted entry door. Next, I bleached the front of her hair like Deborah Harry, slicked her hair back, and made up her face. She looked like a little eleven-year-old Kewpie doll, another photograph. *Zip zip* . . . the film came out the Polaroid camera, proof of a happy moment.

Broke and sick again. "We need to get back to the hospital," I said.

"Fine," K agreed. "Call them."

They took us back.

Three days later, K wanted out and I followed.

I was at the *Ks* in my old rumpled address book.

"Hi, Rachel Kerlan . . . it's me, Carrie."

She sounded happy to hear from me. I gave a story of woe, made my request for two hundred dollars. Rachel said she had to ask Doc, her husband.

"No, I'm sorry, he said we can't support the life you're living."

I sank. The Kerlans had cared for me like one of their own. They were so generous to me with their Lakers floor seats. How did he know how I was living?

More calls, more rejections. When I got to the *Ps*, Linda Pincay, the wife of jockey Laffit Pincay, came through with four hundred dollars. The money was gone in ten minutes, except fifty dollars I saved for gas and food for the kids. All four hundred dollars meant was a few more days I would not have to beg on the phone for money from another person I hadn't spoken to in years. We had twelve more days before K's next trust check came in.

It was a miracle I remembered where the Winklers lived. I pulled up to their big black iron gates and pushed the gate-box buzzer.

"Hi, is Margo in?"

I hadn't spoken to Margo in four years. She'd loaned me money before, maybe she would do it again, but I still owed her.

"The Winklers are in Europe," the houseman said.

I turned to K. "Maybe Ann-Margret's home."

K didn't know who any of these people were, or how degrading this begging was for me. And she didn't care as long as we got our fix. I drove up Benedict Canyon and made a left turn across the street from my first home with Richard. I couldn't look; I needed to prepare myself for this next acting job. I pulled into Roger and Ann-Margret's entrance. I got out of the car like I was expected. *She's an artist—she doesn't look back.* This day I was a con artist. I took a deep breath and knocked. Roger opened the door.

"Hi," I said, surprised he'd opened his door so quickly.

"Oh, Carrie, come on in."

"Who is it?" Ann-Margret's voice rang in from the other room.

"Honey, it's Carrie White."

Roger and Ann-Margret had been so good to me through the years, from Ann-Margret's television special with my big screen credit, to *The Last Remake of Beau Geste*, where Universal didn't want to give me screen credit, so Roger made them pay me double.

"Honey, what happened to your fingers?" Ann-Margret hugged me.

"Oh, I accidentally burned them on the stove, it's nothing, I'm fine." I forgot what I looked like. I wanted to break down and tell them everything but instead, "I'm in trouble with my mortgage, I moved to Malibu, you know Richard and I divorced."

"Yes, and we were sad to hear that . . . Roger, help Carrie."

"How much do you need?" Roger said.

"About a thousand dollars."

"Is that all? I thought I was going to have to call our business manager, I'll write you a check now."

I thanked them and got back into the car. K was huddled into a ball. "Did you get anything after all this fucking time?"

"Look, a thousand dollars!"

"A fucking check . . . how can we buy drugs with that?"

"Who wouldn't take a check from Ann-Margret?"

I was already thinking about who could be my next money target.

We got in the car with my last fancy bracelet and K's Piaget watch that she'd worn when we first met. We were regulars at the Beverly Hills Loan Company. I called the owner Uncle Louie, a nice elderly man, always dressed in a smart suit in a Beverly Hills office. K and I looked quite out of place wherever we went—even our dealers were getting concerned with our disintegration.

"We'll pay you in a few weeks," K assured him.

"I'll help you," he said. "But you need some other kind of help also."

"Good night, girls, time for sleep now." I climbed up the ladder of their bunk bed. Aloma and Pitita were nestled in one bed, reading to each other. "Oh, is that the Moon book I got you? I love the draw-ings, especially the Big Button that buttons up the day-sky for the night-sky."

I heard K calling. *"Where are you?"*

"I better go. I love you girls, thanks for being so good and so quiet all the time."

Beverly Glen Hospital. "I see you girls have tried to get clean before," the administrating doctor said, reviewing our papers. We sat in his office, shuddering and sick. My girls were back at Jeannie's.

"Yes, yes," I said. "Can we get started? We're very sick right now."

"Yes," the doctor said, thumbing through our records. "However, no drugs in here other than the ones we give you, is that clear?"

"When do we get *yours*?" K said.

Day 1. Lots of drugs. IVs. Stayed in bed.

Day 2. Drugs, and made us walk around in our pajamas.

Day 3. Went to group meetings in the afternoon. I couldn't listen.

Day 4. Shuffled through halls from one gathering to another. Still, people talked and I heard nothing. A counselor named Charlie wanted us to meet individually as part of the Get Well program. K refused. I said, "We need this."

"You go then." K needed more drugs. We watched TV in the television room, barely eating, waiting for meds.

Day 5. "They are not giving me enough drugs for my pain," K complained. "I'm calling Jimmy."

"K, *no*," I said, but my mouth watered at the thought of heroin. I had pain too.

Day 6. K knew her check was in at the downtown bank. She called Jimmy and arranged a meeting. I forgot everything but my cravings; I'm in on the caper. We talked the hospital into driving us to get her money with a security guard. We got to the bank, stood in line for the teller, spotted Jimmy waiting in the corner of the bank. The guard watched us from the side. K got her money but put two hundred bucks in her pocket and handed me the envelope of cash. I walked over to distract the guard, and K walked another way. "Hey!" the guard said, spotting K. "She has to go to the bathroom," I said. "And so do I. Do you want to come with us?" "No . . . I'll wait at the door." K was in the bathroom stall like our first night at Flipper's. She'd copped from Jimmy and passed the packet of smack to me; I take a big hit and then snort another. K said. "See, you want it too."

We washed our hands, laughed at our success, and walked out.

"You girls sure picked up," the guard said.

"We're happy to be away," K said smugly.

We got into the elevator and *holy crap* . . . there was Jimmy, waiting to get into the same elevator. K and I put our heads down, the door opened. "After you," Jimmy said to the unsuspecting guard. My heart is rushing like the Wonderland rabbit . . . like I'd been asleep and woke up in this elevator . . . in another world. *Oh shit, not again.* K hunched over and started to nod. I looked at the guard, oblivious to the trio he was riding with, and then I get pissed—dammit, I'm high again. "This is it," the guard says. We got out. Jimmy stayed. We walked to the van and drove back to the hospital.

Whew.

Day 7. I stopped a kitchen lady pushing the food cart. "Excuse me, can I have some tinfoil to cover my Jell-O?"

She came back with a small piece. In order to hide and get high, we created a tent out of our pillows and blankets. I passed in the tinfoil and looked at the others in the room. They knew what was up. I motioned for them to leave and put my finger to my mouth for silence. They walked out. For a cover-up, I lit a stinky Gauloise. Still, I could smell the wafting heroin escaping from K's bed, wrapping itself around hairs of my nostrils. I'd been a week without this smoke in my every breath, a huge accomplishment. "Come here." K passed the tinfoil with a generous amount of Persian brown. My heart fluttered. I bent down, took the lighter, held the straw in my teeth, closed my lips, lit the foil underneath, watched the smack melt into maple syrup and I sucked up the smoke of euphoria.

We got busted, were booted out of the hospital, and went back to Malibu.

We were on our way to the loan company to beg for cash on already hocked items. Uncle Louie was fed up with us, but we thought we'd try. We were on Sunset Boulevard when I spotted the Bel Air sign above the entrance.

"Copa d'Oro," I said, and made a hard left through the gates.

"What you are doing now?" K said, huddled in the passenger seat.

"I might be able to cut someone's hair who lives up here."

"Who?"

"A good client, Peter Bogdanovich."

"*Who?*" K said again.

"He's a great director—ever see *Paper Moon . . . What's Up, Doc?*"

"Just remember, I'm fucking sick. Don't be long."

I drove up to the electric gate box. I had no fancy house-call bag like the good old days and I reeked from stomach acids, beer, and cigarettes. I raked my dirty hair back with my fingers, took another swig of my warm beer and pulled a few bangs down for a veil.

Buzz. Pause. Buzz, buzz.

"Is Peter in?" I said, trying to sound normal. "It's Carrie White."

"Who?"

"*His hairdresser,*" I said, irritated with the effort to be polite. I dropped my head on the steering wheel. "Shit. I don't know how I'll even cut his hair if he says yes."

"*Carrie?*" Peter said through the gate box. "What are you doing here?"

I sat up with a shot of adrenaline hearing his voice. I flashed on the first time I cut Peter, when he was living with my client Cybill Shepherd, when he came strolling down his staircase, dapper as a black-and-white film star, an ascot tied at his neck in his Hampton Beach robe.

Yeah, *what was I doing here?* That was the same question I asked myself every day wherever I was. "Hi, Peter, I was just in the neighborhood and, well, I thought, what the heck, maybe Peter would like a haircut . . . would you?"

"Sure, why not? Come on in."

I parked and went in. We set up in our usual spot as if the years hadn't passed, Peter in his special chair with his name on it. Peter got on the phone, leaving me the left side of his hair for me to chisel. His assistant came in. "Is it still two hundred?" I nodded yes and kept cutting the left side, not to disturb the phone on his right ear.

The assistant came back and set the money on my side table. I nodded thanks, screaming inside, *whoopee.* I was nervous about K and Peter was *still* on the phone. I whispered to him, "I'll be back in a second."

He kept talking, his head wet and half cut. I picked up the two bills and went out to the car. K was brewing in misery. I waved the bills at her. "We're going to be okay."

She grabbed it out of my hand. "What you doing . . . fucking him?"

"I'm just cutting his hair."

"I'm fucking sick out here."

I did not want more of a crazy scene at Peter's. And I certainly didn't want him to know what I was doing these days.

"Oh fuck," I said. "Let's go. I'll never see him again anyway."

Last Call

We were out of jewelry, promises, and payments. We schlepped our scuzzy selves into the loan company like dogs, I saw Uncle Louie bicker with his brother behind the glass doors. It was about K and me and no more loans. But Uncle Louie continued to have mercy, and each morning at the crack of dawn, dope-sick, we would creep up his driveway for money from his own pocket that he would put under the doormat at his home.

One morning there was nothing under the mat. I timidly knocked. Uncle Louie's wife, Pauline, answered. She was not so sympathetic.

"Weren't you a popular hairdresser?" she asked. "And don't you have young children? You should be ashamed." I couldn't argue. "We just have to get through this week, then we're going to a hospital." She looked at me and shook her head, "Well . . . you better." Uncle Louie came out. "This is it . . . no more after this." He handed K an envelope. "I don't know what you're doing, but you both frighten me. I won't have your death on my conscience." And that money was good for *one* day only.

"I have one last idea," I said, twitching from spinal pain. "But I don't like it."

I drove up Benedict Canyon and made a right on Melvin Sokolsky's street. There were a bunch of cars and a sound truck lined up on the wide brick driveway of his grand English-cottage-style home.

"The good news is . . . he's here," I said. "The bad news is . . . *he's here.*"

"Just get some money."

I remembered seventeen years ago, the first time I'd met Melvin at the Beverly Wilshire Hotel and the bright future that had opened for me. Now I was groveling for a few hundred bucks. My body insisted I ring the bell. I was shaking and clammy and reminded myself to hide my hand so he wouldn't see my damn fingers that never healed.

The door blasted open and two guys barreled out with a piece of plywood, almost knocking me over. "Oh, sorry," one said, and they rushed off to the grip truck. I rang the bell again. A girl poked out her head. "Yeah?"

"I'm looking for Melvin." She looked me up and down, I knew I looked like a bag lady.

"He's directing a commercial right now, can I help you?"

"Tell him Carrie White is here."

She looked taken aback. "Didn't you work with Melvin a long time ago?"

"Yes, that's me," I said, with a flicker of joy to be remembered, but I sensed my nose running and wiped it with my cuff. "Okay, I'll tell him."

The door looked partially closed, not partially open anymore. Someone else walked by and did a double take at me. I mumbled, *"I used to be one of you, so don't look so fuckin' uppity."*

Then the fair-skinned freckled hand of Melvin pulled the door open. He backed up a split second and refocused. "Jesus, what happened to you? I heard you were hitting it hard, but you look terrible."

My feelings sank, but I was not surprised he didn't empathize. "Melvin, I know, and I'm working on getting better, but I'm real sick now and I need your help."

"Hey, Melvin," someone called, "we need you in here a minute."

"Wait here," Melvin said.

He closed the front door. I stood rocking myself for what seemed like a half hour before he returned.

"So, you've turned into a damn junkie?"

"Well, I guess but . . ." I cowered.

Melvin jumped in again. "I'm from New York, *and we know junkies.* Let me give you an example—"

Oh no, not the *Let me give you an example* part. I'll die before he gets to the point. I interrupted him, "Melvin, please, I just need two hundred dollars."

"*Just* two hundred dollars? And when that's gone? Listen to me, there was this guy Joe, that used to work for me, and Joe was a junkie. I told Joe, you quit that shit or it'll kill you."

"Melvin, *I know*, I'm going to a hospital—"

"I'm not finished. So Joe started shooting up in his leg . . . then it got infected . . ."

"Melvin, I don't use needles—"

"You're interrupting me again . . . and Joe ran out of veins, so he shot up in his neck . . . then he had to have his leg amputated and—"

"Melvin, I'm so sick, just two hundred dollars, please."

"Let me finish! So do you know what happened to Joe?"

"No Melvin," I said, my nose running like a kid's, squirming like I had ants in my pants. "What happened?"

"Joe died," Melvin said. "Anyway, I don't have cash on me."

"Melvin, I'm gonna die I'm so sick, can't you get cash from someone in there?"

"I'll see . . . you wait here."

Melvin finally came back and I reached out my hand. "Button doesn't have any cash either," he said.

"Melvin, are you going to help me or not, because if *not,* I gotta go."

"Okay, I'll ask Kenny Duskin. Remember Kenny? You worked with him many times." He walked back in the house.

Another eternity went by.

"Here, two hundred," Melvin said, coming out the door counting twenties.

"Oh, Melvin, thank God, thank you so much."

I started to hug him, he stepped back, "Don't ever come back here and ask me for money again. I mean it."

I was too drained to cry. I sniveled a bit and acknowledged *understood,* but also I knew he loved me and he was upset. "I won't Melvin, don't worry." I hobbled up the brick driveway.

"One more thing," Melvin called out. *Of course, one more thing . . .* I wanted to run, but I stopped and looked back. "I've never seen a *junkie* make it yet!"

Mick Jagger was saving me with "Emotional Rescue," his voice ringing out from the tape player on the windowsill, kept company by beer bottles, Bic lighters, torches, and pipes. One pipe was wrapped with Scotch tape from throwing it out of the window because *I quit,* then a half hour later I ran outside down the hill looking for it and taped it back together.

K was oblivious to me, staring at her pipe at the other end of the windowsill. I took a greedy hit off my pipe to erase Melvin.

At first I was fine, then my body shifted into panic mode, over-amped, beyond a rush. I lay down carefully and slowly, monitoring the condition of my throbbing heart and its irregular racing.

There was a warm line marching from my left wrist, up my forearm, moving past my elbow, and headed straight for my heart, oh shit shit shit . . . *Dear God, please don't let me die, please, please, please . . .*

Maybe if I have a hit of smack, that would calm me down, yeah, or no, better not, but . . . *oh, dear God, no, no, no.* Maybe a drink, that always relaxes me from too much coke. *No, no alcohol, don't add one more chemical,* a voice said. Okay, okay, but *please, dear God . . . don't let me die here, not here, not like this, not now.* I kept begging, and breathing. K had no idea what I was going through; I was afraid to lift my head to see her, or speak to call her.

No, this was between me and God, my life and me . . . and then I noticed, the line to my heart started to subside . . . just a tiny bit. *Oh, dear God, thank you, thank you, thank you.* Still I was afraid to move. There was intense pain around my heart muscle but I felt the line reverse itself and go toward my hand. Breath seeped through my half-open mouth, *I'm going to live, I'm going to live, thank you, God.* My temperature was on its way back to normal, the hot line went past my wrist.

Grateful, I lifted my head and slowly sat up. I realized why I *really* didn't tell K what was happening to me; I didn't want her to tell me I shouldn't have any more cocaine. I saw myself in the dark cavity of myself, like a little person hanging inside myself, clutching my ribs, wanting to stop words that I knew were about to come, that would escape off my tongue and out of my mouth to K . . . but I couldn't stop them. *"Where's the pipe?"*

"I have a plan," I said, more sick than not these days, counting change and waiting for a check. I decided to see William, my ex-assistant. He'd left me over ten years ago to work at Ménage à Trois and became one of the three owners. His salon was down the street from my closed Burton Way salon.

I walked in wearing black sunglasses, a black hat, and a gold lamé pantsuit I'd bought on Melrose, trying to be disco-hip. But my outfit seemed dead as disco once I was in this bright, large salon.

"Surprise."

"I'll say," William said, cutting a lady. "Wow, Carrie White! You remember Joan Quinn?" Of course I knew her, she was one of *my* first clients, and her husband was my divorce lawyer. We used to be good friends. William finished her quickly and excused himself. "It's Carrie White," William said to the other owner, Setsu. "I used to be her assistant." I smiled, a tarnished crown and tilted star hanging over my head.

"What if I wanted to work for *you*? Only a few days a week . . ."

"Everyone will be excited, I'll put a banner up with your name."

"Could I get paid . . . daily?"

"Do you need money? I heard you were with a rich lady."

"Things change, I just want to do hair and, well . . . get paid as we go along."

"Whatever you want," William said, lovingly.

He leaned over the reception desk. "Patti, book Carrie White starting a week from today." He turned to me. "What hours?"

I was thinking I'd drive in from Malibu at 7:00 AM, get to the dealer, he would front us, I'd take enough to not be sick and not get high, leave K there, drive to Beverly Hills, pick her up later with my cash, and pay the dealer. Repeat daily.

"How about nine-thirty . . . no, make it ten, wait, eleven is best. Okay? I better go, someone's waiting in the car."

"Who?" William said. "The Princess? Bring her in."

"William, it's not like you think, *whatever you think* . . . trust me."

My girls were happy I was going back to work. I even called Daisy. Their hope was mine. I tried to dress, but I'd had a rough bout getting through the night. I got to Cyrus's, got rid of my sickness with the first two hits, but I took two more hits I hadn't planned on.

I never called William.

There was always a line of degenerates waiting for the phone booth at the corner of Sunset and Laurel Canyon, which now included me.

"Fuck, man, come on," I said, loudly hunched over in line. "You Mr. Heinz, calling fifty-seven people?"

"Fuck you, sister," he said, on his way out. "My mom's dyin'."

"Yeah, sure," I mumbled, wiping my runny nose. Only two more, *dialing for dealers,* to go, then my turn.

I slid my dime in. *Rrrrring Rrrrring Rrrrring.* No answer. "Fucking Cyrus . . . pick up, will you?" I shouted in the glass booth. "Shit."

K honked the horn. I tried again. No answer.

Then . . . like a miracle, I saw a red pill in the corner of the phone booth floor. I picked it up. It looked like a Seconal or something that could help me. I wasn't going to share it with K either. I swallowed it. Nothing happened. It must have been a Tic-Tac.

I was so sick I couldn't make it up the stairs. I was glad the umbrella was down and last month the kids and I had actually done something together as we'd thrown all the sand from the living room out of the back door. I collapsed on a big pillow on the floor. I was kicking hard. My teeth were chattering. My cramping turned to diarrhea. I had to crawl to the girls' bathroom a few feet away. I sat curled over their toilet, then crawled back to the living room. K set up camp on a blanket and more pillows next to me. She was in her worst shape too. We smoked smack fumes off ashes on tinfoil. I crawled back to the little girls' bathroom, this time to dry-heave. They would be coming home from school soon; this would be scary for them.

I heard the front door creak open. They threw their books on the kitchen table and were chatting away. They stopped in their tracks and gasped, seeing me on the floor. "Mom, what's wrong?" Pitita asked. "What happened?"

"She's just sick again, Pitita," Aloma said, walking away.

"Honey," I moaned. "Please don't . . ."

Pitita called to Aloma, "Mom said she was only going to do a quarter."

She had no idea what *a quarter* meant. My heart broke for them. Aloma was mad at me and I was *furious* at me, sad for us all. "I've had nothing for over a day," I squeezed out. "I'm *really* sick." Pitita stared at me on the floor, flattened out like a pancake. "I'm sorry you have to see me like this, my angels."

"Shut up, will you?" K grumbled without moving. "*I'm sick too.*"

Dusk. We were still paralyzed on the living room floor. Aloma came through to see what she could find for dinner.

"Aloma," I begged, "Please, before it's dark, go call Cyrus for us, *please*."

She glared at me. The last thing she wanted was to be a part of this. I told her the number and she left on the dreaded mission. It wasn't the first time she'd called for us, but we were never this ill and she knew that.

She came back, red-faced and sweaty from the bike ride.

"He wasn't there, and yes, I called a bunch of times."

"Thanks, honey," I whined. "I'm so sorry."

No one came to our rescue. K and I puked in shifts in the girls' bathroom. More time passed.

K and I puked in towels; we couldn't get up anymore. I had defecated in my pants. I was paralyzed in agony, my guts, bones, and muscles were melted. Pitita came out again, distraught from my uncontrollable moaning.

"Mom, you want water?"

"Thanks." I barely had wind in my lungs to speak. I was a dead person with a heartbeat. I sipped the water she brought, then gagged and vomited on myself. Pitita went for a cold washcloth. Aloma came out and went for paper towels for both of us. K was heaving on her side. The stench from us was deplorable.

This was more shameful than my mother on the cot in County General Hospital. I swore my kids would never see me die like her. Pitita stood with the cloth in her hand while Aloma wiped the spilled water and moved the dirty ashtrays and foils away from my space on the hardwood floor.

Day three. No Cyrus. No Rita. The girls made themselves some scraps of food and went into their bedroom as if walking past carnage was normal.

"Girls," I said, faint as a whisper, seriously wondering how my heart was going to pump another round. "Please . . . please come give Mommy a kiss."

Pitita put her plate down and bent down. As much as I wanted, I couldn't even reach out to her, it was like my arms were cut off. I waited to feel her sweet little lips touch my cheek. Aloma forced herself to walk over and kissed my forehead quickly; she didn't want to be near me, but she felt she had to.

I felt a warm involuntary tear roll down from the corner of my left eye. It was a sign of life. "I'm so sorry . . . I'm so sorry," I whimpered.

They petted my forehead, and then went back to their room. I could hear Pitita tell Aloma, "See, Mom's going to be okay."

Aloma was almost thirteen, Pitita was just ten—no parties, no cakes. I had surpassed my mother's awfulness.

My tears of regret could have filled an ocean.

Knocked Out

Jeannie was out of town and I needed to figure out a place for my girls while we went to rehab. Richard was a good man regardless of our problems, but he couldn't take care of himself, let alone our girls. He was fighting his own demons and living from couch to couch. I would always think of him as the love of my life, but more irresponsible than me. I took a big chance and called Bucky. Reluctantly he consented.

"When are we going to Bucky's?" the girls asked.

"Tomorrow. Isn't that great? And you'll be with Daisy. And this time, I promise not to come out of the hospital until I'm detoxed."

They looked at me with the *yeah sure* eyes. But Aloma softened. "I hope so." Pitita had believed in me a few days ago, but now I was fucked up again and she was silent.

The next morning, I took a quick last hit, then packed up the girls and myself using large green Hefty garbage bags. I stuffed a few spandex pants, a glitter gossamer shirt, some scarves, my army surplus shiny olive green jumpsuit, a skirt, four pairs of shoes, my electric rollers, and makeup that I hadn't used in years.

K was still sitting on the bed smoking. "Where you going . . . to a party?" she asked.

"Clothes for thirty days."

Inside, I was getting eager. I believed this time was going to be different. I looked at myself in my gray flannel jumpsuit with beer stains and cigarette burns, and thought I looked like an aerial view of Vietnam. I clutched the rail and walked down the spiral staircase.

The girls were ready to go.

"Don't you want to take these books?" I held up books I had bought them, *Alice in Wonderland* and *Goodnight Moon*. Pitita grabbed one and threw it into her pillowcase full of clothes and notebooks. "Don't forget your violin, honey."

We marched out of the house like soldiers who'd survived a dangerous war. K was in the car waiting.

We walked in together, two worlds apart, connected only by our drug addiction. The doctor came in with a clipboard.

"Hello, I see from your records you've tried recovery before." We stared at him, no comment. "I'm going to get you started on your detox; however, with your past history, I have to separate you girls if you expect any success."

That sounded very correct to me. K's mouth curled down. "What you mean? We're always together."

I looked at the doctor's world I was sitting in, the PDR book on his bookshelf, his degrees on one wall, family pictures, his kids hugging an Irish setter. I flashed on my only happy family years with Richard. I saw how alcohol had soaked us to death.

"Maybe we should . . . don't you want to get free?" I said to K. "Aren't you tired of the way we live?" K looked at me like I was speaking Greek.

K nodded okay. "Well, I need some drugs."

"Yes," the doctor said.

"When?" K said.

"Right now, then we will take you to our sister facility in Pasadena." K scowled at him. "It's *very nice*." He turned to me. "You will stay here."

We stood up. I hugged her. "It will be good." She gave me a blank look, not so tough anymore. I exhaled.

"Let's get this over with," she said, and walked away from me, a nurse guiding her out the door.

"'Bye, K," I hollered down the hall. She didn't turn around. I watched K's back go out the door. Then I collapsed.

The next day I woke up shaking and sweating and freezing. Nurses and doctors were around me. "You're doing great," the main doctor said. "In fact, we're going to try something new with you. It's been very successful for heroin addicts in Sweden. It's called the ACE inhibitor."

Day 5. "Doctor said only six shots today."

"And Klonopin?"

"No more Klonopin. Darvon will be enough."

"I can't sleep. I'm hurting bad."

"You just need a meeting."

"*Fuck you.*"

"What did you say?"

"I said . . . *thank you.*"

I came to, hours later, with the buzzing of a man's voice in my head.

"Now, here's an example of what could happen to you, if you continue to go down the path you were headed," a man announced.

I cracked my eyelids. There was a crowd of real people gawking at me from the foot of my bed. The man in a white lab jacket must have been a doctor who had brought patients to view me as a warning. Well, I'm good for something. My second thought: *How's my hair?*

We shuffled down the hall where ten people were seated in a circle waiting to begin. I laughed at myself as I immediately spotted the cutest guy. His name was Leland. "I'm too young for rehab," he shared to the group, pissed off. "My family forced me here."

The *sharing* continued, and I was called on. I mumbled, "My name is Carrie, I used to be, uh, I had a . . ."

"We can't hear you," the leader said.

"Look," I barked. "I'm sick, I don't wanna be here."

When the group broke and we went outside to smoke, the cute guy came over.

"What the hell is in your arm?"

"I know, gross, huh? It's an invention from Sweden . . . I get it out tomorrow."

He stared at my bandaged plug sticking out of my arm. "Does it hurt?"

"I hurt everywhere or I can't feel a thing. I'm used to it . . . how old are you, anyway?"

"I just turned eighteen, that's why they put me in this adult ward."

"Eighteen?" I burst out laughing. "Jesus."

I went to the desk and begged for my shot and something from my detox wardrobe that was locked in the front closet.

"What do you want first?" the nurse said.

"What do you think?"

I accomplished a giant feat: I showered and got dressed—the first time in a week. I dolled up as well as I could, which meant a shirt top over my pajamas, my hair in a ponytail, and I crunched my eyelashes—the few that were left. My teeth were rotting from the inside out, so I had better not smile too big. I took lipstick for cheek blush, then to my lips. Perfume? I forgot perfume. I laughed.

I walked out for my first dinner in the rec room. As I passed the nurses' window, I heard one say, "Well, look who's going to live."

I smirked. "I'm trying. I figure I got a long time to be dead."

"You look really nice," Leland said as I sat down next to him. "Hey, it's Friday night, you know what that means?"

"No," I said, thinking, *Oh, right, days with names* . . . "It's been one long day for me that turned into four years."

"We get to stay up late weekends, and Friday night is music videos."

"Bob Dylan is my poet." I lit up to the word *music*. "What about 'The Wall' . . . *Hello, anybody out there?* And do you know 'The Fuse' by Jackson Browne . . . that's my prayer song . . . *And the years I spent lost in the mystery* . . . What music do you like?"

"Van Halen. I hope they play 'The Jump' tonight."

"I never heard of them."

Two o'clock in the morning. I couldn't sleep. No meds after 11:00 PM. The ACE inhibitor thing had been out of my arm for a week already. I couldn't get comfortable in my bed, probably because I wasn't comfortable in my skin. My methadone roommate had bailed. I understood why. I feared I didn't have what it took to stay, either . . . I battled one second at a time. I knew this was my *last* chance. I realized I should have died on my living room floor a month ago.

I put my children's faces in between me and my urge to run.

I put my dried bloody fingers and Melvin's disgust for me in between my urge to run. I put the kiss on my cheek from Aloma and Pitita, the groveling scumbag I had turned into . . .

Bridgette came in for the nightly check.

"Carrie . . . are you all right?" she whispered. "Carrie?"

I didn't want to talk . . . I had no energy. She walked out. I heard her tell another tech, "I think she's sleeping, standing on *top* of her bed! What should I do?"

"Nothing. Let her sleep."

The next night she couldn't find me and rushed out. I heard her say, "She's not in there."

"Check again."

She found me in a ball under my bed. "Are you okay?"

I played possum. She walked out, I heard her, "She's sleeping *under* her bed. What should I do?"

"Nothing. Let her sleep."

They told me I was allergic to alcohol, that a drink set off a reaction that made "one *too many,* and a thousand *never enough.*" They told me that this allergy created an obsession in my mind for more. They told me that it was on a cellular level. I knew my family bloodline was soaked in *alcohol.* I knew that I was different. But I didn't understand this concept fully. I did resent being told that I could *never* drink again because of an *allergy.*

Leland and I laughed at the new recovery language, like anyone we knew ever said *Fellows, nil, sought,* and other weird terminology. But what I knew for sure was that every time I promised myself I wouldn't start drinking until noon, or five—once I started I wouldn't stop drinking like other people. I thought it was because I didn't want to, not because I couldn't.

Day 28. "I'm almost off the Darvocet," I said to Leland. "Then I get to leave."

He was staying sixty days. We had a fire-charged crush going on. Everyone knew about it, including the doctors and nurses. We got in big trouble when we were caught stealing a kiss. I was punished because it happened in my room; I was older and supposed to have known better. They said I behaved like a schoolgirl, so they made me sit at a school desk, in the hallway, in my pajamas.

Bridgette smuggled me a cigarette and a love note from Leland. I never told him that my son was almost his age.

I collected my possessions, except for the army surplus jumpsuit, which I gave to my latest roommate, Robert from The Gap Band, because he wanted it.

I signed out. I stood in front of the big glass hospital doors, holding my two green Hefty bags and waiting for Bucky. Aloma had gotten me into a recovery house that she insisted upon. Bucky was willing to watch the girls a little longer.

It was 9:00 AM and a whole thirty days later.

On the way out, a doctor told me that my friend, meaning K, had bailed from her hospital treatment. I figured she went to Sasha's, a dealer nearby. While I was waiting, the idea of going over to Sasha's was creeping into my mind like a snake up my pant leg . . .

At that moment, a taxi coasted by. My arm flew up, and the taxi stopped. I told someone to watch my stuff, that I'd be right back. I jumped into the cab and gave him directions.

"Wait here," I told the cabbie, out front at Sasha's.

Bang, bang, bang.

"Who is it?" a voice through the peephole.

"It's me, Carrie."

The door opened and one whiff of the smoky room permeated my whole body. K was sitting on the couch, getting high. She lifted her head and looked up at me, then back to her pipe without a word. I walked over; I wasn't sure if she knew who I was.

"Helloooo? I heard you left the hospital."

She nodded but didn't speak to me.

"I still have your car, have something." Sasha handed me a pipe with cooked rocks and a foil of smack. Maybe *one* hit of each, I can handle that. I took the pipe. I took three hits in a row like thirty days never happened. K looked up and glared. I inhaled the smack off the tinfoil like dessert.

"K, how are you?" I said, like hello to a stranger, but then she always was . . .

"How do I look?" she said, so stoned . . . she'd been there for a week.

"I just came to say good-bye anyway."

The room started spinning. I had to get my bearings and get out of there. "Sasha, can I borrow twenty bucks? I've got a cab waiting . . . I'll pay you when I get back my car." He handed me a twenty.

K didn't look up. I ran out while I could.

I got to the hospital, retrieved my stuff, and bumped into the glass door going out. "You okay?" the receptionist called out.

"I just slipped." I certainly did. "Did anyone ask for me?"

"No."

I was awake in a bad dream. I couldn't believe what I had just done. I'd have to fake *not* being loaded *one more time*. I had done that for as long as I could remember. I wouldn't talk to Bucky all the way to his house. I would see my girls for one big minute, and Aloma would come and drive me to the recovery home, whatever that meant.

I had a new prayer. *Dear God, make this high wear off soon . . .*

Starting Over *Again*

"Where's this place you're taking me?" Aloma was driving east on Franklin. I saw Jimmy the Junkie's street sign and the spot I'd parked on so many sick mornings waiting for him to bring our gram of smack. It made me nervous to be so close to Jimmy's, then my second thought: it made me feel better in case of an emergency.

"I know a dealer right over there."

"You won't be needing dealers anymore," Aloma snapped.

My body twitched, my mouth watered, and a shiver went up my spine that was poking out of my skinny back.

"I've missed you so much. You're going to love the Friendly House."

Aloma made a right on Normandie, south of Third Street. She parked in front of a big house, probably built in the early twenties.

"Ready for your new life?" Aloma said, her eyes tearing up, her tone changed. "You are going to love Peggy; she runs the place."

I looked at the house again. I saw two girls sitting on the balcony, swinging their legs off the railing, looking down at me, *the new girl,* like I was from Pacoima to Hollywood; only I wasn't tough anymore.

A jovial lady with twinkling blue eyes, blondish overpermed short hair, and a padded motherly body in a conservative silk printed dress, greeted us at the door with arms opened wide. "Come in, honey . . . hi, Aloma," she said, and looked at me. I lowered my head and stepped over the threshold.

"I'm Peggy, you must be Carrie," she said, with a sweet bouncy voice. "Aloma has told me so much about you."

"Hi," I said.

Aloma believed that this place was the only way I could save my life. Aloma had lugged in my Hefty bag suitcases. "These are Carrie's things."

"Set them right there," Peggy directed and turned to me. "It's our policy to inspect all belongings. You can have them back after you're settled in your room."

While Aloma and Peggy hummed about how I was going to be fine, and blah blah blah . . . I checked the place out. I didn't like the dark woodwork I saw in the living room, or the old dying ivy plants on the mantel. The style of this house wasn't for me, either, old-fashioned, or maybe it was *no style.* Then I had a humbling thought: what about the stylish rat's nest of a home I had left in Malibu?

Two other girls popped by us in the hallway. "We're going to the store, we have passes." Peggy looked at their papers. Aloma whispered to me, "You're so lucky to get into the Friendly House. Peggy is doing me a huge favor."

I nodded that I understood and looked at the girls talking to Peggy. They were almost twenty years younger than me, wearing sweatpants, T-shirts, tennis shoes, and had lots of tattoos on their shoulders. I had never owned tennis shoes; or maybe once, when I was trying to learn how to play tennis at Warren Beatty's house. Otherwise, it was high heels, platform boots, or roller skates. These girls looked very healthy. I was tired of holding my head up.

"Come into my office," Peggy said, after Aloma left. It was a little past noon. I wanted to go to bed. I'd made it past everyone, fooling them, now I had to get past Peggy. I sat across from her desk. She began.

I felt my head encased in an upside-down fishbowl, water filled to the top, ferns floating at my ears and a lonely goldfish swimming by my eyes. I sat, fighting a nod, and every once in a while a few words would clang in my brain from Peggy, then goldfish came by for another lap.

"Are you willing to stay for thirty *consecutive* days?" Peggy said, very seriously.

Consecutive? That's an awfully big word, I thought. I smiled in robot fashion and agreed to anything she said, I just wanted to lie down. I kept staring at this woman through my mental fishbowl . . . *I ought to do her hair.* I cracked myself up. Hell, I hadn't brushed my teeth for years, let alone *my* hair.

"By the way," Peggy said. "How are you planning to pay? Not that we turn any woman away who wants to get sober."

"My ex-husband is loaning me the money."

"Well, isn't that good of him?" Peggy said.

"Surprisingly, because he pretty much hates me."

Peggy went on about the house and the rules. I tried to listen, but another voice started rising in my head: *When is she going to shut up?*

Finally she asked, "Do you have any questions?"

"Do you have a pay phone here?"

My nose began to run and I couldn't focus. Peggy looked at me curiously.

"Are you all right, my dear? You did complete a hospital detox, didn't you?"

"Yeah," I said, switching my concern that she might throw me out. "I just feel anxious."

"I like to remind everyone, we didn't get in our condition overnight and we don't *get well* overnight."

"Are you sober too?"

"Oh yes, I have been for almost thirteen years."

That was too much time in between drinks and drugs for me to compute.

She got me settled in my room and told me, "You rest."

I missed dinner and stayed in bed.

Sure enough, I came to around 6:00 AM, sweating and aching. I was in the Pink Room, named after the painted walls, with two other girls. The Blue Room and the Yellow Room also had three girls each. I tried to muffle my moans.

"Do you want me to get the house lady?" my roommate Bonnie said. She was about twenty-three, as fit as an aerobics instructor, with big blue eyes and springing curls from a shag haircut.

"I don't know . . . I don't care, I can't move right now."

"I'm getting Faye," she said, and left.

"What's wrong with you?" Faye said when she came in.

"I feel really sick."

"What kind of sick? I thought you just got out of a hospital?"

"I did," I defended, lying through my rotten teeth that looked like they were made out of wood. "I must be coming off those Darvocets."

"Well, stay in bed till Peg gets here."

Peggy came up to see me a few hours later. By then I was in damp sheets and huddled in a fetal position, kicking hard and white as a ghost.

"Get her in a very hot tub right now," Peggy called out to a few girls. By the time the tub was full, I was cramped over. The girls helped me to the scalding bathtub. A tub of fire would have been fine, just so I wouldn't feel my body's misery. Peggy held my back, and the girls lifted my left leg, then my right. I sat slowly into the water and I melted.

When the water got cool, I started to shiver. They took me out and spoon-fed me water with honey until I could drink a whole glass without gagging. Then it started all over again, back to soak it out in the tub. Peggy and the girls then took shifts watching over me like midwives, telling me I could do it. I didn't believe I could, but their belief got me to hang in.

It was a bad night, but I could remember worse ones.

On the second day, I noticed the pay phone was just outside my room. The energy to score smack propelled me past my disability. I looked for a dime, found one, and dialed Jimmy. No answer.

I got into another scalding hot tub. I tried calling again after the bath. No answer. I cut my tubs short and pushed myself back to the pay phone, wet, wrapped in a towel. I tried in between other girls using the phone. No answer. Bed-phone-bath-phone-bed-phone-bath.

That night Faye came upstairs to see that we were all in bed. I was making the day's final attempt to call Jimmy.

"You're not supposed to use the pay phone until you have been here *one week*—who are you calling anyway?"

"My mother. She's very sick, maybe even in a hospital by now."

"Well, I'm sorry," Faye said, and took the phone from my clutches. "You need Peggy's permission, we have *rules* here."

Defeated and drained, I crumpled off to bed, trying to figure how long ago my mother died.

On the third day, I was still very shaky, but I recognized progress. I was even glad Jimmy wasn't home to set me back. I stopped calling him.

I decided to try to go downstairs. I looked at my skinny wrist hanging onto the old wooden banister. I could see through my thin skin, my pulse beating in my veins, my heart making its effort to keep me alive. I'd invested a lifetime in drinking and doing drugs, thinking they were my tools for living, when the truth was they had taken my life and everything good away from me.

Peggy saw me walking cautiously, and came up to help me the rest of the way. She lovingly put her arm around me for support and said something crucial to me, something I prayed I would never forget—they weren't just words.

"*Remember, my dear . . . you never have to do this again.*"

I stopped. I believed her. I choked up. I hoped I would remember.

A few days later, during a routine meeting in her office, Peggy said, "By the way, the Pasadena hospital told me your friend has left the country, she's with her family now."

K was no longer in America? This fact *really* made me believe I had a chance at this *sobriety* thing. I exhaled in renewed safety.

I was approaching my *real* thirty days clean and sober, a huge milestone. It was celebrated with a colored plastic chip like a poker chip, except it hung on a key chain, had the number *30* on one side and the words *Keep Coming Back* on the other. The order of chips to collect were 60 days, 90 days, then a big leap to six months, then nine months . . . then the biggest goal of all, one year, and we get a cake! After that, just cakes to honor different lengths of sobriety.

At the recovery meeting above the Guitar Center on Sunset, I recognized the man from Pasadena who had brought patients to the foot of my bed to gawk. He was passing out chips. "Who would like to take a chip for 30 days?"

I walked up for mine. "Do you remember me?"

"*Damn*," Nolan said, digging in his tin box for my chip. "I can't believe *you* made it." He put the treasured chip in my hand. "Congratulations."

That was worth everything. I waved my chip in the air and thanked the roomful of strangers for my life. They yelled, "Yay," like they do for everyone. It was extremely emotional. *Maybe* I was going to be able to keep my promise to my children and stay sober.

Little by little, day by day, meeting by meeting, I could actually see *life* after alcohol and drugs. It was unbelievable to me that I loved the way I felt . . . human.

On weekends, with the help of my beloved Big Aloma, and my dear friend Jeannie Blackburn, my daughters visited me. We played

Scrabble outside at the picnic table and chatted about how they were doing at Bucky's, how was Daisy, and did they see Adam? They didn't understand where I was, and why I had to stay if I wasn't sick anymore. "How much longer, Mom?"

"Until they tell me I won't fall down on my own, sweetheart."

I clung to the idea of the caterpillar that spins off to its death, that shows no sign, no scientific proof that it could ever become the free beautiful butterfly.

"What about a job?" Peggy said. "Where will you work?"

"I was thinking Fatburger, the night shift, maybe I would run into Mick Jagger or Tom Waits."

"Fatburger? Weren't you a popular hairdresser with your own salon? I bet more people remember you as a good hairdresser than as a good alcoholic."

I laughed and doubted that.

"I didn't open my mail for five years, my license has expired."

"Can't you get a new one?"

Go back to beauty school? I was petrified to imagine being in a salon, the den of my drinking and using. My ears started tuning her out.

"I believe we have a graduate at the Santa Monica Vidal Sassoon School."

"Vidal has *beauty schools*? I always wanted to open one. I was a guest on his television show."

"Wonderful, my dear, but we have a saying: *Your ego is not your amigo.*"

I bristled. "You have a *saying* for *everything.*"

"Let's stay in the moment, shall we?" Peggy continued. "You *do* have to be self-supporting, and you have children to take care of. I will call Caroline tomorrow and find out what you'll need to get started."

This was moving too fast . . . tomorrow?

Peggy lined the whole thing up: I could make payments and start school in a few weeks. She pushed me to ask Bucky to help me get my car back from Sasha's and an advance for school so I could work and repay him.

After the call to Bucky, I called William at Ménage à Trois and apologized for never showing up. I told him that I was clean and sober, could he give me another chance?

"Of course," William said. "Brenda Vaccaro sent you a huge bouquet for your comeback last time, but you never came back!"

"I'll call her too. First I have to get my license back . . . and please put me in a quiet corner, so I can learn how to do hair without coke or Bloody Marys."

I did not feel ready to be *Carrie White* on the hairdressing floor, but William said, "Just say when."

My head goes in circles with memories, guilt, and grief. My unraveling emotions made me anxious, and without a drink or drug to soothe me, going to meetings and Peggy's words were my only relief, "You were a bad alcoholic, not a bad person. Being sober will change your thinking, which will change your feelings. You are being Restored to Sanity, that is the second step."

Looking back, my behavior seemed crazy to me. But my crazy guilt and grief . . . would those ever ease up?

I hadn't forgiven my mother, why would I forgive myself? Would my children ever forgive me? My skin crawled.

To escape, my roommate Bonnie, her friend Dan, and I went to Ah Fong's on Sunset, ordered tea, and ate little spoonfuls of the hot Chinese mustard, just to blow our heads off and laugh. It burned our noses and made our eyes tear like strong cocaine hits. "See how much fun we can have without drugs?" Dan said.

Soon afterward, as part of my exit plan, a few of the Friendly House girls with longer sobriety drove me out to my Malibu home to get it ready to rent. My anxiety flourished as we came up the Pacific Coast Highway, my mouth watered for drugs and I got light-headed. I was glad I was with all my Friendly House sisters. We drove up my rambling driveway and the girls oohed and ahhhed, but I just saw misery, darkness, and my little girls' suffering.

I opened the front door to reveal the trashed world I had called home. I was embarrassed for them to see the horrifying mess. Silently they took it all in. Then Sally said, "Looks just like my apartment when I left for Friendly House." "Yep, me too," Karen said. "Only my kitchen was smaller, so it looked worse."

I was sick to my stomach from the memories of the nights, the years, of cooking coke with those saucepans. Next my friends trailed me to my girls' room.

It was worse than I remembered, their remaining little shirts and dresses falling off hangers, worn-out pajamas on hooks, schoolbooks scattered on the floor, piles of rat droppings, dirty plates and drinking glasses left on chairs. I looked at their toy trunk with its broken lid and dolls jammed facedown, broken.

"What's upstairs?" Becky asked, through the hovering gloom.

Chills ran up and down my spin. We tromped up the metal staircase.

"Well, you beat me here," Vivian said. We waded through the crap on the floor, tinfoil, sliced straws, beer bottles, cassettes with their tapes streaming out, the mile-high bed with the pee- and beer-stained sheets and mattress on top.

"Jesus," Faye said. "We need to get going on this."

"Where's a broom and garbage bags?" Karen said.

"How about Ajax?" Vivian said, walking into the bathroom.

"I don't know," I said. "I doubt there is any."

"Where's a store then?" Faye said.

"A few blocks away, Trancas Market," I said, staring at my gross bathroom.

"We'll find it," Becky said.

"Will you be all right alone here?" Faye said.

"Sure," I said, rummaging for salvageable outfits. "I'm fine."

"Okay, we'll be right back."

I heard the front door slam and went to the window to see them drive off. Then a charge went through my body. Like a robot, I dashed to the closet and rifled through coat pockets. In my plaid jacket I found the stored McDonald's straws I couldn't find before our last hospital trip.

I grabbed them all and fell to the floor, where there was still plenty of tinfoil. Shit, nothing to cut the straws with. With another surge of adrenaline, I leapt up and found a single-edged razor blade and frantically sliced the straws down the middle and scratched the crusted smack onto the foil. Huddled on the floor in the dimly lit closet, I scrambled for a lighter.

Bingo . . . matchbook under a shoe.

I struck the match and melted my heroin scrapings into the familiar delicious golden syrup, then pulled in one large lucky hit. The aroma filled my head before my mouth filled with the smoke. I took in as much as I could until my cheeks popped like a stockpiling chipmunk. The more smoke I could get in, the bigger, the better the hit. And just when I decided to suck it all down my throat into my lungs and head . . . a loud deep voice rang out.

"*Carrie* . . . are you going to get *sober* or what?"

Busted!

The smoke flew out of my mouth as if someone had slapped me on my back. I turned around. No one was there. I blinked. I looked again. I was alone. But I had heard a strong voice—it wasn't in my head—it was loud and clear.

It shook me up to see that I was back on the floor, my head in my navel, the dark small place I lived in for years.

I panicked that the Friendly House girls would find out I had a SLIP, which stands for Sobriety Loses Its Priority.

No, I almost slipped . . . No, you slipped, loser . . . I didn't inhale . . . YOU SLIPPED, you big dummy . . . a million chattering monkeys screamed in my head.

I kicked the monkeys aside and prayed I would never, never do this again. I hurried to clean up any signs, spraying my mouth with some old mouthwash I found on the skanky bathroom counter, thinking about another damned saying I had heard over and over at the Friendly House: *We are as sick as our secrets.* But I had to keep this secret.

I heard the front door open. "We're back!"

I charged down the staircase.

"You know, this cleanup job is really too big," I said, not looking them in the eyes. Vivian and Becky stopped short. They were carrying a mop and a bagful of cleaning products.

"Carrie says it's too much for us," Vivian turned to the group getting out of the van. "So . . . can we go?" Becky said.

"Yeah, let's go," I said, speaking calmly to conceal my nervousness. Faye walked up. "Why didn't you tell us before we went to the damn market?"

"I figured it out while you were gone."

"What's Peggy going to say?"

"I'll tell her," I said, getting everyone out and slamming the door behind me. "I need a cleaning crew . . . professionals."

Every day I thanked the Universe for keeping my secret. My original sobriety date fell on February 14, but my secret *slip* fell on May 4, making my new sobriety date Cinco de Mayo. Ha! It's always a holiday for me.

Ring . . . Ring . . . Ring . . . Ring . . . Ring . . . I put my eyelash curler down, walked out, and answered the pay phone.

"Carrie, is this you? It's Gloria."

"*Gloria?*" How did you get this number?"

Gloria was Dana Magnin's mom, a gorgeous, grand, very wealthy woman who lived in San Francisco. When she came to Los Angeles, she always had me do her hair. I hadn't seen Gloria in years. Since I was in the Friendly House, I had called Dana, wondering if she wanted to come get sober with me. Dana was not interested.

"Dana gave me this number, is this a new salon?"

"Uh, no, I'm with friends . . . until I get settled back in town . . ."

"Dana mentioned you were retired, but she thought you might be working again," Gloria said, sweet and motherly. "I was hoping you'd have time for me."

I held back a burst of laughter. Time? That's all I have! But my next thought sent a volt of fear through me: *Hair without a drink*? I took a deep breath. I'd have to ask Peggy.

"I'll be in town next week," Gloria said. "I have a bungalow at the Beverly Hills Hotel. Would a thousand dollars be enough to get you out of your retirement to do my hair and makeup? You know I don't trust anyone but you."

I saw the gift. I was *getting* to do my first hair job without a drink . . . with a lovely, kind, and understanding lady.

"Yes, Gloria," I said, I wanted to trust me too. "When?"

"Next Friday around lunch, you'll order whatever you like, do my hair, we'll eat and then do my makeup."

"Sounds perfect," I said. "I gotta go now, and thanks."

I walked downstairs to Peg's office and got permission to do Gloria's hair. It was a big deal that Peggy *trusted* me to collect a thousand dollars. Of course I would come right home to the Friendly House.

I got my LeBaron back and Peggy loaned me money to put together a makeup kit from the nearby beauty supply store, adding the leftover hair stuff in my car trunk: scissors, cutting cape, clippies, and combs.

I cleaned up my old case and I was prepared for Friday. It was like my first *Vogue* job, except I couldn't remember the last time I had looked at a *Vogue* magazine.

"I'm so nervous," I told Paula.

"Why? Didn't you do hair all your life?"

Friday arrived like Christmas morning, my stomach full of butterflies. I spruced myself up as best as I could, given my rotten teeth. I would get to them later and not smile too big so as not to horrify Gloria.

I fixed my hair with my electric rollers, to be current with the new eighties look, imitating from music videos. Cathy, in the Blue Room, told me she used egg whites on her hair. "They make my bangs stiff and stick up higher than Aqua Net." I stuck my comb into her bowl and she was right. It wasn't *my* look, but I'd try to get with it.

My lifetime rule still applied: *If your hair is right . . . life works better.*

The week before, I'd put a little lightening bleach in my hair; when I got sober, I found my brown hair had gone gray. I dressed up in some *dead lady's clothes* that someone had dropped off at Friendly House as a donation from a dead relative. I didn't have time for my identity crisis; it was time to go to the Beverly Hills Hotel. I checked in with Peggy.

"You can do this," Peggy said. "Call on your higher power, call me if you need to and come straight home."

Peggy seemed so naïve, but her spiritual strength spread over me like a bucket of honey. "Okay," I said. "Here's to the Big Hairdresser in the Sky."

Gloria greeted me like a countess in a fabulous Christian Dior silk robe and her hair in a towel turban. "I'm so thrilled to be with you," she said, and hugged me. "The hairdressers in San Francisco just aren't *you*." I blushed.

Dana was there. "Wow, what a great surprise," I said, though she was a using buddy and triggered some feelings. She hugged me and handed me a menu, looking as beautiful as ever, but hungover, her bright blue eyes not so bright.

"We're calling in drinks, I'm having a Ramos Gin Fizz, what do you want?"

"Coffee for me."

"Plain coffee?" Dana said. "No cappuccino with a shot of something?"

"Oh no, just coffee." My heart started beating fast. I put my case down.

"The dressing room is set up," Gloria said, and she went in.

I walked over to Dana and whispered, "Dana, I'm not drinking anymore, I'm clean. That's why I'm in a recovery home."

"I thought it was just till you felt better, so no cocaine either?"

"God, *no*, I can't have anything . . . *anything makes me want everything.*"

"How can you do nothing? I tried once, it's not for me."

"I'm ready for my new do," Gloria said, popping back in the doorway.

She sat like a perfect model. I swung my haircutting cape over her shoulders like a bullfighter and flipped my comb through her hair like I was conducting an orchestra. Like a rock star hairdresser, I was on!

"Your hair is so fine, we need to keep you timeless, nothing tricky."

"You're right, and isn't fine hair your specialty?"

"Absolutely. Now tell me what's been going on with you."

Gloria's talk was like music to my ears. Styling a demanding young hip chick would be a challenge. Going back to beauty school and getting my license would be a challenge. But Gloria was no pressure, she loved my hairdos and I knew she loved me. I didn't tell her I didn't have a license anymore.

"You are still the best," she said after I finished her makeup. I appreciated her kindness but didn't feel deserving of the pedestal she put me on. I packed up my supplies. "I need to come back regularly and get my Carrie fix." The word *fix* gave me goose pimples.

"I love you too, Gloria."

She handed me a Beverly Hills Hotel envelope. "And thank you so much."

"I feel it should be more," Gloria said. "You've been here for hours."

"Stop it," I said, and hugged Dana good-bye. "I wish I could do hair for free."

I had an epiphany the minute my arm had reached out for the envelope. I knew exactly where I needed to go—Benedict Canyon . . .

I raced back to the Friendly House, sticky and sweaty, smiling from ear to ear. I felt such a rush. I knew I was late as I ran to the front door, pushed it open, and found Peggy there with her hands on her hips and a stern face.

"Peggy! You won't believe—"

"I trusted you. You've been gone a very long time, why didn't you come right back?"

"Yes, but—"

"Did you drink?"

"No, but—"

"Did you use drugs?"

"No! No, but—"

"Do you have the money?"

"No, but—"

"*No but?* We have *no buts* around here. You didn't follow instructions. Where have you been?"

"After I finished my job, I realized I was around the corner from important friends that I owed exactly *one thousand dollars* to." Peggy started to say something, but I cut her off. "I'm sorry I didn't call, but when Gloria gave me the cash, I thought: oh . . . I get it, God . . . it's *not my cash*, it's Roger and Ann-Margret's cash. So, I drove right up Benedict Canyon."

Peggy sat down to hear me out.

"I pulled up like I did two years ago, when they loaned me one thousand dollars and I said I'd pay them back in two days. They were both home, and as shocked to see me as they were when I had appeared before, a total junkie. *'I'm here to pay you back and I'm so sorry it took me so long.'* Roger opened the door wider. 'Come in, I'm glad to see you looking so well.' Ann-Margret said, 'We're so happy to see you in one piece.'

"When I told them how sick my life had become, tears welled up in their eyes, it was unbelievable, Peggy. I can't wait to pay off all my debts, especially to Melvin Sokolsky."

Peggy believed me but revoked my weekend pass for breaking my word.

Grace Period

"How'd you find this place, Mom?" Aloma said.

Pitita asked, "What school do we go to?"

We stood in the living room of our three-bedroom triplex, in an area called the Miracle Mile, close to all my meetings. Daisy wanted to continue living with Bucky and graduate from University High. Adam was on his own, living with friends, and I wasn't sure where.

"Whatever school you want, I guess."

"Mom," Aloma said, "it doesn't work like that."

All I knew was that I had my girls and we all had to go to back to school.

Peggy gave me money to get my last bracelet out of hock and I sold it for my first and last month's rent. She still had to cosign my lease; I had no credit. I would be working at Ménage à Trois, down the street from the mad ghosts of my past, my old salon, and back to the street where I was born, Burton Way, as soon as I got my license back.

The girls would be starting John Burroughs Junior High.

I would be starting the Vidal Sassoon Academy.

Caroline was English, very professional, and of course she had a sharp short haircut. She greeted me. "I'm very very anonymous, so mum is the word."

"Mumm was my word for champagne," I joked.

She set me up and I went to my first class. The staff were all English, all proper and serious. Everyone's scissors were half the size of mine. Also, being left-handed didn't help me; they all held their scissors differently than I did. I had always spun around and cut hair like a sculptor. Chisel here . . . take a look and a chisel there. The Sassoon method was so organized, a precision step-by-step diagrammed technique. This was going to be difficult. My brain was still sloshing around, trying to reconnect its neurons.

I wanted to defend myself—"I cut Elvis for years" and "I was a guest on the *Vidal Sassoon Show*"—but most students hadn't been born during those days.

When lunch break came, the instructor gave a cheery pitch on where to find the best margaritas. The class listened eagerly.

I went to my LeBaron, locked the doors, and clutched my 12-step book to my chest, breaking only to smoke cigarettes. I stared at the dashboard clock waiting for lunch to pass. I wasn't hungry. I couldn't imagine doing this every day until I could pass the state board.

The next day wasn't easier. I was in the advanced cutting class. The kids were aggressive and competitive, talking about their future in hairdressing. They whizzed by me with their fancy *little* scissors. I knew the look they gave me when they asked me, "And what kind of scissors are those?" I'd given that *same* look to older hairdressers doing side flips twenty-three years ago.

I bit the bullet after arguing with myself to bail on class: I picked up my out-of-date scissors and I cut the Vidal Sassoon wedge, the bob, and the *Rosemary's Baby* cropped Mia Farrow cut. I didn't bother to tell anyone I'd had dinner with Mia twenty years ago either. It seemed everything I knew about myself *was from* twenty years ago.

Lunch break again.

I had had it, from the drinking conversations to my fashion time warp to my talent insecurities. I went out front to the pay phone on the Santa Monica boardwalk and called Peggy.

"I'm leaving the school, I can't do this."

"My dear, did you do your Third Step prayer?"

"What's that got to do with anything? I feel like a dinosaur."

"You've done half the day already—do two more hours and call me again. You can do two more hours."

"Okay, okay, two more hours, then I'm leaving."

"Fine, just call me first."

I hung up the phone. I looked up and saw an old friend walking my way, the crazy using madman Dennis Hopper. He looked great!

"Dennis!" I called out. He squinted to see who was yelling at him. "It's me . . . Carrie White."

"What are you doing here?" he said. "This isn't your neighborhood."

I gave him a snapshot version of my saga. He was proud of me. He too had gotten clean. I was ashamed of my rotten teeth.

"I walk here from Venice, why don't you come over, hang out, look at some art, and have a lemonade," he laughed. "Can you believe we've come to having *lemonade*?"

I drove us to his place. Dennis shared some of his journey down the rabbit hole and how cool it was to be clean. We laughed at our stubbornness in getting off drugs. I followed him into his heavily alarmed gates. I knew why when we got inside. He had an incredible contemporary art collection nestled away in a very unpretentious Venice city block. Lichtensteins and Warhols lined the walls and other artists, plus his own fantastic photographs, from *Easy Rider* to old Hollywood from the sixties, when he was married to Brooke Hayward.

"It's an underground museum," I said.

"Glad you like it."

Dennis still talked as fast as ever and seemed the same: funny, cool, and chic. He made me feel back in the world again, my world of art and fashion.

"You almost finished with school?"

"Almost," I said nonchalantly. "Well, this is my second day, what time is it anyway? I gotta go."

"If you freak out again, come back here," he said, walking me out. "and when you're back working . . . I'll come get a haircut."

"Really, Dennis?" I said, and gave him a big hug.

"Yeah, sure. Why not? Just let me know."

Funny how meteorites could land on my head and I wouldn't feel them, but a little spark was enough to light my fire. I was still full of fear, but I felt more like myself than I had in a very long time.

My girls and I went back and forth to school every day. I went to meetings before school and after, to ensure my stability. Unfortunately, I wasn't a stable mother yet. "Girls, I'll be back in a few hours, love you," I said, ready to fly out to catch my 8:00 PM meeting. "Mom," Aloma said, "it's not much different than when you left us for the dealer every day. We're sitting at this same table—okay, no pipes, but we're still eating from McDonald's bags."

I stopped in my tracks. I'd thought we were all so close, on the same page, and understanding this period of transition *for me*. I hadn't realized *I was still missing* from their lives.

And I was missing *everything* going on in theirs.

"I'm sorry, sweetheart, try to hang in a little longer . . . I mean . . . are you okay? Do you need anything?"

The Test

My chair faced a big open window with a view of the Blessed Sacrament Church, a landmark near Hollywood High. It helped me to pray before marking an A, B, or C in each box. After I penciled in my answers, I thanked Bill Wilson, the founder of the 12-step program, who gave me my sobriety and the ability to show up to take this test.

After the written exam came the test for hair, facial, and manicure. The same rule applied as it had twenty-one years ago: when in doubt, sanitize. This gave me time to remember my next move while the cosmetologist police roamed and hovered over our procedures.

My friend Laura modeled for me. When I got to the manicure part, I clipped her nail too close and she let out a yelp. I coughed so the supervisor didn't hear. If ever I needed a drink, this was the day.

At the end, all I had to do was wait in the hall for my results, not wait months like in 1963. They graded us on the spot and we would leave with a pass or fail. I waited with a hundred other hopefuls. The W's were way down the list.

Hours went by. If I wasn't called by 6:00 PM, I would have to come back tomorrow. The waiting area had thinned out to around seven people.

At 5:40, "Is a Carrie White here?"

I leapt up. "Here."

I walked to the small desk where two people were stamping and stacking papers. One reached out with a piece of paper toward me, never looking up. It was slow-motion torture until I heard her say: "Welcome to Cosmetology, you passed."

"Oh, *thank God,*" I said, my eyes welling up with tears for this second chance. I took my paper, my great incredible wonderful hair-dressing license, and promised the heavens I would never let it lapse again, if I lived to be ninety-nine.

Sunday noon. Rose Avenue. But instead of going to that hellhole, the Venice methadone clinic, I could finally honor one of my many promises to my girls: lunch across the street at the Rose Café.

How many times had I looked at this café from the clinic, shivering and dope-sick, and dreamed of being one of those people who enjoyed lunch and wore shorts in the summer? The day had come. Aloma, Pitita, and I were at the glass counter deciding on pasta salads and gourmet desserts.

"Pick *anything* you want, girls." I had been working one month at William's salon. It was awkward coming back. I was still shaky, but my confidence was building every day.

We collected our trays, found a table, and sat down. I looked out at the poor souls across the street at the methadone clinic, so grateful to be on the other side. Just then, the café door opened and my attention snapped. A very tall handsome man entered, basketball player tall. "Girls, girls"—I scrambled up—"I'll be right back."

Aloma looked at Pitita like *here we go again.* "I promise, *right back,* I have to say hi to someone." I fluffed my hair and practically ran into him as he was seating himself.

"Michael," I blurted, bubbling like a schoolgirl. He leaned back to focus. "It's me, *Carrie White,* and I'm not on heroin anymore!"

His twinkling blue eyes got bigger, his jaw slightly dropped, and he said, adjusting after the sudden invasion, "That's probably a very good idea."

Michael Crichton was probably the most normal guy I knew.

"I *wondered* what happened to you," he said.

"It's a long short story, but I'm working again . . . at Ménage à Trois, just down the street from my old salon—and, well, I won't keep you, but please come see me."

"Carrie used to cut my hair," he told the pretty young lady seated across from him. I forgot my rotten teeth and smiled from ear to ear.

"I'll find you," Michael said. I hugged him and walked back to my girls, glowing.

"Mom, you're too excited," Aloma said.

"Yeah, who was he?" Pitita asked.

"One of your mom's favorite people in the *whole world.* How's your salad? Save room for that carrot cake you wanted."

Slowly my clientele grew. My paychecks were just covering my new life: rent, food, gas, school clothes, and a few updated outfits for me.

I was paying Bucky back for keeping my girls in food, and for the gas and laundry soap he spent on them. He had grumbled and complained, but he did come through. I would be forever grateful to him.

My big priority was paying back Melvin Sokolsky. I urgently saved tips. It tortured me that I had disappointed him. And after all his doubt, I was excited to show him I'd made it back. He was surprised to hear from me. He said I could come over that day.

Melvin greeted me at the door and told me to come downstairs, where he and Button were reading the Sunday paper. They were casual, lying on their bed, and friendly with me like it was 1970. I gave my spiel, my apology, and handed him the two hundred bucks. Melvin said, "Okay, fine. Now, come upstairs, let me show you what I've been working on."

I laughed. Was that it? End of subject? *Let's go see what he's been doing?*

Of course, Melvin wanted to debate the idea that alcoholism was a disease while he showed me his new work. It was hard for me to accept that the world may never acknowledge alcoholism as a genetically predisposed condition and that it is ancient and insidious. Peggy had told me, "Alcoholism kills more people than tornadoes, hurricanes, wars, and traffic accidents." I remembered the hospital's denial when my mother died and they wrote cause of death: Pneumonia.

Melvin asked for my number, in case he needed me for a job.

I left his home with a warm happy heart, knowing it wasn't important if Melvin understood my condition, it only mattered that *I* understood my condition. And *I* knew *my* life depended on my knowing that I don't drink like a normal person.

Not all amends went as well as my first ones. An old friend, who now owned a fancy store on Rodeo, was at a book-signing party at Trumps restaurant for the chef Michael Roberts. I had Jerry on my amends list, but closer to the bottom. When I saw him, I laughed. I figured my Higher Power did the prioritizing and he was next. "Hi," I said. "It's me, Carrie White."

I gave him the speedball version of my destruction derby and said, "Even though your wife told me I didn't owe you guys anything, in my heart I knew you gave me the money, and I want to pay you back."

"Oh, don't worry about it, we all have crazy pasts."

That was a relief, because five thousand dollars was a lot of haircuts.

"Where are you working these days?" he asked.

The next day at Ménage à Trois, over the loudspeaker I hear, *"Carrie White, come to the front desk please."*

I excused myself from my client. At the front desk stood a pair of U.S. Marshals with guns, who handed me a paper. It read, pay immediately or wages will be *garnished*. I thought that word was just for parsley around a steak.

"This is a mistake," I said, embarrassed, while everyone in the salon listened. I called my friend from the desk phone. He casually told me that the money he'd given me five years ago was out of his hands; the check he had given me was from his business, and the debt had doubled to $10,000 over the years.

I hung up. The marshals left. I called Peggy, and money was garnished from my paycheck for the next year to resolve the matter.

The most important and hardest amends to make were to my children. They were teenagers, and I was a case of arrested development. I struggled and cried that I could never fix this in a lifetime. Peggy drilled into me that by staying sober I *was* making amends.

"If you stay sober you will become the mother you always wanted to be, and wanted to have."

Tuesday nights, my sober friends and I rushed to hear a young woman, Marianne Williams, translate *A Course in Miracles* in a big church on Franklin Avenue in Hollywood. I learned something there that made great sense to me: *All healing occurs through forgiveness.* Except, how could I expect my children to forgive me, if I couldn't forgive myself or forgive *my* mother?

As far as anyone knew, my big day was coming—my first year of sobriety. I needed to tell Aloma that I had that *slip* at my Malibu home, but it was too late. She told me, "Wait till you see the red plates and invitations I bought for your Valentine's Day birthday party."

I would *have to* maintain my façade for one more month.

I was coming out of Mayfair Market in West Hollywood when I spotted an old guy that looked like Billy Grimes. I ran through the parking lot, screaming "Billy, Billy?" The man's shoulders went up and his head went down, like he was ducking from my shouting, but he turned around to see who was yelling.

He was a skinny old guy, holding a paper bag, unshaven and homeless-looking, but he wore beads and chains around his neck with hanging trinkets, and a beat-up straw cowboy hat with his scruffy wispy hair poking out. It was him!

"*Billy*, it's me, Carrie!" I charged over to him. I put my head on his chest and wrapped my arms around him, groceries and all. "*I love you!* I'm so happy to find you."

"Wall I'll be got'damn." Billy smiled, his eyes magnified behind his thick-framed reading glasses. His jaw was messed up and he had no bottom teeth. "What the hell are ya' doin' in this neighborhood, baby doll?"

"Billy . . . come to my sober birthday party at Aloma's house in Beverly Hills."

"Sure, dahlin', but what's that mean? I'm not feeling so great, when is it?"

"It's just a party, the day before your birthday, on Valentine's Day. Hey, isn't it weird . . . my sober date is on Richard's and my wedding day . . . like I could have planned that," I laughed.

"Aw hell, I'll be up and runnin' by then . . . will Richard be there?"

My life with Richard flashed by me like one of Billy's decoupage wall paintings. It was still too hard to look at.

"I doubt it, sweetie, he sees the girls when he can or they meet him, or someone picks the girls up for him. We don't talk, just hi and 'bye."

"That's too bad, I thought you'd work that dumb shit out by now."

"We'll always love each other."

"*I heard that*, and hey, I haven't heard from him either." Billy shuffled his grocery bags that were getting heavy in his arms. "Well, Barbara's waitin' fo' me, we finally got married."

"Billy, that's so great. She always loved you to pieces."

"Can you blame her?"

I gave him my card. "You better call me, Billy, or I'll stick pins in a voodoo doll and your hair will fall out!"

"Too late, that's already happenin' . . . I got a *little* cancer, I'm fine now . . . and you know what they say: *Cancer cures smoking.*"

I watched him toddle down the street.

Billy had survived himself.

I walked back to my car, grateful, healthy, feeling *my life* was so perfect.

The day before Valentine's Day, 1985. I found a red silk shirt at Fred Segal's that had written across it in black: *Stay Alive in '85*. The night before the party, I went to bed extremely excited and reflected on my whole year clean and sober. Dawn swept away the night, brought my new day and my new year.

Ouch. What the *fuck*?! I couldn't open my eyes. They were stuck shut. I went to my bathroom and turned on the hot water and splashed my face.

Pitita wandered in, "What, Mom?"

"My eyes . . . look at my eyes, I can't see."

I rinsed my eyes a million more times, frantically trying to unseal them. I finally got a peek in the medicine chest mirror—muck and oozing yellow crap were in my tear ducts. Conjunctivitis? I hadn't had this since beauty school 1962.

Then I burst out laughing. What could be more of a message then waking up blind on my *not real* birthday day? "Okay, God . . . I get it. But taking a cake and going to my party without getting to wear eye makeup? What kind of punishment is that? And yes . . . thank you for my almost one year *of keeping myself safe*."

My wounded ego and I made it through the cake-onstage ceremony at the meeting without anyone yelling, "Hey, where's your mascara?"

After the cutting of my gigantic, beautiful triple-layer chocolate cake with real live flowers, Jim Frank came up to Aloma and me and said, "There're cops at your front door." Busted by the Beverly Hills police. Very chic.

"This is my *sober* party, what's the problem, Officer?"

"Too many people, you're creating a fire hazard."

I laughed. "I've been called a lot of things, but never a fire hazard."

"We'll be ending soon," Aloma said.

"Good," the handsome Beverly Hills cop said. "Its one AM and your neighbors are complaining."

Aloma and I laughed, knowing the mayhem of our pasts.

In 1987, Billy Grimes died. He died of everything. His services were on a hill and everyone showed up but Richard, who was very ill with liver problems.

On one of my worst mornings, I came into my little Aloma's bedroom and found her sitting on her bed with the telephone and a notepad, on the verge of tears, but keeping her composure so she could continue talking on the phone. I looked to see what she had written on her pad.

The first word had a line through it: *Morgue.*

The second word on her list had a line through it also: *Jail.*

I sat down and put my arm around her. "What's going on, honey?"

"Dad's missing."

"How do you know?"

"*Okay, thank you,*" she said, hung up the phone, and drew a line through the last word: *Hospitals.*

"I can't find him anywhere. Can we go look for him?"

"Of course, honey."

I panicked inside for my children. I didn't know what it was like to love a father.

Richard hadn't been able to give up drinking or drugs, and his liver was in terrible shape, bulging out. His mind was getting lost more and more often. The girls would tell me stories about the police finding him wandering near Park La Brea when he didn't live there anymore. They would tell me he kept forgetting that the doctor had told him to stop drinking, that his life depended on this. When they went to restaurants, the girls would say, "Dad, you can't drink." But he would contest, "I always have a beer with my Mexican food," or "I always have sake with sushi."

We had been through repeated trips to UCLA emergency with him, and when he moved in with his mother, we flew several times to San Francisco, thinking he was on his deathbed. Miraculously, he had always pulled through. Richard was on a list for a liver transplant, but each time one became available, he was too sick for surgery.

Seeing Richard sick was like seeing my mother in a hospital bed. "You're going to be okay, Richard, sweetheart," I would say. "You can do this, you can make it." I wanted to scream and cry, *"Richard, don't die, don't leave us. Please. I love you."* But I never did.

It was horrifying to see him in this condition, his once beautiful olive skin turning a dark ashy black from his blood being poisoned from cirrhosis. My handsome king of yesterday was now emaciated and deformed, with sunken cheeks and fading eyes. His hands still looked beautiful, though—limp but beautiful.

I acted strong. I stood tall by his side. I held my girls' hands and smiled at him, with all the love in my heart. When he became conscious, he would make jokes or just smile and be so happy to see us all together. Our rides home were always so sad.

One time, Aloma broke the screaming silence. "Remember the night Dad had us all come out to the front yard on Mulholland, and it was a full moon?"

"I do," Pitita said.

"Remember how he had all of us sit on the front lawn," Aloma continued, "and he went into the house and came out with a big bowl of water?"

"Yes, I do, too, sweetheart," I said.

"And he put the big bowl of water on the grass where he could get the reflection of the moon in the water, and he made us pass the bowl around to each other, so we all held the moon's reflection in our own hands?"

I tried not to cry so I could drive safely. Pitita was quiet.

"And remember how after that night, and for years later, Dad would say to us, '*Remember the night I gave you the moon?*'"

APRIL 27, 1988

I got a call from Richard's mom in San Francisco. He was in her care full time now, back in the house he grew up in. "You better come up *tonight*, as fast as you can. I think this is really it." She was sobbing.

"Okay, Mary, okay, sweetheart," I said, holding my own emotions. "I will leave work, get the girls, and be right up. Where are you?"

"San Mateo Hospital. Please hurry. I know he's hanging on just for you and his girls, I know it."

I didn't want to believe that this was really it. I called the airlines. I picked up my girls. We ran through the airport as fast as we could, my little angels with their overnight bags swinging in their hands. We sat sadly in our airplane seats waiting to land.

"Do you think Dad's still alive?" Aloma and Pitita asked me throughout the flight. "I hope so, my darlings . . . and we are getting there as fast as we can, just remember that."

We ran into the hospital, down the aisle to his room, took a fearful deep breath, and walked in. Everyone was silent. Richard's mother was holding Richard's hand. His cousin Tillie moved aside for us.

"You just missed him," Tillie said. "He waited for you, he really tried."

Aloma and Pitita burst into screams. I put my arms around my girls . . . *his girls*. He looked like he was out of pain. I had never looked at my mother's face after she died or my grandmother's, but I couldn't stop staring at Richard.

He had one tear in his right eye, a whole tear that no one had wiped away. It sat perfectly in the hollow between his tear duct and his beautiful nose, just sitting there like the tiniest pool in the universe. My girls were crying and crying. I just kept staring at the lonely tear in his eye. It held everything neither of us could say. It was the last tear he would have to shed. It was his elegant way.

"Never say good-bye when you leave a party," I could hear Richard whisper. "That way no one knows you've left and your spirit lingers on. It's the Indian way."

One Door Closes and Another Opens

On April 10, 1990, at 11:30 AM, the phone rang while I was doing my reclaimed client Sandra Moss at William's salon. It was my first husband, Jordan. He knew where to find me because I had made my amends to him for ignoring him all the previous years, so as not to acknowledge my past with him. I couldn't imagine what he wanted. I took the call.

"What? Oh, my God . . . *yes.*"

I hung up in shock. My mouth went dry and I froze.

"What was that all about?" Sandra asked.

"My first child had dinner with her father last night, and he asked if he could give her my number . . . she's looking for me."

"You never told me you had another child!"

I had told only my other children, and only a few years prior.

That night, I heard her voice for the first time, because she left a message on my answering machine. The next night, I drove to meet her after work. I thanked my sobriety that she hadn't found me earlier, when I was drooling on myself at the Venice methadone clinic, I tried not to visualize her slamming the door shut with: *Mom? . . . oh, never mind . . .*

I pulled up to her little Craftsman house in Burbank, where she had lived all her life, and there was my first child, standing on the porch. I got out of my car and walked slowly to her, my heart racing in anticipation of her response. We were wearing the same outfit: black T-shirts, jeans, silver hoop earrings, silver buckled belts, and silver bangle bracelets. She hit her forehead with her hand, spun around, smiled, and said, "Well, this explains everything."

We hugged, we cried, and she said the greatest thing a mother who gives up her child for adoption could wish . . . "I know you must have loved me a lot, to have had the courage to do what you did."

"And you also had a lot of courage to look for me," I replied.

Tyler entered my life and was welcomed by her brother and sisters.

On July 1, 1995, Jordan and I walked down the aisle, this time giving away our daughter in holy matrimony. On July 23, 1998, she gave birth to her first child, a daughter, and then another daughter, on September 25, 2000. In them I get to see the daughter I missed, Tyler. By the way, Jordan and his partner, David, have been together twenty years, longer than all three of my marriages put together.

PART 7

Let's Begin at the End

2001 to the Present

I Never Dreamed This Far

"Carrie White Hair. This is Michaelis, thank you for holding. How can I help you?"

Three years after opening my new salon, I had taken my DJ pal and put him to work until I could find another real receptionist. Michaelis was charming and the ladies all walked a little lighter when they saw his broad smile and sexy eyes greeting them. He was twenty-nine and looked like a young Brando in his tight white shirt and tattoos up both arms.

After roller-skating out of my Burton Way salon twenty-six years ago in my Spandex pants; after ten years of managing a salon next door to Spago for Tova Borgnine, selling her hair care system and doing model makeovers live on QVC; after more than twenty years of sobriety, believing that I could go back into my own business because I had my trusted assistant of sixteen years, Chad Simpson, by my side, in 2005 I opened my own salon again.

I found an old skin care studio and gutted it to turn it into a sleek modern two-person operation. I put up a 42-inch plasma screen to run films on my wall—*Auntie Mame, Ashes and Snow, Casablanca, Breakfast at Tiffany's,* and, of course, *Shampoo.* I play the movies without sound so I can pump up my favorite CDs through my salon speakers—William Orbit, Citizen Cope, Hôtel Costes, MC Solaar. The Rolling Stones and Bob Dylan are still always in the mix.

This second chance in hairdressing has taken me traveling again, from Austin, Texas, to Sydney, Australia. Naomi Campbell flew me to Saint-Tropez for her birthday party in 2004, and I danced my ass off every night until 5:00 AM. People kept asking me, "What are you *on*?" I just laughed and said, "Don't worry 'bout me. It's all in here. I just add water."

Michaelis walks over to me with the appointment book. "I need you to figure out where to put Jason Patrick. He has to get in before Tuesday."

"How much longer do I have to sit here with this crap in my hair?" Lili Zanuck hollered from the color-heating machine behind me, her head full of tiny bleached highlights that I had just wrapped in tinfoil.

I laugh. "Come on—you just got under there."

I looked at Lili in her hat of aluminum. The fact that I could touch tinfoil today and not freak out made me laugh too. I remembered the early days of my sobriety, when my girls, Aloma and Pitita, would tease me with the word *tinfoil.* "Don't say that, you know that makes my skin crawl," I'd yell at them. They would laugh harder. I was glad they could joke, but just the thought of tinfoil had made me nauseous.

"I'll check you in twelve minutes, Lili."

"Don't forget," she demands in her funny executive manner, like a little girl stomping for her way. "I hate this."

Maribel, my other assistant, is preparing my chair for my next client.

"Nana!" screams my three-year-old granddaughter Olive, bursting into my salon followed by her mother, my precious Pitita.

"Who's the apple of my eye?" I grab Olive and swing her up in the air. She's wearing a pink tutu over her pink leotard and matching pink ballet slippers.

"Me!" she answers as I give her a big squeeze.

I thought of my nana, my other children, all my grandchildren, and what my mother has missed, having died so much younger than I was now, her life robbed by the drink. I remembered her dying days in County General Hospital and how unpresent I was for her, between my own drinking and my disdain for her drinking. Yet somehow my soul had recorded the details—the thin sheet over her emaciated body, lying on that metal cot, barely able to take in another breath and exhaling with that horrible sound, that "death rattle" in her throat.

I had never even liked her name. Grace. It always reminded me of *Gracie* Allen and dumb jokes. But at my second recovery meeting outside of the house with all the girls from the Friendly House, a meeting that is as old as Los Angeles, I heard the speaker say, "You can have your *excuses* or you can have a life." I identified with making

excuses and not having a life. I was always aware of my deep relationship with alcohol, yet even when I saw my mother die from this, giving up drinking seemed *impossible.*

I turned around and looked at the meeting room of people, and
then my eyes focused on a banner that was tacked up on a wall. I
started to cry for the first time. It was nothing fancy, just six words in
bold letters: *But by the Grace of God.* I realized at that moment that
my mother had shown me, in her death, that I must escape from alcoholism, so I could live. I went home and looked up the word *grace.*
It read: *An unmerited divine assistance.*

I thought about what was divine for me, throughout my life,
from childhood to any of my darkest, saddest, most fearful mo-
ments . . . somehow, I always *respected* my hope.

I see alcohol and drug abuse all around and I often hear a normal
person say, "Why did she do that again . . . what is wrong with her?"
Exactly—there is something terribly *wrong: alcoholism.* The doctors
wrote on my mother's death certificate that she died of pneumonia
instead of what really killed her. But it is not a moral issue, it is an
illness, and it is ancient. It kills neighborhoods and countries. It kills
families long before anyone dies.

I lost my beloved Dana from this illness on my birthday, August
25, 1996.

A few years after Dana died, Rita's ex-boyfriend Perry called me.
"Can you try to help Rita? She's drinking herself to death." I called
Rita and invited her to come with me to a 12-step meeting, as Big
Aloma had invited me many years ago. Rita answered, "What are you
trying to do . . . *harass me?*"

Six weeks later Rita was dead. Why had I made it, and not Rita
and Dana, or Billy Grimes, Beverly Foster, Rosalind Frank, or my
wonderful Richard, my father, or my mother? I am certainly not a
better person.

The list of my friends who did not die of old age goes on.

I haven't heard from K in over twenty-three years. I thought I saw
her a few years ago at the Bank of America on Sunset, but the person
I saw was just a twin ghost of my past.

I cannot measure my gratitude to my friend Aloma, who truly

saved my life with her unfailing concern for me, and her faith in the 12-step recovery program.

"Mom, what should we order for lunch?" Pitita asks. "Daisy, Aloma, and the boys are meeting us here."

"Ask Michaelis to call Roni's down the street and order pizzas."

Olive tugs on my shirt. "And guess what, Nana?" she shouts. "I'm gonna be in a ballet."

I help Olive onto my work chair. As Gnarls Barkley's "Crazy" streams in my speakers, I look in the mirror. I see my all-white salon with white orchids on my custom wall-length station of white enamel car paint, and more orchids above the shampoo bowls behind me and on my product case. Pitita is talking to Michaelis. Chad is busy blow-drying his client Loree Rodkin. Maribel is shaking out the cutting cape, about to put it on Olive. Narine, my manicurist, is giving Margo Winkler a pedicure. Margo is talking to Lili. Lori Petty is waiting on my couch, reading *Vanity Fair*. I see the sheer Mylar curtains and my white Afro headdressed mannequin that I sprayed silver, in my picture window facing the gorgeous view of the Peninsula Hotel across the street, with its brick entry drive, enhanced by a parked maroon Maserati and a beige Bentley convertible under purple-flowered trees, under a perfect blue California sky. I look at myself, smiling with my perfect new teeth after years of sitting for repair in my dentist's chair, my contemporary haircut with blond highlights that have become my calling card, my once shattered body that is now physically fit because I do Pilates with Laura, my instructor upstairs, and I am tan because the Glitz Girls studio next door sprays me up when I feel like a glow would be nice. I have on tight J Brand jeans, a comfortable chic shirt from Zara's, and sensible black flats by Stella McCartney for Adidas. I pick up my comb and scissors. I see something else from my insides. Gratitude. I love my life.

"I know, Olive, sweetheart, and I'm gonna do your hair."

Acknowledgments

In addition to my eternal gratitude for my true heroes, each of my children and grandchildren, I could fill another book around all the people named (and unnamed) throughout the past twenty-two years who have given me encouragement while I have been birthing this book.

Thank you to my countless clients and friends who came for haircuts and who I pressed to read chapters of my book and who even fixed typos (including Carol Bootsby Arnold, who in 1989, typed my first draft into my first computer as I read from my handwritten steno pads to Linda Feferman, who helped me carefully cut six hundred pages from the book).

Johannes Gamble, for his generous time and extreme talents entering my photo collection.

My lifetime friend, Aloma Ichinose, whose continued faith in getting me to the recovery program made all of this possible.

To Peggy Albrecht, for lovingly guiding my recovery for twenty-seven years.

My treasured work partner, Chad Simpson, for his endless support beyond call of love and duty.

My wise writing teacher, Jack Grapes, for everything he taught me and for introducing me to—

My brilliant writing coach, Chiwan Choi, who sat by my side for over three years, controlling my A.D.D. and my dyslexia, directing me to expand on this or you don't need that and telling me to never write from wisdom, but instead to write from truth.

My final gratitude to Michael Crichton, my beloved friend and client for thirty-eight years, who introduced me to my great agent, Lynn Nesbit, who got me to my genius editor, Greer Hendricks, and the amazing team at Atria Books of Simon & Schuster.

Clearly, I did not achieve this alone.

Afterthought

You would be surprised how close you can get to someone in only one hour . . . when you have a pair of scissors in your hand.

Sandra Bullock	Natalie Wood	Petula Clark
Oprah Winfrey	Courtney Wagner	Candy Clark
Wallis Annenberg	Joanne Woodward	Suzy Parker
Lucille Ball	Diahann Carroll	Jean Shrimpton
Louise Fletcher	Dyan Cannon	Lauren Hutton
Stefanie Powers	Claudette Colbert	Amber Valletta
Marla Maples	Rosalind Russell	Rene Russo
Aretha Franklin	Betsy Bloomingdale	Beverly Johnson
Dusty Springfield	Pamela Churchill	Jenny Shimizu
Elizabeth Taylor	Hayward (Harriman)	Dayle Haddon
Sharon Tate	Babe Paley	Veronica Hamel
Abigail Folger	Edith Mayer Goetz	Cheryl Tiegs
Jennifer Jones	Sherry Lansing	Kirsty Hume
Arlene Dahl	Elsa Peretti	Maud Adams
Lana Turner	Loree Rodkin	Joey Adams
Roberta Flack	Jacqueline Bisset	Jolie Jones
Ruth Gordon	Dinah Shore	Ulla Jones
Julie Christie	The Pointer Sisters (all)	Peggy Lipton Jones
Goldie Hawn	Jane Fonda	Verna Harrah

Brenda Vaccaro

Jill St. John

Peggy Fleming

Suzanne Somers

Capucine

Lizabeth Scott

Ursula Andress

Mama Cass

Michelle Phillips

Chynna Phillips

Geneviève Waïte Phillips

Alana Hamilton Stewart

Rachel Hunter

Betty Furness

Katharyn Ross

Faye Dunaway

Barbra Streisand

Barbara Feldon

Barbara Bain

Barbara Parkins

Barbara Bach Starr

Barbara Harris

Barbara Barrie

Barbara Eden

Barbara McNair

Barbara Luna

Barbara Rush

Barbi Benton

Lee Grant

Annette Funicello

Cheryl Holdridge

Chris Evert

Tippi Hedren

Pat Crowley

Zsa Zsa Gabor

Mae West's Wig

Suzanne de Passe

Ann-Margret

Angie Dickinson

Neile McQueen

Terry McQueen

Ali MacGraw

Anna Maria Alberghetti

Joanie Sommers

Ruta Lee

Rona Barrett

Melinda Dillon

Anthea Sylbert

Sally Kellerman

Sally Field

Sally Kirkland Sr.

Sally Kirkland Jr.

Carrie Donovan

Nancy Dinsmore (W.C. editor—*Harper's Bazaar*, '60s–'70s)

Eleanor Phillips (W.C. editor—*Vogue,* circa '60s–'70s)

Lori Petty

Kathleen Wilhoite

Mary Tyler Moore

Valerie Harper

Lily Tomlin

Susan Powter

Donna Dixon Aykroyd

Donna Mitchell

Geneviève Bujold

Connie Stevens

Joey Heatherton

Shelley Fabares

Jean Seberg

Anjelica Huston

Angela Cartwright

Dorothy Provine

Vanessa Redgrave

Raquel Welch

Teri Garr

Toni Basil

Annie Marshall

Carol Eastman

Helena Kallianiotes

Bobbie Gentry

Vikki Carr

Sue Mengers

Ronee Blakly

Susan Blakely

Susan Tyrrell

Cloris Leachman

Jessica Cauffiel

Polly Bergen

Joan Collins

Samantha Eggar

J. P. Morgan

Brittany Morgan

Marilyn Erskine

The Cranky Secretary from *The Beverly Hillbillies* (Nancy Kulp)

Marilyn McCoo

Diana Ross

Natalie Cole

Diane Baker

Christine Lund

Kelly Lange

Phyllis George

Nancy Allen

Joanna Pettet

Carolyn Jones Spelling

Joan "Culture Queen" Agajanian Quinn

Donna Reed

Alice Faye

Phyllis Kirk

Madeline Kahn

Bette Midler

Karen Black

Cybill Shepherd

Ingrid Boulting

Lola Folana

Pat Morrow

Anouk Aimée

Terry Moore

Tatum O'Neal

Farrah Fawcett

Kate Jackson

Cheryl Ladd

Shelley Hack

Lindsay Wagner

Donyale Luna

Emma Roberts

Courtney Burness

Courtney Kennedy

Lee Remick

Janet Leigh

Jane Powell

Abbe Lane

Norma Shearer

Karen Carpenter

Ruth Buzzi

Judy Carne

Angela Bowie

Joan Hackett

Marsha Mason

Leslie Caron

Lesley Ann Warren

Anne Archer

Joan Tewkesbury

Katharine Ross

Carol Lawrence

Cathy Lee Crosby

Joanna Cassidy

Elayne Boosler

Donna Mills

Yvette Mimieux

Camilla Sparv

Sarah Buxton

Diane Baker

Blythe Danner

Charlotte d'Amboise

Stockard Channing

Heather Locklear

Valeria Golina

Penny Marshall

Cindy Williams

Ellen Burstyn

Candice Bergen

Sharon Kay Ritchie (Miss America 1956)

Carmen Worth (owner of Hassler Hotel, Rome, Italy)

Mrs. Bob (Sarah) Dylan

Mrs. Danny (Fawn Hall) Sugerman

Mrs. Ronald (First Lady Nancy) Reagan

Mrs. Pierre (Nicole) Salinger

Mrs. Robert (Ethel) Kennedy

Mrs. Sidney (Joanna Shimkus) Poitier

Mrs. Miles (Frances) Davis

Mrs. Henry (Ginny) Mancini

Mrs. Larry (Pat) Gelbart

Mrs. Jack (Bobbie) Elliot

Mrs. George (Joan) Axelrod

Mrs. Walter (Carol) Matthau

Mrs. Gregory (Veronica) Peck

Mrs. Ed (Dana) Ruscha

Mrs. Sly (Sasha) Stallone

Mrs. Johnny (Joanne & Joanna) Carson

Mrs. Freddie (Janet) De Cordova

Mrs. Bill (Camille) Cosby

Mrs. George (Jolene) Schlatter

Mrs. Nick (Felisa) Vanoff

Mrs. Milton (Ruth) Berle

Mrs. James (Gloria) Stewart

Mrs. Robert (Rosemary) Stack

Mrs. Edgar (Frances) Bergen

Mrs. Kirk (Anne) Douglas

Mrs. Bob (Toby) Rafelson

Mrs. Nat (Maria) "King" Cole

Mrs. Robert (Rachel) "Doc" Kerlan

Mrs. Bing (Kathryn) Crosby

Mrs. Ernest (Tova) Borgnine

Mrs. Karl (Mona) Malden

Mrs. Hall Bartlett, 1st (Anna Marie), 2nd (Rhonda Fleming), and 3rd

Mrs. Tim (Susan) Hardin

Mrs. Vilmos (Susan) Zsigmond

Mrs. Frank (Nancy) Sinatra

Mrs. Horst Buchholz

Mrs. Ray Milland

Mrs. Otto Preminger

Mr. & Mrs. Melvin (Button) Sokolsky

Mr. & Mrs. Irwin (Margo) Winkler

Mr. & Mrs. Milton (Amy) Greene

Mr. & Mrs. Tony (Christine Kaufmann) Curtis

Mr. & Mrs. Richard (Lili) Zanuck

Mr. & Mrs. Robert (Julie Payne) Towne

Mr. & Mrs. Peter (L. B.) Bogdanovich

Mr. & Mrs. Marvin (Joan) Worth

Mr. & Mrs. Saul (Shirley) Turteltaub

Mr. & Mrs. William (Babs) Shoemaker

Mr. & Mrs. Lafitt (Linda) Pincay Jr.

Mr. & Mrs. Andrew (Heather Lowe) Prine

Mr. & Mrs. Andrew (Irene) Robinson

Mr. & Mrs. Robert (Sandra) Blake

Mr. & Mrs. William Schallert (Patty Duke's TV dad)

Mr. & Mrs. Jeff (Susan) Bridges

Mr. & Mrs. Pat (Karen) Proft

Mr. & Mrs. Kenny (Eva) Loggins

Mr. & Mrs. Stuart (Fiona) Copeland

Mr. & Mrs. Elvis (Priscilla) Presley

Michael Crichton

David Steinberg

Buck Henry

Jack Nicholson

Warren Beatty

Robert De Niro

Harvey Keitel

David Bowie

David Scott (*Apollo 15* Commander)

Peter Sellers

Hal Ashby

William Friedken

Marlon Brando

Joe Eula

Sonny Bono

Robert Altman

Jerry Moss (The M of A&M)

Paul Cummins

Dewey Nicks

Jason Patrick

Seymour Cassel

Bruce Dern

Balthazar Getty

Eric Dane

Alan Greisman

James LeGros

Peter Allen

Michael Paré

Howard Hesseman

Michael Butler (producer of musical *Hair*)

Davis Gaines (Michael Crawford replacement in *Phantom of the Opera*)

Neil Diamond

Elliot Gould

Merv Adelson

Harpo Marx Jr.

Richard Mulligan

Gram Parsons

Todd Rundgren

Dean Stockwell

Wallace Berman

Dennis Hopper

George Hermes

Don Feld

Governor Jerry Brown

Senator John V. Tunney Jr.

Ted Ashley (president of Warner Bros., circa '70s)

Paul Williams

Paul Sands

Paulo Costanzo

Gene Wilder

Michael J. Pollard

James Edward Olmos (Eddie James)

Lorne Michaels

Orny Adams

Garrett Graham

George Hamilton

George Chakiris

Joe Namath

Keith Carradine

Mark Rydell

Miko Brando

Wolfgang Puck

Matthew Mellon

William Orbit (Madonna's Grammy-winning producer)

Robert Lamm (Chicago)

The Bee Gees (not Andy)

Anthony Kiedis (Red Hot Chili Pepper)

Bill Mosely (*The Devil's Rejects*)

Shane Brolly (*Underworld*)

Giorgio Veroni

Chris McMillan (Jennifer Aniston's hairdresser)

And Brad Pitt

Few, I did once.

Most, I did for many, many years.

Many, I still do.

Some, I forgot I did or forgot to mention.

And a million others in the past forty years have passed through my fingers without famous names that have touched my life as well.

To all I say: *Thank you and I'm sorry if I kept you waiting.*